PEARSON CUSTOM
ANTHROPOLOGY

Research Methods and Society:
Foundations of Social Inquiry, 2/e
Linda Eberst Dorsten
and Lawrence Hotchkiss

Managing Editor
Jeffrey H. Cohen
Ohio State University

Associate Editor
Douglas E. Crews
Ohio State University

Contributing Editors–Cultural Anthropology
Randal Allison
Blinn College

Lee Cronk
Rutgers (New Brunswick)

Donald C. Wood
Akita University Medical School

Contributing Editors–Biological/Physical Anthropology
Susan Kirkpatrick-Smith
Kennesaw State University

James Stewart
Columbus State Community College

D1509430

Executive Editor: Stephen Frail
Program Manager: Mayda Bosco
Editorial Assistant: Caroline Beimford
Vice-president/Director of Marketing: Brandy Dawson
Marketing Manager: Nicole Kunzmann
Production Editor: Barbara Reilly
Production Manager: Fran Russello
Cover Art Director: Jayne Conte
Cover Design: Bruce Kenselaar
Manager, Rights and Permissions: Charles Morris
Composition/Full-Service Project Management: Mogana Sundaramurthy/
  Integra Software Services Pvt. Ltd.

Credits and acknowledgments borrowed from other sources and reproduced, with permission, in this textbook appear on appropriate page within text.

Library of Congress Cataloging-in-Publication Data
Dorsten, Linda Eberst.
   Research methods and society : foundations of social inquiry / Linda Eberst Dorsten,
SUNY Fredonia, Lawrence Hotchkiss, University of Delaware.—Second edition.
      pages cm
   Includes bibliographical references.
   ISBN-13: 978-0-205-87991-5 (alk. paper)
   ISBN-10: 0-205-87991-8 (alk. paper)
   1. Sociology—Research—Methodology.   2. Social sciences—Research—Methodology.
   I. Hotchkiss, Lawrence.   II. Title.
   HM511.D67 2014
   301.072—dc23
                                                          2013011063

10 9 8 7 6

ISBN-10:   0-205-87991-8
ISBN-13: 978-0-205-87991-5

Table of Contents

INTRODUCING SOCIAL RESEARCH

INTRODUCTION: LOOKING AT HOW THE SOCIAL WORLD WORKS

"If I can talk my parents into buying a new car, then...."

"If I call my parents before they hear about this from someone else, then...."

"If I work out in the gym every day, then...."

The people at your local automobile dealership would love to persuade you that buying their newest auto will do all sorts of wonders for you, particularly "improving" your love life. If you believe that a new car would help your love life, and you could afford it, would you be tempted to buy one?

What do the above snippets of conversation with one's self have to do with social research? Each one contains an *if...then* statement. The goal is to predict what will happen next, based on current conditions—*if A occurs, then will B follow?* This abstract question defines the fundamental goal of social research, and of all of science. In highly simplified terms, it captures the notion of **cause and effect**, but there is more to cause-and-effect relationships than just comparisons. The point is that we all engage continually in our own informal social science!

Goals of This Chapter

This chapter introduces fundamental goals and issues in social research by considering several examples. The first three examples come from everyday experience; the next three come from published research. Despite the apparent diversity of the examples, most, but not all, share a unifying theme: *comparisons*. For example, compare people who work out with weights every day to those who don't work out with weights to see which group has a more active social life.

As you read each of the examples below, make a list of whether or not it implies a comparison. If so, what is compared to what? What cause-and-effect question might the comparison suggest?

From Chapter 1 of *Research Methods and Society, Foundations of Social Inquiry,* Second Edition. Linda Eberst Dorsten, Lawrence Hotchkiss. Copyright © 2014 by Pearson Education, Inc. All rights reserved.

SUCCESS IN EVERYDAY LEARNING: THREE EXAMPLES

How does "trial-and-error" success in everyday learning determine the conclusions we draw about how our world works?

Fixing a Meal

The first example of an everyday learning activity is "fixing a meal." Suppose you've never done it. How long would it take you to fix a meal that would satisfy your hunger—given that you have food items in your kitchen and you aren't too picky about what constitutes a "meal"?

The motivation is there (hunger) and you probably have or can readily locate some information about how to prepare the food. If you decide to have macaroni and cheese, for example, instructions probably are printed on the package. And, if you cook it too long or not long enough, you'll probably make a mental note about what to do differently next time. In this type of everyday learning, you are likely to have a high level of success in one or two tries, if success is measured as "not hungry."

How Late Is "Late for Work"?

A second example is a little more complicated. Suppose your job requires you to be at work from 8 A.M. to 5 P.M. During the first week on the job, you are 10 minutes late one day, and no one seems to notice. A week or so later you are 20 minutes late, and no comments come up. You might begin to wonder, *How late is "too late" to come to work on this job?* How many trials of being late do you think it will take before you learn the answer?

Of course, a specific answer depends on your boss and other job characteristics, such as how visible your absence is and how much it affects the work setting. Although it probably requires a few more trials than fixing a meal, success in finding out "how late is too late" will come with relatively few trials, but you might be looking for another job after you find out!

"Why Can't Some People *Understand*?"

Have you ever been pursued by another person to be close friends when that is not what *you'd* like? Suppose you've dropped what you believe are clear hints about your preferences. You next confront the person and gently explain that you're not interested, but the person still attempts a relationship with you. You tell a friend, "I'm not interested in him or her! Why can't some people *understand*?"

It might take several tries before you "get rid of" this person. The number of needed trials is harder to determine than in the other two examples. Why?

Perhaps the other person didn't understand your comments and behaviors because you've been unclear (too indirect). Maybe you are secretly flattered—ever so little—by the attention and are not really sure you want the person to go away. Or the person and you have different expectations about relationships because you've been socialized under different cultural or subcultural norms about how many times to keep trying. Perhaps the hints and direct statement are ignored by the other person, who hopes that you'll change your mind, or even are misinterpreted as a challenge—you're playing hard to get!

THREE PUBLISHED EXAMPLES—AND ONE MORE

Excerpt: *Drugs on Campus*

Next, look at a report in a university newspaper about drug use on campus. The ellipses (...) in the excerpts indicate where text from the original article was deleted.

> An informal survey conducted by *The Review* of drug usage and attitudes among university students found that while hard-core drugs are rare, marijuana and tobacco use is common on campus.
>
> The poll of 100 students, conducted in-person in the *Scrounge* [an on-campus, fast-food place], found almost all students felt they could easily obtain marijuana.
>
> Nearly half of the students surveyed believe they could get cocaine and more than 25 percent think they could get heroin. All students surveyed said they felt cocaine and heroin usage is dangerous if done more than once a month.
>
> Marijuana used more than once a week was also considered harmful, according to 52 percent of those surveyed. Of those surveyed, 94 percent felt they could easily obtain marijuana.... "I know lots of people who use marijuana and a few who use cocaine," [a sophomore male student] said. "They seem to have no problems getting it." "If you want something bad enough," [a sophomore female student] said, "you can always find it." ... Illicit use of hard-core drugs (cocaine and heroin) is not as widespread. Eight percent of students surveyed said they have used cocaine and 2 percent admitted to previous heroin use. All those surveyed said they no longer use the drugs.
>
> However, 66 percent of those questioned said they have used marijuana at least once in their life. Thirty-six percent of surveyed marijuana users smoke once a week or more. Those who use marijuana between once a week and once a month account for 21 percent of the marijuana users. The remaining 43 percent said they use marijuana less than once a month. (Weaver, 1994)

Before evaluating the Scrounge data, let's look at another type of informal survey about college drug use. Below is a recent excerpt from a website that advertises itself as a service providing "college reviews by students for students." The excerpt is a summary of student opinions about the "drug scene" on that campus written by a student author of the online service.

The most-used drug among students is alcohol by far....Some students...(say) marijuana and cocaine are a problem, but for the most part no one sees heavy drug use. Some sororities and fraternities are known for certain drugs, but again, if you don't know about it, you don't see it. (College Prowler, 2010)

The goal of the Scrounge study was to describe student use of and their beliefs and attitudes about illegal drugs on the campus. This is **descriptive research** and therefore doesn't attempt to identify any causes of drug use on campus. How well do you think the goal was accomplished? For example, is 25 percent a good estimate of the percentage of students on the campus who know where to get heroin? Can you tell whether or not 25 percent is a good estimate for that campus, based on information from 100 students found in the Scrounge?

In comparison, the online service website does not provide sample size information, although it does offer 17 student ratings of the "drug scene" on that campus that presumably were used to produce the summary. Would you know much about drugs on campus from reading the above summary or from reading the 17 student ratings?

Excerpt: *Prostitutes in Jail?*

An interesting study about the treatment of prostitutes offers a controversial conclusion: Putting prostitutes in jail is not a good policy.

> "...get tough" policies are often counter-productive. For example, arresting prostitutes increases the level of violence both against these women and by them. Rehabilitation programs based on the lives and experiences of street prostitutes that will provide a path into legal employment need to be developed. (Norton-Hawk, 2001, p. 403)

Norton-Hawk conducted extensive interviews with 50 prostitutes while they were serving time in the county jail. Some of the questions were short, asking for basic information like age and when they got started in prostitution. Other questions were open-ended and complex, intended to reveal how the women got started practicing prostitution, and why they continued in it.

The author offers several arguments for her proposal. Here are three.

■ *Argument 1:* For 200 years, the city has used incarceration to discourage prostitution. It hasn't worked. Prostitution continues unabated. Why hasn't incarceration worked?

The women in Norton-Hawk's sample had no job skills that would permit them to make more than the minimum wage, except for working in the "sex trade." Therefore, most of them returned to prostitution soon after release from jail, considering the risk of "doing time" a cost of business. Also, the women grew up in a poor environment. Many had limited formal education and few job skills. Nearly 50 percent had left home by age 16, and 25 percent first ran away from home before age 10. Why did they leave home at such young ages and without completing their educations? Reasons include drug- and/or alcohol-abusing parents, severe verbal abuse and physical abuse. Forty-two percent reported sexual abuse, and 26 percent had been raped (p. 406).

> *Argument 2:* Fear of arrest forces the women to work alone, because the presence of many prostitutes in one place draws the attention of police. Yet, working alone increases the danger of physical and psychological abuse. Moreover, reporting abuse is likely to end up with the victim in jail and no punishment for the perpetrator.

Fear of arrest and the fact of doing time in jail put the women in an environment that draws them into drug addiction, subjects them to danger and often results in their working for pimps. The women did not originally work in prostitution to support a drug habit. Although most respondents had tried drugs at an early age, they didn't become addicted until after they first were paid for sex.

> *Argument 3:* Alternatives to incarceration would cost less than the cost of policing and maintaining the women in jail. The author cites several statistics about the cost of incarceration—for example, the average cost of law enforcement alone per year per city is $7.5 million, as reported in one 16-city study.

Excerpt: *Proximity of Schools and Use of Contraceptives*

Is there a connection between contraceptive use and living close to school? A study conducted in the Himalayan nation of Nepal reports a surprising finding.

> A woman's proximity to a school during childhood dramatically increases permanent contraceptive use in adulthood. This finding is largely independent of whether the woman subsequently attended school, whether her husband attended school, whether she lived near a school in adulthood, and whether she sent her children to school. (Axinn & Barber, 2001, p. 481)

What does the finding mean? The first sentence implies that living close to a school as a child influences a woman to use contraceptives after she grows up. The authors also imply that living close to a school as an adult reduces the fertility of women. Here is a sketch of this connection:

proximity to school → *contraceptive use*

read as "proximity to school leads to contraceptive use."

Axinn and Barber base their conclusions on a survey of 1395 married women in Nepal. The authors argue that girls living in a neighborhood with a school encounter many more family, friends and neighbors who support the idea of small families. The girls—and boys—tend to adopt the ideas of people around them.

Are there likely to be many differences between neighborhoods with and without schools that might lead to differences in attitudes about contraceptive use? The answer is—Yes! Before reading further, write down one characteristic of neighborhoods that might influence attitudes toward contraception.

Parents of girls living close to a school likely are more highly educated than parents in neighborhoods without a school, and highly educated parents influence their children to use contraceptives when they grow up. Therefore, parental education should be "controlled" before we can confidently conclude that living close to a school as a youth actually does influence adult contraceptive practices. As the contraception study suggests, the idea of control in social research is very important.

The notion of **control** is basic in science. It means to "hold constant" one or more factors that might affect both the presumed cause and the effect. *The point of control is to avoid misinterpreting a relationship that is not a causal relationship as if it were a cause-and-effect relationship.* This mistake is very easy to make when studying the social world.

In the Nepal study, for example, living close to a school as a child is one presumed cause of contraceptive use as an adult; parental education is one factor that might need to be controlled, because it probably affects both residence near a school and contraceptive use.

Unlike the descriptive research of the campus drug survey, study of cause and effect—such as in the research about residence and contraception use—is called **explanatory research**. Two types of control are used in explanatory social research: *physical control* and *statistical control*.

Using **physical controls**, *the researcher sets the values of all causes thought to affect the outcome*. In the contraception study, the researcher would need to exercise physical control over (a) where each subject lived and (b) how much education her parents achieved. As this example illustrates, researchers typically have limited ability to use physical controls in studies of social life. Therefore, most social research is based on *statistical control*.

Statistical control is an approximation of physical control. The researcher has no control over any of the factors that affect the outcome. Instead, the relationship between a presumed cause and presumed effect is examined separately under constant levels of other factors thought to influence the outcome.

For example, using statistical controls in the contraception study, the researcher would examine data showing the relationship between residence near a school and contraceptive use *only* for women whose parents had less than 6th-grade education, then *only* for women whose parents had between 6th- and 10th-grade educations and so forth. In each comparison, parental education is "held constant" (approximately) using statistical techniques, even though the researcher had no physical control over it.

One More Example: "Sticky Theory"

Quentin is a strong supporter of the death penalty. He participated in a psychology experiment. For the experiment, he read an article containing compelling evidence that the death penalty has almost no deterrent effect. At the conclusion of the experiment, *his support of the death penalty increased.*

Jared is a strong opponent of the death penalty. He participated in the same experiment and read an article containing compelling evidence that the death penalty deters crime. At the conclusion of the experiment, his *opposition to the death penalty increased.*

What's going on here? These two cases illustrate the findings of an interesting experiment in which two versions of "compelling" evidence were included. Half the subjects were *assigned* (using a statistically random method) to read an article supporting the effectiveness of capital punishment, and the other half read an article undermining it. Here is a summary of the findings.

> At strategic points in the reading of these two studies, the two groups completed ratings dealing both with their evaluations of the two studies and with their own changes in attitudes and beliefs. These ratings dramatically revealed the capacity of theory-holders to interpret new evidence in a manner that strengthens and sustains their theories. First, both proponents and opponents of capital punishment consistently rated the study that supported their beliefs as "more convincing" and "better conducted" than the study that opposed those beliefs. Second, and in contrast to any normative strategy imaginable for incorporating new evidence relevant to one's beliefs, the net effect of reading the two studies was to polarize further the beliefs of the death penalty opponents and proponents (Ross & Anderson, 1982, p. 145).

What *does* it take to discredit existing beliefs? Are humans always so seemingly irrational in the face of evidence? Perhaps not always, but often enough that we are going to give it a name: **sticky theory**—sticky because some ideas stick so tightly that no amount of contrary evidence dissuades people from them. *Do you know anyone whose beliefs appear to fit the idea of "sticky theory"?* No one is immune— although some ideas seem to stick better to some people than do other ideas.

A revealing video shows an example of sticky theory. It looks at the question, *Why don't even the brightest students truly grasp basic science concepts?* Researchers studied Harvard University graduates (including science majors) and compared their beliefs about a science topic to beliefs of high school students, some with no known formal education on that topic. The video shows how each person's "private universe" of misinformation persisted, even after learning the correct information (Harvard-Smithsonian Center for Astrophysics, 1987).

SIZING UP EVERYDAY LEARNING AND SCIENCE LEARNING

Except for the campus drug study, all of the examples, including the one you just read on capital punishment and "sticky theory," make comparisons designed to test an *if...then* statement. The *if...then* comparison generally implies some idea about a causal influence, or a **cause-and-effect relationship**. *If* prostitutes are put in jail, *then* they are more likely to develop a drug habit. *If* girls are reared close to a school, *then* they are more likely to use contraception as adults. *If* one reads an article about capital punishment, *then* it is likely to reinforce one's preexisting view, no matter what the content of the article.

An important thread running through the above examples is the continuity between everyday learning and science learning. The common thread arises because both the layperson and the scientist *look to experiences to identify rules*, such as, "If I do A, then B is the result." *If* the rules are cause-and-effect rules, *then* they provide reliable ways of making decisions. This is true, almost by definition, of the notion of causation.

So, how does the scientific approach to learning differ from the everyday approach? Not surprisingly, they blend into each other, as you probably noticed in the above examples. Not all everyday learning is useless—and not all science finds "the truth." But science does extend everyday learning in very important ways.

- In scientific research, extensive attention is given to *producing reliable and valid measurements*—much more than is attainable by any one individual.

- Scientific research pays close attention to *how to get a fair sample and how to avoid* **overgeneralization** *of sample information beyond the sample.* Overgeneralization from just a few, often unrepresentative, cases is a common error made in everyday life.

- Science pays close attention to *control of competing explanations for what seem to be cause-and-effect relationships.* Scientific research can afford to be much more deliberate and systematic than can any individual.

- Science expands the natural reasoning power of people by relying on formal reasoning—particularly mathematics and, to a lesser extent, formal logic.

- *Science subjects its conclusions to formal and public review*, called "peer review." Given the avalanche of claims and counterclaims we encounter in our everyday lives, the importance of peer review in science learning is difficult to overstate!

- Science *keeps much better records about its findings* than individuals are able or inclined to do. Typically, findings are written down and published in scholarly journals and books. Consequently, scientific findings are more cumulative than common sense.

But keep in mind that the line between a scientific approach to learning and common sense is not always clearly delineated. An interesting way to view science

> - **Written records:** Recipes usually are written down.
> - **Peer Review:** Recipes are passed from generation to generation.
> - **Formal Reasoning:** Recipes often are explicit and relatively precise, even containing some basic mathematics.
> - **Control of competing explanations for causation:** They have been subjected to many test to ensure an "if...then" outcome. (But tests are mostly informal and their results are not recorded.)
> - **Measurement:** Except in larger food producing firms, there is no explicit "measurement" of the taste. And, no one pays any attention to how to measure the outcome. We just want to know—Does it taste good? But some measure of taste is possible if we construct repeatable rules for doing so—a rating scale, for example.

FIGURE 1   Science and Recipes.

is as an institution that over many centuries systematized and institutionalized the way people learn naturally.

Here's an example of everyday learning that has several characteristics of scientific knowledge. What is your favorite holiday food? Do you have a recipe for it? Usually we don't classify recipes as scientific. But they do exhibit some of the characteristics we associate with science, as shown in Figure 1.

Recipes also illustrate how much we can learn without doing formal science. In fact, it's probably the case that most recipes would never have been invented if we had imposed rigid experimental rules on their development! Yes, even if we don't use it for cooking our meals, we still believe in a scientific approach—at least most of us probably do.

We end this chapter comparing science and "everyday learning" with a puzzling question: *What is the appropriate role for science in everyday life?* Think about it.

SUMMARY

This chapter presents several examples, some from everyday experience and some from published social science research. Except for the campus drug survey, all of the examples contain *if...then* comparisons, and except for the campus survey, all imply a search for cause-and-effect relationships. The capital punishment study also illustrates the idea of "sticky theory," which applies to all of us at least sometimes.

Sticky theory is a phrase we invented to try to capture the widespread observation that people sometimes hold ideas so strongly they refuse to acknowledge evidence that contradicts them. In science, however, skepticism is a strong norm. Still, science is conducted by humans; sticky theory creeps in.

If...then rules propose uniform expectations, so that we can use past observations as a guide to the future. Consequently, there is no way to "prove" a cause-and-effect rule—we have to wait to see whether it keeps on working. Our willingness to bet on it increases as it passes more and more of the observational tests it could have failed.

In this chapter, why did we include experiences from everyday life and published research? The main intent is to point out the *similarities and the differences between everyday approaches to learning and social science*. The same types of questions arise in both instances, but there are important distinctions between scientific investigation and everyday learning. The social sciences obviously have more resources and more refined methods for answering questions than does any individual, but social science still encounters many obstacles to achieving definitive answers.

YOUR REVIEW SHEET

1. The goal of the campus drug study was to describe students' beliefs and attitudes about illegal drugs on their campus. How well do you think the goal was accomplished? Do you believe 25 percent is a good estimate of the percentage of students on the campus who know where to get heroin? How can you tell?

2. There are likely to be many differences between neighborhoods with and without schools that might lead to differences in attitudes about contraceptive use. One example presented in the chapter is that parents of girls living close to a school may be more highly educated than parents in neighborhoods without a school, and highly educated parents influence their children to use contraceptives when they grow up. Offer one other explanation for why living in neighborhoods with and without schools could lead to differences in contraceptive use.

3. What is "control"? Briefly explain in your own words the purpose of control in discovering cause-and-effect relationships, both in everyday learning and social research.

4. How does a scientific approach to learning differ from an everyday approach to learning? How is it similar?

5. This chapter ends with the question, "What is the appropriate role of science in everyday life?" Write a short statement about how science plays a role in decision making in your life.

STUDY TERMS

cause-and-effect relationship Change of the cause is followed by a change in the effect, "everything else being equal," as illustrated by *if...then* statements. The study of cause and effect is called explanatory research.

control To "hold constant" one or more influences that might affect both the presumed cause and the effect. The purpose of using controls is to avoid mistaking a chance "relationship" for a cause-and-effect relationship (see **physical controls** and **statistical controls**).

descriptive research Research intended to present a summary of subjects' characteristics, one subject at a time, such as in the campus drug study. This drug study does not present comparisons designed to identify causes of drug use.

explanatory research Research with the goal of identifying cause-and-effect relationships (e.g., residence close to a school affects contraceptive use). Compare to descriptive research, which does not attempt to discover cause-and-effect relationships.

overgeneralization Concluding that a pattern observed in too small a number of instances and/or atypical instances is typical of other situations. For example, you observe in 100 lottery drawings that the number 22 turns up more often than any other number, and conclude that future drawings are more apt to turn up 22 than any other number.

physical control Control in which the researcher determines the values of all causes thought to affect the outcome. To use physical controls in the study of contraceptive use and residence, the researcher would need to (a) assign each subject to live close to *or* far away from a school and (b) assign girls to parents with low *or* high education. Neither of these requirements is possible, particularly assigning children to parents. Thus, social researchers have limited ability to use physical controls and must rely on statistical control instead.

statistical control An approximation of physical control based on the idea of observing relationships between a presumed cause and an outcome within constant levels of the control variable. For example, the relationship between living near a school and contraceptive use might be examined for each category of a third measure, such as parents' education (e.g., less than 6th grade, between 6th and 8th grade, more than 8th grade).

"sticky theory" A phrase we invented to try to capture the widespread observation that people sometimes hold ideas so strongly they refuse to acknowledge evidence that contradicts them. In science, no norm is stronger than the norm of skepticism, which should overcome sticky-theory thinking. Still, science is conducted by humans; sticky theory creeps in.

EXERCISES

Exercise 1. Evaluation of Research: Overgeneralization

Directions: First, read the following excerpt. Then, answer the questions that follow.

Bossiness in Firstborn Girls *by Beverly Capofiglia**

A total of 40 girls and 40 boys, ages 4 to 5 years, participated in this research; all of them were firstborn and had at least one younger sibling.... Protagonists were 3- and 4-year-old younger siblings of the study participants.... Each firstborn child was paired with another younger and unrelated child. The two were introduced to each other and were instructed to play while their mothers were "right outside talking to the teacher." Half ($n = 20$) of the firstborn girls were paired with other girls, and half ($n = 20$) were paired with boys. Half of the firstborn boys ($n = 20$) were paired with boys, and half ($n = 20$) were paired with girls. [Play] [s]essions lasted 20 min.

Ratings of bossiness were made from the videotapes. A Checklist of Bossy Behaviors was constructed for this research.... When contrasted to firstborn boys... the data clearly show that firstborn girls are significantly more bossy than firstborn boys. The bossiness ratings of the girls were higher when they were interacting with other girls than they were when interacting with boys... Not only does birth order make a difference in the trait under inquiry, but it has a differential effect on boys and girls. (Meltzoff, 1998, pp. 207–209)

*Capofiglia is Italian for "boss-girl." Excerpted from a fictional article developed for research education.

Questions

1. What are the two comparison groups in this excerpt?
2. Why do you think subjects were paired with younger children, rather than with older children?

3. Do you agree with the conclusion presented? For example, could differences in "bossiness" be explained by some characteristic of children other than gender? Briefly explain.

4. Does the conclusion overgeneralize? If so, list the sentence that implies overgeneralization and briefly explain how.

Exercise 2. Evaluation of Research: "Sticky Theory" in Everyday Life

Directions: First read the following overview. Then, answer the questions that follow.

Shortly before Thanksgiving 2010 the Transportation Security Agency (TSA) instituted full body scans at airports. The scans provided views of travelers' naked bodies. The alternative was "pat downs" that included touching of breasts and genitals of air travelers of both genders. A short but intense "thunderstorm" of criticism broke out targeted directly at the TSA and more broadly against the Obama administration. The criticisms came mostly from Republicans and conservatives. Shortly thereafter a comment appeared on the editorial page of *The New York Times*:

The opinion stated two main ideas: (1) If precisely the same policies had been implemented during the George W. Bush administration, the same loud howls of protests would have been leveled against the TSA and the Bush administration. But the source of the protests would have been Democrats and liberals, and the defense would have come from Republicans and conservatives. (2) Excessive "sticky theory" notwithstanding, the partisanship "does have one modest virtue." It serves as a brake on the growing potential for abuse of authority in Washington and state capitols (Douthat, 2010, p. A25).

Questions

1. What are the two comparison groups in this opinion?

2. What was the main argument by each group? How did each group choose their argument?

3. Does either argument display evidence of "sticky theory" beliefs? Briefly explain.

4. Do you agree with the conclusion presented? Why or why not?

Exercise 3. Examining Everyday Learning: Observation in a Crowded Room

Directions: Locate a room that is fairly crowded with people and items, and that you can easily enter and leave. Choose a room in a setting that you seldom visit. Examples of settings include an exercise or workout room at a busy time, a produce market, and a dining area during mealtime.

    a. Enter this room and look around for about 2 minutes.

    b. Now leave the room. Make a list of the items that you can recall.

    c. Answer the questions below.

    d. Be prepared to hand in your lists.

Questions

1. Briefly describe your setting.

2. Rewrite items you recall from your list into categories that have a common theme. What do you conclude about your observations?

3. The assignment did not provide a specific goal for your observations. For example, if you observed in a frame gallery, your focus might have been primarily on wall decorations.

4. When conducting scientific study the first step is to establish a research goal, often written in the form of a question. Write one question that you could use to focus your observations in the room that you selected. (*Example:* What types of clothing items does this campus bookstore sell?)

5. Return to the same room. Keeping your research question in mind, again look around for about 2 minutes. After leaving the room, make a list of the items that you can recall. If needed, rewrite the list into categories. Compare your two lists. What do you conclude about the differences between the two lists?

6. Did your research question help you to focus on specific items to answer your research question? Briefly explain the importance of having a research goal.

7. Why is comparison important in social research?

Exercise 4. Examining Everyday Learning: Using a Control

This exercise helps you to see the importance of considering alternative explanations for relationships. You are asked to "statistically control" potential age differences by limiting the *second* set of observations to one age group: people 25 years old or younger.

Directions: Select a busy entrance to a building. Hold the door open for one person who is following you, and then walk through the doorway. Record the characteristics (e.g., age, gender, race) of each person, and whether or not he or she said "thank you" (or "thanks"). Repeat this procedure 15 times. Then, answer the questions below. Be prepared to hand in your notes.

Questions

1. What *personal characteristics* differentiate those who said "thank you" from those who did not? For example, did more males than females say "thank you"?

2. Suppose you found that a higher percentage of males than females thanked you. However, you also noticed that most of the males were older than the females. You might wonder, Did gender or age make the difference in how they responded?

   Repeat the procedure, but this time hold the door open *only for people who appear to be 25 or younger*. Again record each person's gender and whether or not he or she said "thank you." What can you say now about whether gender or age makes the difference in responses?

3. Describe a control other than age from your list of personal characteristics that you could use to conduct another door-opening procedure. Briefly explain how your control would help you to see a relationship between saying "thanks" and gender.

4. Look again at the information for the first procedure. In everyday life we typically don't record people's behaviors and characteristics. Suppose that you held the door for the same 15 people, without recording, or even noticing, their characteristics, and whether they said "thanks." What do you think you might recall in a week or two? How would your recollections affect your conclusions?

5. How confident are you with results based on 15 people? Explain briefly. (Hint: overgeneralization).

Exercise 5. Skills Building: Overgeneralization in Everyday Life

Find an example of overgeneralization in your newspaper. Explain the conclusion and then add your critique. Be prepared to hand in a clipping of the article.

DOING SOCIAL RESEARCH: STRATEGIES AND ETHICS

INTRODUCTION: LOOKING AT HOW THE SOCIAL WORLD WORKS

Did you know that societies around the world with the highest levels of maternal education also have the highest rates of infant survival?

In an extensive review of research on illness behavior in the developing world, one study reports that many mothers in the less-developed nations have between 1 year and 6 years of primary schooling (Christakis, Ware, & Kleinman, 2001, p. 148). Before reading further, jot down how schooling for women might reduce the risk of death for their children and generally improve child health.

Perhaps you wrote that students, as future mothers, might learn basic health practices, such as hand washing, keeping away from sick people and getting immunizations. You might also have said they learn the value of nutrition and to avoid behaviors such as smoking and drinking alcohol during pregnancy. Past research has associated good maternal nutrition and avoiding smoking and drinking during pregnancy with favorable outcomes for infants and children.

Research also suggests spacing births farther apart increases child survival. Why? Two reasons are that infants can be breastfed longer and there is less competition from a subsequent child for the family's resources. Christakis and others also point out other circumstances that improve child survival, including postponing marriage and childbearing, using schooling to obtain greater economic resources and learning assertiveness to seek health care for oneself and one's dependents (pp. 148–151).

These are intriguing explanations. But the positive association between maternal education and child health is not certain evidence that mother's education actually *affects* the health of her children. Women who achieve high levels of schooling also tend to live in locations where sanitation standards, diet and medical care are above average. Maybe these factors are the primary determinants of both child health *and* women's education.

What does it take to produce believable explanations? A finding is not true automatically because it's in print. A study reported by Desai and Alva (1998), summarized in the next section, confronts the question head on: "Does maternal education actually affect child health or is the association between the two just incidental?" See how they address this question.

Goals of This Chapter

This chapter introduces the major topics in social research methods: (1) two strategies of social research (basic research and applied research), and (2) the increasingly important need for careful attention to ethics in research.

If you're assigned a research project as part of your methods course, this chapter can help you by providing an overview of the two major research strategies and a summary of ethical issues in research with human subjects with emphasis on how to avoid unethical practices. These topics are very important to understand before you begin to develop a research project.

STRATEGIES OF SOCIAL RESEARCH

How might one begin to study a topic like the effect of maternal education on child survival or, more generally, on child health? A researcher can choose one of two fundamental research strategies: conduct *basic research*, or perform *applied or evaluative research*. These strategies are distinguished by (a) the goals of the research, and (b) the intended audience for the results.

Basic Research

Basic research is research undertaken with no immediate practical application as the goal. Sometimes this type of research informally is described as "asking the question for the question's sake." In the social sciences, most basic research is undertaken by faculty and staff at colleges and universities or in research institutions, sometimes supported by research grants from government, foundations or corporations. All types of data collection are used in basic research—surveys, direct observations, indirect observation and experiments.

For example, another study also examines the relationship between maternal schooling and positive health outcomes of children (Desai & Alva, 1998). The authors point out that although there is a strong association in past research, unanswered questions remain. Specifically, they argue that maternal education could be a substitute for (a) socioeconomic status of the household, and (b) characteristics of community of residence—like sanitation standards, access to health care and diet. They include *statistical controls* for these alternative possible influences on child health. Using these controls, they examine three measures of child health—likelihood of death before 1 year of age, height-for-age and number of vaccinations for children at least 1 year of age.

This study was based on a theory that predicts a positive effect of maternal education on the well-being of their children. The goal is basic research—to clarify unanswered questions about the importance of maternal education to the well-being of their children.

Excerpt: *Maternal Education and Child Health: A Strong Causal Relationship?*

> Maternal education [is] statistically significant for children's immunization status in about one-half of the countries even after individual-level and community-level controls are introduced. (Desai & Alva, 1998, p. 71)

Because mother's education does not affect child's height-for-age or reduce death in the first year of life, the data only partially confirm the theory. The researchers did include statistical controls for alternative possible causes of mortality and height, such as father's education, access to piped water and community of residence. However, mother's education does have a direct effect on immunization in about half of the countries in the sample. The study does (a) provide some support for the importance of mother's education in the well-being of her children, and (b) clarify the pathways by which education might improve child health, such as through immunizations.

As basic research, there is no immediate practical application offered as a goal of the study. However, the findings might be combined with other research to produce practical applications for policy, such as increasing access to primary health care and clean water.

Applied Research

A second research strategy is to assess the outcomes of projects, programs and policies associated with social interventions. A *social intervention* is an activity undertaken to produce an intended practical outcome, such as programs to reduce teen birth rates (Figure 1). The investigation of a social intervention is called **applied or evaluation research**.

Evaluation research is not a method of data collection or analysis. Experiments, surveys, personal interviews and other methods of data collection are used in evaluation research, just as they are in basic research. And any method of data analysis that is used to test theory might also be used in applied research.

To evaluate a social intervention, the researcher must know the intended outcome. However, individuals involved with a social intervention ("stakeholders") do not necessarily agree on an outcome, its definition and measurement or the time period required to achieve it. For example, teachers, administrators and parents might not agree about how to measure improvement in "student learning" or how long an innovative teaching technique takes to achieve desired learning gains: A semester? A school year? Several years? A researcher undertaking the evaluation must consider the different viewpoints of many "stakeholders."

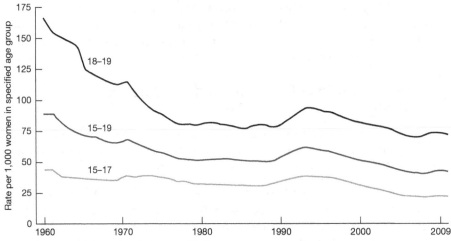

FIGURE 1   Trends in U.S. Teen Birth Rates, 1991–2009.

Source: Ventura and Hamilton, 2011.

Excerpt: *Evaluation of a Pregnancy-Prevention Program for Teenagers*

An interesting study evaluated a school-based program for the prevention of pregnancy among inner-city adolescents in Baltimore, Maryland (Zabin et al., 1986). For nearly three school years, the program offered education and counseling about sexuality and contraception, and medical and contraceptive services to students attending one of two schools—a junior high school and a senior high school. Students in two other schools (one junior high and one senior high) received no such services; they were included to provide *comparison data*.

The evaluation was designed to compare changes in the knowledge, attitudes and behaviors between students who were offered and those who were not offered pregnancy-prevention services. Data were collected from the students through self-administered questionnaires. The researchers conclude thus:

> [O]ne of the most striking findings from the project is the demonstration that boys in the junior high school used the clinic as freely as girls of the same age.... Increased and prompt clinic attendance and the resulting increased use of effective methods of contraception appear to have had a significant impact on pregnancy levels....
>
> One of its [the project's] major effects...is that it appears to have encouraged the younger sexually active teenagers to develop levels of knowledge and patterns of behavior usually associated only with older adolescents. This accelerated protective behavior, coupled with evidence that first coitus was not encouraged but, in fact, postponed, should provide solid support to the current movement toward the introduction of school-based clinics. (Zabin et al., 1986, pp. 124–125)

This evaluation excerpt suggests the two school-based clinics did influence students' behaviors and attitudes, as anticipated.[1] Although the researchers imply that other schools might benefit from similar programs, the primary goal of evaluation was to assess the contributions from the specific program studied.

In contrast, a goal in basic research might be toward clearer understanding of the role of school clinics in pregnancy prevention. Basic research might attempt to learn, for example, the *cause-and-effect relationship* between components of the program, such as whether individual counseling or the availability of nursing staff in school-based clinics reduces the risk of pregnancy.

Despite their differences, there is a common theme in both basic and applied research. Both types of research nearly always focus on *comparisons*, as illustrated in the examples presented so far in this chapter:

1. *Study of child well-being:* compared infant mortality, height-for-age measures and immunization among mothers with differing maternal education levels.

2. *Evaluation of pregnancy-prevention program:* compared various outcomes such as age at first coitus between students in the experimental program and students not in the program.

3. In basic research, however, the comparisons derive from theory. In evaluation research, comparisons come from the goals of the program being evaluated—that is, assessing program effectiveness substitutes for theory. Nonetheless, social interventions nearly always are based on some theory about what affects the outcome. In the pregnancy-prevention study, the selection of the services offered to students surely was based on some theoretical notion about influences on the sexual behaviors of students, such as knowledge of risks associated with sexual activity and contraceptive practices.

Note: *Basic research* and *applied research strategies* should not be confused with *explanatory research* and *descriptive research methods*. Explanatory research is also called *cause-and-effect research*. Both the maternal education–child health excerpt and the evaluation of the pregnancy-prevention program in this chapter are examples of explanatory research. Descriptive research is investigation that records what happens and describes how it is recorded, but does not attempt analysis of cause and effect. Both basic and applied research strategies can use explanatory and descriptive research methods.

ETHICAL ISSUES IN RESEARCH

Most social research is comparatively benign—but not all of it is. For example, the infamous Milgram (1974) experiments had subjects administer fake electric shocks to persons who knew that the shocks were fakes but were told to pretend otherwise. *You might be able to locate an online video of the Milgram experiment.*

The Belmont Report

Attention to the treatment of human subjects has intensified in recent years. The National Commission for the Protection of Human Subjects of Biomedical and Behavioral Research was created in 1974 by the National Research Act. The Commission was charged with codifying protections that must be afforded to human subjects in research.

Basic Ethical Principles. The Belmont Report summarizes the principles formulated by the Commission. The report identifies three ethical principles: "respect for persons," "beneficence," and "justice."

1. *Respect for Persons.* The principle of respect stipulates that each person must be considered an independent person, capable of looking out for his or her own welfare. Persons with handicaps limiting their capacity have the right to protection.
2. *Beneficence.* The principle of beneficence (compassionate behavior) imposes two obligations on researchers who use human subjects: (a) do no harm to the subjects, and (b) strive for maximum benefit for the subjects.
3. *Justice.* The principle of justice identified by the Commission is difficult to summarize. The basic idea is to strive for equitable distribution of benefits and burdens of research. But, in practice, determining what is equitable is very difficult. Equitable is not necessarily the same as equal. Factors such as age, experience, deprivation, competence and merit enter into equity judgments. The Commission lists five considerations: (1) to each person an equal share, (2) to each person according to individual need, (3) to each person according to individual effort, (4) to each person according to societal contribution, and (5) to each person according to merit. These principles are not necessarily consistent and often must be balanced against each other (Figure 2).

The Belmont Report is online at: *http://ohsr.od.nih.gov/guidelines/belmont.html*. It is very important to understand the expectations for research with human subjects, such as "do no harm," *before* planning a research project. Researchers are likely to need permission from an **institutional review board (IRB)**.

On college campuses, the IRB group often is called the **human subjects review board** (or human subjects committee). IRBs review research proposals for potentially harmful impacts on research participants (social, psychological, emotional, physical) and advise researchers about required changes in procedures before research may begin. IRBs pay special attention to subjects such as children, prisoners, pregnant women, mentally disabled persons and the economically or educationally disadvantaged, who might be unduly coerced or influenced to participate.

---

1. *Informed Consent.* It implements the first ethical principle, *respect for persons*.
   - It requires that each subject be given a fair summary of the research, its potential risks and benefits, and that each subject sign a formal consent document. Few persons dispute this requirement in the abstract, but, as you might imagine, many disputes arise in its specific application.

2. *Assessment of Risks and Benefits.* It is intended to help ensure the second ethical principle, *beneficence.*
   - It requires careful consideration of whether the potential benefits of research offset the risks to subjects. This consideration often may stipulate comparison of alternative methodologies for achieving the same knowledge. Review boards are expected to discuss explicitly these issues before approving a proposed research study.

3. *Selection of Subjects.* This must be designed to satisfy the principle of *justice.*
   - Procedures must be adapted that do not put same individuals or groups at unfair risk of being subjected to dangerous research procedures. The implementation must be free of personal favoritism and generalized prejudice against classes or groups of people, such as racial minorities or one gender.

FIGURE 2   Three Types of Activities Designed to Ensure Protection of Human Subjects.
Source: The National Commission for the Protection of Subjects of Biomedical and Behavioral Research, 1974.

These codes require **informed consent** from research subjects. Subjects have the right to know about the risks and benefits of their participation. Informed consent is obtained and documented from each prospective subject or the subject's legally authorized representative (e.g., parent).

Confidentiality and Anonymity

Two terms are important in research with human subjects. **Confidentiality** means the researcher knows respondents' identity, but does not reveal any information in any way that can be linked to individual respondents. For the researcher to reveal any answers of a respondent outside the research team is a breach of trust.

Ethical considerations aside, confidentiality often is important in a practical way to the success of research. Suppose someone you know earned money for college selling stolen merchandise. How likely is your acquaintance to reveal this in an interview? Undoubtedly there is no chance if the respondent believes his or her answer might be broadcast to the world.

Anonymity, a term sometimes confused with confidentiality, means the researcher keeps no records that can link respondents with their answers (e.g., on a questionnaire). Therefore, the researcher is not able to reveal any answers given by individual respondents. Anonymity is an important consideration for the study of highly personal experiences, illegal activities and other sensitive topics.

Practical Dilemmas

In practice, the principles of the Belmont Report are not easy to implement. They generate a lot of controversy and a lot of bureaucracy. For example, is it harmful to ask people about respondents' age, level of education, weight or how many alcoholic drinks they consumed last week?

As you likely have anticipated, "harm" can depend on a variety of considerations, such as who is being asked the question, who is asking the question, and how the question is asked. At the same time, the requirement to "do no harm" is of increasing concern to universities, to sponsors of research such as federal agencies and to the public.

Disaster research illustrates many of the conflicts arising from the requirement of informed consent. Disaster researchers are interested in how a community responds during natural disasters, such as an earthquake, hurricane, flood or fire and human-generated disasters like the destruction of the World Trade Center buildings in New York City.

In the past, disaster researchers typically explained the purposes of their research, promised confidentiality, asked for permission to tape interviews and answered questions from prospective interviewees (Tierney, 1998, pp. 5–6). Today, workers at a disaster site usually are required to present written documentation that explains the research in detail and to obtain written consent from research participants. People living in disaster-stricken communities during a disaster and also the disaster workers are likely to be considered "disaster victims," who require special protection. Yet, highly formalized approaches to obtain informed consent are inconsistent with the informal data collection approaches used in postdisaster studies (Tierney, 1998, pp. 6–7). Moreover, time-consuming procedures for ensuring informed consent often conflict with the need to move quickly to keep up with unfolding events.

The requirement of informed consent also poses particularly knotty problems for observational research. For example, should an on-site researcher inform potential participants they will be research subjects? This question is of special concern for participant–observers who need to blend into a group appearing as a bona fide group member. Being known as a researcher during data collection can influence responses. Subjects might choose behaviors and comments to please or displease the researcher.

Researchers have made important contributions from studies in which they were not known as researchers, such as accounts of how the American nursing home industry is producing great profits at the expense of the well-being of residents. Yet, to *not* disclose one's role as a researcher violates the norm of informed consent.

Excerpt: *Piercing the Darkness: Undercover with Vampires in America*

A recent book explores vampire culture, in part because the author became intrigued about how and why people increasingly adopted this unusual lifestyle (Ramsland, 1998). The book, *Piercing the Darkness,* describes how contemporary culture reflects aspects of the image and mythology of the vampire, and who the people are that integrate some aspects of vampire culture into their everyday lives.

To collect her data, the author sought out vampires—"people who claimed to live by a vampire's code" (p. x). She says she talked with many people and offered to listen to anyone who wanted to talk with her. This is how she decided to manage confidentiality and anonymity of the individuals she talked with.

> I gave each person the choice of using his or her real name or a pseudonym....
> [For those who preferred not to be known] I altered identifying details to the extent
> I deemed necessary. (Ramsland, 1998, p. xii)

So, what approach *should* one take to ensure confidentiality? Punch (1986) notes that in ethnographic and observational work there are no easy answers to many situational ethics. He suggests seeing research subjects as "collaborators" in the research, and behaving toward them as we are expected to behave toward friends and acquaintances in our everyday lives (p. 83). Lofland and his coauthors (2006, p. 53) emphasize that "… your research plans…the code of ethics of your academic discipline, your local IRB protocols, and any current federal or state statutes relative to privacy" should be considered before making exceptions to promising confidentiality. Should you use names in field reports and other social science endeavors? They also state, "When in doubt, the best advice remains: disguise or obscure."

Summary

This chapter introduces two major topics in social research: research strategies and research ethics. It begins by asking how one might study a critically important social science question, such as the effect of maternal education on child health and survival. The example is used to illustrate several basic issues in social research.

Two research strategies are presented: basic research and applied or evaluation research. When conducting basic research, typically there is no formal intent to evaluate a specific social policy. Applied or evaluation research assesses the outcomes of social interventions. A social intervention is an activity undertaken with the explicit goal of producing a specified outcome. In practice, however, the dividing line between basic and applied research often is blurred.

Ethical issues must be weighed carefully in social research. Researchers generally need permission from an institutional review board (IRB) before initiating a study involving human subjects. IRBs examine research proposals for potentially harmful influences on research participants and advise researchers about needed changes before research may begin.

YOUR REVIEW SHEET

1. List two influences not mentioned in this chapter that might reduce the risk of child death and generally improve child health. For each influence, is physical control or statistical control more appropriate to control (hold constant) each influence? Briefly explain.

2. Is evaluation research a method of data collection? Why or why not?

3. If information is obtained at an all-boys school, does gender vary among these students? Briefly explain in your own words the type of control implied by this type of study.

4. Should a researcher inform potential participants that they will be research subjects? Provide one reason why and one circumstance under which one might not inform participants.

5. What is an IRB? Summarize its activities.

END NOTES

1. A limitation of this study, common in evaluation research, is "clustering" of students in the two groups, which increases sampling error. It's not a fatal flaw, but one that must be considered.

STUDY TERMS

anonymity The researcher does not know the identity of respondents, and the researcher therefore cannot link data to specific individuals (compare with confidentiality).

applied (evaluation) research Investigation of a social intervention designed to find out whether it works. Evaluation is a goal or objective, rather than a method of data collection (compare with basic research).

basic research Investigation for which the goal is to expand the level of knowledge rather than to change or evaluate a social intervention or social policy. The study of the possible effects of maternal schooling on child health is an example (compare with applied research).

confidentiality The researcher knows respondents' identities, but does not reveal information in any way that can be linked to individual respondents (keeps their information confidential) (compare with anonymity).

human subjects review board See **institutional review board**.

informed consent Formal signed statement obtained from research subjects prior to starting the research. The statement affirms that the subject agrees to participate with full understanding of the risks and benefits of participation.

institutional review board (IRB) A formal committee that examines research proposals for potentially harmful impacts on research participants (social, psychological, emotional, physical). The IRB advises researchers about needed changes before research may begin. On college campuses, this group might be called the human subjects review board (or human subjects committee).

EXERCISES

Exercise 1. Evaluation of Research: Practical Dilemmas

Directions: Read the excerpt on "evaluation of a pregnancy-prevention program" in this chapter and answer the following questions.

Factual Questions

1. What is the research question? What are the comparison groups?
2. What are the main findings?

Questions for Discussion

1. Is it harmful to collect student information about sexuality and contraception attitudes and behaviors?
2. Briefly discuss at least one advantage and one disadvantage relevant to the pregnancy-prevention program.
3. Explain the benefits of informed consent for this study. Are there disadvantages? Why or why not?

Exercise 2. Skills Development: Writing Research Questions for Quantitative Research*

The goal of this exercise is to develop skills in writing research questions, so you might need to rewrite a question several times. For example, "What are children's problems?" is too broad. Better questions are "What types of behavior problems do children display between the ages of 3 and 5 years?" (descriptive research*) or "Does mother's job type influence child's behavior between the ages of 3 and 5 years?" (explanatory research). To be operational, you must specify the specific types of behaviors and how they will be measured. Of course, there may be causes of a child's behavior problems other than the mother's job, such as family problems and health of the child, for example.

Directions: Choose a social science topic. You may use one of the topics discussed in this chapter (exclude topics from an excerpt) or select one of your own.

1. Write your topic here (e.g., *children's behavior problems, ages 3–5*).
2. Write a one-sentence research question for a *descriptive study*.

---

* Qualitative research doesn't require nearly as much focus at the beginning of a study.

3. List the information needed to study the topic for a *descriptive study* and how it might be obtained (e.g., *types of behavior problems for children, ages 3–5. Data from observations of children or from questionnaires completed by children's preschool teacher*).

4. Write a one-sentence research question for an *explanatory study*. Use the *If…then* format.

5. List the information needed to study the topic for an *explanatory study* and how it might be obtained (e.g., *types of behaviors for each child ages 3–5 in the study, obtained from parent or teacher reports; and job type for each child's mother from telephone interviews of mothers*). (*Hint:* Recall that you need *two pieces of information* for an explanatory (cause-and-effect) study: the "cause" and the "effect.") In the example, "job type of mother" is considered to be the cause of "child's behavior problems," which is the effect. The idea is to study whether the mother's type of job has an effect on her children's behavior.

SCIENTIFIC METHOD AND BASIC CONCEPTS

INTRODUCTION: LOOKING AT HOW THE SOCIAL WORLD WORKS

Jenny says she is going to stop smoking. Chad says he is going to lose 15 pounds. The sign says: "Speed checked by radar." The government said it is safe to bury nuclear waste in Yucca Mountain, Nevada.[1] A total eclipse of the Sun will occur over the continental United States on August 21, 2017.

Which of the above statements do you consider the most likely to be correct? Why? Assuming astronomers have predicted a total eclipse of the sun for the United States on August 21, 2017 (which they have), most people probably judge this statement to be the most likely. As far as we know, astronomers have never been wrong about a predicted date and location for an eclipse. On the other hand, lots of people say they will stop smoking and fail to do so. Many cars exceed the speed limit on a section of road posted as "monitored by radar" without being issued a ticket. Many people intend to lose weight but don't. And we know the government hasn't tested the integrity of the Yucca Mountain site over the million years that nuclear waste will remain dangerous.

Your judgment about each statement depends on predicting what will happen, given what you know currently. And each judgment is based on experience—the more regular the pattern in the past, the more confidence you have that the pattern will continue. Astronomers' predictions of eclipses also are based on experience. Of course, the way astronomers learned how to predict eclipses is a lot more elaborate than the way we learn common-sense rules.

Goals of This Chapter

A prominent theme of this chapter is this: *Science learning is an extension of what all of us do continually: look for predictability.* In science, the idea of predictability is expressed in the concept of "causal law." The definition of causal law isn't a settled issue, but highly technical scientists generally don't worry about how to define a causal law. They look for patterns in data that can be used as rules for prediction.

A second important theme of this chapter is: *The best strategy for finding out is to search continually for new information and to update current understanding continually as new information is produced.* And note—continual searching for new information and ongoing updates of current understanding are in clear contrast with "sticky theory" beliefs. "Sticky theory" is the idea that people sometimes hold ideas so strongly that they refuse to acknowledge evidence that contradicts their ideas. The complexity of the world is one important reason for a skeptical attitude and for developing the habit of continually updating our understanding of it.

The chapter begins by defining a few key terms that are essential to the rest of the chapter and used throughout this chapter: *variable, element, case* and *relationship*.

VARIABLES, ELEMENTS, CASES AND RELATIONSHIPS (STATISTICAL, NOT LOVE)

The concept of *relationship* depends on understanding the term *variable* and is closely connected to the concept of an *element* and a *case*. So we start with these three terms, and then use them to define relationship.

Variables and Elements

A **variable** is a way of describing people or objects by assigning a category or a number to each person or object. For example, the word "color" can describe houses, flowers, animals, automobiles and numerous other items. To create the variable "color" to describe houses, we can assign a color category to each house (e.g., white, blue, gray, brown) or a number code (e.g., a blue house is a "1," a gray house "2," and so forth).

In the social sciences, gender probably is the most frequently cited example of a variable, because it is easy to define. There are two gender categories: female and male. Each person fits into exactly one. With few exceptions, there is little ambiguity about gender classification, and nearly all social research can proceed on the assumption that gender classification is unambiguous.

The people or objects being described are **elements**. Examples of elements include individual people, couples, families, cities and countries. Every variable is defined by at least two categories, and *every* element fits into *exactly one* of the categories. That is, the categories must be exhaustive and mutually exclusive of each other. **Exhaustive** means that all possible categories for elements are included as part of the definition of the variable. **Mutually exclusive** means that each element fits into only one category (Figure 1).

Height, weight, age and income are examples of *numerical variables* often used in social research. Each individual is assigned exactly one height, one weight, one age and one income (mutually exclusive), and every possible value of these variables can be represented by one number (exhaustive).

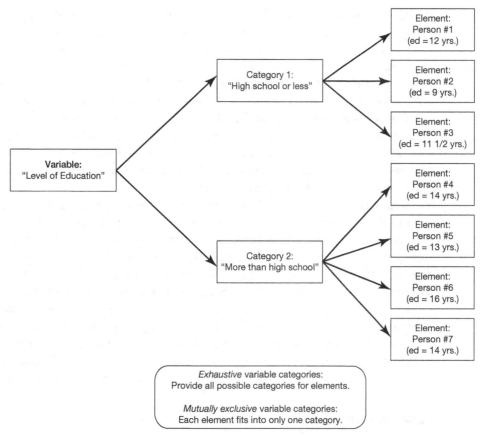

FIGURE 1   Schematic Illustrating Variable, Category, Element.

Another frequently cited social science example of a variable is race. Defining the categories of race is more controversial than is defining the categories of gender, or height, or weight. A commonly used collection of categories is Asian, black, white, Native American/Pacific Islander, Other. However, decision rules must be established to ensure that each person fits into exactly one racial category. Inclusion of the "Other" category is necessary to ensure that the categories are exhaustive—that is, accommodate everybody.[2]

The **value** of a variable is the category or number assigned to it for one element. For example, the monetary value of your 1992 "heap of junk" car is $300. In 2013, the year of this writing, the value representing its age was 2013–1992 = 21 years (or 22, depending on the exact current date and the date of manufacture).

Defining and Constructing Variables. If you are studying income differences among racial groups, define the racial categories carefully. For example, if for convenience, you use two categories "white" and "other," you tend to eliminate possible racial differences. This is because the "other" category contains racial groups with both high (e.g., Asians) and low incomes (e.g., blacks).

Often the definitions are long-standing in a discipline, so the individual scientist may take them as given. Newer scientists—including student researchers—can look in published research to learn long-standing definitions. Sometimes new variables must be constructed and their definitions developed or old definitions revised.

Concepts or **constructs** are variables that are not directly measurable (by one or more of the five senses of touch, taste, smell, vision and hearing). Variables such as prejudice, self-esteem, occupational status and intelligence are examples of constructs. To assign numbers or codes to abstract concepts like *prejudice* or *self-esteem,* explicit, detailed rules must be devised.

Codes are numbers or letters representing values of a **categorical variable**, such as the categories of male and female for the variable gender. For example, you may decide to assign the letter "F" to represent female and the letter "M" to represent male. More commonly, especially in computer-based statistical software, *numeric* codes are used, for example, "1" for male and "2" for female. The rules for assigning the numbers or codes comprise the **operational definition** of a variable.

Of course, when numbers are used as arbitrary codes for categories, they lose their meaning as numbers. Rather, they are simply symbols. For example, the code of "0" assigned to represent male gender is not ranked lower than "1" for female gender. This type of coding is very convenient and used so frequently that this type of variable is given a special name: *dummy variable* (or *binary variable).*

Case and Relationship

In the English language, the word *case* is used in many contexts. In this section, we give it one specific meaning—a **case** is the collection of values for all the variables in a study for one element. Cases can be people, couples, organizations and so on. In short, a case provides a profile. The word **observation** is a synonym for case. For example, here are two hypothetical cases:

| Case #1 | 23 years old | female | white race | $12.50 per hour |
| Case #2 | 21 years old | male | black race | $12.75 per hour |

A **relationship** (or **association**) is defined for two or more variables. By definition, *two variables are related if knowing the value of one of them reduces uncertainty about the value of the other one*. For example, knowing the age of an automobile reduces uncertainty about its monetary value.

When knowledge of one variable reduces uncertainty about the other variable to *zero*, there is a **perfect relationship**. For example, there is a perfect relationship between your age and your mother's age. Knowing both your current age and your mother's age when you were born predicts exactly your mother's current age.

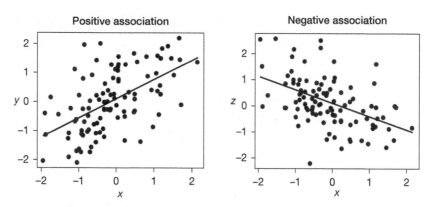

FIGURE 2   Examples of Positive and Negative Association.

Relationships also can be positive or negative. A **positive relationship** is one in which the two variables are related so their linkage "travels" in the same direction. As the value of one variable goes up, the value of the other variable goes up, and vice versa. For example, as city size increases, traffic congestion increases. A **negative relationship** is one for which the direction of change of the two variables is opposite. As a car gets older, its monetary value declines: as age increases, price decreases. Figure 2 illustrates positive and negative relationships.

WHAT ARE CAUSAL LAWS?

A loose definition of a causal law is a "rule for prediction." The rule is a *relationship*, based on what is already known. But the concept of cause-and-effect is more subtle and complex.

In everyday conversation, the word *cause* generally carries some connotation of *produces*. For example, the microwave heats the popcorn which produces enough pressure to cause the corn kernels to explode. But careful analysis reveals that the idea of *produce* is not necessary. *If* popcorn kernels are heated, *then* they pop. More generally, a **cause-and-effect relationship** occurs where knowledge of the cause reduces uncertainty about the effect. If I smile at a friend, the chance my friend will smile at me goes up.

In science, the ultimate determinant of what is (and is not) a cause-and-effect relationship is examining what happens in the physical world, called an *empirical test*. The empirical test is important because you don't "understand" unless your explanation "works." For example, if you claim rattlesnakes don't strike unless they shake a rattle at you first, no matter how reasonable the explanation sounds, the ultimate test is an empirical test—go out and check what happens!

Two terms you will encounter repeatedly in social science are **independent variable** and **dependent variable**. The independent variable is the expected cause in a relationship, and the dependent variable is the expected effect.

Cause and Effect: Universal Laws and Specific Instances

Cause-and-effect terminology is used in many ways. For example, what attribute do all of these statements share?

1. Tom is tall because his father is tall (Tversky & Kahneman, 1982, p. 120).
2. The average hourly wage of women is less than the average for men.
3. The more people associate, the more they like each other (Homans, 1950).
4. The fire was caused by a 3-year-old playing with matches.

Each statement implies some kind of *cause-and-effect relationship between two or more variables*. The first one relies on expecting a positive relationship between the heights of fathers and sons, and the "cause" of the son's height is the father's height. In example 4, the 3-year-old plays with matches, which "causes" the fire.

Although each statement expresses a cause-and-effect relationship, there are three important distinctions among them.

1. *Some are universal rules, and others are specific applications of these rules.* Example 4 is a *specific application* of universal rules. The fire was caused by a 3-year-old playing with matches. The particular situation has to do with *specific* sources of heat and fuel. (Oxygen is nearly everywhere, so here it is a constant.) In this example, heat from a match set in motion a chain of causes and effects.

2. In contrast, example 3 (association leads to affection) illustrates a *universal rule* about human behavior. Science focuses on finding universal rules. Applications such as forensic science and police work rely on identifying specific instances of the universal rules.

3. *Many of these relationships are between two numeric variables, like height and weight. But some of them refer to categorical variables, like gender.* With either type of variable, the idea of a "relationship" remains—*knowing the value of one variable (the cause) reduces uncertainty about the value of another variable (the effect).*

4. *Some of these relationships refer to change over time.* For example, "the more people associate with each other, the more they like each other" implies a process that unfolds over time.

Do cause and effect ever occur simultaneously? For most practical situations in social science, we can assume there is at least a very short time lag between cause and effect.

Spurious (Noncausal) Relationships and Their Control

If people eat ice cream mostly in the summer, it does not mean that eating ice cream causes summertime. In other words, just observing a relationship between two variables isn't convincing evidence for a cause-and-effect connection between them. In the ice-cream example, however, probably there is a cause-and-effect relationship, but it runs from the warm summertime weather to eating ice cream.

The term **control variable** defines a variable that is held constant. If a relationship between two variables, say A and B, is observed within constant categories of a third variable, call it C, we say C is *controlled*. Therefore it cannot account for a relationship between A and B. For example, look at the relationship between eating ice cream (A) and season of the year (B) controlling for outdoor temperature (C).

Why is a control variable important? The control variable might affect *both* the dependent variable (possible effect) *and* the independent variable (possible cause), so that actually *the independent variable has no causal effect on the dependent variable*.

For example, there is a negative relationship between wearing a dress and wearing a beard because both are affected by gender, as shown in Figure 3. (At least three variables must be considered together for one of them to be called a control variable.) In the case of wearing a beard and wearing a dress, the control variable is gender. In this example, gender is a **confounding variable**—a variable producing a **spurious** (noncausal) **association** between wearing a dress and wearing a beard.

Control can take place (1) by physical manipulation or (2) statistically. An example of *physical manipulation* is chilling several sodas to a specific temperature before conducting a taste test. The idea is to keep the temperature of all drinks the same (constant) so it can't affect judgments of taste. *Statistical control* may be used when physical control is impossible. Social scientists can't physically control the gender of a person, in contrast to control of the temperature of sodas, but they can examine the relationship between wearing a dress and wearing a beard separately for each gender (e.g., first for women and then for men). This is one type of statistical control. Also control of a variable can be approximated by (3) random assignment to categories of the independent variable.

How do you know what should be the control variable, for example, for a project assigned by your supervisor in a future job? As with most social research, the selection of a control variable is specific to the situation.

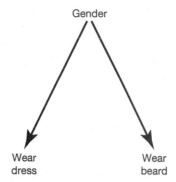

FIGURE 3 Spurious Relationship: Gender Affects Wearing a Dress and Wearing a Beard.

Qualitative Science and Causal Laws

Not all scientific investigations look for causal laws, at least not directly, and not all science is **quantitative (numbers-based) research**, that is highly quantitative and mathematical. **Qualitative (meaning-based) research** is relatively unstructured, with an interpretive, naturalistic approach to its subject matter. Often the goal is to make sense of, or interpret, concepts according to the meanings people bring to them. Qualitative science generates invaluable information about topics as varied as experiences of patients in nursing homes; humans coping with disasters; and the mentality of street gangs.

Many qualitative studies are conducted in the social and behavioral sciences. As in biology, many aspects of human behavior are difficult or impossible to study with quantitative methods. The Disaster Research Center (DRC) located at the University of Delaware maintains an ongoing research program that depends heavily on qualitative methods. For instance, a quick-response team was deployed to the site of the disaster at the World Trade Center on September 11, 2001. Here is a short excerpt from the DRC website:

> On September 13th, a quick-response field team from the Disaster Research Center traveled to New York City to observe the efforts underway in response to the tragic attack on the World Trade Center. Since that time, faculty and staff from the DRC have been returning to New York City to systematically observe emergency management activities, conduct informal interviews, attend planning meetings, collect documents, and employ other unobtrusive field work strategies in the impacted area. Settings in which fieldwork has been conducted include the City's Emergency Operations Center, incident command posts in the Ground Zero area, the FEMA Disaster Field Office, supply and food staging areas, bereavement centers, and hospitals (*http://www.udel. edu/DRC/Quick_Response_Studies/2001_WTC.html*).

The potential importance of documenting the kinds of activities mentioned in this statement is clear. Yet, quantitative methods often associated with science do not apply. Neither are causal laws likely to be an immediate outcome of such activities. The descriptions are done with the expectation that others will find them useful—probably not in developing explicit causal laws, but in helping determine effective policy related to disasters. "Useful policy" has to do with reducing uncertainty about the future based on what we know today; cause-and-effect relationships are implicit in most policy.

Qualitative science provides at least two important functions.

- Qualitative science documents what has happened, either in human affairs or in other matters.
- Qualitative science provides important perspective for current decisions and strategies. The documentation provides the "input" for the perspective. Without information, there is no perspective—that is, where to focus our attention, a narrowing of possibilities.

Qualitative methods may be combined with quantitative data in dynamic study of recovery from disasters. For example, the DRC currently is conducting a long-term study of recovery from major hurricane destruction, Hurricane Katrina and Hurricane Charley:

> This literature offers rich cross-sectional insights into recovery at a given point in time, but limited views of changes over time or systematic, quantitative empirical descriptions of recovery over large areas.
>
> An opportunity exists now to address some of these limitations using newly available high-resolution satellite imagery, previously underutilized statistical data, and field survey techniques that capture a detailed geographically-referenced record of recovery through photographs, video, and observations. (*http://www.udel.edu/DRC/ current_projects/PostDisasterRecovery.html*)

SCIENTIFIC APPROACH

Science proposes rules about how the world works and checks to see whether they are correct by observing whether they describe what happens. The proposed rules are formulated as relationships called **hypotheses**.

An example of a hypothesis is, rattlesnakes strike only after they warn you with their rattles. In a test of a relationship, the presumed cause is called the **independent variable**, and the effect is called the **dependent variable**. The determination of independent variable (e.g., rattlesnake shakes its rattles) and dependent variable (e.g., rattlesnake strikes) has meaning only when we think there is a causal connection between two variables—warning followed by strike. In this instance, however, probably both the rattle and the strike are instigated by the snake's detection of a threat.

Scientific Theory

The term *theory* as used in science doesn't mean exactly what it means in every-day conversation, such as "I have a theory about why people ride motorcycles." But the two meanings of theory are similar. Scientific theory isn't easy to define, however.

One way to think about **theory** is as a collection of hypotheses about a coherent topic. A set of hypotheses about the cause-and-effect relationships among parental status, mental ability and educational degrees on occupational status and earnings, for example, has collectively been called a "theory of status attainment." A random collection of hypotheses isn't a theory, however. The hypotheses must "belong together." For example, hypotheses about the behavior of the planets and the behavior of children with a learning disability do not belong in the same theory.

Parsimony Is Simplicity. Suppose you have two theories that make the same predictions. Which one would you choose? In science, the simpler theory is preferred. This principle is called **parsimony**. The principle of parsimony often is associated with William of Ockham (1285–1347/49) and sometimes is called "Ockham's razor," because he used it so frequently to dispense with what he viewed to be redundancy. But the principle predates even William Ockham and has been used often in subsequent scientific debate.

The impulse for parsimonious theory can be seen in many aspects of social science. For instance, stratification theory is aimed at developing a comprehensive explanation of inequality encompassing class, race, gender, ethnicity and many other factors that give rise to inequality among people. The intention is to identify the common processes among these apparently distinctive threads. A theory that creates a new hypothesis for each new case it can't predict is difficult or impossible to falsify.

Serendipity: Surprise in Science

An important component of scientific development might ironically be called "finding the unexpected"—an irony (contradiction) because most scientific discoveries come after long, arduous and tedious work. But an element of surprise, often called **serendipity**, also is thought to figure prominently in the history of scientific discovery.

The discovery of penicillin is a well-known example of serendipity. Alexander Fleming discovered penicillin by noticing that a particular bacterium did not grow on mold which had infested cultures of the bacterium. Notice that the investigator Fleming was immersed in the research. There was an element of serendipity in his discovery, but it's hard to imagine this discovery would have been made "out of the clear blue" by someone not engaged in the research. Hard work and expertise definitely are essential.

Science as Public Knowledge

Are social support groups of benefit to breast cancer patients? *The New York Times* published a summary of a study—with findings opposite to the common thinking at the time. The summary stated that women with advanced breast cancer do not benefit from support groups, a commonly held, powerful belief (Kolata, 2001). If most of the general population believes there *are* benefits from "social support," why was this study undertaken?

The investigators began their study because they were concerned that many patients felt obligated to join support groups to fight their cancer, whether they wanted to or not. Many were convinced of the benefits of support groups by a small and inconclusive study published more than a decade prior to the study reported in the *Times*. The earlier study indicated that support groups could substantially prolong patients' lives. *The New York Times* article quotes leading medical researchers praising the revised findings, because they are based on a much larger sample and use better methods than the original study.

The debate about the benefits of support groups to cancer patients illustrates a basic aspect of science. *Scientific research is open to public scrutiny, particularly by other scientists with the same or related specialties as those who conducted the research.* Findings are published in scientific journals. Each paper must be reviewed critically by peers before it is published. In contrast, as "lay scientists," we often keep our "findings" private. At most, we may try them out on a few family members, friends and acquaintances.

But the process of accumulating findings in science is much more systematic. In science, written records are kept, and the whole process is very deliberate. Because of these steps, erroneous ideas are less likely in science than in the general culture. Scientific process, however, is far from perfect. Yet science embodies a built-in mechanism designed to be self-correcting in the long run, because of the open competition in the "marketplace" of ideas.

Skepticism and "Sticky Theory"

In science, even the most extensively tested ideas are not final. Thus scientists seldom use the word "prove" when describing their findings. Some theories and their associated hypotheses have passed so many tests that we are willing to bet they'll pass the next one—but the next test necessarily will happen in the future. There's nothing that guarantees test results will be duplicated in future studies.

Because of this indirect way of doing tests of scientific theories, hypotheses associated with a theory must be **falsifiable**. That is, they must be stated so that findings could invalidate the theory. If a hypothesis can't be falsified at least in principle, it isn't a scientific hypothesis (Popper, 1968). Can the claim in Figure 4 be falsified?

Skepticism is one contribution of science to everyday learning—the mind-set to reserve judgment, minimizing "sticky theory." However, people have to act, often before compelling evidence is in. So a part of "good judgment" is knowing when to act—and still reserve judgment.

FIGURE 4 World's Best Coffee?

Summary

This chapter opens with several illustrations of how each of us looks for relationships in everyday learning. For example, what is the relationship between studying hard to get good grades and going out every night with friends? The idea is to use experience to develop rules for reducing uncertainty in everyday life and in scientific research. The second section reviews several basic concepts that are needed in the remainder of the chapter and in the social sciences generally. This material includes definitions of the fundamental concepts of variable, element, case and relationship. A variable is a way of describing differences among people or objects; examples include gender and age. An element is the people or objects being described. A case is a profile showing the value of one or more variables for a single person or object, also called an observation. Two variables are related if knowing the value of one of them reduces uncertainty about the value of the other. *Association* is another term for relationship.

Much science has to do with identifying cause-and-effect relationships. A cause-and-effect relationship is a rule for expectations about the future based on current knowledge. But discovering cause-and-effect relationships isn't easy. One of the primary reasons for the difficulty is that an observed relationship between two variables might be due to another variable. Wearing a dress and growing a beard *are* related, but only because both of them depend on gender, for example.

In a cause-and-effect relationship between two variables, the cause is called the independent variable and the effect is called the dependent variable. A cause-and-effect relationship must persist when other variables are held constant (controlled). Also, the effect can't precede the cause in time in a cause-and-effect relationship and changing the cause is *followed* by a change in the effect (or, at least the effect does not precede the cause).

Scientific investigation doesn't proceed by observing every detail in the world but depends on hypotheses. A hypothesis is a proposed cause-and-effect relationship (usually). Hypotheses must be formulated so that they can be falsified by empirical test. One way to view scientific theory is as a collection of hypotheses about a topic. Theory is an essential guide indicating where to look for useful relationships. Often theories contain unmeasurable variables, like the economic concept of utility, which are used in models to predict relationships among measured variables. Theory ties together (provides a unifying framework for) broad classes of behavior.

Parsimony refers to the preference for simplicity. Given that two theories make the same prediction, the simpler theory is preferred. Serendipity is a fancy name for the role of luck in research: finding unexpected relationships. But, most discoveries probably arise from long, arduous investigations with much trial and error. And scientists engaged in hard work are the people who spot serendipitous findings. They are the only ones in a position to observe the unexpected events and with the expertise to recognize their importance.

Generally, qualitative investigation is used when the subject matter is too complicated to be quantified. Qualitative research documents what happens and describes the structure of what is seen, such as human emotional reactions and the meanings people attach to events or circumstances. Qualitative research also provides many insights into cause-and-effect relationships that we likely would overlook otherwise.

What can you learn from the ideal of scientific approach? In short, be flexible, learn from experience, be skeptical and avoid the fallacy of "sticky theory." Be aware that a limited sample of cases might not be typical of the rest of the world. *Always be on the lookout for possible alternative explanations of relationships that you do observe.*

YOUR REVIEW SHEET

1. What is "theory," and what role does it play in science?

2. Suppose you have two theories that make the same predictions. Which one do you choose? Why?

3. How does science differ from how people learn informally—that is, from common sense? How are they similar?

4. Suppose your 10-year-old cousin asked you, "What is science?" Summarize your answer to the question.

5. In your own words, what are the contributions of qualitative science?

6. In social science, perfect relationships almost never are observed. Why not?

7. Are even the most extensively tested scientific ideas ever considered to be final? Why or why not? (*Hint:* Consider falsifiability.)

8. What is a hypothesis? Why can we *reject* a hypothesis but never prove a hypothesis?

9. Observing a relationship between two variables is not convincing evidence for a causal connection between the two variables. Why not, if you've observed it? Offer an example to illustrate. (*Hint:* Think about control.)

10. In a summary sentence, how does social science differ from other sciences?

END NOTES

1. The plan to bury nuclear waste in at the Yucca Mountain site has been the target in a long history of political and legal dispute. The Obama administration canceled the Yucca Mountain nuclear-waste burial site.

2. The 2000 and 2010 U.S. Censuses permitted people to select more than one racial category. This means that the collection of answers to the race question do not form a single variable. A sequence of variables, each with two categories, must be constructed. Each racial category (e.g., white) may be assigned a yes or no. In this case, for example, one may be both black and white, but there are two variables to handle this possibility. Race, for most purposes, probably is best viewed as a social category rather than biological. For example, if you view yourself as black and are defined as black by others, you fit the social category of "black," irrespective of the exact shade of your skin and the mix of biological races in your ancestry.

STUDY TERMS

association See relationship.

case A collection of values for every variable from one subject or respondent in a study, or, more generally, for every element. If elements were households, for example, each case might contain variables like size of household, number of children under age 18 in the household, gender of the "head of household," household income, square feet in the house or living quarters, whether the living quarters are owned or rented, etc.

categorical variable A variable with categories that are different from each other, but one category is neither greater nor less than any other category, e.g., gender contains two categories; marital status contains several. But married is neither less than nor greater than single, for example.

cause-and-effect relationship A relationship that occurs where current knowledge of the cause reduces uncertainty about the effect at some time in the future. Change in the cause is followed by a change in the effect, "everything else being equal."

concepts (constructs) Variables that are not directly measurable; examples include prejudice, self-esteem, occupational status, and intelligence.

confounding variable A variable producing a *spurious* (noncausal) association between two other variables.

control Studying a relationship between two variables while "holding constant" at least one other variable that might threaten a cause-and-effect interpretation of the relationship (see **control variable**).

control variable A variable that is held constant when observing the relationship between two other variables. The two other variables are considered the dependent and independent variables. The purpose of the exercise is to see whether the relationship between the dependent and independent variables still exists within constant categories of the control variable.

dependent variable The effect or outcome variable in a relationship.

elements The people or objects being described.

exhaustive categories Set of categories that accommodate every person or object; no person or object is left unclassified.

falsifiable Hypothesis formulated so that empirical tests might show it is wrong.

hypothesis Speculation about how the world works. In science it's usually a proposed cause-and-effect relationship that, at least in principle, can be checked against observation.

independent variable The variable that is hypothesized to be the cause in a relationship between two variables.

mutually exclusive categories Set of nonoverlapping categories defined so every person or object fits into exactly one category, no more.

negative relationship Direction of change of two variables is opposite. As one goes up the other goes down, and vice versa.

operational definition Collection of rules for obtaining information that will become a variable.

parsimony Simplicity; in science, the simpler theory is preferred when two theories make the same predictions.

perfect relationship Relationship for which knowledge of one variable reduces uncertainty about the other variable to zero.

positive relationship Direction of change of two variables is the same, as one goes up the other goes up, and vice versa.

qualitative research ("meaning-based" research) A relatively unstructured approach to social science, involving an interpretive, naturalistic method, attempting to make sense of, or interpret, phenomena in terms of the meanings people bring to them.

quantitative research ("numbers-based" research) Comparatively structured research that emphasizes cause-and-effect relationships among variables, using data represented by numbers.

relationship (or association) A relationship exists between two variables when knowing the value of one variable reduces uncertainty about the value of the other variable. Knowledge of gender, for example, reduces uncertainty about hair length.

serendipity Finding the unexpected, thought to figure prominently in the history of scientific discovery.

spurious association A *non*-cause-and-effect relationship between two variables, generated by their common dependence on another variable.

theory In brief, a collection of hypotheses about a coherent topic.

value (of a variable) Category or number assigned to one variable for a single case.

variable Way of describing people or objects by assigning a category or a number to each person or object. There must be at least two categories, and every person or object must fit into exactly one of the categories. We say the categories must be exhaustive and mutually exclusive of each other.

EXERCISES

Exercise 1. Evaluation of Research: Testing the Relationship between Variables

Directions: Read the journal article by Rand D. Conger, Frederick O. Lorenz, Glen H. Elder, Jr., Ronald L. Simons, and Xiaojia Ge. (Lorenz, 1993). "Husband and wife differences in response to undesirable life events." *Journal of Health and Social Behavior, 34*, 71–88. Your instructor will provide instructions for obtaining the article.

Factual Questions

1. In your own words, state the general hypothesis(es) tested in the study. In each hypothesis, underline the dependent variable and circle the independent variable (or its categories).

2. Is this study an example of qualitative or quantitative research? Explain your answer.

3. Summarize in your own words the findings of the study.

Question for Discussion

1. How well do you think the results from this sample generalize to all married couples? Why?

Exercise 2. Skills Building: Operationalizing Concepts

Directions: This exercise gives you chances to practice converting abstract concepts into measurable variables, the process called "operationalization."

Example: Hypothesis: Black males who assault white women are more likely to be sent to prison than are white males who assault white women.

Concept 1: racial background (of males)

Concept 2: sent to prison (for assaulting white women)

Independent Variable: race categories: black and white*

Dependent Variable: sent to prison (yes, no) or categories: years (in 5-year time intervals)[*]

Topic 1: Are males or females more likely to be admitted to medical school?

What is the independent variable?

List its categories. _____

What is the dependent variable?

List its categories (consider as a dummy variable).

Topic 2: Do younger or older teens spend more time on household chores?

What is the independent variable? _____

List its categories. _____

What is the dependent variable?

List its categories (collapse it into three categories and explain why the three you chose are sensible).

Exercise 3. Skills Building: Evaluating Hypotheses

Directions: For each of the following hypotheses:

1. Identify the variables.
2. Define operational definitions for each variable.
3. Determine whether or not each hypothesis could be tested as written, and briefly explain your answer.
4. Identify at least one variable that should be "controlled" before accepting a causal connection between the variables.

   a. High school students with good grades are more likely to attend college than students with low grades.

   b. Opinionated people live shorter lives than open-minded people.

   c. Men who participate in organized sports are cocky.

[*]Other categories could be proposed, depending on the study design.

Exercise 4. Skills Building: Writing and Evaluating Hypotheses

The goal of this exercise is to develop skills in writing and evaluating research hypotheses using a basic data table, the "2 × 2 table." A 2 × 2 table has two rows and two columns: one row is for each category of a two-category variable (in this text, the dependent variable) and one column for each category of a two-category independent variable.

Directions: Choose one of the topics listed below.

- Smiling at a friend, friend smiling
- Wearing a magnet for pain relief
- Attending religious services, praying at home

1. Write a one-sentence hypothesis for an *explanatory study*. Use "if-then" format. You might need to rewrite a hypothesis several times (or re-draw your 2 × 2 table).

2. Underline the dependent variable and circle the independent variable.

3. Create a table that looks like the one shown below.* Put dependent variable categories in rows, and independent variable categories in columns. Invent *hypothetical* (but sensible) data for your table, using percentages.

4. Write a one-sentence finding about your results like the one for Table 1.

Finding: "Those who go out frequently are much less likely to study hard (10%) than those who go out infrequently (85%)." Here, the independent variable is going out, and the dependent variable is level of studying.

Do you think that the decision to study hard might affect frequency of going out? If so, the independent variable is studying hard and going-out frequency is the dependent variable.

Hint: For an explanatory study (cause-and-effect study) you need two pieces of information: the "cause" and the "effect". In Table 1 the idea is to study whether going out (here, the independent variable) has an effect on studying.

TABLE 1. Sketch of the Relationship between Studying and Going Out (Hypothetical Data)

	Go Out Frequently (%)	Go Out Infrequently (%)
Study Hard	10	85
Neglect Studies	90	15
Total	100	100

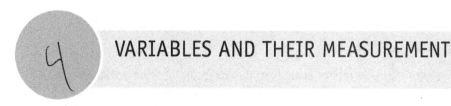

VARIABLES AND THEIR MEASUREMENT

INTRODUCTION: LOOKING AT HOW THE SOCIAL WORLD WORKS

"The Eagles have 'Big Mo' on their side—momentum, that is. The Chiefs have team chemistry."

"Hey! Go after it, man! Work hard and you'll get rich!"

"You've got to believe in yourself."

"Study hard and you'll make it. America is the land of opportunity!"

What do these claims have in common? They all imply we have in ourselves the capacity to succeed against high odds, in the greatest *Star Trek* tradition. But to succeed, we have to believe in ourselves and work hard! The notion of "controlling your destiny" by hard work and ability is more apparent in most of these statements than in the one about team chemistry. What is "team chemistry"? It's not an easy term to define, but it seems to include several components:

- Team members like each other.
- Team members anticipate what their teammates will do next.
- The team exhibits high team spirit—there is an atmosphere of joking and confidence.
- Each team member "goes at 110 percent, 110 percent of the time."

A key idea implied in the phrase *team chemistry* seems to be that good team chemistry fosters team success, and that team chemistry is something that coaches and "team leaders" can nourish to improve the fortunes of their team. It does appear that winning teams tend to have better team chemistry than losing teams. Even supposing this appearance is correct, it's not clear whether teams win because they have good team chemistry, or teams have good team chemistry because they win, or a little of both.

Goals of This Chapter

The notion of team chemistry is an everyday example of what social scientists call a **construct**—a concept or idea that is abstract and not directly measurable. The construct, "team chemistry," probably is too complex and poorly defined to be used in research.

This chapter helps to show how to turn abstract constructs into variables. A **variable** has *unique* categories that must include every person being studied (or other study object, such as couples, agencies, schools, etc.). The process of converting abstract concepts into variables is called **operationalization**.

The next section summarizes a study that illustrates how variables are used in research.

EXAMPLE: SELF-ESTEEM AND SUCCESS IN SCHOOL

An interesting study examines the cause-and-effect relationships among the abstract concepts of "self-esteem" and "personal control." Look at how the authors operationalized these concepts.

Excerpt: *A Study of Self-Esteem and Grades*

Most previous research on adolescent self-concept has included self-esteem or, less commonly, the sense of personal control, but not both. Using three waves of panel data from the National Educational Longitudinal Study, the authors examined the effects of academic achievement in the 8th grade on the sense of personal control and self-esteem in the 10th grade and the subsequent effects of control and esteem in the 10th grade on academic achievement in the 12th grade.

They present evidence that the sense of personal control affects subsequent academic achievement, but that self-esteem does not. Earlier academic achievement and parental support increase self-esteem and the sense of personal control. (Ross & Broh, 2000, p. 270)[1]

In this study, "personal control" refers to one's generalized belief about how much influence the person has over her or his own successes and failures in life. Personal control and self-esteem aren't directly *observable*. That is, no one can directly see, hear, feel, or touch either personal control or self-esteem. Yet there is pretty good indirect evidence that people differ on tendencies thought of as personal control and self-esteem. For example, people tend to classify each other along such dimensions as "high self-esteem" or "low self-esteem," often based on subtle cues.

In place of subtle cues, Ross and Broh depended on answers to questionnaire items as operational definitions. For "personal control" the questions asked whether respondents believed (1) they had no control over life, (2) luck is important, (3) others stop their personal progress and (4) their plans rarely (or always) work out. Questions for "self-esteem" were respondents' beliefs about whether they (1) are a person of worth, (2) do as well as others, (3) are satisfied with self, (4) feel useless at times, (5) feel no good and (6) are not proud. Higher values for the personal control and self-esteem variables represent higher sense of personal control and self-esteem, respectively. Grades probably seem concrete because we are familiar with them. But grades also might be viewed as imperfect indicators of an abstraction: student learning.

The authors posed several questions, one of which is *Do students with high self-esteem make good grades because they have high self-esteem or do they have high self-esteem because they've made good grades in the past?* Figure 1 summarizes the main ideas.

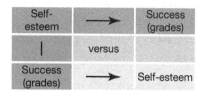

FIGURE 1   Direction of Effect between Self-esteem and Success (grades).

In general terms, what are Ross and Broh trying to accomplish? They're trying to unravel the old question of how achievement affects one's attitudes toward oneself, and how one's attitudes affect achievement. This is another version of the theme in the first paragraph about success and sports: The way people think of themselves affects whether they succeed, rather than success breeding confidence. Ross and Broh conclude that it is the latter—Success leads to higher self-esteem.

The theory tested by Ross and Broh depends on operationalizing complex constructs such as self-esteem, personal control and parental support, turning them into variables. Of course, not all social science variables are from complex constructs. For example, "age in years" is pretty straightforward to operationalize—it is just the number of years between your date of birth and your most recent birthday. A variable like age poses fewer operational difficulties than complex, abstract constructs like self-esteem. And much social research depends on complex constructs. Consequently, most of the discussion in this chapter focuses on measuring constructs that are abstract and not readily observable.

VARIABLES: DEFINING, CREATING, CLASSIFYING

S.S. Stevens defines measurement as *the assignment of numbers to objects according to rules* (1946; 1958). For the most part, Stevens's formulation is accepted in the social sciences, except that assigning numbers to objects is implicitly generalized to assigning numbers *or* categories.

Defining Variables: Indicators and Indexes

The first step in creating a variable is to define what you want to measure. This is easy for concrete variables like age and gender; definitions already exist. But it is more complicated for constructs like morbidity, personal control, or team chemistry, none of which can be observed directly.

Because constructs such as "team chemistry" can't be physically observed, their measurement depends on **indicators**. Indicators, such as a question on a survey, are observable and are used as *indirect measures* of a construct. The assumption is that the unobservable construct "causes" or influences the answers that people give to the indicators.

Generally, constructs are developed from everyday ideas, with specific rules about how they'll be turned into variables. For example, an **index** is created by combining two or more variables, usually by adding or averaging the values of the variables.[2] In the Ross and Broh paper, self-esteem and personal control were defined as indexes, comprised of six items (questions) and four items, respectively.

Ultimately, variables are judged by how useful they are—*Do they support a prediction or serve as diagnostic tools?* The paper by Ferraro and Farmer (1999) shows an example of what appear to be "useful" variables derived from complex ideas.

Excerpt: *Physician Assessments or Patient Self-Report of Patient's Health?*

Kenneth Ferraro and Melissa Farmer (1999) compared physician evaluations to patients' own answers about their health. They used the first survey of a highly regarded national data collection called the National Health and Nutrition Examination Survey (NHANES-I). The paper poses the question "Does self-reported morbidity better predict a patient's health status as well as does physician-evaluated morbidity?" (Morbidity is the tendency toward or presence of ill health or sickness.)

For the "cause" variables (morbidity), four independent variables were measured at the first data collection survey: (1) general medical exam (physician-based), (2) physician-evaluated morbidity (physician based), (3) self-reported serious illness (respondent-based), (4) self-reported chronic illness (respondent-based). The research used two constructs to create the independent variables.

    ■   *Construct 1: Physician-evaluated morbidity* Two physician evaluations of morbidity were conducted containing extensive measurements.

        The first physician instrument was a *general medical exam* consisting of eight components: Examinations of (1) head, eyes, ears, nose and throat; (2) thyroid; (3) chest; (4) cardiovascular function; (5) abdomen; (6) musculoskeletal systems; (7) neurological function and (8) skin.

The second physician instrument consisted of *physician-evaluated morbidity* using the *International Classification of Diseases* (ICD). The ICD contains 15 categories, such as infectious and parasitic diseases, cancers and neoplasms and diseases of the respiratory system.

■ *Construct 2: Patient self-report morbidity* Self-report morbidity was measured by 36 items contained in an interview administered to patients by the survey staff. For example, "Has a doctor ever told you that you have...hypertension or high blood pressure?" (p. 307). Two variables were constructed from the answers to the 36 questions: (1) *self-reported serious illnesses* (e.g., heart attack), and (2) *self-reported chronic illnesses* (e.g., arthritis).

The analyses use two dependent variables: (1) *mortality*, and (2) *self-assessed health*. Both dependent variables were collected 15 years after the first survey, ensuring that the "effect" (mortality and self-assessed health) occurred after the "cause" (morbidity measures). Mortality is defined by whether the patient survived until the follow-up survey or, if not, by the date of death. Date of death was taken from death certificates and therefore should be quite accurate. Self-assessed health was based on the answer to a single survey question: "Would you say that your health in general is excellent, very good, good, fair, or poor?"

Recall that Ferraro and Farmer defined "self-reported morbidity" to include both serious and chronic illnesses. Their research findings seem unexpected. The authors summarize as follows:

> It is not surprising that self-reported morbidity is the stronger predictor of self-assessed health, given that the outcome was a subjective appraisal of health. Yet even when mortality [death] is the outcome, physician-evaluated morbidity was not the superior predictor. Self-reported serious illness and morbidity from the general medical examination predicted mortality among white respondents, but neither type of physician-evaluated morbidity was predictive of mortality among black respondents. In summary, the evidence shows that self-reported morbidity is equal or superior to physician-evaluated morbidity in a prognostic sense. (Ferraro & Farmer, 1999, p. 313)

For white (but not black) patients, a patient's self-estimate of health predicts risk of death at least as accurately as do physician assessments. This result illustrates what we mean by "useful" variables. Does the study invalidate medical checkups? No, because no single variable for "health" exists and there is no unambiguous criterion for it. For example, a person in "perfect health" can be fatally injured in a car crash or even struck by lightning and killed.

Classifying Variables

In the social sciences, variables are classified into types according to the math operations that sensibly can be used with them. The type of data analysis for a study depends heavily on the types of variables. For example, some variables are created by addition, such as the 6-item index for self-esteem by Ross and Broh, discussed earlier.

Stevens (1946) introduced a classification scheme consisting of four types of variables: nominal, ordinal, interval and ratio.

A **nominal variable** classifies persons/objects into different categories. The categories are not "greater than" or "less than" each other. Examples include gender, color, marital status and make of an automobile. No math operations are sensible—you can't add, subtract, multiply or divide with nominal variables such as gender or marital status. Two values of a nominal variable are either equal to each other or they are not. If two automobiles are Fords, make of car 1 is equal to make of car 2. If one is a Chevy and the other a Dodge, make of car 1 is not equal to make of car 2.

Ordinal variables rank persons/objects in one category as "greater than" or "less than" persons/objects in other categories, but they don't support math operations like addition or multiplication. The place (1st, 2nd, etc.) in which a person finishes a marathon is an example of an ordinal variable. It isn't sensible to subtract 2nd place from 1st place, for example. One can only say that one individual is faster or slower than another.

In social research, ordinal variables include responses to attitudinal scales that have response options like "strongly agree" to "strongly disagree." The categories clearly imply order, but they do not support statements like these: Ashley agrees twice as strongly with statement A as Matt does, because Ashley's score is 2, and Matt's score is 1.[3]

Numeric variables *without a natural (meaningful) zero point* are **interval variables**. The most frequently cited example of an interval variable is temperature measured on the Fahrenheit or Centigrade scale. The zeros on these scales are arbitrary points—they don't indicate the complete absence of heat. With interval variables, one can sensibly add and subtract the numbers, however. For example, the "high temperature today is 10 degrees warmer than it was yesterday." But multiplication and division don't make sense: "The high temperature yesterday was 20 degrees, today it is 40 degrees; it's twice as hot today as it was yesterday." "Pure" examples of interval-scale variables in the social sciences are rare or nonexistent.

Numeric variables containing a natural zero are called **ratio variables**. The zero stands for complete absence of some physical quantity. For example, wage = 0 means you earn nothing, so wage is a good example of a ratio variable. And addition and subtraction are sensible; ten dollars per hour is one dollar less than 11 dollars per hour. Multiplication and division also are meaningful; 40 dollars per hour is twice as much as 20 dollars. Figure 2 summarizes Stevens's classification scheme.

So why are these types of variables worth knowing? Many statistical procedures depend on calculating an average or mean score (requiring addition and division) or other math operations. Consequently, the types of variables in a study determine the type of data analysis for that study.

Type of variable	Characteristics
Nominal	Unordered categories: The only mathematical operation supported is equal or not equal (e.g., gender, marital status).
Ordinal	Ordered categories: Each category is either greater than or less than each of the other categories (e.g., agree-disagree: I am a person of worth).
Interval	Numeric variable with no natural zero: Addition and subtraction are supported (e.g., Fahrenheit temperature).
Ratio	Numeric variable with a natural zero: All mathematical operations are supported (e.g., wage, age).

FIGURE 2   Stevens's Classification of Variables.

MEASUREMENT ERROR

Suppose you are the interviewer, and a 69-year-old man insists he is 49. You might be a little skeptical, but must report the information as given. This is an extreme case of measurement error. In this example, the standard is wage reported by one's employer. **Measurement error** (ME) is the difference between an observed value of a variable and its "true score": ME = **observed score—true score**. In this example, the man's reported age minus his actual age (49–69 = −20 years) is the measurement error. Hopefully, errors of this magnitude don't occur often.

Measurement error makes it difficult to detect a relationship between two (or more) variables that might actually exist. For example, Ross and Broh (2000) were surprised to find that self-esteem does not predict later grade-point average. Perhaps a better-measured variable would show that self-esteem does predict academic achievement. If it did, we might be inclined to accept the new variable as an improvement. But—and this is an important but—we don't want to accept the measurement of a variable (or a relationship between variables) just because it supports our own beliefs.

How can one ever know whether an unobservable construct like self-esteem is measured accurately? There's no way to know for sure, but there are several methods for evaluating variables, including use of the *correlation coefficient*, as discussed in the next section. However, none of the methods, taken singly or together, provide a definitive answer to such questions as these: Is self-esteem measured without error? Do we have an accurate measure of "health"? Have we measured "team chemistry"?

Ultimately, constructs are best evaluated by whether they *predict* more concrete variables, like academic achievement or longevity. We don't know precisely how well self-reported serious illnesses measure the abstraction called "health." But we do know that one's health status predicts mortality 15 years later with reasonable accuracy. Our ability to gauge the extent of accuracy and consistency of variables depends on the concept of *correlation*.

The Correlation Coefficient

Correlation is a generic term standing for "relationship" or indicating some measure of the strength of a relationship. In technical writing, usually, when the term *correlation* is used to refer to a specific measure of a relationship, it's understood that the **Pearson product-moment correlation coefficient** is the specific measure. The remainder of this chapter uses the term *correlation* or *Pearson correlation* as shorthand for the Pearson product-moment correlation.

The relationship between total cost and quantity of gasoline purchased is an example of a **positive relationship**. Here, positive relationship means the more you buy, the higher the cost. Figure 3 shows an example of a perfect positive linear relationship (where "perfect" means if you know the value of one variable, you know exactly the value of another variable). Price is a constant in this example. The two variables are gallons and total cost of the purchase.

A **negative relationship** is one in which two variables move in opposite directions; as the value of one goes up, the value of other goes down. For example, "the more you spend the less you save" is a perfect negative relationship, by definition. Most relationships aren't perfect, however. For example, the quantity of gas left in your gas tank declines as the distance you've driven since the last fill-up increases. But you can't predict exactly how much gasoline is left just by knowing the distance you've driven.

The Pearson correlation measures how accurately one variable predicts another variable using a straight-line approximation. It ranges from -1.0 (perfect negative correlation) to 1.0 (perfect positive correlation). A correlation of zero indicates there is no straight-line relationship between two variables: $r = 0$ (where r stands for "correlation calculated from a sample"). The closer a correlation is to $r = -1.0$ or $r = 1.0$, the stronger the linear association between two variables. The strength of the relationship does not depend on whether the correlation is positive or negative. For example, the *strength* of a relationship where $r = -0.50$ is exactly the same as the strength of a relationship where $r = 0.50$!

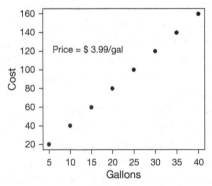

FIGURE 3   Perfect Positive Association.

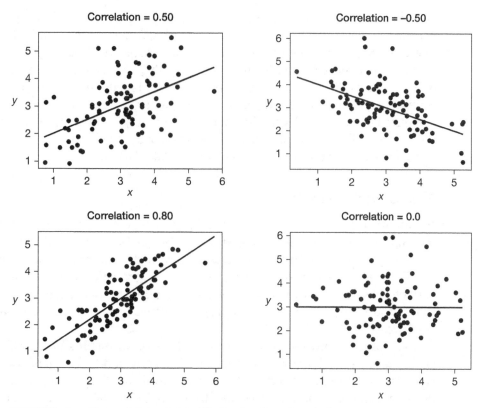

FIGURE 4   Plots of Data Points Illustrating Four Correlations.

Figure 4 shows examples of imperfect linear relationships. It illustrates a scatterplot for four correlations, including one where the correlation is zero ($r = 0$, no linear relationship), two with a positive correlation ($r = 0.50$ and $r = 0.80$), and one with a negative correlation ($r = -0.50$). The diagonal line running through the points on each plot is the predicted straight-line relationship. The more closely the points cluster around the line, as measured by the vertical distance between the line and the point, the higher the absolute value of the correlation.

What relationships might these correlations represent? The positive correlations might represent the association between height and weight. Height and weight are *positively correlated* (but it's not a perfect relationship). Here is an example of a negative relationship: The more you smoke tobacco, the poorer your health. As tobacco consumption goes up, health status goes down. Another example of a negative relationship is the one we just mentioned: The more miles you have driven since your last fill-up, the less gasoline left in your gas tank (also not a perfect relationship). There probably is near-zero correlation, however, between height and musical talent!

What happens to the correlation if variables are measured with error? The *correlation is reduced* between the two variables, *if* the error is entirely random. The error adds a random component to each variable, and the random components are not related to each other, lowering the association between the two observed variables. But if the error is *systematic* (not random), all bets are off. The correlation could even be inflated. For example, suppose respondents who have completed many years of schooling but earn a low wage exaggerate their reported hourly wage. The correlation between education and wage is inflated, because the measurement error is positively related to level of education.

Assessing Reliability

Reliability refers to *consistency*. A variable is reliable to the extent it yields the same answer each time it is used in the absence of change in the true score. Reliability is measured by the test–retest method and by internal consistency.[4]

Test–retest reliability is evaluated by the correlation between the same variable observed at two time points, in the absence of change in the "true score" and the "absence of memory." This correlation is called the *reliability coefficient*.

Suppose you measure the heights of students in Mr. Short's third-grade class at 9:00 A.M. and 2:30 P.M. on the same day. The correlation between the two variables should be nearly perfect—a "true score" for height, depending on precision of the measurements. It's pretty certain that the children's heights haven't changed in a few hours, and memory doesn't affect height. In contrast, suppose you ask Mr. Short's students at 9:00 A.M. and 2:30 P.M. on the same day about the grade they think they'll get in math for the current 6 weeks. It would be hard to argue that the second measurement was done in the "absence of memory." And students' "true-score estimate" of their math grade might have changed, particularly if they took a math test between the two times they were asked to estimate their grades.

Internal consistency is the second way to measure reliability. Internal consistency means to compare more than one measurement of a construct when all the measurements were taken at the same time. The agreement of thermometer readings illustrates the idea of internal consistency. Not all thermometers give the same reading when placed together. In fact, they often vary by a degree or two, quite noticeable if you look at several cheap models on display in a store. If you really wanted to know the best estimate of the room temperature in the store, you could calculate the average of all the readings. We expect that this average reading would be more reliable, and its reliability coefficient higher, than the reading on a single thermometer.

Is there a single measure of internal consistency, rather than many correlations among the self-esteem and personal-control variables in the Ross and Broh study, for example? *Cronbach's alpha* is a summary based on all correlations among the items.[5]

Evaluating Validity

Validity is the *accuracy* with which an observed variable measures the construct it is designed to measure. The correlation between the true score and the observed score is called the *validity coefficient* (Lord & Novick, 1968, p. 261). However, here's an important point—a variable can't be valid unless it is reliable (consistent, e.g., over time), but a reliable variable is not necessarily valid.

In the health study, Ferraro & Farmer were trying to determine whether patient or physician information had greater validity. Of course, if one knew the "true" score (e.g., that 69 is the true age of the man described above), there would be no need to worry about measurement error. Because there's no way to know for sure how accurate a variable is, validity must be evaluated indirectly. There are three main forms for evaluating validity indirectly: content validity, criterion validity and construct validity. And there are two aspects of content validity: face validity and domain coverage, as summarized in Figure 5.

Content validity	Validity assessment based on researcher's judgment.
Face validity	Type of content validity: Assessment of whether a specific indicator measures some part of the construct. Is the measure valid "on the face of it"?
Domain coverage	Type of content validity: Assessment of whether a collection of indicators measure all the content of the construct (e.g., 3rd grade math test contains addition, subtraction, multiplication and division).
Criterion validity	Validity assessment based on prediction of a criterion or standard (e.g., self-report age predicts age calculated from birth certificate).
Construct validity	Validity assessment determined by whether a measure behaves as predicted by a theory (e.g., measure of occupational prestige predicts earnings).

FIGURE 5   Types of Validity Assessment.

Content validity is a method of evaluating validity based on the judgment of researchers. Content validity includes two components: (1) face validity and (2) domain coverage. A single item (e.g., a survey question) has **face validity** when there is general agreement that the variable represents the underlying idea. For example, asking "How old were you on your last birthday?" appears to contain the definition of the concept. But, "How old is your mother?" provides inadequate information about the respondent. It is clear "on the face of it" that the second question doesn't measure the respondent's age. **Domain coverage** refers to how well a variable captures the *entire range of content* (or domain) for the construct. A concept like "age" is unidimensional—it has one dimension—age at a specific date. In contrast, "math achievement" is multidimensional. It contains several specific skills. For example, math skills for third-graders probably include addition, subtraction, multiplication and division. Therefore, subtraction questions on a third-grade math test do exhibit face validity, as subtraction is one third-grade math skill. But if the entire test contained only subtraction questions, the test would be invalid because it wouldn't cover the full *domain* of the content for third-grade math achievement.

Criterion validity is the second method for assessing validity, and it is based on whether a variable predicts a *criterion* (or standard). The correlation between self-report wage and wage reported by one's employer is an example of criterion validity.

Construct validity is the third method for assessing validity of a variable. Here, researchers check to see whether the variable operates as predicted by *theory*. In the Ross and Broh (2000) study of personal control and self-esteem, these variables illustrate *construct validity,* though the researchers don't mention the term. The variables do show relationships with other variables, as predicted by their theory. For example, personal control does predict academic achievement, but self-esteem does not. However, the strength of these relationships is modest, so construct validity is not compelling in this instance.

Be sure to note the difference between validity and reliability: Validity = accuracy in measuring the construct. Reliability refers to consistency. It's impossible to have highly valid variables unless they are reliable. But it's easy to imagine highly reliable variables that are not valid. A ruler used to measure the length of one's index finger is very reliable, and probably would be positively correlated with height, but it's obviously not a perfectly valid measure of height.

LINKING THEORY AND VARIABLES

An interesting study with limited previous research illustrates some of the close connections between theory and measurement of variables. The study also provides intriguing findings about the relationship between type of child care chosen and characteristics of mother's job.

The primary hypothesis is that maternal job characteristics influence type of child care:

Employing a theoretical framework suggesting that different family resources are associated with different types and quality of child care, Parcel and Menaghan (1994) hypothesized that mothers with more prestigious occupations place a lower value on conformity in childrearing. They also earn adequate incomes which permits them to purchase higher-quality child care. The researchers chose four categories for one of their dependent variables, type of child care: formal group care in centers or schools, caregiver relatives, non-relative caregivers and other arrangements. A variety of control variables were included.

Here, one of the independent variables for maternal job characteristics, *maternal wage*, is a ratio scale variable; the dependent variable *type of child-care arrangement* is a nominal scale. Maternal wage was measured by the mother's hourly wage at several predetermined time points, such as when type of care was assessed at child's ages 1 and 3 years.[6]

The researchers cite research evidence presented by Kohn and others. Kohn and colleagues theorize that parental values about the importance of conformity versus creativity for their children are determined in part by how much autonomy the parents have on their jobs. Working-class jobs tend to be repetitive, with little room for variation. In contrast, middle-class jobs tend to require individual decision making and provide higher job autonomy. The theory is that repetitive jobs influence parents to emphasize conformity in their children, and job autonomy influences parents to value creativity over conformity. These ideas have received extensive development and testing by Kohn and his associates (Kohn, 1977; Kohn & Slomczynski, 1990).

Parcel and Menaghan found that mothers with higher paying, more complex jobs, higher cognitive skills and higher levels of education are more likely to use out-of-home child-care arrangements and more likely to have a nonrelative caregiver. Perhaps surprisingly, fathers' occupation had minimal influence on type of child care. They conclude, "Rather than compensating for initial differences and disadvantages, nonmaternal care arrangements are apt to reflect other existing inequalities among families" (Parcel & Menaghan, 1994, pp. 179–191).

This line of research quite obviously depends crucially on the definition and measurement of complex constructs like "job autonomy" and "child-rearing values"!

Summary

This chapter outlines the process of turning abstract concepts such as self-esteem, health and job autonomy into measurable variables. The first section includes an excerpt from a research study about self-esteem, personal control and school grades. This study is used to illustrate many of the basic terms having to do with measurement, such as *validity* and *reliability*.

The type of variable determines the types of mathematical and statistical operations that are appropriate, and shapes how one formulates theory about the variables. Four types of measures generally are identified: nominal, ordinal, interval and ratio variables. Nominal variables are defined by unordered categories like gender (male, female) or type of cheese (Colby, Swiss, cheddar, . . .). Ordinal variables are defined by categories, each of which is either greater than or less than each of the others, but ordinal variables contain no indication of how much their categories differ, for instance, first place, second place, third place in a race. An interval variable measures quantity, but has no natural (meaningful) zero, for example, the temperature scale. A ratio variable measures quantity, and the zero means the absence of some physical quantity, for example, annual earnings.

Reliability refers to consistency. A variable is reliable to the extent that it gives the same answer on repeated measurements in the absence of change in the "true score" and in the absence of memory. Reliability is measured by the test–retest method and by internal consistency. Test–retest reliability is determined by the correlation between the same measurement taken at two different times in the absence of change in the true score and in the absence of memory. Internal consistency is measured by the correlation between/among two or more variables each of which is intended to measure the same construct when all the variables are measured at the same time.

Validity refers to the accuracy with which a variable measures the construct it is intended to measure. Three forms of assessing validity are discussed: content validity, criterion validity and construct validity. Content validity depends on a judgment of whether a variable measures what it is designed to measure. Criterion validity is an assessment of validity based on how accurately a variable predicts a criterion. Construct validity is an assessment based on how closely a variable matches theoretical predictions about its relationship with other variables.

Remember: *A valid variable must be reliable, but a reliable variable is not necessarily valid.*

The last section of the chapter includes an excerpt from research about the relationship between mother's job type and child-care arrangements. The excerpt illustrates the close interdependence among variables, theory and analysis in social research.

YOUR REVIEW SHEET

1. Some often-used independent variables in social research include gender, age, race and ethnicity (ethnic background). Identify the type —nominal, ordinal, interval or ratio—for each of these variables.

2. The following statement is made in this chapter: "We don't know whether we really measure self-esteem or personal control." However, the real question is "Are the variables useful?" How can usefulness of variables be determined?

3. What might one learn about room temperature in a store by looking at several thermometers? How is your answer related to the topic of measurement?

4. Why is it important to know the types of variables to be used in a research study?

5. Why should we be a little skeptical about procedures that claim to "measure" a complex idea such as self-esteem, even if the researchers combine the answers to seven questions on a survey?

6. What happens to the correlation between two variables if they are measured with random error?

7. What does a positive correlation indicate about the relationship between two variables? A negative correlation? Does a correlation of 0.60 indicate a stronger relationship than a correlation of −0.60? Explain your answer.

8. Give an example for each term: content validity, face validity, domain coverage, criterion validity and construct validity.

9. Provide one question other than those discussed in the chapter that does not have good face validity, and briefly explain why not. Try to think of a realistic example.

10. List two examples each of a nominal and an ordinal variable, other than examples mentioned in this chapter.

11. What is a "natural zero"? List at least one social or behavioral variable that has a natural (meaningful) zero and one that does not. Why is the distinction useful between a natural zero and no natural zero?

12. How are variables related to theory?

END NOTES

1. In this excerpt, the authors do not indicate whether academic achievement has a positive or negative effect on self-esteem or personal control. Neither do they indicate the direction of any of the other effects. But it is fairly clear from the context that all are positive relationships (e.g., as academic achievement goes up, so does self-esteem). It's a good practice to state the direction of effects when summarizing relationships, even when it is fairly evident from the context.

2. If none of the components of the index are missing, the difference between a summed index and an averaged index is trivial. But if a respondent skipped some of the items comprising the index, then the difference isn't trivial. Adding together the nonmissing

components is equivalent to setting the missing values to zero, but averaging the nonmissing components is equivalent to setting the missing items to the mean of the nonmissing items. Clearly, the average is more sensible in most instances of missing items. If you prefer the metric of a sum, you can multiply the average by the number of items comprising the index.

3. In practice, numbers (e.g., 1 through 4) usually are assigned to agree–disagree responses, and the results treated as if they were numbers, as in the study of self-esteem, personal control, and high-school grades by Ross and Broh (2000).

4. Measurement theory first developed in areas of intelligence and knowledge testing, so a combined score was called a "test." This terminology sometimes carries over into attitude measurement, so that the term *test* sometimes includes both knowledge tests and attitude assessments.

5. The most elementary way to measure internal consistency is to randomly divide the items in the "test" into two halves, called the split-half method. If r = correlation between the two halves, then the predicted reliability of the entire test is given by the "Spearman-Brown prophecy formula" defined by

$$r_{xx} = 2 \frac{r_{x_1 x_2}}{1 + r_{x_1 x_2}}$$

where r_{xx} is the estimated reliability and $r_{x_1 x_2}$ is the correlation between the two halves of the test.

Cronbach's alpha is a generalization of this measure equal to the average of all possible split-halves.

6. Parcel and Menaghan wanted a statistical analysis that would assess how increasing maternal wage affects the probability of each of the types of child care. This is a different type of analysis than an analysis to check whether a variable affects the actual value of the outcome, such as race affecting wages, and it requires a different type of statistical method.

STUDY TERMS

categories (of a variable) Classes of a variable; values of a nominal variable, for example, state of residence, with categories: Alabama, Alaska, . . . , Wisconsin, Wyoming.

concepts (or **constructs**) Variables not directly measurable; examples include prejudice, self-esteem, occupational status and intelligence.

construct validity Method of evaluating validity by observing whether a variable representing a construct exhibits relationships with other variables as predicted by theory.

content validity Method of evaluating validity that relies on researchers' judgments about whether a variable measures the construct it is designed to measure.

correlation (Pearson product-moment correlation) Number ranging from −1 to 1, which measures the degree of linear relationship between two variables. A correlation of 1.0 indicates a perfect positive linear relationship. A correlation of −1.0 indicates a perfect negative linear relationship; a negative relationship means that values of the variables change in opposite directions—one increases as the other decreases. A correlation of 0.0 indicates no linear relationship.

criterion validity Method for assessing validity by testing whether a variable predicts a criterion or standard. For example, does self-reported age predict the age calculated from one's birth certificate?

domain coverage Degree to which a set of variables measures the entire range of content (domain) of a construct. A math test for third-graders should cover all the math operations they have learned, not just addition, for example.

face validity Judgment of researchers about whether a specific item measures at least part of the construct it is intended to measure. An addition test for third-graders measures skills in addition but not multiplication.

index Variable defined by combining two or more other variables, usually by adding or averaging the values (e.g., on questions about health). However, some indexes are not created by addition. Body-mass index (BMI) $= W/H^2$, where W = weight in kilograms and H = height in meters. BMI is a well-established measure of underweight, normal weight and overweight.

indicators Variables such as a survey question that partially measure complex, abstract **concepts** such as "self-esteem" or "parental support."

internal consistency Comparing more than one measurement of a construct when all the measurements were taken at the same time, usually measured by a single correlation-based calculation (see endnote 5 about Cronbach's alpha).

interval variable A variable whose values are numbers but which does not include a natural (meaningful) zero, such as the Fahrenheit temperature scale. Addition and subtraction are sensible with an interval scale, but multiplication and division are not.

measurement error Difference between an observed value and the "true" value of a variable.

negative relationship Relationship in which values of two variables move in opposite directions. As the value of one variable increases, the value of the other variable decreases, and vice versa.

nominal variable Variable that classifies *all* objects or elements into one and only one class or category; the classes simply are different (e.g., color).

observed score Value of a variable obtained through data collection procedures (e.g., personal interview or questionnaire) (compare with **true score**).

operationalization Process of converting abstract concepts (e.g., academic achievement, self-esteem) into measurable variables.

ordinal variable Type of variable defined by a set of categories, each of which is either greater than or less than each of the other categories, but with no indication of the magnitude of the differences among the categories (e.g., agree–disagree questionnaire item).

Pearson product-moment correlation See **correlation**.

positive relationship Relationship in which values of two variables move in the same direction. As the value of one variable increases, the value of the other variable also increases, and vice versa.

ratio variable Variable defined by values that are natural numbers *and* zero indicates the absence of some real-world quantity (e.g., wage).

reliability (consistency) The degree to which a measurement gives the same result each time it is used, in the absence of change in the true score and in the absence of memory.

test–retest reliability Correlation between the same variable at two time points, in the absence of change in the true score and the absence of memory.

true score Correct value of a variable, for example, age = number of full years since the date of birth on one's birth certificate (compare with observed score).

validity Accuracy with which an observed variable measures the concept it is designed to measure.

variable An operationalized concept. Set of categories or numbers defined so that the categories are *mutually exclusive* (unique) and *exhaustive*. Each case (e.g., person, object) fits into exactly one category, and all needed categories are included. An example is gender (two unique categories); other variables include race, age and self-esteem.

EXERCISES

Exercise 1. Evaluating Research: Linking Theory and Measurement

Directions: Refer to the discussion on "child-care arrangements" in this chapter to answer the following questions.

Factual Questions

1. State the research hypothesis.
2. Identify the dependent variable. What is the level of measurement (nominal, ordinal, interval, ratio)? In your own words, explain the justification for this level of measurement, referring to the researchers' specific use of this variable.
3. Identify the independent variable(s). How is each measured?

Question for Discussion

1. Based on the findings, briefly suggest one topic for future research (if needed, modify the theoretical framework). Offer a research hypothesis for your topic.

Exercise 2. Skills Building: Operationalizing Variables

Directions: Choose three variables that are not discussed in this chapter, one nominal, one ordinal, and one interval or ratio. Provide the following information for each: (1) a variable name; (2) categories or values for the variable; (3) level of measurement, with a brief explanation; (4) a short explanation why the variable satisfies the definition of a variable and (5) a way to operationalize the variable (an indicator and its values).

Example:

Variable name:	Gender
Categories:	Male, female
	Each case can be classified into only one category, and there is a category for everyone.
Level of measurement:	Nominal scale, because female and male describe different categories, no more, no less.
Explanation:	No operation is sensible except a test for equality— Are two people the same gender or different?
Indicator:	Are you male or female? (survey question, two gender categories)

Exercise 3. Skills Building: Developing Hypotheses

Directions: In your own words, provide the requested information. Review sections in this chapter.

1. List as many categories as you think are needed for a variable called "type of religion" (religious denomination). Tailor your categories to your answer to question 2.

2. Choose a second variable. It can be either the independent or dependent variable for a relationship with "type of religion." List the categories you think are needed.

3. Construct an *if . . . then* hypothesis stating your proposed relationship between "type of religion" and your other variable. Circle your independent variable and underline your dependent variable. Be sure to state the comparison group in your hypothesis.

4. Select an appropriate population for testing your hypothesis (i.e., one that would provide some members for all categories of both variables). Revise your categories for one or both variables, if needed.

5. Construct a second hypothesis of a relationship in which the categories of "type of religion" might have to be different from those for your original hypothesis. Again, identify your independent and dependent variables, and a population to which your hypothesis applies.

6. Define an ordinal, interval or ratio variable about some aspect of religion. Propose a hypothesis, identify the dependent and independent variables, and specify a population.

Exercise 4. Skills Building: Examining Measurement Error in Variables

Directions: Refer to the discussion on "measurement error" in this chapter to answer the following questions.

1. Choose an interval or ratio social science variable other than age and describe a hypothetical but realistic example of error in its measurement (see example below). Then, calculate how much your (hypothetical) variable differs from its "true score." Offer a plausible brief explanation why the ME might have occurred.

a. *Example of ME:* During an interview, a man reported his age as 49 years. For a validity check, the interviewer visited the local department of vital statistics and found that the "true score" for the man's age was 69 years.

b. *ME = observed score–true score.* ME is 49–69 = −20 years.

c. *Plausible explanation for the ME*: The age question for the man followed questions about the man's son, so the man misunderstood the question, thinking that the interviewer asked for the age of his son.

2. The researcher checked the accuracy of the man's age by checking with the vital statistics department. How might a researcher include a reliability (consistency) check as part of the interview? (*Hint:* How do you assess reliability?)

3. Briefly describe one way to evaluate the reliability for your variable.

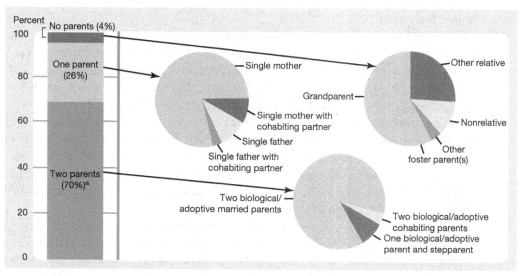

5 DESIGNING SOCIAL EXPERIMENTS

INTRODUCTION: LOOKING AT HOW THE SOCIAL WORLD WORKS

"He lives with only one parent. That's why he keeps getting in trouble with the law."

"She's pregnant? No surprise—her parents got a divorce and both immediately remarried."

"The twins' stepfather mercilessly picks on them. Both the boy and the girl have threatened to run away from home more than once."

Figure 1 shows Census Bureau estimates of percentages of children 0–17 years old living in various family arrangements. Do nonintact homes cause these disadvantages, or are they due to something else that also affects marital breakups, or are these disadvantages coincidental?

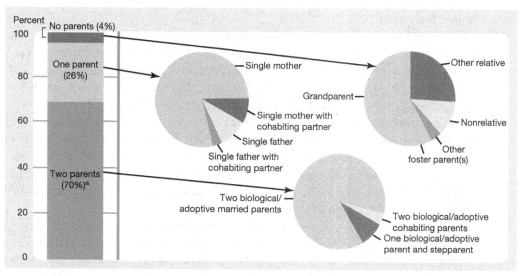

Percent

- No parents (4%)
- One parent (26%)
- Two parents (70%)ª

Single mother
Single mother with cohabiting partner
Single father
Single father with cohabiting partner

Other relative
Grandparent
Nonrelative
Other foster parent(s)

Two biological/adoptive married parents
Two biological/adoptive cohabiting parents
One biological/adoptive parent and stepparent

ª Includes children living with two stepparents.

FIGURE 1 Percentages of Children 0–17 Years Living in Various Family Arrangements, 2009.
Source: U.S. Census Bureau, *Current Population Survey*, Annual Social and Economic Supplement.

Painter and Levine (2000) report the following:

[O]n average, youths living with a single mother are roughly twice as likely as other youths to drop out of high school, become pregnant, and be arrested. Moreover, most studies find that youth living with a biological mother and a stepfather are almost as disadvantaged. (Painter & Levine, 2000, p. 524)

However, Painter and Levine also quote Charles Manski and his coauthors on this subject:

It may be, as the [cross-sectional] empirical evidence suggests, living in a nonintact family has adverse consequences for children. On the other hand, it may be that some unobserved process jointly determines family structure and children's outcomes. For example, parents who are less committed to their family may be more likely to divorce and may also provide less support for their children. Behavioral and/or medical problems such as alcoholism, depression, or drug addiction may make a person more likely to divorce and less effective as a parent. (Manski et al., 1992, p. 25. Quoted in Painter & Levine, 2000, pp. 524–525)[1]

The Manski quotation is a good example of why *control of alternative explanations is necessary when attempting to establish a cause-and-effect relationship.* Determining the effect of family structure on children is not a simple matter—there are many possible explanations for the observation that children from broken homes fare poorly.

Controlled experiments (using physical controls) generally are thought to set the standard for deciding *cause and effect*—a conclusion that an observed relationship is due to the effect of the independent variable on the dependent variable. Using **physical controls** in an experiment, the researcher determines what is changed, by how much and what is not changed (kept constant, i.e., controlled).

An **experiment** is a process whereby a person physically changes at least one variable and watches to see what happens to one or more other variables. For example, substitute a low-calorie sweetener for sugar in a recipe for peanut-butter cookies, and compare that taste with the taste of cookies made with sugar. In the cookie-baking experiment, what is controlled? All the ingredients, the temperature of the oven and the length of time the cookies bake.

In sharp contrast to the process of baking cookies, however, no one knows the "complete recipe" for determining the outcome of nearly all social experiments, including trying to find out whether nonintact homes might cause juvenile delinquency. Consequently, it is impossible to control all causes. How, then, can one identify a cause-and-effect relationship in social research if many alternative explanations are possible?

The short answer is, use **random assignment** to different treatments. In an experiment, the independent variable is called a **treatment** variable, and the dependent variable is the outcome of the experiment. Random assignment means that each subject is assigned at random to categories of the treatment variable. Random assignment is an ingenious device, but as we'll see, it's definitely not a cure-all for finding cause-and-effect relationships. Nonetheless, it does set a very useful standard.

In the simplest experiment, there are just two categories—an experimental treatment and a control; the treatment variable is defined by these two categories. Subjects are assigned to one of two alternatives: an **experimental group** or the **control group** using a pure chance method. The experimental group receives some type of treatment, like a drug, and the control group gets no treatment or a placebo; the control group (no treatment) is included simply for comparison.

There is a potentially confusing aspect in this description of experiments. We started by saying that an experiment involves "changing something and watching what happens as a result." But the cookie-experiment example does not involve change for anybody. One group gets cookies baked with sugar; the other gets cookies baked with artificial sweetener. Nothing is changed for either group. But notice: the cookies differ *from one group to the other group*, and we then look for a difference in the outcome, the taste-test results.

Since subjects were assigned at random to eat cookies with sugar or sweetener, the average preference for all aspects of cookies is the same in the two groups before the experiment, *within limits of sampling error*. Therefore, the difference between the two groups after eating the cookies is a close estimate of the true effect of sweetener versus sugar, since the two groups were nearly the same at the beginning. Increasing the sample size of both groups obviously improves the accuracy of the experiment.

Ethics and Experiments

The researcher must understand the expectations for research with human subjects, such as "do no harm," *before* planning a research project. If someone were gathering data from you via an experiment, probably you would want your data—and perhaps even your involvement—kept in confidence.

Goals of This Chapter

Goals of this chapter are (1) to examine the reasoning of experiments, and (2) to evaluate threats to drawing valid conclusions about cause and effect. First, contrived and real-world examples are presented. The chapter then gives a systematic summary of the standards of experimental design, including some of the basic types of experimental and related nonexperimental designs. The review emphasizes both the power of *randomized experiments* (or *random assignment*) and their very substantial limitations.

TWO EXAMPLES: ONE CONTRIVED, ONE REAL

A Contrived Little Experiment

Suppose you conduct an informal cookie experiment with a handful of people to find a low-calorie cookie many people actually will buy. How likely are you to be successful?

Your chance of success is not very high, partly because you (and everyone else) don't know all the factors that influence people's personal tastes. You just know that different people have different taste preferences. Consequently, it isn't possible to control every variable that might influence people's preferences for the cookies.

Suppose, however, that the cookie experiment is laid out as shown in Figure 2. What does the experimenter physically control in this example? The *only* difference between the two recipes is whether they contain sugar or (non-sugar) sweetener, and that is what the experimenter controls. "Sugar" and "other sweetener" are the two categories of the **treatment variable** for this experiment. Neither category is called the control in this instance; the two categories permit comparison, however.

Since you can't control subjects' preferences for the cookies, random assignment to sugar and sweetener groups is critical. To see how critical, suppose you allow the subjects to decide for themselves which type of cookie to eat. What do you think might happen? One possibility is that a high percentage of cookie lovers choose sugar-baked cookies, thereby skewing the results against the sweetener-baked cookies.

The remarkable aspect of random assignment is that no systematic (regularly occurring) process puts people who are extra fond of cookies—or who dislike or like artificial sweeteners—into one group or the other. Random assignment eliminates all possible explanations for the average differences among the treatments except the effect of sugar versus sweetener and random variation.

Stop for a moment to absorb this point! It's really quite remarkable *that random assignment can eliminate the systematic effects of all other independent variables except the treatment.*

But, it still is possible that one group or the other might, by chance, like sugar or sweetener better than the other group. That's where statistical tests enter in—to calculate the chance the difference might have occurred by chance. If the chance is small, attribute the difference to difference in preference for sugar or sweetener. Nothing is certain, even with a very big sample. But the bigger the sample, the more confidence we have in the result.

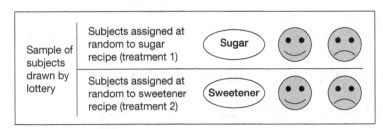

FIGURE 2   Cookie Experiment.

In our cookie-tasting study, the taste-scale response is the dependent variable (outcome). Suppose the outcome is measured by a 10-point rating scale that is asked of all subjects, such as in the following question:

On a scale from 1 to 10 please rate how much you liked the cookies. (Circle 1)

Don't like   *Like*
1   2   3   4   5   6   7   8   9   10

Further, imagine the average of the ratings for people who ate the cookies with sugar is 8.1, and the average of the ratings of people who ate the cookies with sweetener is 7.7. Rather than informally decide ("eyeball" the results), statistical tests (based on probability) can be used to decide whether the difference of 0.4 (8.1–7.7) is due to "real" difference between the sugar recipe and the sweetener or just due to random variation in individual tastes. Of course, the larger the sample, the easier it is to distinguish between a random difference and a "real" difference.[2]

A Field Experiment: Does Having a Job Reduce Crime?

An article by Christopher Uggen (2000) reports an intriguing field experiment about the influence of employment on criminal behavior.

> Sociologists have increasingly emphasized "turning points" in explaining behavioral change over the life course. Is work a turning point in the life course of criminal offenders? If criminals are provided with jobs, are they likely to stop committing crimes? (Uggen, 2000, p. 529)

Many studies of criminal behavior show people with jobs commit fewer crimes. But the interpretation of this relationship is far from settled.

> Taken together, existing theory and research point to a complex and perhaps conditional relation between work and criminal behavior. Whether this relation is causal remains unresolved, as does the direction of causality. (Uggen, 2000, p. 530)

Citing others (Rubin, 1974; Winship & Mare, 1992), Uggen thus concludes:

> Experiments on the effect of employment on crime convert uncontrolled variation in personal criminal propensities into random variation....(Rubin, 1974). Therefore, designs that randomly assign people to work and nonwork statuses are preferred over nonexperimental designs, especially when a convincing model of selection into employment is unavailable. (Winship & Mare, 1992, as quoted in Uggen, 2000, p. 531)

What are they saying? They are saying that maybe a lifetime of experiences determines *both* whether a man is inclined to be a criminal *and* whether he is inclined to get a job or is even employable. *And field experiments with random assignment are needed to help sort out the causal connections, if any, between paid employment and criminal behavior.*

If Winship and Mare are correct, it suggests a *spurious (negative) relationship* between working and crime. What's one possible confounding variable—one variable that might determine both having a job and not committing a crime? Two examples might be religious upbringing and being reared in a high-crime neighborhood, or not.

Uggen subsequently analyzes data from a nationally funded field experiment called "The National Supported Work Demonstration Project." This project was conducted on a sample of more than 3,000 men whose work and arrest history was traced during the period from March 1975 to July 1977. The sample was selected from men with an official arrest history.

Each member of the sample was randomly assigned to either (1) a *treatment group*, with subsidized employment, or (2) a *control group*, with no subsidized employment. As in the cookie experiment, the terms *treatment group* and *control group* are used generally to distinguish between subjects who are given a special treatment of some sort (the treatment group) and the control group—those who are given no special treatment or sometimes a **placebo** (a nonreactive agent such as a sugar pill given in medical research).

During the study, Uggen compared the arrest history of men in the treatment group to the arrest history of men in the control group. To see whether age might be a confounding variable, he split the sample into two age groups: those 26 years old or younger, and those over 26. He found that older men who held a job were less likely to be re-arrested than older men who didn't hold a job. But this association was *absent* for younger men. In this example, the variable *age* is a specifier: It specifies for whom the job–crime relationship operates—only for older men, as shown in Figure 3.

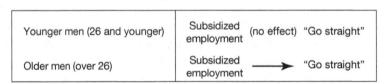

FIGURE 3   Field Experiment Showing the Importance of Controlling for Age.

In Uggen's study, much previous theory and research suggested that he divide the sample by age. Had Uggen not split the sample by age, what would he probably have concluded? Differences between arrest rates of those in the treatment and control groups would be averages of "no effect" in the younger group and the "fairly strong effect" in the older group.

In a long-running experiment like Uggen's, events that affect the outcome may occur *after* the beginning of the experiment. Uggen uses statistical controls for three other possible confounding variables: dropping out of the treatment, getting a job outside the supported work, and attending school. All three events took place after the experiment began, so they cannot be controlled by random assignment, and all three activities likely affect whether subjects commit another crime. In short, experiments are not automatic finders of cause and effect, particularly in long-running, complex real-world situations.

The Zimbardo prison study used random assignment of college students in a prison-like setting. You might be able to locate a video of the Zimbardo prison study by using a search engine such as Google. Consider the ethical issues of this experiment. Would you be willing to be a guard or a prisoner in this study?

DEFINITIONS AND BASIC DESIGNS

Definitions

As the above studies illustrate, experimental design uses a special vocabulary. But sometimes the interchangeable terms can be confusing: (a) *treatment/treatment variable/independent variable,* (b) *outcome/outcome variable/dependent variable* and (c) *control/control variable/alternative explanation.* Also somewhat confusing are the terms (d) *random assignment* and *random selection,* and (e) *internal validity* and *external validity.* Definitions of these terms appear in the next few paragraphs.

First, recall that *treatment variable* often is a synonym for *independent variable.* But the term "treatment variable" usually is used only in an experimental study. In experiments, the treatment variable is manipulated by the researcher and is the presumed cause. In a nonexperimental study, the presumed cause is called the independent variable and cannot be manipulated by the researcher.

The simplest treatment variable has two categories, frequently called "treatment" and "control." Subjects assigned to receive the treatment often are designated the "treatment group" or "experimental group," and those assigned to the control are designated the "control group." But if the treatment variable contains more than two categories, they may be labeled treatment 1, treatment 2 and so on. Or, there may be two or more treatments, plus a control—for example, aspirin, buffered aspirin, ibuprofen and the control, perhaps a sugar pill.

So, the word *treatment* is used in multiple ways: (1) as part of a phrase meaning independent variable (treatment *variable*), (2) as a label for one category of the independent variable (treatment) and (3) to identify subjects assigned to the treatment category (treatment *group*).

Outcome or *outcome variable* often is a synonym for *dependent variable* in an experiment, but not elsewhere. Similarly, the word *control* is used (1) to designate one category of the treatment variable (control), and (2) to identify subjects assigned to the control category (control group) (see Figure 4). The term *control* also is used to designate the role of a variable in an analysis, for example, the relationship between wearing a beard and wearing a dress, controlling for gender.

Uses of the term "treatment"	Uses of the term "control"
• as the independent variable (treatment) variable • as a category of the independent variable (treatment and control) • a group of subjects (treatment group)	• as a category of the independent variable • a group of subjects (control group)

FIGURE 4   Uses of *Treatment* and *Control* in Experimental Research.

To explain types of random processes, the cookie experiment makes a good springboard. The first random process is **random selection**. Subjects for cookie-tasting experiment were selected from a predetermined population using a lottery, but any random process could be used. In an experiment, random selection eliminates bias in generalizing results from the subjects to the population providing the subjects. Using random selection means there is no tendency to overestimate or underestimate the results from the sample when the results are applied to its population. That is what is meant by the term *unbiased*. For example, a study of sugar–sweetener preferences using a sample selected from a population of tenth-graders is not a random sample of the adult population, and it might produce biased estimates of how adults react.

The second random process is **random assignment**. After subjects are selected, they are assigned at random to one of the two experimental groups— sugar or sweetener cookies. The sweetener group might be designated the treatment group and the sugar group the control group. Random assignment eliminates bias in estimating the difference between the two treatments. That is, observed differences are due to differences between subjects' preferences for sugar or sweetener and random variation, and nothing else.

The difference between random selection and random assignment is closely related to two important concepts: **external validity** and **internal validity**. In a classic work about experiments, Campbell and Stanley (1963) define *external validity* as follows:

> External validity asks the question of generalizability: To what populations, settings, treatment variables, and measurement variables can this effect be generalized? (p. 5)

They define *internal validity* using these words:

> Internal validity is the basic minimum without which any experiment is uninterpretable: Did in fact the experimental treatments make a difference in this specific experimental instance? (p. 5)

In short, *random selection is for external validity,* and *random assignment promotes internal validity.* Figure 5 summarizes the differences between these two random processes.

Random Selection
- Select a sample of subjects at random from the population
- Eliminates bias generalizing from sample to population
- Supports external validity

Random Assignment
- Assign subjects at random to categories of the treatment variable
- Eliminates bias estimating differences among treatments and control
- Supports internal validity

FIGURE 5   Comparison of Random Selection to Random Assignment.

FIVE BASIC RESEARCH DESIGNS

1. Classical Experimental Design. Campbell and Stanley (1963) define their preferred design to be an experiment that includes (1) *a pretest* to measure the dependent variable (outcome) before the treatment is administered, (2) *random assignment* to treatment and control groups and (3) a *posttest*, a second measurement of the dependent variable. They present a handy diagram for what they call the **classical experimental design**, which is sketched in Figure 6.

		Pretest	Treatment	Posttest
Classical experiment:	R	O_1	X	O_2
Pretest-posttest				
control-group design:	R	O_3		O_4

FIGURE 6   Classical Experimental Design.
Source: Campbell and Stanley (1963).

The symbols in Figure 6 are as follows:

R denotes random assignment.

X denotes treatment; its absence stands for no treatment (control).

O denotes observation, meaning some type of measurement of the outcome variable (e.g., the cookie-rating scale).

O_1 denotes pretest measurement for the experimental group.
O_2 denotes posttest measurement for the experimental group.
O_3 denotes pretest measurement for the control group.
O_4 denotes posttest measurement for the control group.

What is the goal of this design? That is, which measures should be compared to determine whether one type of cookie is judged to be better tasting than the other? Look again at Figure 6 before reading further.

The goal is to compare pretest–posttest changes in the outcome for the treatment group (O_2–O_1) to changes for the control group (O_4–O_3). In the cookie experiment, the classical design requires feeding everyone cookies twice. Both the control group and the treatment group get sugar-baked cookies for the pretest (time 1), then the initial taste-rating measurements (O_1 and O_3) are taken for both groups. Next, the treatment group gets sweetener-baked cookies, and the control group again gets the standard sugar-baked cookies. Then the taste ratings are done again—posttest measures, O_2 and O_4.

Generally, comparisons are done with averages (or percentages for non-numeric outcomes) calculated for each of the groups. In the usual notation, a sample average is indicated by an "overbar" So the change in the average for the experimental group is

$$\overline{O}_2 - \overline{O}_1$$

and the change in average for the control group is

$$\overline{O}_4 - \overline{O}_3$$

The experimental research question is

Did the treatment-group mean (average) change more than the control-group mean?[3]

Note: At the pretest, the average ratings for the experimental group should be about equal to the average rating for the control group:

$$\overline{O}_1 - \overline{O}_3 \approx 0$$

(The symbol $\approx$ stands for approximately equal.) How close to equal the two pretest averages are at the beginning of an experiment depends on random variation in the subjects. Random variation is reduced as the number of subjects in the study increases.

We expect that the pretest (time 1) averages are the same, which leads to a very interesting conclusion:

With random assignment, the difference between the posttest means is a good estimate of the difference in change from pretest to posttest.

With random assignment to treatment and control groups, the expected mean pretest difference between treatment and control groups is zero. *Therefore, a comparison of posttest means is a good estimate of the difference between the changes of the two groups.* See the next subsection.

2. Posttest-Only Control-Group Design. Have you noticed that the original cookie experiment differs from the classical experimental design? Look back to the "contrived little experiment" section to see how it differs before reading further.

No pretest was mentioned in the original description of the cookie experiment. In the language of Campbell and Stanley, the original cookie experiment is the **posttest-only control-group design**. Figure 7 illustrates this design. For the cookie experiment, the posttest-only design may be quite a bit better than the classical experiment. Considering that the subjects are eating cookies, can you think of one reason why? Here are two reasons. First, subjects taste cookies for the pretest and rate them. This experience could alter their posttest ratings. For example, completing the ratings may sensitize subjects to pay closer attention to the taste of the cookies at the posttest than they otherwise would. Second, tasting cookies twice may affect the sensitivity of the subjects' tastes.

			Posttest
Posttest-only control-group design:	R	X	O_1
	R		O_2

FIGURE 7 Posttest-Only Control-GroupDesign.
Source: Campbell and Stanley (1963).

Since the pretest average ratings should be about the same for treatment and control groups, the posttest-only design is nearly as good as the classical design. In many circumstances, as in the cookie experiment, it may be better.

In all, Campbell and Stanley describe 16 experimental designs. In addition to the two already discussed, three others are important in social research: the **static-group comparison**, the **one-group pretest–posttest**, and the **one-shot case study** designs.

 3. Static-Group Comparison Design. Probably the most often–used design in social research is not really an experiment at all. It's a comparison between naturally occurring groups, as indicated in the sketch in Figure 8. Notice that this design looks like the posttest-only design—but what's missing?

R is absent; the dashed line "—" indicates no random assignment. Here, the idea is to compare natural groups, such as those defined by occupation, gender,

			Posttest
Static group comparison:	—	X	O_1
	—		O_2

FIGURE 8 Static Group Comparison Design.
Source: Campbell and Stanley (1963).

age and marital status. For example, we could compare the speed of pizza-delivery drivers to the speed of other drivers. The natural groups take the place of treatment group and control group.

The static-group comparison requires statistical controls for variables that might affect the independent and dependent variables. However, the two randomized designs use random assignment to approximate physical control. What variables should be controlled for pizza-delivery drivers' comparison? At least age, gender and traffic should be controlled.

4. One-Group Pretest–Posttest Design. The one-group pretest–posttest comparison is laid out in Figure 9. What is different in the design of Figure 9 from the previous designs?

	Pretest		Posttest
One-group pretest-posttest design:	O_1	X	O_2

FIGURE 9   One-group Pretest–Post test Design.
Source: Campbell and Stanley (1963).

The one-group pretest–posttest design has no control group and no comparison group. Therefore, random assignment can't be used—random assignment to what?

In this design, the researcher observes change after an event occurs. The event may be a treatment administered by the researcher as in the cookie experiment without the sugar-baked cookies or a naturally occurring event. For example, one could compare the speed of automobiles one mile before a speed trap and one mile after the speed trap. In this case, the speed trap is the treatment, or X. The one-group pretest–posttest design also requires statistical controls for variables that might generate change during the time between pretest and posttest.

5. One-Shot Case Study Design. The most basic design consists of a single measurement made after an event has occurred or a treatment has been administered. Campbell and Stanley call it a "one-shot case study." It decidedly is not an experiment. Figure 10 illustrates the one-shot case study.

Campbell and Stanley judge this design to be more or less useless. For example, measure the speed of drivers one mile after the speed trap. The average obtained is 55 MPH, exactly the speed limit. Did the speed trap slow drivers down? There's no way to know for sure. No measure of speed was taken *before* the speed trap. But most of us might suspect it did, because we think most drivers

	Posttest	
One-shot case study:	X	O_2

FIGURE 10   One-shot Case Study.
Source: Campbell and Stanley (1963).

exceed the speed limit most of the time. So the value of the one-shot case study experimental design in this example depends on what we know informally about the topic. However, in the case of the speed trap, without knowing more about weather, road conditions, and other factors affecting speed, it would be risky to draw any more than very cautious conclusions.

The Importance of Comparison

The one-shot case study design helps to bring out this important point again:

A critical aspect of nearly all research—whether it is an experiment, survey or observational study—is that some implicit comparison nearly always is involved. Even when the comparison is not formally laid out, comparisons nonetheless are implicit.

In the speed trap example shown in Figure 10, what can be compared? Only informal comparisons can be made between the observations of driving behavior in the study and knowledge about driving behavior from other sources.

Consider another example.

Paradoxically, Hurricane Andrew also brought new opportunities to some women.... We learned, for example, of women earning equitable construction wages, developing new employment skills, and using relief monies to leave violent relationships.... (Morrow & Enarson, 1996)

What comparison groups are implied here? There's no explicit reference to any comparison group, but the implied comparisons are between ordinary circumstances and disaster circumstances brought on by a hurricane. The "treatment" is the hurricane, and the "control" is the absence of a hurricane, that is, ordinary circumstances.

Comparing ordinary and disaster circumstances, the implications are that some women earn higher wages, learn different job skills and more readily escape from abusive situations after a disaster than they otherwise would. Abundant research exists about women's wages, job skills and ability to escape abuse in ordinary everyday circumstances, and findings from this body of research serve as an *informal base of comparisons*. Another comparison also is implied—between men and women and how they differ in ordinary times versus how they differ in disaster times.

A caution: As with the differences between "everyday learning" and "science learning," experimental and nonexperimental designs should not be put into separate "mental compartments." Both are subject to the same rules about avoiding threats to valid research results: (1) threats to internal validity (affecting cause-and-effect relationships), and (2) threats to external validity (affecting ability to generalize results from a sample to a population). These threats are examined in the following sections.

THREATS TO VALID RESEARCH RESULTS

Campbell and Stanley (1963) identify 12 much-cited threats to drawing sound conclusions from research results. These threats are divided into the two types of validity: (1) eight threats are to internal validity and (2) four threats are to external validity.

Notice: The term *validity* doesn't mean the same thing here as it does when applied to measurement.

Threats to Internal Validity

Recall that internal validity refers to whether or not the treatment had an effect on subjects who participated in the experiment—*internal to the experiment*. Many factors threaten the internal validity of research when random assignment is absent. Table 1 summarizes the threats to internal validity identified by Campbell and Stanley. The table classifies the many ways we can be fooled into thinking a treatment had an effect on the outcome when, in fact, it didn't. Each threat is discussed, with examples, in the paragraphs that follow.

TABLE 1. Threats to Internal Validity (Valid Cause-and-Effect Conclusions)

1. Selection	Subjects choose to be in the treatment or control group. Measured differences between the treatment- and control-group outcomes due to subject preferences are mistaken for a difference due to the treatment.
2. Mortality	Some subjects do not complete the study. Therefore, there is no posttest measure for them. Measured differences between the treatment and control group due to differential dropout are mistaken for a treatment effect.
3. History	A natural event occurs between pretest and posttest. Its effect on the outcome is mistaken for an effect of the treatment.
4. Maturation	Subjects change due to natural growth/decline. The natural change is mistaken for an effect of the treatment.
5. Testing	The pretest affects measurements at the posttest. The difference between pretest and posttest generated by testing is mistaken for an effect of the treatment.
6. Instrumentation	Calibration of the measuring device (instrument) changes between pretest and posttest. The resulting difference between pretest and posttest observations is mistaken for an effect of the treatment.
7. Regression	Subjects selected from one or the other extremes of the distribution of scores for the outcome variable gravitate naturally toward the middle. This natural result of selecting from one extreme is mistaken for an effect of the treatment.
8. Interaction of selection and history, maturation, testing, or instrumentation	Treatment and control groups react differently to history, maturation, testing, or instrumentation. The difference in the posttest measure due to differential reaction is mistaken for a treatment effect.

Selection. Most social research is done using the static-group-comparison design. Remember that the static-group design uses comparisons among naturally occurring groups—with no random assignment.

The most frequent source of a false or spurious relationship is a mechanism called selection. **Selection** occurs when subjects select (choose) to be in the treatment or control group, or otherwise are selected by a nonrandom process. Consequently, outcome differences between the treatment and control groups due to selection are likely to be mistaken for a difference due to the treatment.

Consider the spurious relationship between wearing a beard and wearing a dress, which is due to a common influence of gender on both beards and dresses. Men sometimes choose to grow a beard but rarely choose to wear a dress. Women sometimes choose to wear a dress but, with rare exceptions, cannot grow a beard. The idea generalizes as shown in Figure 11.

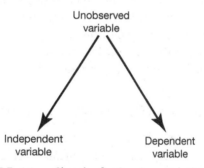

FIGURE 11   Sketch of a Spurious Relationship.

The Uggen study about the effect of employment on re-arrest, cited earlier in this chapter, shows how selection might work. Without random assignment, the men might choose to work (select themselves into jobs) and decide not to be criminals for reasons unrelated to whether employment influences committing crimes. This possible confusion of the *effect of selection* with the *effect of working* is part of Uggen's argument for the strength of his data, because respondents were assigned at random to a supported work program or to the control group.

However, selection doesn't always refer to deliberate choices made by subjects. It just means some selection process other than a random one is occurring. When random assignment isn't possible, as in most research, statistical controls are essential.

Mortality. Mortality does not mean physical death, though it might occasionally be due to physical death. In this context, it just means that the rate of dropping out of a study differs among the treatments; the differential dropout rate is mistaken for a treatment effect.

For example, suppose students in a low reading group are offered a chance to take a remedial reading course. At the end of the course, compare the average score of those who completed the course to the average of those who did not.

Those who completed the course did better on the reading test than those who didn't. Success! Parents, teachers and students are pleased!

But there's a problem. Participation is voluntary—students were offered a chance to take the course. Who might be more likely to leave the study before the posttest? Probably students who leave have the most difficulty with reading, learn the least and consequently become frustrated. Since readers who learn the least drop out before the posttest, their scores are omitted from the average for those who have completed the course. As a result, the average change in the reading scores for completers is too high, suggesting that taking the class had a stronger effect than it did.

Weight-loss programs, aerobics classes and similar programs also tend to have overestimated positive outcomes. Many such programs are promoted during a blitz of television commercials just after the December holidays—with lavish praise from the testimonials of "happy" (and likely well-paid) clients. Furthermore, "sticky theory" suggests that once established, beliefs fueled by such commercials are likely to persist. But enrolling in a weight-loss program might be a good predictor of future enrollment, regardless of whether or not weight loss occurred. The belief that weight-loss programs work "sticks" in the minds of the hopeful—despite research indicating they don't work.

Four Other Threats (Mostly from One-Group Designs)

Campbell and Stanley classify these threats into four types: history, maturation, instrumentation and regression to the mean (average). These threats apply primarily to the one-group pretest–posttest design with no control or comparison group.

Recall that in the one-group pretest–posttest design, the same group of subjects is compared at different points in time, once before the treatment and once afterward. Therefore, threats to valid results involve some change or event (other than the treatment) that happens between the pretest and posttest. **History** is a shorthand term for the idea that events or circumstances other than the treatment that occurred between a pretest and posttest might account for observed changes in the outcome.

For example, your high school does a drug-use survey on students aged 13 and older, and finds an "alarming" rate of marijuana use. The school district quickly implements an elaborate campaign to reduce marijuana use, and repeats the survey at the end of the school year. The reported rate of marijuana use declined by 10 percent, implying that the campaign was effective. But, unbeknownst to school officials, a rumor spread a month or so before the follow-up survey that undercover police agents were looking for peddlers of illegal drugs. The rumor was influential enough that many suppliers decided to lie low for a while. Consequently, the percentage of students reporting they used marijuana during the last month was noticeably lower on the posttest than it was on the pretest, due to the effect of the rumor, *not* the antimarijuana campaign.

With no control or comparison group, history effects threaten the cause-and-effect conclusions of the pretest–posttest comparison. And "sticky theory" beliefs are not unusual in conclusions from one-group research designs.

Maturation is the idea that changes in subjects between a pretest and posttest would have occurred with or without the treatment (or any other external events). Individuals get older, wiser, healthier and so forth, without treatment. For example, feed massive vitamin C supplements to a group of adults with bad colds; then see whether the cold symptoms subside after 2 weeks. Most colds in healthy people will subside within this time period without vitamins.

Testing is the idea that the experience of a pretest might influence results on a posttest. The cookie experiment is one example of potential effects of testing. And examples abound in educational research. The experience of taking a test usually improves performance on a second test, even without any information about which questions you missed.

Another example of potential testing effects is shown in Table 2. Are "plots hatched in secret places"? Perhaps, but our point here is that without careful consideration, questions on attitudinal surveys might reveal the hidden intent of the research and thereby skew the responses. Can you tell what the question in Table 2 is trying to find out? Many respondents also probably would recognize what the survey is getting at and might adjust their answers on a second test.

TABLE 2.   Example of Attitude Survey Question with "Hidden" Intent

Most people don't realize how much our lives are controlled by plots hatched in secret places by politicians.

Disagree Strongly	Disagree Mostly	Disagree Somewhat	Agree Somewhat	Agree Mostly	Agree Strongly
[ ]	[ ]	[ ]	[ ]	[ ]	[ ]

Source: T.W. Adorno, et al. *The Authoritarian Personality*, 1950, p. 249.

Testing effects threaten primarily the pretest–posttest-only design because of the absence of a control or comparison group.

Instrumentation is a term meaning change in the measuring instrument between pretest and posttest. It primarily threatens the pretest–posttest design. Here is an everyday example of instrumentation effect: after the winter holidays you weigh yourself at the fitness center; come back a week later and weigh yourself again—you've lost weight. But oops—the fitness center bought a new scale the day after your first visit, and it's calibrated too low!

Another example is using the same questions at two exam sittings is likely to show artificial "learning," because you remember questions from the first administration. To avoid this problem, exams, tests or surveys administered to the same subjects at more than one time often use "alternative forms" to avoid effects of memory. But to avoid the effects of instrumentation from alternative forms, multiple forms must have the same mean score and variation.

Regression to the mean (average) is a very interesting phenomenon that can easily be mistaken for a treatment effect. It occurs whenever a variable is imperfectly correlated with itself over time. In general, regression to the mean doesn't threaten internal validity, but with a one-group pretest–posttest design, results due to regression to the mean can easily be mistaken for a treatment effect.

Suppose you choose your elementary school to administer a reading test to all 150 third-graders. You then pick the 25 students with the lowest scores for special remedial classes. At the end of the school year, you administer the same (or equivalent) reading test again. Sure enough, the average scores of the treatment group increased. The remedial class worked—or did it?

These 25 students—chosen for their low scores—would have had a higher average score on the posttest than on their pretest due to regression to the mean. In actions such as remedial education, in which subjects are selected because of their extreme initial scores on the outcome, regression to the mean is almost certain to be mistaken for a treatment effect unless you (a) know to look for it and (b) design the experiment to avoid it. How can you design an experiment to avoid confusing regression to the mean with a treatment effect? The suggested design is to pick 50 of the lowest-scoring students and assign them at random—25 to special remedial classes and 25 to regular classes. (You might need more than 50 students.)[4]

Coaches often seem to yell at their players; does yelling get a better performance? Coaches find that if they praise players for a good performance the players do worse the next game, but if they yell at players for doing poorly, the players do better the next game. So, is the formula for a winning team to withhold praise when players do well and yell at the players when they make mistakes? The coaches' observations likely are correct, but the implied cause-and-effect relationship almost certainly is *not*. Quality of play naturally waxes and wanes because it is not perfectly correlated with itself over time. Therefore, regression to the mean occurs when both exceptionally good *or* exceptionally poor play is followed by mediocre play. This happens whether or not the coach yells!

Regression to the mean does not imply that every individual subject with an extreme pretest score is closer to the mean on the posttest. It just means that the *average score of subjects in either extreme* is closer to the mean score on the posttest than it was on the pretest.

Selection interaction *or* **selection ✕ (one of the "four other threats")** (or just **interaction**) refers to the possibility that selection into treatment and control groups occurs in such a way that subjects in the treatment group react differently than subjects in the control group to one of four threats: maturation, history, testing and/or instrumentation.[5]

Suppose a vigorous jogging program improves the cardiovascular health of people with healthy cardiovascular systems, but reduces cardiovascular health of those with clogged arteries. However, healthy people are more likely to *select* a vigorous jogging program than people with cardiovascular problems and thereby distort the general effect of a jogging program – selection ✕ exercise program interaction.

NOTE: *Threats to internal validity from selection-x interactions are different than threats from the "main effects" of maturation, history, testing and/or instrumentation in Table 1.* Main effects threaten valid results when there is *no control/comparison group*, such as the one-group pretest–posttest design. The selection interactions mainly threaten valid results from designs *with a comparison group but no random assignment.*

Threats to External Validity

Internal validity addresses the question Does the treatment have any effect in the particular experiment? External validity, however, addresses the question *Can the results of the experiment be generalized to people other than those in the experiment?* See Table 3.

Random selection means that subjects were chosen from the larger population by a pure chance process. Random selection is for external validity of the experiment: Does the observed effect generalize to populations other than the one from which subjects were chosen? For example, does an experiment with college students generalize to the entire adult population? Would an experiment assigning people to compare advertising in *Sports Illustrated* magazines generalize to ads in a fitness or home repair magazine? And would information from adults in Buffalo, New York, apply to adults in Galveston, Texas or Minneapolis, Minnesota? The results typically are limited to the population from which the subjects were randomly selected.

TABLE 3.   Threats to External Validity

1. Interaction of testing and *X*	The effect of treatment is different in the absence of testing or measurements than it is when testing/measurement is done—a "sensitizing effect."
2. Interaction of selection and *X*	The effect of the treatment is different for those who participate in the research than it is for those who do not—the "susceptibility effect."
3. Reactive arrangements	The artificial nature of an experiment and subjects' knowledge of being a "guinea pig" prevent generalization to settings outside the experiment—a "guinea pig effect."
4. Multiple-X interference	More than one treatment is given to each subject. Effects of early treatments last longer than the elapsed time between treatments. Effects of early treatments are confounded with effects of later treatments—an "overlapping-treatment effect."

Source: Campbell and Stanley (1963).

Interaction of Testing and X. This difficulty is that something about the measurements tends to skew the results of the experiment. Suppose a marketing class conducts an experiment intending to assess the effectiveness of an ad campaign for a new product. The objective of the research is to estimate the effectiveness of the ad and to measure the effect of perceived "hype" in the ad on reactions to it. A questionnaire is administered before and after students in the treatment group view the ad. The questionnaire asks pointed questions about hype in the ad which sensitizes subjects to the ad in such a way that they are less influenced by its appeal than they would have been had they watched the same ad outside the classroom and therefore did not complete the questionnaire.

Interaction of Selection and X. The basic problem here is that volunteers for an experiment are selected, most likely inadvertently, in a way that they are more, or less, susceptible to the treatment than is the general population. The result is an exaggerated estimate of the effect of the treatment.

For example, students in introductory psychology classes are asked to volunteer for an experiment involving reactions to violent content in TV and in movies. Appeals for volunteers contain a *Star-Wars*-like image and subtly emphasize the entertainment value of the experiment. Students who already like shoot-em-up video games are substantially more likely to volunteer for the experiment and are pretty much inured to violence in video images. Subjects are divided at random into a treatment group that watches a violent video and a control group that watches a more sedate video.

A before-and-after battery of questions are administered to both groups to assess, among other things, tolerance of violence against women. The result is an underestimate of the effect of violence in video images on tolerance for violence in the general population.

Reactive Arrangements. This threat is an umbrella term covering a variety of experimental manipulations that might not mirror real-world settings.

The idea of reactive arrangements is easier to illustrate than to define. Recall the example earlier in this chapter of selecting only low-scoring students for a remedial-reading program. The selected children likely would figure out that they were doing something different than other children, and this knowledge might affect the outcome. Also, teachers undoubtedly know the difference.

Multiple-Treatment Interference. Multiple-treatment interference occurs when several treatments are administered to the same subjects, and the effects of early treatments last longer than the time between treatments.

Suppose several pain-killers are administered in sequence, not at the same time, to a sample of subjects with chronic pain. A pain questionnaire is given to each subject at several time points after administering each drug. If the effects of drug A have not worn off completely by the time drug B is given, the effects of drug B will be confounded with the effects of drug A.

In summary, there are many threats to valid research results, whether the observations come from an experiment, from nonexperimental research or from everyday life. Clearly, not just any experiment offers convincing evidence for a valid cause-and-effect conclusion, and many important issues cannot be verified beyond a reasonable doubt. *In both everyday life and science, the trick is to know when to reserve judgment, to always look for new evidence, and to know how to evaluate evidence.*

SUMMARY

This chapter is about experiments and what can be learned from them about standards supporting valid cause-and-effect conclusions.

An experiment is a process in which a researcher manipulates or changes the value of at least one variable (the treatment variable) and watches to see what happens to another variable (the outcome). For example, the treatment might be to show a commercial ad to people, and the outcome might be whether subjects purchase the product shown in the ad.

A relationship between the treatment variable and the outcome might be due to effects of the treatment on the outcome or it might be due to the dependence of both treatment and outcome on one or more other variables. In the latter case, the observed association is false or spurious. Usually it's impossible to identify and measure all the variables that might affect both the treatment and the outcome, but valid cause-and-effect conclusions nonetheless depend on it.

How can an experiment control for *all* variables that might account for an observed relationship between the treatment variable and the outcome? The short answer is, by *random assignment.* Random assignment is for internal validity of the experiment. Half the subjects get the treatment and half of them don't, and assignment is done using a random procedure, such as a lottery. The result is that the *expected* average score before the treatment—on all variables, known and unknown—is the same for treatment and control groups. After the treatment, the difference between the treatment and control group average for the dependent variable can't be due to anything other than treatment effects and random variation.

Random assignment doesn't guarantee exact equivalence at the outset between the treatment and control groups. Random assignment also does not guarantee equivalence among the treatments over the duration of an experiment. For example, consider long-lasting evaluation research, like the field experiment about the impact of jobs on criminal activity. In long-lasting studies there may be an overtime drift away from the initial average equivalence between the two groups expected with random assignment. Larger samples can reduce initial average differences between groups, at least in principle, to near zero. Statistical tests can be used to assess the effect of random variation, while statistical controls can help to compensate for differential drift over time between treatment and control groups.

Random selection means that subjects were chosen from the larger population by a pure chance process. Random selection is for external validity of the experiment: Does the observed effect generalize to populations other than the one from which subjects were chosen? For example, does an experiment with college students generalize to the entire adult population?

Social experiments using random assignment with people usually are not feasible, due to ethical and other reasons, as illustrated in this chapter. Therefore, most interesting social science questions are not amenable to experiments. However, the study of experiments provides important insights about how to evaluate nonexperimental research, as well as how to evaluate information from everyday life.

Generally, a useful experiment is possible only after much is known about a topic. Then a well-designed experiment may answer a perplexing question. However, it is possible to study many complicated issues, even if the barriers to valid results seem to be hopelessly high. The discussion in this chapter is intended to help you become a better judge—in your everyday life and in your professional life—of what is and is not likely to be true.

YOUR REVIEW SHEET

1. What is an experiment? Provide an everyday example not discussed in this chapter.

2. In the cookie example, what does the experimenter physically control? Why are these controls important?

3. Explain the difference between random selection and random assignment to your 13-year-old cousin. What form of validity is increased by each type?

4. Explain how random assignment "controls" for all possible confounding variables, both known and unknown. (*Hint:* Look back at the cookie experiment.)

5. Summarize the classical experimental design. What is the basic comparison of this design?

6. Why is the posttest-only random-assignment design nearly as good as the classical design? In what way is it inferior?

7. Compared with the "posttest-only control-group" design, what's missing in the "static-group" design? Why is this missing element important?

8. The "one-shot" design has only one group and no pretest. What could be compared when using this design?

9. Suppose students voluntarily take a remedial reading course. Who might be likely to leave the study before the posttest? What effect is this likely to have on the data analysis?

END NOTES

1. Reprinted with permission from the *Journal of the American Statistical Association*. Copyright 1992 by the American Statistical Association. All rights reserved.

2. Often one or more variables is controlled statistically even with a random-assignment experiment. The controls improve the precision of the experiment by reducing the size of the random variation due to random assignment.

3. Remember the terms *average* and *mean* are synonyms.

4. *Grouping* is not one of the threats to internal validity explicitly named by Campbell and Stanley. But many experiments are conducted in group settings, and the consequence of grouping is not appreciated widely. Grouping effects occur when observations are not independent of each other. When observations are not independent, special statistical procedures are needed, because standard statistical analysis is based on the assumption of independent observations.

5. The term *interaction* (statistical interaction) is a technical term, meaning that an effect operates differently in some categories of a control variable than in others. Recall the findings of the Uggen field experiment—the supported work program reduced arrests for men over 26 years of age, but not for those 26 and younger. In this case, statistically controlling for age revealed the differential effects of the work program for the younger and older groups. This is an example of interaction, not of selection effects.

Study Terms

classical experimental design (pretest–posttest control-group design) Experimental design in which pretest–posttest changes for the experimental $\overline{O}_2 - \overline{O}_1$ group are compared with changes for the control group $\overline{O}_4 - \overline{O}_3$, and subjects are assigned at random to the treatment or control group (the O with an "overbar" refers to the mean or average score of observations at the two time points and for treatment and control groups).

control group In an experiment, the group that receives no treatment or a placebo; it is included simply for comparison.

experiment In its simplest form, an experiment is a process whereby a person "changes" one variable (e.g., gives a sugar or sweetener cookie to each subject) and watches to see what happens to another variable (e.g., differences in a taste test).

experimental group In an experiment, the group that receives some type of treatment.

external validity (generalizability) Degree to which findings apply beyond the experimental setting.

random selection Done to improve external validity.

history Events or circumstances occurring between a pretest and posttest (other than the treatment) that might account for changes in the outcome; a threat to **internal validity** in the absence of a comparison group.

instrumentation Change in the measuring instrument between pretest and posttest, which is mistaken for a treatment effect; a threat to **internal validity**.

interaction The possibility that selection into the treatment and control groups leads to a different response for the treatment group than for those not recruited into the experiment.

internal validity Degree to which the treatment had the expected effect in an experiment; random assignment is undertaken to protect **internal validity**.

maturation Changes in subjects between a pretest and posttest that would have occurred with or without the treatment (or any other external event); maturation may be mistaken for treatment effects and therefore is a threat to internal validity.

one-group pretest–posttest design Quasi-experimental design with no control group or comparison group; the researcher observes change between a measurement taken before an event occurs and a second measurement taken after it.

one-shot case study Most basic design, consisting of information from one group after an event has occurred or a treatment administered; usually, informal or implied comparisons are made between the group and other information not gathered as part of the study.

physical control The researcher determines what is changed, by how much, and what is not changed (i.e., is kept constant). Includes "control" by random assignment (where only the expected initial differences among mean scores of variables are controlled).

placebo Nonreactive agent, such as the sugar pill given in medical research, to provide a baseline comparison group in experiments.

posttest-only control-group design Random-assignment design comparing differences between the experimental group and the control group after the treatment is administered to the treatment group. Subjects are assigned at random to treatment and control groups.

random assignment (*randomized design*) A pure chance procedure to determine which subjects are in the treatment group and which subjects are in the control group. The purpose is to improve **internal validity**.

random selection A pure-chance procedure for including subjects in a study. The purpose is to improve **external validity**.

regression (to the mean) Regression to the mean threatens internal validity if subjects are selected for their extreme score (very high or very low, often for remedial treatment), and subjects are not randomly assigned to the treatment. The average for extreme scores at the pretest moves closer to the middle score at the posttest, due to positive but imperfect correlation between pretest and posttest scores.

selection The result when subjects choose the treatment group or control group or are selected by any nonrandom process; the most frequent source of a spurious (false) relationship.

static-group comparison A design with no random assignment; comparison is between naturally occurring groups. For example, compare earnings of college graduates to earnings of non–college graduates.

testing A pretest might influence results on a posttest and be mistaken for the effects of the treatment. For example, the experience of taking a test usually improves performance on a second test; a threat to internal validity.

treatment In experiments, one category of the independent or treatment variable.

treatment variable Terminology generally used in experiments as an alternative name for *independent variable*.

Exercises

Exercise 1. Evaluation of a Hypothetical Experiment: Schools and Sexual Norms

Directions: Read the statement about a proposed hypothetical experiment and answer the questions that follow.

Statement: Suppose a researcher wants to find out whether school norms influence the age of first sexual intercourse. Further suppose that each student in a hypothetical experiment is randomly assigned to a school by a fair lottery—not by the parents/guardians, the students or the school staff. In this experiment, school is the treatment variable, an indicator of school norms associated with first sexual encounter.

Factual Questions

1. With random assignment to schools for all students, would gender, race, age composition, and even unknown factors such as home environment or religious beliefs be nearly the same in all the schools at the beginning of the study? Why or why not?

2. Which research design is suggested by the above statement? Briefly explain. (*Hint:* The experiment uses random assignment.)

3. What would be compared in this experiment? Briefly discuss, based on the research design you selected for your answer to Question 2.

Questions for Discussion

1. This experiment in everyday life wouldn't work at all. Why not? (Other than students and parents, which social groups might object to the experiment, and why?)

2. Even if random assignment were possible, it wouldn't yield sound evidence about the effect of school norms on student sexual behavior. Why not? (*Hint:* Suppose the experiment lasted for 5 years. What in schools might change that could affect sexual practices?)

3. What do you think can be learned about real-world limitations of social research from this fictitious experiment?

4. If students are assigned at random to the schools, how might differences in school norms between the two schools be generated? After all, school norms should be nearly the same in all the schools at the beginning of the experiment.

Exercise 2. Skills Building: Developing a Nonrandom-Assignment Study

Directions: Read each of the following hypotheses and answer the questions that follow.

1. Roman Catholics are less likely than Protestants to approve of capital punishment.

2. Residents in a nursing home who receive regular visits from relatives report greater satisfaction with the nursing home than other residents.

3. A college policy of mandatory class attendance leads to higher student achievement.

Questions

1. What are the two variables in each hypothesis? What are their categories?

2. Could the hypothesis be tested in an experiment using random assignment? Briefly explain.

3. Propose a study of your own that does not use random assignment. Identify the independent (treatment) variable and the dependent variable (outcome). Referring to the schematic layout used by Campbell and Stanley, draw a sketch of the design, replacing the *X*, O and the blank in the Treatment column with specific categories of the variable you chose. For example, replace Figure 8 with Figure 12.

	Pretest	Treatment	Posttest
Static group comparison:	—	Catholic	% Catholics who approve of capital punishment
	—	Protestant	% Protestants who approve of capital punishment

FIGURE 12

Source: Campbell and Stanley (1963).

4. Describe who will be the subjects for your study, and how you plan to get a sample of them. (The treatment is the independent variable. Note that variables must have at least two categories, and each category must have an adequate number of cases, or subjects/individuals).

5. Referring to Table 1, why did you choose this design?

6. Is this design externally valid or not? Briefly discuss.

Exercise 3. Skills Building: Randomized Experiment Using the Posttest-Only Control-Group Design

Do you prefer Pepsi or Coke? Could you tell the difference, if you didn't know which one you were drinking? Do you think most people could—or might this be an example of "sticky theory"?

Directions: For this assignment, use the posttest-only control-group design with random assignment. Pepsi and Coke define the two categories of the treatment variable (independent variable) for the experiment. The colas are poured into two identical pitchers, with no identifying information other than an "A" on the pitcher containing Pepsi and a "B" on the pitcher containing Coke. (Subjects don't know what "A" and "B" stand for, only that the test includes the two colas; neither does the administrator of the experiment.)

Suppose you use a lottery to select 100 subjects from the student population at your college and another random method to assign each of these 100 students to taste either Coke or Pepsi. Assume that this puts 50 students into each group.

Hypothesis: *People can't tell the difference between Pepsi and Coke.* Use the following taste-identification indicator.

Please tell me which cola you drank. (Circle 1)
Pepsi   Coke

Questions

1. How many groups define the treatment variable? What are they?

2. What type of random-assignment strategy will you use to assign subjects to the two groups? Describe it. What type(s) of invalidity does your strategy avoid?

3. Describe your *O*s. What are its categories?

4. Suppose 56 percent of Pepsi drinkers said it is Pepsi, and 40 percent of Coke drinkers claimed they drank Pepsi—a difference of 16 percent. Based on this difference, can you safely conclude that people can differentiate between the two colas? Samples do vary; perhaps the 16 percent difference is due to the particular sample selected. What type of statistical procedure is needed? *Hint:* Think about sample size and what a statistical test does.

Exercise 4. Skills Building: Recognizing Grouping Effects

Grouping is not one of the threats to internal validity explicitly named by Campbell and Stanley. But many experiments are conducted in group settings, and the consequence of grouping is not appreciated widely, so we are going to introduce you to the idea in this exercise.

Directions: Read the discussion and example below, and answer the questions.

Grouping effects occur when observations are not independent of each other, when scores are more similar *within groups* (e.g., cities, dorms, classrooms) than across all observations.

As an extreme example, think about a sample of 30 students from a *sample* of just 10 classrooms, 300 students in all. But the students in each classroom get exactly the same score as every other student in their class on a reading-achievement test. Scores do differ among the 10 classrooms, however. How many observations do you really have, 300 or 10? Of course, this extreme situation probably never has and never will occur in fact. The idea is that the more averages vary between classrooms, and are therefore correspondingly similar within classrooms, the fewer effective observations you have for estimating the overall average.

It is important to keep in mind that the 10 classrooms are just a sample of all the classrooms in the country. This is a key feature of grouping effects. The problem would not occur if you had all the classrooms in your study.

For another example, suppose you select Bismarck, Helena, Fargo, Minneapolis and Sioux Falls for a "weather cure," and send a cadre of oracles to each city on December 31, 1999, to do a "warm-weather dance." Table 4 shows the temperatures for these five cities. The table also reveals that the average temperature increased compared with the original readings taken before the dance, and the effect persists for 2 years. The dance worked!

TABLE 4. Temperature Measurements for U.S. Cities with the Five Lowest Temperatures on January 25, 1999

	January 25, 1999	January 25, 2000	January 25, 2001
Bismarck, ND	21.6	14.1	13.5
Helena, MT	0.6	21.6	20.7
Fargo, ND	1.5	13.1	7.7
Minneapolis, MN	10.1	16.5	9.3
Sioux Falls, SD	10.3	17.1	4.2
Average	4.18	16.48	11.08

Or did it—would people pay for your "weather cure?" Probably not, because no one expects the dance to work. Our theory about weather change is better than that. In the case of these cold-weather cities, all are fairly homogeneous in weather because they are located in northern Midwestern states and influenced by the same weather systems. Consequently, the temperatures of Bismarck, Helena, Fargo, Minneapolis and Sioux Falls are not independent measurements. Grouping effects occur because temperature data from cities in close geographic proximity are more homogeneous than those from a random selection of cities.

And, at least as important, choosing five cities with the coldest (or warmest) temperatures leads to natural drift back to the mean temperature after the weather dance, an example of *regression to the mean* that easily can be mistaken for a treatment effect.

Why is grouping a threat to internal validity? When observations are not independent, special statistical procedures are needed. Describing these procedures is well beyond the scope of this chapter, but you should be aware of the grouping phenomenon; standard statistical analysis is based on the assumption of *independent observations*.

Currently, most researchers are well aware of the need to use specialized statistical procedures when data are collected from intact groups, have access to the needed software, and know how to use it.

Questions

1. Which research design is used? How can you tell?

2. What is the treatment? Briefly explain.

3. Is there a pretest? If so, what is it? What is the posttest?

4. In your own words, briefly explain the grouping effect of this study.

5. Select an example from this chapter in which scores are likely to be more similar within groups than across the groups, and briefly describe the grouping effect.

Exercise 5. Skills Building: Preparing a Field Experiment

Directions: You have been hired by Decision Research, Inc., to evaluate the effectiveness of an anti–cigarette smoking campaign in Marlboro School District. The target population consists of all students in the school system 11 years old or older.

1. Identify the outcome variable. How will you measure it?

2. Describe the treatment. (Unless your instructor indicates otherwise, limit your answer to one approach of an antismoking campaign.)

3. Sketch a one-group pretest–posttest design. Briefly describe how you will use this design to check the effect of the antismoking campaign.

4. Is random assignment possible? Explain your answer.

5. Using the one-group pretest–posttest design, identify at least three variables whose effects on smoking might be mistaken for effects of the antismoking campaign. Briefly describe why the effects of these variables might be confounded with effects of the treatment (the antismoking campaign).

6. Describe one intervention to reduce smoking that might be assigned at random to individual students.

6 OBSERVATION AND ETHNOGRAPHY

INTRODUCTION: LOOKING AT HOW THE SOCIAL WORLD WORKS

Home! What did you notice about your home the last time you entered it? Did you detect any fragrances or aromas that you didn't expect? Could you hear music or voices as you entered the door? Or, was everything still? Suppose you opened the door and someone was standing there whom you didn't expect, what would you do? Immediately you would begin trying to determine: Do you know the person or not? If you do, does the person seem happy to see you? How could you tell? Of course, you might use several of your senses—vision, hearing, and perhaps touch. Smell or taste might be helpful to interpret social life in other situations. For example, what is your favorite food? Can you tell whether someone has prepared it before you see it on the table?

We continuously make observations of our everyday world, whether or not we are actively aware of it. Regularities often are so commonplace that we scarcely notice many actions and reactions—unless something unexpected occurs or we are required to recall the actions. Did you ever drive down a street or road so often that you couldn't tell another person whether a sign indicating its name is present or not?

A lot happens in the social world that cannot easily be quantified. Disciplines such as anthropology and sociology have evolved in part to understand the "other" as well as the "self," requiring observation and communication of the results to others (Vidich & Lyman, 2003, p. 56).

Observational study is a method of data collection in which the researcher obtains information by directly watching social interactions and behaviors. Frequently, the observations are done for an extended time and include direct involvement in the lives of subjects.

Ethnographic research has been described as "...the direct observation of social realities by the individual observer" (Vidich & Lyman, 1994, p. 25). It "entails an attitude of detachment toward society that permits...(observation of) the conduct of self and others,...(understanding of) the mechanisms of social processes, and...(comprehension and explanation about) why both actors and processes are as they are" (Vidich & Lyman, 2003, p. 56).

Ethnographic research often uses *unstructured data*, "that is, data that have not been coded at the point of data collection in terms of a closed set of analytic categories" (Atkinson & Hammersley, 1994, p. 248). Ethnographic researchers typically investigate a small number of cases (e.g., individuals, couples, groups and so forth) for an extended period of time, sometimes years. They look for the meanings and functions of human actions using verbal descriptions and explanations. The goal is to understand as fully as possible every aspect of a culture or subculture.

The fundamental strength of observation and ethnography is their ability to see things that almost certainly cannot be observed using surveys or experiments. A central goal is to understand the meanings attached to life events by the actors themselves. As Corbin and Strauss (2008, p. 163) emphasize, "Thinking is the heart and soul of qualitative analysis. Thinking is the engine that drives the process and brings the researcher into the analytic process."

Goals of This Chapter

The methods used in observation and ethnography often are called qualitative methods and stand in contrast to quantitative methods. **Qualitative methods** do not rely heavily on mathematical and statistical analysis; whereas, **quantitative methods** rely primarily on these methods. Also, field workers in qualitative research decide moment to moment exactly what questions to ask, what to observe and what to record. The **field** is the location of an observational or ethnographic study. Only broad guidelines are set before the fieldwork begins.

Qualitative methods bring to light the constraints faced by people in their daily lives and their emotional reactions to these constraints. They help us understand the continuity of people's dreams and feelings in highly varied circumstances.

The goals of this chapter are to help you gain a sense of the value and the limitations of observational and ethnographic research approaches and to show how qualitative and quantitative approaches complement each other. Exercises at the end of this chapter offer an opportunity to discover details about your social life—details you might not have noticed previously.

Ethics in Observation and Ethnographic Research

Note that *before planning a research project, the researcher must understand the expectations for research with human subjects, such as "do no harm."* If someone were studying your conversations and behaviors, would you like *your* information to be protected?

As you read this chapter, think about possible ethical issues of each study. We'll examine ethical issues of observational and ethnographic research in detail at the end of this chapter.

OVERVIEW OF QUALITATIVE/DESCRIPTIVE RESEARCH

The definition of qualitative research has taken different meanings during the past one hundred years (Denzin & Lincoln, 2005). Authors Denzin and Lincoln give one definition of *qualitative research:*

> ...a situated activity that...turn[s] the world into a series of representations, including field notes, interviews, conversations, photographs, recordings, and memos to the self....[Q]ualitative researchers study things in their natural settings, attempting to make sense of, or interpret, phenomena in terms of the meanings people bring to them. (Denzin & Lincoln, 2005, p. 3)

In comparison with quantitative research, which emphasizes theories and cause-and-effect relationships, qualitative researchers

> ...stress the socially constructed nature of reality, the intimate relationship between the researcher and what is studied, and the situational constraints that shape inquiry. Such researchers emphasize the value-laden nature of inquiry. They seek answers to questions that stress how social experience is created and given meaning. (Denzin & Lincoln, 1994, p. 4)

Qualitative researchers target all aspects of the social settings they choose to study and attempt to describe how the varied parts fit together. For instance, if the topic is "police academy curriculum," what topics might qualitative researchers investigate? See Figure 1 for some examples.

Over the years, numerous qualitative designs have emerged. For example, Denzin and Lincoln (1994, 2005) identify 10 qualitative designs and eight historical periods. Creswell (2007) describes five approaches—ethnography, grounded theory, phenomenology, biography, and case study. Janesick (1994) lists 18, and notes that the list isn't inclusive of all possibilities.

- Quality of a selected curriculum or program:
  - length of training time; grading on exams
  - certification of academy instructors
- Meaning or interpretation of some component of the curriculum:
  - patrol procedures; practical police skills
- Political, economic or sociopsychological aspects of academy training:
  - prison system chain of command; human relations skills
- Instructors' implicit theories about teaching and curriculum:
  - police ethics; moral issues (See Lofland, 2007.)

FIGURE 1   Examples of a "Police Academy Curriculum" that Qualitative Researchers Might Investigate.

This chapter reviews three frequently used approaches: *ethnography*, *participant observation* and *nonparticipant observation*. Also, a newer approach to qualitative research is examined: *Internet-mediated communication*.

An Example: Observation in Disaster Research

An important research question about disasters is: *How do emergency-services groups such as the Red Cross coordinate search and rescue efforts and communicate with hospitals and social service agencies?*

This research question is an example of the description of qualitative research by Denzin and Lincoln, as quoted above, "qualitative researchers study things in their natural settings, attempting to make sense of, or interpret, phenomena in terms of the meanings people bring to them" (2005, p. 3).

The Disaster Research Center (DRC) at the University of Delaware applies this type of "holistic" approach to nearly every type of disaster:

> DRC was established at Ohio State University in 1963,...and moved to its current location at the University of Delaware, in 1985. The Center was the first in the world devoted to the social scientific study of disasters. Researchers at DRC have conducted over 600 field studies since the Center's inception, traveling to communities throughout the United States and to a number of foreign countries....
>
> Past DRC studies have focused on such topics as emergency medical and mental health service delivery in disasters, community responses to acute chemical hazards, mass evacuation and sheltering, preparations for and responses to major community disasters by lifeline organizations, community earthquake mitigation and emergency preparedness...and the utilization of earth science information in earthquake risk decision making. (Disaster Research Center home page, 2010)

The first considerations in investigating a disaster in the field are (1) access to key people and organizations and (2) provisions for recording data. When horrific events occur, what do disaster researchers do? According to Kaplan (2010), first they check media for information about what has happened and where. Then they try to get access to off-limits places—sometimes even "pulling strings"—although they wait until search-and-rescue operations are complete, which could take hours or even days. When they do enter the field, they bring all kinds of recording and safety equipment, such as cameras, GPS devices, even water purification tablets, and of course, sturdy shoes.

Below are summaries of DRC's activities after Hurricane Katrina in 2005, and after the Haitian earthquake in early 2010, both of which employed observations.

> About three weeks after Katrina hit the Gulf Coast, DRC deployed eight researchers to various places in the impacted region for between five and ten days per team, to engage in several forms of data collection, including interviews (*n* = 150), participant observations, and systematic document gathering. Field teams visited a variety of locations...[in]Texas (the Astrodome and the Reliant Arena); Mississippi...and

Louisiana....DRC teams talked to local, state, and federal officials; relief workers; evacuees; and others who responded to the hurricane and consequent flooding.

When a 7.0 earthquake struck Haiti on January 12, 2010, millions of people were impacted. Hundreds of thousands of people died or were severely injured, and there was widespread and severe damage to property and infrastructure. Within two weeks, researchers from the University of Delaware's Disaster Research Center (DRC) traveled to Florida and the Dominican Republic to begin to understand the immense humanitarian operation underway to assist the devastated nation. (Disaster Research Center quick response studies page, 2010)

THREE QUALITATIVE METHODS AND A NEWER ONE

How do the daily embarrassments, cultural clashes and racism experienced by ghetto residents working in legal jobs in the white upper-class world lead them to seek employment in a local crack house? How does an ethnographer obtain answers to such questions, and at what personal and professional risks? Such questions are addressed below.

Researcher as Ethnographer: *In Search of Respect: Selling Crack in El Barrio*

Philippe Bourgois, an anthropologist, decided to study crack houses, focusing on one house he called "Game Room." "Game Room" is located in a "bogus video arcade" in El Barrio, an East Harlem neighborhood. Bourgois was particularly interested in studying the "underground economy" of drug sales and what he calls the "inner-city street culture of resistance" of socially marginalized populations. The culture Bourgois studied is

> ...a complex and conflictual web of beliefs, symbols, modes of interaction, values, and ideologies that have emerged in opposition to exclusion from mainstream society. Street culture offers an alternative forum for autonomous personal dignity....This "street culture of resistance" is not a coherent, conscious universe of political opposition but, rather, a spontaneous set of rebellious practices that in the long term have emerged as an oppositional style....Purveying [supplying] for substance use and abuse provides the material base for contemporary street culture, rendering it even more powerfully appealing than it has been in previous generations. (Bourgois, 1995, pp. 8–9)

Bourgois used participant-observation ethnography to learn about the street culture, establishing long-term relationships that permitted him to "...ask provocative personal questions, and expect thoughtful, serious answers" (p. 13).

> I spent hundreds of nights on the street and in crackhouses observing dealers and addicts. I regularly tape-recorded their conversations and life histories. Perhaps more important, I also visited their families, attending parties and intimate reunions—from

Thanksgiving dinners to New Year's Eve celebrations. I interviewed, and in many cases befriended, the spouses, lovers, siblings, mothers, grandmothers, and—when possible—the fathers and stepfathers....I also spent time in the larger community interviewing local politicians and attending institutional meetings. (p. 13)

Bourgois struggled with a variety of intellectual and methodological issues. For example, he decided to tackle what he calls "historically taboo" topics in anthropology, such as self-destruction, personal violence, alienation and addiction, which he argues are taboo in part because

...the methodological logistics of participant-observation requires researchers to be physically present and personally involved. This encourages them [ethnographic researchers] to overlook negative dynamics because they need to be empathetically engaged with the people they study and must also have their permission to live with them....[O]n a more personal level, extreme settings full of human tragedy, such as the streets of East Harlem, are psychologically overwhelming and can be physically dangerous. (p. 14)

Yet, Bourgois also reveals his conflicts, both professional and personal, about sharing his results with others who did not witness the entire spectrum of inner-city street culture.

I feel it imperative from a personal and ethical perspective, as well as from an analytic and theoretical one, to expose the horrors I witnessed among the people I befriended, without censoring even the goriest details....[Yet] I continue to worry about the political implications of exposing the minute details of the lives of the poor and powerless to the general public. Under an ethnographic microscope everyone has warts and anyone can be made to look like a monster. (p. 18)

Avoiding personal danger is another issue for ethnographers, what Bourgois calls "learning street smarts," and it is a continual risk in some settings. For example, after more than two and a half years of crack house experience, he had secured a "close and privileged relationship with the 'main man' of 'Game Room.'" Bourgois wanted to impress him and his followers, raising his credibility as a "real professor," rather than a "stuck-up professor," a closet drug addict, pervert or long-term undercover drug dealer. So, while surrounded by the man's followers and employees, he showed him a newspaper photo of himself and then talk-show host Phil Donahue, taken after a prime-time debate on violent crime in East Harlem. But, the man didn't know how to read and therefore was "disrespected" by Bourgois. However, the "main man" recovered his dignity the next time the two met by using the event to give Bourgois a warning about the risks to security from media attention:

Felipe (Bourgois), let me tell you something, people who get people busted—even if it's by mistake—sometimes get found in the garbage with their heart ripped out and their bodies chopped up into little pieces...or else maybe they just get their fingers stuck in electrical sockets. You understand what I'm saying? (p. 22)

Was Bourgois able to present his findings about the poor and powerless without offering a sensationalized account of violence and racism? Bourgois's answer is "...ultimately the problem and the responsibility [of interpreting the findings] is also in the eyes of the beholder" (p. 18).

Researcher as Participant Observer: Everyday Life in Nursing Homes

Participant observation is one of several essential data-collection strategies used in disaster research. A **participant observer** is a researcher who is completely immersed in the regular activities of the group under study. Almost all projects seek multiple perspectives of those involved—a complete picture of the event is of greatest importance, so individual and group interviews aim to collect information from people with every possible vantage point and every conceivable perspective on the event (Quarantelli, 1997).

Prior to developing a study, the participant observer might be a member of the group to be observed. For example, suppose for research purposes you observe some aspect of life in your campus residence hall—you would be a participant observer. Often, however, the participant researcher joins the group only for the purpose of conducting a study.

Other types of observation are done by the **complete observer** (where field workers' roles as researchers are unknown to subjects) and the **partial observer** (where a field worker's role as a researcher is known by subjects, but the field worker is not a member of the group). Sometimes these roles run together, for example, when the researcher becomes known only to some group members (Atkinson & Hammersley, 1994).

A participant observer whose role as a researcher is known to subjects could affect the events being studied. When a participant observer does not reveal his or her role as a researcher to subjects, it's possible to obtain information about the group that otherwise might not be revealed. Timothy Diamond describes his observations in nursing homes:

Initially, I indicated on my job applications that I was a researcher interested in studying nursing homes...not once was I offered a job....Eventually, I began to emphasize my training as a nursing assistant rather than as a researcher. Using this strategy, I was soon employed...yet...my presence was never without suspicion. It was one of the administrators who...asked, "Why would a white guy want to work for these kind of wages?"

I worked in both private and state-subsidized homes....Given present economic arrangements for long-term care, a patient moves along a path: the more time in long term care, the poorer one becomes....Many patients told me of their fears as those last weeks of Medicare drew near and, for example, that "damn hip wouldn't heal"....

The women and men I met at the expensive home started out in the posh two lower floors. When their money had run out they were moved to the public aid wings, there to receive noticeably inferior care.…The management had made it clear that they preferred more short-term Medicare patients, since these patients were worth more. One could feel a murmur of fear among the public aid patients that many would be asked to leave or go to another home. No doubt this would happen to some. I know because I met women and men in the poor homes who had started as private pay residents in other homes and had been forced to leave them. Meeting them made me understand that there is a distinct economic progression in nursing home life—the longer one stays the more impoverished one becomes, and the more unstable one's environment becomes.…

I came to change my image of nursing home life as a static enterprise. It is not sitting in a chair "doing nothing." Rather than being passive, it is always a process. The policies that shape this environment inform every moment of nursing home life. Each person is situated somewhere on an overall turbulent path. Each person sits in a chair, or lies on a bed, often appearing motionless, but is moving and being moved, however silently, through the society.…Their [nursing assistants' and patients'] standpoint, I conclude, is often opposed to the organizational logic of business that increasingly encases nursing home life (Diamond, 1986, pp. 1287–1289; see also Diamond, 1992).

The interaction between a participant observer and members of the group being studied might influence the social events in the group. However, a researcher could study an event without becoming a part of it, as the next excerpt shows.

Do you think Diamond should have revealed his identity to administrators and others at the nursing homes? The question of unannounced (or covert) research is examined later in this chapter.

Researcher as Nonparticipant Observer: An Unobtrusive Study of Arousal–Attraction

Have you ever sat in a shopping mall people-watching? Sitting in a mall to observe patterns of communication between children and parents, for example, isn't likely to influence subjects, particularly if the researcher unobtrusively records information about them as they go about their regular activities. Nonparticipant observation, sometimes called *complete observation*, is done without informing the subjects they are being studied—the research is not announced. It usually is undertaken in public settings, where the researcher is unlikely to know most other people, and the subjects might not even know they are part of a research project.

The following excerpt from a journal article reports a study that uses nonparticipant observation to investigate whether the public behavior of couples is affected by the level of emotional drama in a movie they have just viewed.

The present study attempted to generalize previous findings [that emotional states are a function of physiological arousal and one's perception of the precipitating event] beyond the laboratory by observing the impact of arousal on interpersonal attraction among people attending a movie.…

It was hypothesized that couples leaving the high-arousal (suspense) movie (*52 Pickup*) would engage in significantly more affiliative behaviors than couples leaving the neutral movie (*True Stories*, a mock documentary on middle-class life in America that includes no violence or nudity). It was further predicted that couples watching the high-arousal movie would engage more in affiliative behaviors (i.e., talking, touching) when exiting the theater than when entering the theater but that couples watching the neutral movie would not exhibit increased affiliative behavior when exiting the theater....

Seventy-nine mixed-sex dyads were unobtrusively observed entering, and 70 mixed-sex dyads were observed leaving the two movies. The dependent variable, level of affiliation, was measured by the number of couples who were either talking or touching, both talking and touching and neither talking nor touching. In order to record patron behavior unobtrusively, three observers kept a mental count of the number of couples fitting each of the four categories. The totals were recorded as soon as all the patrons were seated or had left the theater....

These results indicate that couples leaving the high-arousal movie were more affiliative than couples leaving the low-arousal movie. The results from the pre-arousal measure of affiliation reduce the possibility that behavior while leaving the movies was due to preexisting differences in affiliative tendencies between the two groups. (Cohen, Waugh, & Place, 1989, pp. 692–693)[1]

Notice: Although illustrating qualitative methodology, this study shares important features with quantitative methods. It combines an observational method of data collection with quantitative analysis.

In their study design couples decided for themselves which movie to watch. That is, *no random assignment was used to determine which movie each couple would watch.* Therefore, how might "selection"—a threat to internally valid results—affect the findings?

Maybe couples who were more affiliative before watching the movie chose to see *52 Pickup* and the lesser affiliative couples decided to watch *True Stories*. If this were the case, couples viewing *52 Pickup* would be more affiliative after the movie than couples seeing *True Stories*, even if the movies had no effect on affiliative behaviors. How do before-and-after measures help to reduce this threat to internal validity? Some settings require more detailed information about the social circumstances or subjects than detached observation might provide. In a hospital emergency waiting room, for example, it might be hard to tell without asking whether the person sitting next to you in the waiting room is a neighbor, friend or relative of a patient, or perhaps a patient waiting to be called by the staff. The **nonparticipant observer** in an ER also is likely to have limited time before being noticed and questioned by hospital staff. In the movie-watching study, what other details would strengthen the findings about level of emotional drama in movies and subsequent affiliative behaviors of couples?

A Newer Approach: Online Qualitative Research—and Its Challenges

The Internet is similar in some respects to other forms of communication, such as letter writing, telegraphing, telephoning and post-it note writing (Markham, 2005). Yet as Markham notes, *computer-mediated communication* (CMC), sometimes also called *Internet-mediated communication* (IMC), still probably is unfamiliar to most researchers as a method of data collection for social research.

For ethnographers, who are used to "going someplace" to physically watch people, their practices, and so on, online ethnography might not readily be seen as equivalent to "getting your hands dirty with data" (Berg, 2009, p. 226). However, online ethnographers, like traditional ethnographers, must find ways to understand the cultures and practices of the group they are studying and ways to explain these to others (Kendall, 2004). Like traditional ethnographers, the online qualitative researcher is not "an objective, politically neutral observer...all inquiry reflects the standpoint of the inquirer...there is no possibility of theory- or value-free knowledge" (Denzin, 2004, p. 5).

Internet technologies also have the potential to shift "sense-making practices," including the ways qualitative researchers think about, gather, evaluate and represent data. For example, researchers collecting information on or via the Internet readily can obtain data from across the globe if they wish. Cut-and-paste methods facilitate transfer for storing, rearranging and transferring data to others. And data collection is economical (Markham, 2005).

At the same time, the online ethnographer can be overwhelmed by the *massive* amounts of conversational data that a computer can record. It's important to establish criteria that can point out what information should be retained and what can be ignored—but like planning to travel unfamiliar roads, be ready to go off-course if an exciting opportunity for new information presents itself (LeBesco, 2004).

An example of online ethnographic research is work by Michael Wesch, a cultural anthropologist and media ecologist at Kansas State University. He is studying the effects of new media on human social interaction. To learn about the basic ideas underlying what people know as Web 2.0, Wesch made and uploaded the video "The Machine Is Us/ing Us" to *YouTube* website (Sasaki, 2008). The video quickly became highly popular, but Wesch became more interested in *YouTube* from an anthropological point of view. So he created a class, part of which involved participant observation by his university students (The video might be located online by typing anthropologist Wesch's name into a search engine.)

Sasaki wrote an article about Wesch and his research, an excerpt of which is given below.

Describing what it's like to watch many of *YouTube*'s best vloggers [video bloggers], he [Wesch] said, "it's like you can see straight through to someone's core without feeling like you have to respond immediately. It almost gives you an artistic perspective about the individual. Even though it's one of the most public spaces in the world, it's also one of the most intimate." That is, Wesch's students were to point their cameras on themselves and share their observations.

...This (the public-yet-intimate nature of vlogging) is also what his students found when they started posting their own diary-like entries. As their class project became more well-known and more public, they began questioning just who they were talking to. The webcam? An invisible audience? A certain person they knew (or assumed) would eventually watch the video? One of the students, speaking quietly into his webcam said, "because I'm not looking at anyone in the eye, maybe that's why I'm able to say certain things I otherwise wouldn't." (Sasaki, 2008)

As Wesch's students themselves began to realize, complex questions can arise with online data collection. How can the online researcher understand others in their particular social contexts, know with certainty anything about those others, such as age, gender, race—which Markham (2005, p. 808) calls "searching for the body behind the text"—or even determine what constitutes data?

Moreover, there are various forms of social interaction that must be considered. Online social interaction can include "emoticons" (e.g., smiley faces); mailing lists, blogs, virtual work teams and similar virtual communities and violent or emotionally charged acts, such as insulting and hostile comments called "flaming" (see a short description of recent research by Markham, p. 798).

Online research also poses special challenges for ensuring ethical practices not only for Institutional Review Boards (IRBs) and ethics committees (whose guidelines vary by country and professional discipline) but also for the researcher trying to make "on-the-spot" decisions (Markham, 2005). How can anonymity be assured for vulnerable populations such as children and institutionalized individuals? If one gains **access** permission today, will the researcher be studying the same population next week or next month (pp. 812–813)? What about online "lurking" (reading posts to newsgroups or other lists) as a means of data collection? And do publicly accessible discussion sites provide public or private information?

Many list moderators and group leaders believe that "observation without participation" (nonparticipant research, a legitimate fieldwork method) is considered unethical in online research (Chen et al., 2004, pp. 165–166). One solution Chen and colleagues mention is that the list owner might be willing to ask the list to vote to gain users' permission. Other scholars believe that development of ethical and legal frameworks for Internet research ethics is well underway, at least between the United States and Europe (e.g., Ess, 2004).

For advice about ethical issues of online research, the Association of Internet Researchers (2012) offers guidelines for ethically grounded decisions. Their document presents a series of questions, some case studies and references and other resources for computer-mediated communication, including a sample consent form for parents and children involved in Internet research (see also Berg [2009] on protecting children and debriefing Internet subjects; Ess [2004]).

Online researchers at the earliest stage of their project also should examine the current ethical guidelines required by IRBs and funding agencies. Above all, "the priority of qualitative research is to protect the well-being of participants" (Mann & Stewart, 2000, p. 63).

SELECTING THE SITE AND THE SUBJECTS

Usually, decisions about the site or setting and selection of subjects for observational study are made when designing a research project. However, sometimes researchers rely on chance encounters in the field.

After a major disaster, where do victims find shelter? How would researchers begin the study of such a topic? Careful thought is needed before choosing the **target population**—the subjects or the specific site(s) in an area struck by disaster. Several sites could be selected: (a) in all neighborhoods where damage occurred, (b) only in the hardest-hit neighborhoods, (c) in the shelters or areas to which residents were evacuated, or (d) some combination of these locations.

The research question is the primary guide to selecting a site. For example, if the researcher wants to know whether women or men are more likely to lack access to shelter and housing aid after a disaster, a sample can be selected of adult males and females living in one or more neighborhoods with the most property damage. On the other hand, if the research question is about differences between people who obtain shelter and others who don't, then one might observe two samples—one sample of victims who found shelter and one sample of victims who did not.

After choosing the field site and subjects, a second issue is access. Researchers reveal that "...in the literature of qualitative methodology, *access* is probably one of the most written-about topics—understandably so, for it remains problematic throughout the entire period of research" (Lofland & Lofland, 1995, p. 22, emphasis in the original).

An "access ladder" of restrictiveness identifies three types of social settings (Lofland et al., 2006, pp. 34–35). "Public places" permit entrée and continuing presence without restrictions on specific activities or characteristics. An example might be public shopping malls. "Quasi-public places," such as restaurants, bars and public restrooms, expect engagement in defined activities or specific personal attributes. "Quasi-private" settings require certain credentials or attributes; examples include employee status and recognized membership. Access to "private places" depends on personal invitation or ownership, for example.

Another way to think about settings and their access is to evaluate the potential to navigate within the setting.

1. Do you, the investigator, want to be close to your subjects or a remote "objective" observer? There are advantages and disadvantages to both stances, and the issue of access depends on what kind of observer you want to be.

2. Contrasting ascriptive statuses between you and the people you study often presents substantial barriers. A young male may have difficulty studying the subculture of a beauty parlor employing only middle-aged women; a black person probably will find it impossible to study white supremacists.

3. Access for a team of observers requires large-scale coordination, as in disaster research (Lofland & Lofland, 1995).

Many settings are difficult to study. Examples include the economic elite, warring sides in a civil war and secret societies. Sometimes it's impossible to gain access to settings like these, but Lofland and Lofland (1995) urge researchers not to give up easily.

Recording Field Data

Observation and ethnography rely on a variety of data sources and methods. One scholar compares seven strategies for making observations, including ethnography and participant observation (Morse, 1994). Other potential data sources include art documents, poetry, diaries, photography, maps, social network diagrams and videotaped observations. Creswell (2009) adds art objects, computer software and videotapes to this list. As examples in this chapter show, many qualitative studies rely on more than one method and several data sources.

In the social network diagram (**sociogram**) shown in Figure 2, the goal is to identify the "stars" or persons who take charge of a conversation. Here, the "tail" of the arrow indicates who initiated the conversation, and the head of the arrow points to the recipient. An exercise at the end of this chapter provides an opportunity to identify some strengths and limitations of a sociogram.

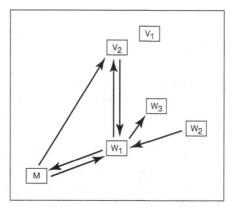

FIGURE 2   Sample Sociogram (Hypothetical Example)
(M = manager, W = worker, V = visitor).

For recording conversations in field observations, Creswell (2009, p. 181) suggests designing a note-taking form ("protocol") as a single page divided into two sections, descriptive notes and reflective field notes. **Descriptive field notes** include conversations, the physical setting and details of activities and events. **Reflective field notes** contain the researcher's thoughts, feelings, ideas, problems and so forth. A sample page is shown in Figure 3.

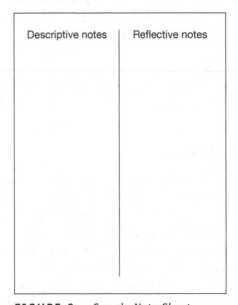

| Descriptive notes | Reflective notes |

FIGURE 3   Sample Note Sheet.

While qualitative research depends on persistence and meticulous documentations by the investigator, beginner researchers should not be discouraged if the project begins to seem too complicated (Morse, 1994, pp. 225–226).

ANALYZING FIELD DATA

Analysis of ethnographic and observational data usually begins by reading the field notes, and paying close attention to major themes and the theoretical framework. During the first reading, look for *patterns or groups of similar themes* that will be used to tell the "story."

The next step is to decide the *meaning* of the conversational patterns, such as how security in the "Game Room" is managed. With text-based data from interviews, initial readings can be used to identify key words and phrases that will be used to organize the information from all interview notes.

Computer software programs are available to assist with coding, retrieval, theory-building and other aspects of **qualitative data** analysis. Many of these programs are compatible with word-processing file formats, allowing field notes entered into a word processor to be imported directly into the software analysis program.

Figure 4 shows a simplified example that was produced by *The Ethnograph*, one of many text-analysis computer software programs. In Figure 4, for example, the code word "SHIPTIME" refers to the amount of time an interviewee spent on board a ship when emigrating from Sweden to the United States. The researcher may sort the interviews by one or more code words, enabling easy comparison of all text coded with the selected code word(s).

It's still up to the researcher, however, to determine which words, phrases, character strings and chunks of text or other information should be coded, what the codes should be and how the result is related to the research question and to theory. Then the software can help to speed through some of the most tedious aspects of making sense of the data. Lacking access to software for qualitative data, you can improvise with MS Excel or MS Access.

```
SEARCH CODE: SHIPTIME
    LINEA: So then we came over, and it      169 #
    took us 14 days to come over. We came    170 #
    over on a steamer called "Stockholm."    171 #
    It was huge. It was one of Sweden's      172 #
    largest ships. I shouldn't say a         173 #
    steamer, because it was a ship. And      174 #
    usually it took 9–10 days, but it took   175 #
    us 14 because we ran into a terrible     176 #
    storm. And I never was seasick but       177 #
    my sister was sick the whole trip, and   178 #
    she was so mad at me because I was       179 #
    having so much fun. And I didn't get     180 #
    sick at all.                             181 #

SEARCH CODE: SHIPTIME
    WILLARD: It was a new one. The            82 #
    "Stockholm." Um, it took about six        83 #
    days. In 1948.                            84 #

SEARCH CODE: SHIPTIME
    RAY: We had an awful storm when          405 # $
    I come over. In three days we only       406   $
    went 75 miles. Oh boy, big waves.        407   $
    Every wave came at you like a big        408   $
    mountain, and the boat overtook into     409   $
    it. I never was sea sick. But the        410   $
    rest of them... It took us almost 20     411   $
    days across. We had an awful storm.      412   $

SEARCH CODE: SHIPTIME
    GUNHILDA: The boat was the "Gripsholm."  210 #
    Took about 10 days.                      211 #
```

FIGURE 4 Sample Interview Text from a Code-and-Retrieve Computer Software Program.

CHECKING RELIABILITY AND VALIDITY

While *reliability* refers to "repeatability," validity refers to how accurately a variable corresponds to what it is intended to measure.

A study of massage parlors illustrates the difference between reliability and validity (Kirk & Miller, 1986). One of the research questions was whether sex-for-hire was part of the operations. The observer on the scene apparently built up a good rapport with the masseuses who consistently told him there were no "extras." Clients of the massage parlors reported the same thing—no sex trade.

But based on extensive experience, the principal investigator of the study operated on the theory that "there's always more immorality than you can see." He insisted that the field worker continue to observe and probe. Finally, one informant, apparently assuming the field worker already knew about the sex trade in the massage parlors, opened up. This one instance opened the floodgates of information. Confronted with the "facts," informants who once had denied masseuses took money for sex now "fessed up."

This case brings out three important principles. First, reliable information from interviews, here, repeated, consistent reports that the masseuses didn't engage in sex with their clients, is not necessarily valid information. Second, what is the likelihood that a survey of masseuses or clients of this massage parlor would reveal the correct extent of the sex trade in massage parlors (i.e., a validity problem)? Of course, it's really impossible to have a very good idea without doing extensive fieldwork comparing survey responses to information from direct observation. Third, whether using qualitative or quantitative approaches, generating valid information depends on a "theory." Why do you believe sex-for-hire was commonplace in the massage parlors? The answer clearly depends on insights about human behavior and about people concealing their secrets until special circumstances prompt them to "tell all."

In the absence of this prior "knowledge" of human behavior, you would have no idea whether the massage parlors engaged in sex-for-hire. All you would have is two sequences of conflicting reports. In fact, maybe there was not sex-for-hire at first, then there was. But we know better, don't we?

Designing concrete, specific methods for achieving accurate observations in qualitative research probably is not possible. And, there are too many unforeseen events in qualitative data collection to justify specific, rigid rules for what to ask, how to phrase it and what to record. Kirk and Miller (1986) do propose a sensible general approach, however: (1) Field notes should be systematic and abundant. (2) The notes should be shared among field workers. Sharing improves reliability and stimulates observers to take careful and comprehensible notes. (3) Create reliable conventions about recording dates and times, and (4) clearly separate observations from speculation and comment.

WRITING UP THE RESULTS

You've completed the needed observations or interviews and have analyzed your data. The next task is to write a paper describing what you found. Below is a summary of suggestions for getting started.

- Begin writing early—even before beginning observations or interviews. Writers who wait until their thoughts are "clear" run the risk of never starting at all.

- Perhaps start by describing the method of your project, the published research you reviewed and the details of how you collected your data. However, most of the write-up of qualitative research should be devoted to the descriptive details and their meanings.

- A good candidate for an opening sentence is, "The purpose of this study is…" If you are stuck here, then the problem likely is lack of focus. Talking to another student or a professor about your research might help define the project. Or, try "free-writing"—write to yourself in order to help pin down your thoughts. Like all writers, you will need to read and revise your written drafts several times.

- You are "telling a story," and your own writing style can be used. However, write for readers who don't know the details of your project (Wolcott, 2001).

If "Triscuits and coffee" are convenient and comforting to get you started writing and keep you writing, perhaps your kitchen table might be a good location, unless such an environment is too distracting—or too fattening (Wolcott, 2009, p. 11).

Integrating Data Collection, Interpretation and Writing

Qualitative approaches often *simultaneously* use data collection, data interpretation, narrative report writing and data analysis (Creswell, 2009).

The "metaphor of dance" has similar features to qualitative research (Janesick, 2000). Both activities have a warm-up period, a total workout stage and a cool-down period. The warm-up period occurs when the researcher selects the study question, the site, the subjects and type of research strategies. In the total workout stage, the researcher is immersed in the statements and behaviors of the participants, adjusting the focus of the study and interpreting the beliefs and behaviors of participants. The cool-down portion includes leaving the field setting, final data analysis and writing the narrative. Janesick points to common "rules of thumb" for the workout stage, on which, she says, most researchers agree.

- Look for the meaning and perspectives of the participants in the study.

- Look for relationships regarding the structure, occurrence and distribution of events over time.

- Look for points of tension: What does not fit? What are the conflicting points of evidence in the case? (pp. 387–388).

At the same time, don't forget to contemplate why you are doing all these detailed tasks—it would be easy to get lost in the details, as the phrase "can't see the forest for the trees" illustrates. A good strategy is to reflect about the meaning of what you're recording at every opportunity. Be sure to record these thoughts, too, but clearly distinguish them from factual descriptions.

ETHICAL ISSUES

Should on-site observers inform potential participants that they will be research subjects? The main tension is between (a) the very important contributions to knowledge often emerging from studies in which observers were *not* known to their subjects as researchers, and (b) the ethical implications of not informing subjects they are participating in a research study.

There is a real threat to reliability and validity in qualitative studies—participant observers can become so embroiled in the social life of the community observed that objective reporting is difficult or impossible. Of particular concern is the unannounced or covert (hidden) participant observation, discussed in the following paragraphs. Subjects are likely to accept and trust the researcher as group member, only to find out later that they were research subjects.

Charlotte Allen presents a thought-provoking essay on covert observation in her article titled "Spies like Us: When Sociologists Deceive their Subjects," published in *Lingua Franca* (Allen, 1997). She depicts the bind confronted by social scientists conducting participant observation—fulfilling research objectives *and* honoring ethical obligations. As part of her review and discussion about covert observations, Allen recounts the controversy generated from a study by Carolyn Ellis.

Ellis investigated social life among a group of Chesapeake Bay "fisher folk," the results of which were presented in her prizewinning book (Ellis, 1986). According to Allen, Ellis spent nearly 10 years of summers and weekends studying the fishing community. Initially, she explained to them she was a college student writing a paper on fishing, which she says nearly everyone forgot over time. She secretly tape-recorded conversations, eavesdropped on conversations and pressed respondents for additional information while pretending to visit them socially.

Although Ellis used made-up names in her writing, it became known to the fishing families who had taken her into their homes as a guest that she had used them for research without their knowledge. In addition to descriptions such as "fishy body odor," Allen states that conclusions in Ellis's book about the region were unflattering, because the area was known for its "white-trash backwardness and marshland criminality" (p. 31). The community was decidedly displeased.

Allen continues, Carolyn Ellis later published a "remorseful essay" that described her deception. According to Allen, although admitting guilt, Ellis still was convinced that the success of the project depended on deceiving her subjects (Allen, 1997, p. 32).

After what Allen (p. 32) calls a "raging debate," the American Sociological Association (ASA) approved stringent new ethics guidelines for professional conduct in the field. Although Carolyn Ellis acknowledged remorse, Allen notes that other researchers insist that scientific research sometimes requires covert techniques—particularly when the payoff is high, and with few negative consequences (p. 32).

Following up the "Unknown Investigator" Issue

Both Ellis's study and Diamond's research bring up an important question: *If you are a known member of an organization, particularly a formal organization as an employee or student intern, is there an ethical problem if you begin collecting data from within that organization?*

For example, perhaps part of your work duties includes making observations of suspects at a police department or observing social services clients during group counseling. You already have access to the information, so can you use these data for your own research?

This question is called the "unknown investigator" issue and has been discussed in some detail by Lofland and his coauthors (Lofland et al., 2006). The seriousness of conducting covert research can vary by type of setting, with the most serious ethical issues often associated with "private settings," described earlier in this chapter. However, Lofland and his coauthors point out social scientists are not in full agreement in either direction with what some call "spy research." They refer the reader to several books, book chapters and journal issues, and emphasize the importance of consulting local IRB requirements and knowing your discipline-specific code of ethics.

Some argue that qualitative research such as observational methods present greater challenges to decisions made by IRBs for research on human subjects than quantitative research, such as surveys.[3] For example, observational studies are more likely to focus on deviant, secret or difficult-to-locate populations, such as drug smugglers (Berg, 2001). In working with these populations, written informed-consent slips and probability samples are impossible to manage.

However, implied consent sometimes can replace a signed consent slip. For example, at the beginning of the interview if the researcher fully explains the nature of the research project along with potential risks and benefits of participation, and individuals permit in-depth, tape-recorded interviews, implied consent has been given (Berg, 2009, p. 90). A benefit of implied consent is the elimination of participants' names in any researcher records. Nonetheless, the researcher still must consider the matter of **confidentiality**—not revealing information about respondents to anyone outside the research project, including location information, such as street, business or other names that might identify participants or make people wary of participation in future research.

Qualitative research is likely to be ongoing and evolving, these many difficulties notwithstanding. So decisions, such as impartial selection of subjects, location, and so on, become more difficult. The role of IRBs also is evolving, with specific details still to be worked out.

Punch (1986) explains there are no easy answers to many situational ethics in ethnographic and observational work. Punch's guideline is worth restating: *See research subjects as "collaborators" in the research, and behave toward them as we are expected to behave toward friends and acquaintances in our everyday lives* (p. 83).

SUMMARY

This chapter is about qualitative methods, as exemplified by observational and ethnographic approaches. Qualitative research makes much fuller use of all our senses than do quantitative methods. This idea is illustrated in the beginning of the chapter by considering the probable reactions of someone who, returning home expecting an empty house, finds someone in the house.

Findings from qualitative research inform us about the emotional content of human interactions; paint vivid pictures of people's daily lives; describe problems people face and how they cope with them and work with special populations such as crack cocaine dealers, homeless people and nursing-home residents. None of this is possible with the methods of data collection and analysis associated with quantitative work. In addition, unstructured observation as qualitative research encourages reporting and interpretation of unexpected events, as illustrated in our review of disaster research.

In addition to reviewing the three main methods of data collection, ethnography, participant observation and nonparticipant observation, the chapter also discusses a newer form, namely, the computer-mediated Internet observation. None of these can be arranged in the way that a survey typically is organized. The study of a crack cocaine house and that of nursing homes illustrate how the observer must be flexible and inventive. Fieldwork also requires intense attention to detail. Accurate notes must be kept, organized and analyzed. Constant attention to maintaining data quality is required. The write-up must reflect the particular nature of the study. Writing should start early and continue throughout the fieldwork and after it is complete.

The chapter discusses each component of observation separately, to organize the presentation. However, qualitative approaches nearly always engage in data collection, data interpretation, narrative report writing and data analysis as ongoing simultaneous activities.

Qualitative work raises special ethical questions, and online qualitative research has special ethical considerations, including verification of status of subjects such as age, among others. Often, informing subjects you are researching them makes it impossible to do the research. Written consent forms might be difficult or out of the question in some instances. Also, qualitative research is labor-intensive. It's arguably more difficult in some aspects than most quantitative research, in part because selecting the research site and gaining and maintaining access to subjects generate an ongoing tension.[4]

YOUR REVIEW SHEET

1. What are some of the important similarities and differences between our everyday observations and the observations of social scientists conducting social research?

2. When does the researcher usually choose a site or setting and select the subjects for an observational study?

3. How does a researcher decide which settings and subjects to choose for an observational study?

4. Summarize the difficulties associated with gaining access to subjects in a qualitative research study.

5. Suppose you want to observe the work activities of the mayor of your city or town. Would access be the same during the height of a hurricane as during a typical day? Discuss the similarities and differences.

6. What is an advantage of concealing your identity as a researcher? A disadvantage?

7. What might happen if a nonparticipant observer interacts with the group being studied?

8. Should members of a group be studied without their permission?

9. Thinking about the observations conducted with nursing home residents, what are some strengths of participant observation? What are some reasons why participant observation might not be the best approach to data collection?

10. Thinking about the observations conducted with couples viewing the two movies, what are some strengths of nonparticipant observation?

11. What are some reasons why nonparticipant observation might not be the best approach to data collection?

12. Are ethical issues different when conducting qualitative observations online compared to other types of qualitative observations? Briefly discuss.

END NOTES

1. Copyright 1989 From "An unobtrusive study of arousal-attraction" by Brett Cohen, Gordon Waugh & Karen Place. Reproduced by permission of Taylor & Francis Group, LLC, *http://www.taylorandfrancis.com*.

2. The Policies and Procedures from the Committee on Professional Ethics, American Sociological Association, can be found at *http://www.asanet.org/about/ethics.cfm*.

3. Institutional review board (IRB) is one of several titles for formal committees in research organizations, such as universities and hospitals. IRBs review ethical concerns of proposed research. Usually, research may not proceed without approval of the IRB.

4. This isn't to say that high-quality quantitative data collection is easy—it isn't. A survey, for example, requires often-difficult coordination of the research team and careful attention to detail.

STUDY TERMS

access Permission or agreement from subjects and/or agencies to permit research at an observational or field setting.

announce Divulge to potential subjects that they are part of a research study; opposite of covert (hidden) observation.

complete observer (nonparticipant observer) Field worker whose role as a researcher is not known by the subjects.

confidentiality Not revealing information about subjects to anyone outside the research project, including location information such as street, business or other names that might identify participants or make people wary of participation in future research.

descriptive field notes Notes that include descriptions of conversations, the physical setting and details of activities and events—facts as opposed to opinions or ideas.

ethnographic research "The direct observation of social realities by the individual observer." Ethnographic research relies on data that have not been coded into a closed set of categories at the point of data collection. Ethnographers typically investigate a small number of sites for an extended period of time, often years. The goal is to understand, as fully as possible, all aspects of a culture or subculture. They examine the meanings and functions of human actions using verbal descriptions and explanations.

field Location of an observational or ethnographic study.

nonparticipant observer See complete observer.

observational study Study using unstructured method of data collection in which the researcher visits a field site for an extended time to obtain information by directly watching human social interactions and behaviors.

partial observer Researcher who is observing and participating as a member but is known as a researcher.

participant observer Researcher who is completely immersed in the regular activities of the group under study, and usually is known as a member of the group rather than as a researcher.

qualitative data (meaning-based) Information collected from unstructured observation intended to represent meanings, symbols, descriptions, concepts and characteristics of people.

qualitative methods Research methods that do not rely heavily on mathematical and statistical analysis. Qualitative research is multimethod in focus, involving a naturalistic approach to topics. Qualitative researchers study people in their natural setting, attempting to make sense of phenomena in terms of the meanings that people bring to them.

quantitative methods Research methods that rely primarily on mathematical and statistical analysis of numeric data.

reflective field notes Notes that contain the researcher's thoughts, feelings, ideas, problems and so forth.

sociogram Method of displaying patterns of interaction, such as friendship networks, cliques and other social relationships. It consists of a diagram with circles or squares representing participants, and arrows or lines connecting interacting participants.

target population Collection of all people who are eligible to participate as subjects in a study.

EXERCISES

Exercise 1. Evaluating Research: Participant Observation

Directions: Refer to the excerpt on "everyday life in nursing homes" in this chapter to answer the following questions.

Factual Questions

1. How did Diamond become a participant observer? Did he have any trouble in joining the group? If so, summarize his difficulties and how he overcame them.
2. What group members did he observe?
3. What was the purpose of the study, as suggested by the findings? How was participant observation a useful method of data collection for this purpose?

Questions for Discussion

1. Describe how Diamond's observations might have been different if he had revealed his identity as a researcher to patients and staff.
2. As a researcher, what rules might you rely on to decide whether or not to disclose your identity?
3. Think of a study in which you believe the accuracy and completeness of the findings would be compromised if subjects knew your identity as a research observer. Briefly discuss. In this situation, is disclosure of your identity after completing the study an acceptable compromise between (a) disclosing it at the beginning of the study, and (b) not disclosing it at all?

Exercise 2. Evaluating Research: Nonparticipant Observation

Directions: A study by two sociologists at Florida International University used observation and qualitative analysis to examine a topic that has not been the focus of very much research: the impact of disasters on women's lives. Read the excerpt below and then answer the questions that follow.

Excerpt: *Hurricane Andrew through Women's Eyes*

The unique experiences of female disaster victims, survivors, and rebuilders tend to be overlooked in disaster studies. Our work analyzes a major natural disaster through the eyes of women....With...notable exceptions...gender rarely appears even as a variable of analysis in disaster studies and a gendered perspective is almost totally absent from the literature.

To help address these concerns we conducted a qualitative sociological analysis of women's experiences in the aftermath of Hurricane Andrew in the southern part of Florida. We focused on the implications of gender and the roles of women in preparation, relief, and recovery efforts at both the household and community levels. Data were collected through...observations in the tent cities used for temporary housing, service centers, provider organizations, and at meetings of emergent community groups....We [also] interviewed immigrant and migrant women from Haiti, Cuba, Mexico and Central America, African-American single mothers and grandmothers, women construction workers, business owners, farmworkers, teachers, social workers, battered and homeless women....

The family caregiving roles of women expanded dramatically at all stages of disaster response. Most of the women we interviewed prepared their family for the approaching hurricane, including stocking supplies and getting the household ready....Women who reached beyond the boundaries of their own homes were crucial to response efforts. They often helped elderly neighbors and friends, either directly or by connecting them with community services....

Households headed by poor, minority women have tended to be the last to recover....According to personnel from the public and private agencies working to help victims find housing, the families who are left in the trailers tend to be the poorest of the poor, most of whom are minority women....

Paradoxically, Hurricane Andrew also brought new opportunities to some women....We learned, for example, of women earning equitable construction wages, developing new employment skills, and using relief monies to leave violent relationships....Women have forged new friendships and found common ground as they struggled to rebuild their homes, neighborhoods, and communities. (Morrow & Enarson, 1996)

Factual Questions

1. What was the purpose of the study, as suggested by the excerpt?
2. What subgroups of women did the researchers observe? According to the researchers, which subgroup struggled the longest to recover from the hurricane?

Questions for Discussion

1. Data from documents and newspaper articles also were incorporated in the report. What might these sources of information reveal that observations alone likely would not? Briefly discuss the value of combining qualitative information (e.g., observations of caregiving behaviors) and quantitative data (e.g., wages from employer payrolls).
2. As a researcher on this study, how might you decide whether or not to disclose your identity?
3. Why do you think there has been limited research on women in disaster studies? Provide one explanation that might be related to women's work roles, and one that might be related to their greater social isolation in communities.

Exercise 3. Evaluating Research: Nonparticipant Observation

Directions: Refer to the excerpt on "study of arousal–attraction" in this chapter to answer the following questions.

Factual Questions

1. In what setting did the researchers conduct their study? Where in this setting did they make their observations?

2. Whom did the researchers observe, and what behaviors did they record?

3. Explain the strategy used to record the subjects' behaviors. List at least one advantage and one limitation that might be associated with this strategy.

Questions for Discussion

1. Why do you think the researchers chose nonparticipant observation to obtain their data?

2. Nonparticipant observing in some settings can produce superficial, sketchy conclusions that lead to misperceptions about the social setting under study. What item of information about the couples might be unknown in this research? Briefly explain how not knowing the information might influence the outcome of the study.

3. Observational studies provide firsthand data about behaviors of subjects in a natural setting. However, a limitation of observational studies is generalizability, or the ability to apply the results to other subjects and locations. Comment briefly on the generalizability of the study.

4. Comment on the ethical issue of studying subjects without their consent in this study.

Exercise 4. Skills Building: Participant Observation of a Familiar Group

Directions: Conduct two types of participant observations of the same group. In your first observation, go as an unannounced participant. Then, either later at the same session or at another time, conduct a second observation of the *same* group as an announced participant.

Before beginning this exercise, review carefully the Code of Ethics. If you are uncertain about any of the ethical expectations, check with your instructor before proceeding with the exercise. Also, be sure to review relevant chapter sections before planning the observations.

1. Select a group in which you are a current and familiar member. Some groups to consider are your dorm residents, a campus or community club or your family. Use the same group for each observation.

2. Choose two times that you can observe the group for at least 15 minutes without interruption.

3. Select a specific topic, such as patterns of verbal or nonverbal communication while the group is holding a meeting, watching television or participating in a sports or game activity. This topic need not be a specific hypothesis as in quantitative research. Observe the same activity and the same group at both times.

4. Use a sample note sheet like Figure 3 to record descriptive information and your reflections about the group and its activities. You might need more than one sheet

per observation. Conversations should be *recorded exactly*, to the extent possible—don't summarize or skip some words or phrases. Your reflections can be added either during the observation or immediately afterward. Be ready to turn in your original note sheets. For each observation, use a form similar to:

Type or name of group _____

Date, time and location of observation 1 (unannounced) _____

Specific *activity* for observations _____

Specific *topic* for observations _____

Date, time and location of observation 2 (announced) _____

Questions

After completing the unannounced observation:

1. How did you arrange yourself in the setting to be able to observe and write your notes? Did anyone ask you to explain what you were doing? If so, what did you say? If not, what do you think their reasons might be?

2. Did you write any notes after completing the observation? If so, why, and what did you write?

After completing the announced observation:

1. How did you arrange yourself in the setting to be able to observe and write notes? Did anyone ask you to explain what you were writing? If so, what did you say? If not, what do you think their reasons might be?

2. Did you write any notes after completing the observation? Why?

After reviewing your answers to the above questions:

1. Which type of observation did you prefer, and why?

2. Was the behavior of the group similar or different for the two observations? If different, provide an example. If the same, briefly explain why.

3. Was your behavior as researcher similar or different for the two observations? Briefly explain.

4. Which observation do you think provides data that are more valid? How can you tell? Refer to the definition of "validity."

Exercise 5. Skills Building: Nonparticipant Observation of an Unfamiliar Group

Directions: Locate a small group (three to four persons) whose members are unfamiliar to you. Choose a group that will be together for at least 15 minutes, as you will need a few minutes to draw and label the symbols on your sociogram and about 10 minutes for your observation. Refer to Figure 2 for a sample sociogram.

Record who initiates verbal communications. Therefore, avoid groups and settings in which participants are likely to have minimal verbal interaction. Be ready to turn in your original sociogram.

Before beginning this exercise, review carefully the Code of Ethics forms. If you are uncertain about any of the ethical expectations, check with your instructor before proceeding with the exercise. Also, be sure to review relevant chapter sections before planning the observations.

1. Plan in advance the symbols that you will use for your sociogram (e.g., letters, numbers or a combination of the two). Bring several blank sheets of paper for the sociogram. You might need more than one page if there are many verbal interactions.

2. After observing the group briefly:
   a. Decide whether you will record only statements, only questions, only answers or all verbal communication.
   b. Choose a symbol to represent each member of the group (e.g., "P_1" for "person 1", etc.).
   c. Place each symbol on your blank sheet in the general pattern of group members (e.g., sitting in a circle). Use the entire page, so that there will be enough space to see each arrow when completed.

3. For each verbal communication, draw an arrow to indicate who initiated the verbal communication. The arrow should start at the symbol representing the initiator and point to the recipient(s). See Figure 2.

Questions

1. Describe the group and location of the interactions.
2. Who is/are the leader(s) of the communication? Looking at the arrows, how can you tell?
3. If the leader(s) spoke more to some persons, were the respondents more or less likely than other persons to initiate verbal communication?
4. Briefly assess the validity of clearly identifying the group leader(s) from your observations. What additional information might be useful? How difficult would it be to record it reliably?
5. Assess how useful the sociogram was for this exercise; write a short statement pointing out the strengths and limitations (two to four sentences).
6. Would the exercise have been easier or harder if you knew members of the group? If you had announced your project to the group? If you had participated in the group as a member?
7. Construct a tabular layout with one row and one column for each person in your group. Mark row and column headings to identify each person. Use made-up names or

symbols. But make notes that permit you to identify mentally each group member later. For example:

		Initiator of interaction			
		Emily	**Rob**	**Ann-Marie**	**Pablo**
Recipient of interaction	Emily		|||		
	Rob	||||| ||		||	|||
	Ann-Marie					
	Pablo						

8. Keep track of interactions by placing a mark in the cell of the table for the column of the initiator and the row of the recipient. In the example, Emily initiated seven communications to Rob, and Rob initiated three to Emily.

INDIRECT METHODS

INTRODUCTION: LOOKING AT HOW THE SOCIAL WORLD WORKS

Sex after Death as a Research Topic?

A recent study examined gender differences in the inscriptions on cemetery markers. Cemetery markers typically display name inscriptions. Many markers include dates of birth and death, and occasionally events such as marriage, social statuses and special words, phrases, poetry and other sentiments. Cemeteries also keep written records of interred persons. Before reading further, make a list of possible key words on gravestones that could be used for a study of gender differences.

As you read the following excerpt, check off each gender-descriptive word on your list that was used in the study, and list others that you didn't record. You will be asked to review your list in the next section of this chapter.

Excerpt: *Patterns of Conception, Natality and Mortality from Cemeteries*

Gravestones yield social data, including gender, ethnicity (at least as surmised by surname), age...marital status and other familial relationships....Inscriptions offer potential insight into the character and demeanor of those buried. Finally, deceased are not often buried randomly but interred in particular (e.g., church) cemeteries because of particular (e.g., religious) affiliations....Cemetery records, as primary data from which questions must follow, are written on paper or cut in stone....

[W]e focus on [a sample of 10] cemeteries in Coles County, Illinois....All Coles County cemeteries were surveyed in the 1930s by the Sally Lincoln Chapter of the Daughters of the American Revolution (DAR), which recorded all gravestone inscriptions. The survey was updated, beginning in 1979, by the Coles County Genealogical Society, which published three of an expected four volumes in 1984, 1985, and 1996....We reread 110 (5.4 percent) of the stones to assess the reliability of the DAR recordings and found only one discrepancy....The cemeteries span sixteen decades, the 1830s–1980s. The smallest contained twenty-one burials, the largest, 804. We did not examine a random sample of burials but all burials in the ten cemeteries....

Sociohistorical considerations of gender must acknowledge expressions of inequality, such as gravestones more often identifying females in the context of familial relationships, reflecting male dominance/ownership since historically women were regarded only as complete persons in their relationships to others, particularly adult males.

Of the 2,021 marked gravestones, 1,041 (51.5 percent) indicated a familial relationship to another person. While only 371 (34.2 percent) of all males had relationships identified, 657 (71.6 percent) of all females had relationships identified, clearly supporting our expectation. Among males with familial relationships specified, 366 were sons; 3, fathers; 2, husbands. Of the 657 females, 433 were wives; 218, daughters; 4, mothers; 2, sisters....Cemetery type and time period offered no substantial variant pattern....

[Yet, q]uantitative assessment of cemetery data, even rudimentary descriptive parameters, misses the tenderness of the human story. For example...[w]as it...vows to never part that claimed Elias and Sarah Bisson, married nearly fifty years at their deaths on February 26, 1877? Despite such limitations, these findings advance our understanding of vital events prior to the creation of national birth and death registries. (Foster, Hummel, & Adamchak, 1998, pp. 473–485)

This sample illustrates four important general points about indirect sources of data. (1) The cemetery data are from a sample that could not have been obtained in any other way. (2) The data collection method is entirely unobtrusive—subjects were unaffected in any way by the data collection method. (3) Both qualitative and quantitative analyses are contained in the excerpt. (4) Comparing archival records to the actual gravestone inscriptions illustrates the *criterion validity* check—whether a variable predicts a criterion or standard, in this case, whether each archival record accurately predicts its gravestone information.

Perhaps even more dramatic, another cemetery study looked at inscriptions on Roman tombstones. The author notes that age at death

...is biased by underrepresentation of children's deaths, exaggeration of ages at death beyond age forty or fifty, and probably by understatement of younger women's ages at death. The inscriptions for males dying between the ages of fifteen and forty-two provide the best basis for mortality estimates. (Durand, 1960, p. 365)

He concludes that life expectancy at birth for the total population of the Roman Empire during the first and second centuries probably was about 25 or 30 years.

As the quotation indicates, historical data require careful scrutiny because of the many possible sources of error. And the data are scarce, so they must be taken from whatever sources that can be found—metaphorically speaking, from "out-croppings" (Webb et al., 2000).

Notice also that there is an implied comparison—why do we find conclusions about longevity in the Roman Empire so startling? This is probably because we automatically compare it with current lifetimes. For example, U.S. life expectancy today is two and one-half to three times longer. Even in nations with the shortest life expectancy—for example, 41 years in the nation of Lesotho in southern Africa and 44 years in Afghanistan in south central Asia (Population Reference Bureau, 2010, pp. 11–12)—longevity is higher today than are these estimates for the Roman Empire.

Goals of This Chapter

This chapter examines three types of *indirect sources of data*: (1) contemporary records (e.g., books, newspapers, magazines, music, TV), (2) archival and historical records and (3) physical traces.[1] Additionally, the chapter reviews the methods of content analysis and unobtrusive observation. Content analysis may be used with any of the three indirect data sources. For example, the cemetery study relied on archival data (archived gravestone inscriptions) *and* used content analysis to convert the inscriptions into variables.

An important theme of this chapter is how data collected by indirect methods complement data collected by **direct methods**, such as surveys and direct observation. It also discusses key issues in obtaining valid and complete information with indirect methods and unobtrusive observation. The last section of the chapter reviews the strengths and limitations of indirect methods.

SOURCES OF DATA

Contemporary Records

Do you like hip-hop music? Heavy metal? Indie rock? Country and western? Regardless of music preferences, you could examine music lyrics from a social science perspective.

Studying lyrics as sources of data requires clarification about what you wish to know and how you will know when you've heard (or seen) it. For example, suppose you are interested in the extent to which popular culture portrays love relationships as a competition between two people: "Love is a game." You decide to focus on musical lyrics as a form of popular culture. To keep manageable limits on the study, you confine the music styles to country and western and classic rock. How might you collect the lyrics data?

One possibility is to use the Internet to obtain song lyrics. Or you can record all songs played on a "country-and-western" radio station and all songs played on a "classic rock" station during a predetermined time period. Then, identify passages indicating "love is a game" by playing back the recordings. This process of converting recorded communication into usable data is an example of content analysis.

To conduct a content analysis of the songs, first *define the basic items to be classified*—the **recording units**. Weber (1990, pp. 21–23) identifies six types of recording units commonly used in content analysis:

- *word*
- ***word sense***—words/phrases that can serve as alternatives for the same meaning (e.g., "applauding" and "clapping") and *word units* (e.g., New York state)
- *sentence*

- *theme*—a clause or sentence that typically has a subject, verb and object (e.g., "snow covers the grass")
- *paragraph*
- *whole text*—for example, stories, news articles, songs and so on.

Second, *define the operational definition* of all variables. The current example is about "competition between two people in love relationships." One notion in this example is that, similar to a competitive game, one must watch out for cheating in love relationships (Berger, 2000). The operational definition of "cheating" must specify concrete criteria for classifying each unit as "cheating" or "not cheating" (two categories of the variable "cheating in love relationships"). This is not a simple task.

Third, answer the question, *what units will you classify: words, sentences, song or other?* You might examine all relevant words and word sense units in each audiotaped song that imply "cheating in love." To help you visualize this process, think about *your* favorite songs—what words or word sense units (words or phrases) suggest cheating in love relationships? Notice that your answer to this question defines an element.

Fourth, *refine your definition*. Is cheating multidimensional? One dimension of cheating in love relationships is deception, such as lying to the other person. Of course, one could choose a few specific words such as "lying" and "deception" and their variants (*lie, lies, lied; deceive, deceived* and so forth), but you might also need other words and phrases that convey the idea of lying. "Being with another" and "saw you with her/him" might impart a visual aspect. What about more symbolic terms such as "evil ways," "hard-bitten," or "cheating heart"?

Then, a qualitative approach is useful. Computer software programs can assist with clerical tasks such as locating and organizing the units you have chosen to define cheating/not cheating in the songs. Or you can record this information manually (see Exercises 1 and 2).

Coding is a qualitative (meaning-based) process, but the analysis might contain *both* qualitative and quantitative (numbers-based) methods. For example, you might want to know whether country-and-western *or* classic rock songs contain a higher percentage of references to cheating in love. To get a sense of both approaches, compare the qualitative process in Figure 1 with the quantitative approach shown in Figure 2.

A mixed-method approach (meaning-based and numbers-based data) offers a lot of potential. Exercise 2 gives you practice in combining qualitative and quantitative approaches.

Historical and Archival Data

Look at your list of gender-descriptive words from the "sex after death" excerpt—how many were you able to identify? Now re-read that excerpt; see if you can find at least two more gender-descriptive words to add to your list. Why was a second reading helpful? In our everyday world,

[a]ll that we take for granted as "natural" is a product of both historical and contemporary processes. Our task as social scientists is to interpret those multifaceted meanings, including their interactions with one another. (Tuchman, 1994, p. 310)

- *Get a sense of the whole.*
  - First, listen to all of the selected songs, perhaps jotting down any ideas that emerge.
- *Pick one song,* such as one that is most interesting to you.
  - Listen to it and write down what you think is the message or underlying meaning. Repeat this procedure for several songs.
- *Make a list of topics from your notes.*
  - Past research or theory might be used to determine categories, or to search for patterns in the data.
- *Cluster similar themes, and list them under a few column headings.*
  - Examples could be: "deceit," "lying," "honesty," "romantic," "sexual innuendo" and so forth.
- Using the list, *listen to each downloaded or recorded song.*
  - Replay sections as needed to accurately understand the lyrics
- *Write down each predetermined word, phrase, or theme under the correct column heading.*
- Using the most descriptive words, *turn the list of words, phrases and themes - into categories* (e.g., lying, cheating, stealing).
  - Then, condense the list by grouping categories (e.g. into "dishonesty").
  Make final decisions about the material within each category; replay songs, if needed.
- *Interpret the results.*

FIGURE 1 Qualitative Approach to Content Analysis: A "Cheating in Love" Study.
Source: Tesch, Renata (1990). *Qualitative research: Analysis types and software tools.* New York: Falmer.

Tuchman offers a revealing example of how we take time-specific meanings for granted. The inscription on a cemetery marker for a man who died in his mid-20s in the late eighteenth century might say, "He lived a useful life." By the nineteenth century, cemetery markers weren't remarking on "useful lives," but were "remembering" the deceased with "love" (p. 313).

What types of sentiments are chosen for cemetery markers today? The next time you pass by a cemetery, take a few minutes to look at markers placed in the past 20 or so years. Compare what you find to Tuchman's statement about the previous two centuries. And, check the older gravestones—see whether you agree with Tuchman's descriptions.

Archival data are recorded information, usually historical, stored in repositories such as libraries or museums. These secondary data (data collected by someone other than the researcher) or primary data (new data collected by the researcher) can be used in historical research.

- *Decide on the topic and form a hypothesis about what you expect to find,* based on theory and past research.
- *Provide definitions in operational (measurable) terms.*
  - What criteria will define lyrics that refer to "cheating" other than the word itself? Similar to qualitative analysis, you might begin by listening to several songs to identify your topics. *Clarify the unit of analysis* (e.g., words, phrases, paragraphs or songs).
- Determine whether to include *all downloaded/recorded songs* or *only a sample.*
  - If a sample, determine a method of selection.
- Define your *variables and categories.*
  - Each category of a variable must be mutually exclusive and together, the categories must be exhaustive—each recording unit (e.g., each word) must fit into only one category of a variable, and there must be a category for each recording unit.
- *Assign a number or code to each recording unit.*
  - For example, in each song. record how many times the word *cheat* and its variants (cheater, cheated, etc) were used.
- *Test your hypothesis using the lyrics data.*
  - Calculate a test statistic, such as percentages of the words/word sense phrases for "cheat" for both country & western songs and for classic rock.
- *Interpret the results.*
  - Was your hypothesis confirmed (e.g., which type of songs had a higher percentage of references to "cheating in love")?

FIGURE 2   Quantitative Approach to Content Analysis: A "Cheating in Love Study."
Source: Adapted from Berger (2000).

What kinds of topics were published in your high school newspaper or your major hometown newspaper during the year you were born? How could you find this information? Someone might already have published a historical study and you could read it as a *secondary source* of information. Where would you find *primary data* (i.e., the original articles in newspapers)? Libraries often keep newspapers in their archives, usually copied onto tape, microfiche/microfilm or in electronic format. The publishers also probably have archival copies, although accessing their files generally requires permission. The Library of Congress has selected issues online for some city, county and state newspapers, some dating as far back as the 1860s.

The authors of this chapter conducted a study that uses primary historical data. Our study investigates the effects of inbreeding (reproduction between close relatives, for example, cousins) on infant mortality among the Amish residing in Lancaster County, Pennsylvania. The data consist of records kept by the Amish, an Anabaptist religious group, for purposes entirely unrelated to research.

Excerpt: *Inbreeding and Infant Mortality among the Amish*

Our data are derived from the member directory of the Old Order Amish of the Lancaster county, Pennsylvania Settlement....The directory represents membership and family records collected and printed by the Lancaster Amish for their internal use. The records include data on births, deaths, marriage dates, residence and church district, and family of origin for nearly every member of the Lancaster Settlement. (Dorsten, Hotchkiss, & King, 1999, p. 265)

The title of the article mentions inbreeding, but these data don't contain any information about inbreeding. So if there are no data in the Amish directory about "inbreeding," how could one study its effects?

Data to measure the indicator for the variable "inbreeding" were obtained from a separate source and matched to individuals in the main source. The source of the data on inbreeding is unusual—it provides information to calculate the presence of intermarriages for up to 12 generations of Amish families.

We produced the inbreeding coefficients using information from the Fisher Family History...which documents genealogy relationships for descendants of Christian Fisher, one of the founders of the Old Order Amish community in the United States....More than 90% of the Amish population is included after 1900. (Dorsten et al., 1999, p. 265)

The "inbreeding coefficients" are numbers. These numbers represent the degree that an individual's ancestry contains children from couples who were related to each other: The closer the kinship and the greater the number of children produced by close-kin ancestral couples, the higher the person's inbreeding coefficient. We included *statistical controls* for birth order, whether first born, gender, survival status of the immediately prior sibling (unless first born), and spacing between the birth of the immediately prior sibling and the infant studied.[2]

What did we find out about the effects of inbreeding? For infants who survive the first week of life, the higher the level of inbreeding, the greater the chances of dying before age 1. More importantly to social scientists, the findings suggest that for infants who survive at least 30 days, several sociodemographic variables—including year of child's birth and church district of residence—predict a greater risk of infant death in the first year of life. Families in some church districts tend to follow more traditional Amish practices and beliefs (e.g., fewer immunizations) than families living in less traditional districts. And economic level differs by church district.

These historical data exhibit three particularly noteworthy features. (1) The records were kept by the Amish for private use by members of the Amish Settlement. (2) Record keeping was done by a private organization (the Amish) with no large research funding from the government or a private foundation. (3) The overall quality (reliability and validity) and completeness of the records provide data sufficient to support a fairly sophisticated quantitative study.

Physical Trace Data

In everyday conversation, the word *unobtrusive* means an action that is low-profile, inconspicuous and restrained. Similarly, unobtrusive data collection is "inconspicuous" to the research subjects. *Therefore, data collected by unobtrusive methods are unaffected by the subjects* as observations are made after the behavior of subjects is complete. In contrast, a personal interview has the potential for influencing respondents to give answers that don't reflect their opinions or to give deliberately inaccurate accounts of their behavior.

Collection of physical trace data is a prime example of unobtrusive measurement. Examples of trace data inform everyday life in many ways. In the field of criminal justice, examples of trace data include physical evidence left at the scenes of crimes, such as fingerprints, footprints, hair samples and DNA specimens; broken windows, bullet holes and other damage to physical facilities and bruises, broken bones and other traumas of victims.

Archaeologists and anthropologists rely on trace measures. Arrowheads found in farm fields provide evidence of early human settlements. Well-preserved family Bibles suggest the importance of Christianity to our ancestors. Disaster investigators study sunken ships and crashed aircraft to determine the reason for an accident, such as the plane crash of the late John F. Kennedy, Jr., into the Atlantic Ocean in 1999, and the loss of the space shuttle *Columbia* over Texas in February 2003. Soup kitchen workers might count the number of bundles of silverware prior to serving a meal and again at the end of mealtime to find out how many meals (or persons) they served.

Trace evidence, especially when combined with other forms of data, can yield important clues about social life and human problems. Mitchell Duneier's *Sidewalk*, a participant observation study, details the ways in which street vendors and panhandlers in Greenwich Village, New York, solve many problems of daily life. For example, when one is homeless and lives on urban streets, or conducts business outdoors all day, and stores and restaurants require a purchase to use their restrooms, how are bodily needs such as urination managed to avoid arrest for violating the local "sewer ordinance"?

One of the street vendors describes his solution—and offers clues for what might be called a "distinctively aromatic" approach to collecting physical trace data.

Excerpt: *When You Gotta Go*

A former mayor of New York City got a lot of publicity for his public stand about the private matter of bathroom use. Mudrick, a street vendor, recounts his creative approach in response to the city's law.

> "I gotta get me a paper cup and I'm gonna be all right."... "Guiliano [Rudolph Guiliani, then the mayor of New York City] says you can't go to the bathroom [directly onto streets, sidewalks and alleys]. I invented this thing. Now everybody out here gets a cup."... "I went to Riker's Island jail for [using] the street.... Now I get a cup."
>
> While Mudrick pretends to be hailing a cab, he holds the cup and urinates under an untucked shirt.... On another occasion, after dumping his urine in the sewer, Mudrick placed the Starbucks cup he had just used in the branch of a tree on Sixth Avenue.... I had occasionally noticed paper cups hanging from tree branches but had

never thought twice about them.... "This is my bathroom.... Everybody do's [sic] it."
(Duneier, 1999, pp. 173–175)

What clues are there in the brief excerpt that could be used to identify the city streets in greatest need of public restrooms? How might you collect the data?

One technique for data collection might be visual. Paper cups in trees at certain heights might suggest an inability to access (or dislike for using) public restrooms. However, despite Mudrick's assertion, not all of the men use a cup. Some prefer the sides of buildings, particularly buildings that have an indented section of a wall, and others hide between cars and around, or even in, trash dumpsters.

Of course, counts of paper cups in trees are only suggestive and must be combined with other data before drawing definite conclusions. So, we might need to broaden our potential sources and types of data. What about olfactory cues—might one be able to "follow one's nose" to identify the street locations most frequently used by the men? Would weather affect visual or olfactory cues? Would this study be an invasion of anyone's privacy?

Example: *"Sneaky Measurement" of Crime and Disorder.* In the United Kingdom, crime "hot spots" aren't well identified, due to imperfect recording of details about location, especially for vehicle crime (Garwood et al., 2000, p. 159). Moreover, recorded data often do not provide adequate information about time, place and circumstance to support specific crime-fighting policies. Underreporting can distort the official record of domestic violence and hate crimes, for example (p. 159).

Garwood and her coauthors propose some unobtrusive sources of data they obtained using "sneaky measurement." They argue these sources supplement official crime records and thereby improve the validity of crime information. Examples of some variables they review include the following:

- *alcohol consumption in public locations*—indicators for the variables include quantity of bottles and cans found in litter containers in parks and other public places
- *vandalism*—indicators include rate of repairs to football stadium seats, bus shelters and telephone booths
- *illegal drug use (heroin smoking)*—indicators include remains of matches and burned foil in bars and public restrooms
- *illegal drug use (amphetamines)*—indicators include high rate of sale of water and soft drinks in clubs (Garwood et al., 2000, pp. 162–63).

Because unobtrusive measures seldom are attached to any single individual, ethical concerns about invasion of privacy are reduced (Garwood et al., 2000, p. 162). Thinking about your campus or hometown, what are some other "sneaky measures" of crime, disorder or misuse that could be added to this list?

INDIRECT METHODS OF DATA COLLECTION

Unobtrusive Observation

Recall that unobtrusive data collection is "inconspicuous" to the research subjects. Webb and his coauthors (2000) report an interesting unobtrusive study of drivers' use of turn signals. The main research question was, "Do drivers copy the turn signal behavior of cars in front of them?"

Observers were stationed inconspicuously beside the road at an intersection. For a period of 4 weeks they recorded (1) whether drivers used turn signals before turning, (2) direction of the turn, (3) whether a turning car in front of an observed car used a turn signal, (4) whether another vehicle was driving 100 feet or less behind the car being observed and (5) gender of the driver.

Do you think drivers copy others' turn signal behaviors? Do you think there could be a gender difference—if so, what do you expect? The researchers found more conformity for left turns than for right turns, and more conformity if drivers of both vehicles were female. Follow-up studies found more erratic signaling among drivers of expensive automobiles and in bad weather. Do you think insurance companies might be interested in results from unobtrusive data such as these?

Content Analysis

Earlier discussion in this chapter described content analysis of song lyrics. Recall that *content analysis* is a method for coding recorded communication into usable form. Generally, this amounts to creating variables from communication found in sources such as books, magazines, journals, newspapers, diaries and other print media, and from audio and audiovisual recordings. Content analysis has been used to study a variety of interesting social science topics such as propaganda, international differences in communication content and cultural patterns of individuals and groups (Weber, 1990, p. 9).

Primary sources of data for content analysis increasingly are e-mail and electronic text and images such as those found at websites and on website "bulletin boards." For example, a study reports that e-mail writers tend to be more informal and more self-disclosing, and to feel more socially equal with others than when using pen and paper (Baron, 1998, pp. 147–148). Indicators include less careful editing of e-mail than with other written documents, use of a more familiar tone in e-mail than in other methods of communication (e.g., use of first names) and use of humor or sarcasm between people who have never met in person.

It appears that reliable information usually can be coded from content analysis of a variety of sources. Nonetheless, it is not easy to produce reliable content analysis. The validity could depend more on the accuracy and completeness of the sources, however, than on the ability to train coders to produce reliable results.

Exercise 2 gives you an opportunity to develop or strengthen skills in doing content analysis.

RELIABILITY AND VALIDITY OF INDIRECT METHODS

Reliability refers to consistency. A variable is reliable to the extent it yields the same answer each time it is used, in the absence of change in whatever is being measured and the absence of memory. High reliability generally is reported for content analysis, despite difficult sources of information and complex concepts. The reliability issue for content analysis is, do the coding schemes produce the same research results across different coders?

Validity (accuracy of measuring a construct) is evaluated by three questions. Examples from this chapter illustrate each type of validity.

1. Is there general agreement (high *content validity*) that the variable measures the underlying idea *(face validity)* and covers all dimensions of the idea *(domain coverage)*? How much confidence should we place in observing cups in trees to indicate the need for public restrooms? Do only people living or working daily on the street use the cup as a restroom?

2. Does the variable predict a standard *(criterion or predictive validity)*? Did the historical records, the primary data source, agree with the inscriptions on the gravestones?

3. Does the variable behave as theory predicts it should *(construct validity)*? Do the selected words or word units of gravestones indicate stable patterns across the stones as predicted by a theory of gender inequality?

ADVANTAGES AND LIMITATIONS OF INDIRECT METHODS

There are three primary advantages and a major limitation shared by the indirect methods of data collection, as summarized in Figure 3. As Figure 3 suggests, the strengths and limitations of indirect methods reinforce the need to rely on many sources of data, use many methods, be alert to the limitations of each data source and method and combine information from many sources.

SUMMARY

This chapter describes several types of indirect sources of data: (1) contemporary records such as music and newspapers; (2) archival and historical records like records of gravestone inscriptions and church records and (3) physical traces. In addition, the chapter describes two indirect methods of data collection: unobtrusive observation and content analysis.

Indirect methods produce data not available from other sources; this is one primary strength. Also, indirect methods sometimes produce more valid data than survey data, because indirect methods avoid contamination from respondent reactions or from inaccurate recall.

- **Access information not available in other sources**.
  - Without historical data, how else could we get a glimpse of over-time differences in infant deaths?
  - Content analysis commentary in popular media can't be duplicated by surveys.
- **No respondent reactions that might contaminate the data**.
  - On your campus, which approach is likely to give a more accurate picture of racial integration?
    - Counting the number of mixed-race groups at the student center or conducting a survey? (The ideal might be to use both.)
- **Direct unobtrusive observation can avoid errors that could results from usual survey methods**.
  - Compare: watching from inconspicuous locations to see what actually happens to interviewing people about their use of turn signals.
- **Primary limitation: indirect data sources seldom contain all needed information**.
  - No details from gravestones other than the content of inscriptions.
  - No information about drivers' education, occupation or political beliefs from unobtrusive observations of turn signal behavior.

FIGURE 3   Advantages and Limitations of Indirect Methods.

But issues of validity are important limitations of indirect sources of data, particularly historical data, for which coverage may be incomplete and sources for checking accuracy limited. Even contemporary data sources often are limited—not all recorded music is available (or remembered, even by the artist), and paper cups can blow away. Perhaps the primary disadvantage of indirect sources of data is the limited amount of information they contain. At best, just a few variables can be retrieved from gravestone inscriptions, for example. Historical records are incomplete, and the content of garbage cans doesn't give a full account of the drinking habits of their owners.

YOUR REVIEW SHEET

1. What gender-descriptive words did you include in the list you prepared as you read the study of gender differences on gravestones? Briefly evaluate your list. What additional words did you add with your second reading? What conclusion can you draw about re-reading materials (including this chapter)?

2. Suppose you plan a study of gender stereotyping in TV commercials. Propose a list of words and phrases you would count as stereotypical of (a) women and (b) men.

3. What words or phrases have you heard recently in songs of your favorite musical type that suggest deception in a love relationship? What are some other words and phrases that convey the idea of "cheating" that were not mentioned in this chapter?

4. Briefly explain how and why one might combine qualitative and quantitative approaches in the same study. Include an example.

5. Referring to the excerpt on paper cups, if weather conditions change either visual or olfactory cues, how would the results of the study be affected? Would weather change produce concerns about reliability or validity?

6. Thinking about your campus or hometown, what are some "sneaky measures" of crime, disorder or misuse other than those mentioned in the chapter?

7. Pick an example from this chapter that is used to illustrate reliability. Discuss how the example helps one think about the importance of consistent measures in research.

8. Using one example from this chapter that is used to illustrate validity, discuss how this example helps one think about the importance of using a measure that reflects the idea (construct) it is designed to measure (validity).

END NOTES

1. Adapted from Webb et al. (2000). Webb and coauthors don't mention contemporary recorded sources and divide observation into two categories: simple observation and contrived observation. In the former, the investigator just watches, unobtrusively. In contrived observation, the investigator intervenes in some way unknown to the subjects.

2. The statistical model we employed is the Cox proportional hazards model.

STUDY TERMS

archival data Recorded information, usually historical, that is stored in repositories such as libraries or museums.

content analysis Conversion of recorded communication into usable form, that is, construct variables using the recorded material as the source of raw data. Recorded communication is found in print materials (e.g., books and magazines) in audio and visual recordings, and in electronic text and images, such as those found at computer websites.

direct methods Method of data collection in which data are obtained personally from subjects or respondents. Examples include interviews, questionnaires and observation of behaviors. Compare with indirect methods.

historical data Data describing the past. Historical research often is used to examine changes over time, such as in pictures or words.

indirect methods Methods of data collection that don't involve contacts between the researcher and subjects. Compare with direct methods.

physical trace data Data such as paths worn in the grass and fingerprints indicative of subjects' previous activity. Another example is checking litter containers for cans and bottles to estimate the extent of illegal use of alcohol in public places.

recording units In content analysis, the basic items to be classified. There are six commonly used types of recording units for text: word, word sense, sentence, theme, paragraph and whole text.

reliability Consistency of a measure; does the same result occur on repeated measurement in the absence of real change and absence of memory?

theme In content analysis, a recording unit as subject/verb/object, such as "Snow/covers/the grass."

unobtrusive observation Watching behaviors in a way that is "inconspicuous" to the research subjects

validity Accuracy with which a measure represents the construct it is designed to measure.

word sense In content analysis, the meaning of words or phrases and phrases constituting a unit (e.g., New York state). Different specific words and phrases often convey the same or nearly the same meaning, for example, "applauding" and "clapping."

EXERCISES

Exercise 1. Evaluation of Research: Historical Analysis

Directions: Read the journal article by Stephanie Shields and Beth A. Koster (1989). Emotional stereotyping of parents in child rearing manuals, 1915–1980. *Social Psychology Quarterly, 52*(1), 44–55. Your instructor will provide instructions for obtaining the article.

Factual Questions

1. What was the research question of the study?
2. Explain in your own words how the researchers selected specific manuals.
3. Why was the time period divided into eras?
4. Did the researchers find "emotional stereotyping"? Explain.
5. Were there differences in parental stereotyping over time?

Questions for Discussion

1. Did the manuals provide appropriate information for the purposes of this study?
2. List two potential sources of historical information about "emotional stereotyping of parents" other than child-rearing manuals.
3. Was the number of books reviewed in each era sufficient?

Exercise 2. Skills Building: Content Analysis of Gender Advertisements

Note: This exercise could be a homework assignment or an in-class small-group project, with each group evaluating the same ads without any consultation. Comparing the results across groups provides a reliability check on coding.

Directions: Select an issue of a popular press magazine that has advertising. Pick at least 30 ads with images of one or more adults. If you don't get 30 ads in one issue, continue through subsequent issues until you get 30.

Code all ads (photographs or drawings) that include images of one or more adults and record the information in a table like the one shown below. For each person in the ad, record "gender" and assign a code for two additional variables:

Variable 1, Strength: three categories—strong, neutral, weak

Variable 2, Sex object: two categories—yes, no

Be sure to define operational criteria that assign every person in the ads to one and only one of the categories for each variable. Consider strength to include both physical strength and social strength, that is, "in control of the situation."

For ambiguous images, assign codes and make a note about your decision on a separate sheet of paper. Also, assign an ad number for each ad.

Sample table:

Ad #	Gender	Strength ("In Control of Situation")	Sex Object
1	Male	Strong	Yes
1	Female	Strong	No
1	Male	Neutral	No
⋮	⋮	⋮	⋮
30	Female	Weak	Yes

In this example, the first three people were pictured in the same ad. You may have quite a few more observations (rows in the table) than ads.

After recording the data, assign numbers to the "strength" and "sex object" variables as follows:

strength: 1 = weak, 2 = neutral, 3 = strong

sex object: 0 = no, 1 = yes

Then calculate separate averages by gender for both variables:

1. Average "strength" for females: Add up the values of "strength" for females and divide the result by the number of females (*not* the number of ads).

2. Average "sex object" for females: Add up the values of "sex object" for females and divide the result by the number of females. Note that this average is the same as the proportion of females you judged to be sex objects.

3. Average "strength" for males: Add up the values of "strength" for males and divide the result by the number of males (*not* the number of ads).

4. Average "sex object" for males: Add up the values of "sex object" for males and divide the result by the number of males. Note that this average is the same as the proportion of males you judged to be sex objects.

Note: The fact that ads may contain more than one picture is an example of grouping. If you were doing a "real-live" study, special methods of analysis would be required to handle the grouping inherent in the pictures.

Questions

1. What is the name of the magazine you chose? In this magazine, which gender had the greater number of ads? Taking the type of readership into account, offer a brief explanation.

2. Which gender had the greater average score on "strength"? On "sex object"? Offer a short social science explanation.

3. Describe any coding problems you encountered and how you solved them. Be specific.

4. Discuss one advantage and one disadvantage of content analysis as a method of data collection, based on this exercise.

5. Did you notice any tendency for the "strength" and "sex object" variables to be more alike in the same ad than they were across different ads? Briefly discuss (grouping issue again).

Exercise 3. Skills Building E-Project: Social Aspects of E-Mail

Directions:

- ▣ Step 1: Review the section on content analysis and e-mail. Then, select a topic and write a one-sentence statement about a finding you expect from study of e-mail messages. You can use a qualitative or quantitative approach or a combination of the two. Review relevant sections in this chapter about e-mail as a source of indirect data, and check qualitative and quantitative approaches.

- ▣ Step 2: Answer questions 1–4 below.

- ▣ Step 3: Look at the e-mail messages on the page below. Answer questions 5–8. Be prepared to hand in your worksheet.

Questions

1. Briefly review the e-mails listed below.

2. Before re-reading e-mails for details, state a topic and your expected findings. If you use a quantitative approach, state a testable hypothesis. Be sure to specify a comparison group (e.g., another form of communication).

3. Describe the steps of your approach.

4. Briefly describe how you decided between a qualitative and quantitative approach.

5. Evaluate the e-mails. Summarize your findings; then consider your findings in relation to what you would expect to find from your comparison group.

6. Summarize what you think are the strong points of your study.

7. Summarize weakness(es) of your study. Mention limitations of the sample of e-mail messages you read.

8. Describe the most difficult part of the exercise, and briefly explain how you overcame this difficulty.

SAMPLE E-MAIL MESSAGES FOR EXERCISE 3

1. Cara, am looking for a website that lists figures for costs of things like groceries, transportation, misc. expenditures per family, either in US as a whole or preferably by state or region. Can you point me in right direction? Tori

2. amanda, 3 women who were part of one of largest u.s. protests for peace will present a symposium 7p mar. 13 in rm. 138 ccenter., part of convocation year "culture of peace" & an event celebrating women's history month. reception w/goodies after p-gram. c u there? megs

   a. 3. kc, only msg I received from u ;o(Kyle
      > > Hi, second test to see if u got my msg :o)

3. hi yourself! Great to hear from you. love to have lunch but this week is really jammed up for a bunch of silly reasons but how about next week? my bberry is downstairs but how about if you give me a few dates when you're available...Suzi

4. hey lindsay, glad you like the p-card. don't you think I look like @@@:??? found it in a batch of old travel things at g-ma's, and thought it would make you giggle! let's do our annual superbowl party at our place. david'll dress up in his special outfit and demonstrate his fawning skills—LOL! david & me!

5. kari, enjoying some freedom from classes? got an opinion? as a beginning nursing student, a group of us did a "pretend" research study on nurse attitudes toward death and dying. i have half a mind to resurrect it and do a real study. from what I saw, there have been few if any changes over time. thoughts??? got notice of amnesty mtg too late to go—again :-/ holly

6. M, wasn't sure if those days are when you will be here, but here's my schedule to help you make a decision, hehe!! Tues: reading at library—morning/afternoon, exercise—afternoon. Wed: reading—morning, class—1–5. Thurs: reading—morning/afternoon, class—2:30–5, group meeting—5:00 until??? Fri: reading morning/afternoon, exercise—afternoon. BTW, could you bring picture of my apt. you took in June? Me!

7. J, Sorry to keep bugging you—now don't need ride to pool. J's friend will pick him up, so have car. Thx much for being willing to help out! R.

8. hey Josh...Sat PM great :-D going to Pitt on Fri—hope *<{:o}) (santa) finds me there—taking my stocking to hang on fp! Talk w/u toward end of week....LUVnXOX Ashley

SURVEYS

INTRODUCTION: LOOKING AT HOW THE SOCIAL WORLD WORKS

"Have you gone to a Lady Gaga concert?"

"Yeah."

"What'd you pay for the tickets?"

People often ask their friends about concerts, movies, cars, restaurants, sports events and many other topics. These are examples of informal interviews. Personal interview is one of the main tools for collecting data in a survey. A **survey** is a tool for gathering data by posing questions to many people. Surveys are a familiar way to obtain data in everyday life, and they are used extensively in social science research.

A great deal is known about survey methods, and sample surveys have been used to learn about people's opinions and behaviors for more than 75 years (Dillman et al., 2009, p. 1). A well-designed survey provides accurate estimates of characteristics of an entire population, based on a relatively small sample. For example, election polls routinely make correct calls of election results using sample sizes of about 1,000 to 1,500 people—a very small percentage of voters (except in very small election districts).

Topics of Surveys

Surveys ask questions about a diversity of topics, including the following:

- behaviors (drug, alcohol and tobacco consumption; criminal activities)
- attitudes (toward death penalty, assisted suicide, civil rights, women's rights, legalizing marijuana, politics, religious minorities, fairness of income inequality)
- opinions (about seriousness of the crime problem, foreign aid, mixed-couple dating and marriage, welfare spending, gay marriage)
- Many large-scale surveys also ask demographic and socioeconomic questions about—
  - gender, race, age and marital status (single, married, divorced…)
  - number of children (and often ages, sometimes gender)
  - education completed, occupation, income/earnings, employment status

There's little doubt that survey data have revolutionized social research. And, *external validity*—**generalization** beyond a study—is comparatively high for surveys. But there are reasons to be cautious when interpreting survey data.

Ethics and Survey Data

A code of ethics requires that *one must understand the expectations for research with human subjects, such as "do no harm," before planning a data collection project*. If you've completed a questionnaire or interview, were you informed about how *your* answers would be protected?

Confidentiality and *anonymity* are two levels of protection of survey data. All survey methods—personal interviews, telephoning, mail questionnaires and Internet forms—must ensure that respondent information remains confidential. **Confidentiality** means completed survey forms contain identification such as a name or a code, but the researcher doesn't reveal any answer from any respondents to anyone outside the research project.

Anonymity means a survey contains no information of any type that identifies respondents; therefore it isn't possible to reveal any individual's answers. Anonymity is an important consideration for the study of highly personal experiences, illegal activities and other sensitive topics. For example, suppose someone "earned" money for college selling stolen merchandise. How likely is this person to reveal in a face-to-face interview that method of financing college?

Goals of This Chapter

Four themes guide the discussion in this chapter: (1) the *flexibility* of survey research for handling many topics, (2) the *standards* for constructing and evaluating surveys, (3) the *strengths and weakness* of survey data and (4) *recent changes* in survey operations.

We'll first look at three excerpts from research journals. Each excerpt shows the process of developing and executing one type of survey, and illustrates some of the strengths and limitations of that survey type. We'll also consider Internet surveys and "mixed-mode" approaches that combine traditional survey methods with high-technology devices, most often a Web survey. Finally, the chapter reviews some of the principles for conducting valid surveys.

Survey data collected by academics typically are obtained to test hypotheses derived from theory. Therefore, the last section of the chapter discusses the linkages between theory and research by looking at an excerpt about the effects of parental education and occupation on attitudes toward child rearing.

THREE FAMILIAR TYPES OF SURVEYS AND NEWER VERSIONS

Three types of surveys are familiar to most people: personal interview, telephone interview and mail questionnaire. Presently, Internet surveys are used extensively.

However, perhaps the most significant change in the last decade is that *multiple-mode survey strategies* are being chosen, not only to collect valid sample surveys but also to better understand the role of respondents in producing their responses (Dillman et al., 2009, pp. 10–11). For example, some populations might receive a survey by mail, while another group receives it via the Internet. This chapter reviews the three familiar types of surveys and Internet and multimode survey strategies.

Personal Interview

Structures of Personal Interviews. It's a beautiful Monday afternoon. You're sitting in the sunshine thinking about what to do during spring break. You know what you'd like to do—see Lady Gaga at the Arena. But you've not gone to one of her concerts and decide to get some information from a friend who has been to several of her concerts, sometimes traveling to nearby states. You start a general conversation:

How'd you like the last couple of Lady Gaga concerts?

Your friend describes her recent experiences in some detail; you ask a few more questions, but mostly listen to her descriptions. You're conducting an informal or unstructured interview. An **unstructured interview** is a "conversation." It is used to learn more about respondents than can be expressed by answers to a few specific questions written in advance of the interview. But, think for a moment about the nature and expectations of this "conversation."

First, an unstructured interview is unlike ordinary conversations. The interviewer (you) provides direction, and the respondent provides the content (Weiss, 1994, p. 207). *Therefore, most of the conversation is provided by the respondent, and the format often is not question–response* as in a more formally structured interview. Second, respondents must have some level of trust in you to share their insights (Maxim, 1999). Typically, friends have that trust, developed over a period of time. However, interviewers must gain trust in a very short time. And if the topic is personal or about deviant behavior, extra caution is warranted.

It's later that same afternoon. You meet another friend you've not seen for a while and decide to ask her about Lady G. concerts. You have the first friend's conversation in mind, and decide to ask more specific questions, including probes, to get additional details. A **probe** is a question or comment used to clarify responses or to request more detail. Although you probably would not have a written list of questions like an interviewer would have, you're providing more structure to this conversation than the previous one. You're now conducting a **semistructured interview**.

> YOU: Hey Brittney, been to a Lady G. concert lately?
>
> FRIEND: Yeah, next one will be my third since I moved here. Wish I had money to go to more.
>
> YOU: How much do tickets cost? And what're her shows like? [open-ended probes]
>
> FRIEND: ...and some of the best concerts I've seen.
>
> YOU: Best you've seen? [feedback probe]
>
> FRIEND: Yeah, her music really gets you moving and grooving! And she's all about everything together.
>
> YOU: What's "everything together" mean? [probe to clarify vague answer]

A semistructured interview that includes several people is called a **focus group** or a focused interview (Krueger & Casey, 2000; Merton, Fiske, & and Kendall, 1990). In social research, focus groups can be used in a variety of ways, such as pretesting questionnaire wording, studying shared experiences of group members, and aiding respondents' recall of events such as celebrations or disasters (Fontana & Frey, 2000, p. 651). Although perhaps more often thought of as a qualitative (meaning-based) data collection method, numeric data also can be obtained from focused interviews. Limitations of focus groups include the possibility that one person could dominate the discussion, group dynamics can be difficult to manage successfully by the less-skilled researcher, and the results are difficult to generalize beyond the group studied (p. 652).

The **structured interview** is the most formal interview form. It basically is a questionnaire administered by an interviewer. But it is less flexible than an unstructured or semistructured interview, there is very little or no probing for additional information, and typically the response categories are provided by the interviewer. The structured interview is designed to return reliable quantitative (numeric) data for use in statistical analysis.

The following excerpt from a recent journal article uses *semistructured* personal interviews to examine the pros and cons of open adoption of infants.

Excerpt: *Open Adoption of Infants: Advantages and Disadvantages*

The term *open adoption* refers to a continuum of options that enables birthparents and adoptive parents to have information about and communication with one another before or after placement of the child or at both times. An essential feature of open adoption, regardless of the extent of the openness, is that the birth parents legally relinquish all parental claims and rights to the child. The adoptive parents are the legal parents.

[A]n open letter inviting prospective participants to contact the researcher was included in newsletters of two New England infertility and adoption-support organizations and...to all parents who had a recent open adoption in [one New England] state.... The letter explained that the interview would be tape-recorded in the respondents' home and that parents would be interviewed jointly as a couple and guaranteed confidentiality....

A semi-structured interview guide...was developed and then pretested to assess the instrument's content validity.... [S]ome items were added to the questionnaire and others were revised.... The interviews...lasted from 1½ to four hours, depending on how much the respondents had to say.... Twenty-one adoptive couples were included in the sample.... All respondents were asked, "What, if any, were your initial fears, anxieties, and concerns about the adoption being open?" and "How did you initially feel about doing an open adoption?"...

...The parents often noted that the issue of openness was eclipsed by the enormity of four other concerns: coping with infertility; finding a baby; dealing with unresponsive or obstructive social workers, lawyers, and medical personnel and dealing with the lifelong issues present in all adoptive families. The parents, whatever level of openness they experienced, thought that openness was simply not a matter of much concern... (Siegel, 1993, pp. 16–20)

Strengths of Personal Interviews. Thinking about the interviews with adoptive parents, what are some strengths of personal interviews?

Generally, respondents are more likely to answer questions in a personal interview than in a **self-administered questionnaire**, and personal interviews produce higher response rates than do other types of surveys. Another important advantage of face-to-face interviewing is that interviewers can follow up on incomplete, unclear or unanticipated responses using a probe. For example, a parent who says "finding a baby" was the most difficult part of adoption could be asked—

Could you please explain?

Why do you think some people might say, "I don't know" to a question such as

Before bringing your baby home, about how many times per week did you talk to family or friends about the adoption process?

Even if they don't know the exact number, they likely have a reasonable estimate. But, sometimes people need a bit of time to think about a question. The interviewer, who is face-to-face with the respondent, might probe by saying,

Would you take a moment to think about the question?

or

If you had to choose one answer, what would it be?

Personal interviews can be conducted in the respondents' own social settings. Most people probably feel more relaxed in their own homes—but there may be exceptions. A respondent might feel intimidated if the interview is conducted within earshot of an argumentative spouse. Regardless of where the interview takes place, the interviewer must quickly adapt to both the respondent and the social setting, so that the respondent feels comfortable during the interview.

Personal interviews also allow monitoring of respondent body language. For example, after observing that a respondent seems confused, bored or angry, the interviewer might restate or rephrase a question. Also, information can be recorded about body language and social context that is impossible to obtain otherwise. Face-to-face interviewing also permits easy use of visual aids such as photographs, advertisements, charts and newspaper clippings. Using a card or list can be an important device for obtaining sensitive information like income, drug use or sexual behavior. Table 1 shows an example of response options for income that can be used on a card that is handed to respondents.

TABLE 1. Low-End Response Categories for Total Family Income Before Taxes, 2008 (General Social Survey)

Dollar Range	Assigned Numeric Code
Under $1,000	01
$ 1,000–2,999	02
$ 3,000–3,999	03
$ 4,000–4,999	04
$ 5,000–5,999	05
$ 6,000–6,999	06
$ 7,000–7,999	07
$ 8,000–9,999	08
$10,000–14,999	09
(remaining response categories not shown)	

Source: http://www.norc.org/GSS+Website/

Limitations and Considerations of Personal Interviews. Why might personal interviews *not* be the best method of data collection? What if the interviewer asked,

Have you ever had a sexually transmitted disease?

Respondents might be hesitant to answer this question in a face-to-face interview. In general, respondents are unlikely to divulge certain types of information, such as deviant or socially questionable behavior.

Also, "being there" during data collection sometimes leads to biased responses (invalidity). Unlike a self-administered questionnaire, the respondent might choose answers to questions to impress or please (or displease) the interviewer.

Interviewer effect is bias resulting when a respondent tries to impress the interviewer or otherwise reacts to the interviewer in a way that produces incorrect or misleading responses—that is, *measurement error*. Furthermore, adapting to the situation may be difficult or impossible, particularly if the interviewer and respondent are poorly matched. For example, a middle-aged, upper-middle-class male interviewer might not know how to act with a young unemployed mother. Sometimes interviewers can be matched to respondents, but it is seldom possible to know ahead of time what the respondent will be like.

Finally, the interviewer needs to carefully consider personal appearance and general demeanor. For example, "dressing up" might be appropriate for an interview with a corporate head, but not with an unemployed person living in poverty conditions.

Telephone Interview

Phone surveys are particularly well suited for studying the pace of rapidly shifting attitudes, as illustrated by election and political-opinion polling. They also are well suited for rapid response to major national events. For example, when a shocking event occurs such as the explosion of the space shuttle *Challenger*, how do "early knowers" find out this information, and where were they when they heard? Do demographic characteristics such as education, gender and age make a difference?

Excerpt: *Who Are the "Early Knowers" of Shocking News?*

On January 28, 1986, the space shuttle *Challenger* exploded approximately one minute after take-off, killing all seven astronauts aboard, including Christa McAuliffe, America's first teacher in space. The news media...gave the shuttle explosion as much coverage as the assassination of a major political figure. This media coverage provides a rare opportunity to better understand how people learn about such events, whether their demographic characteristics are correlated with how they learn about the event, and whether they discuss the events with people whom they know....

Data were obtained from telephone interviews with 538 adult "heads of household" living within the city limits of a suburb of a large Southwestern city. Random digit dialing was used to select households for the sample. The individuals were randomly selected by alternating between female and male when both genders were present in a domicile [residence]. A minimum of seven callbacks were used before substitution by randomly changing the last four digits of the initially chosen number.... The...sample compared favorably with known population parameters of the target suburb.... Interviewing was conducted by the Telephone Laboratory of a large Southwestern university during the period January 30–February 7, 1986.

The questionnaire consisted of items designed to measure 10 variables... [1] time respondents heard of the explosion... [If heard within the first 30 minutes] the respondent was labeled as an early knower.... [2] where the respondent was when she or he heard, coded home, work, or somewhere else.... [3] source from which the respondent heard, coded media or another person.... [4] whether or not the respondent told anyone else....[5] the number of people told....[6] the number of strangers told....[7] the major source of follow-up information, coded television, radio, newspaper, or another person....[8] the person's age....[9] amount of education in years....[10] respondent's sex.

...Descriptive statistics revealed that approximately one half of the respondents heard of the event within 30 minutes...and almost everyone within three hours. About one third...heard of the event at home...[and nearly one half of the rest were at work]. Half the respondents heard through the media and half from another person. About six out of ten respondents told someone else of the explosion, with half of them telling three or fewer people.

...[Our research suggests that] demographic variables do not play an important role in the diffusion [of major national news]....*where* one is affects *how* one discovers the occurrence of a major news event....People at work are much more likely to hear of the event from another person than from the media, while those people at home are more likely to hear of the event from the media....*How* one discovers the event then affects *how quickly* one hears of the event. People who are among the first 50% to hear of the event discover its occurrence through the media, while those who discover the occurrence of the event later hear of the event interpersonally. (Mayer et al., 1990, pp. 113–123)

As the "shocking news" excerpt illustrates, telephone interviewing can be automated by a process called **computer-assisted telephone interviewing (CATI)**. Using a special type of computer software program, CATI uses random-digit dialing and automated recording of responses to questions. CATI speeds the data collection process and virtually eliminates transcription errors. CATI promotes higher data quality by reducing chances for respondent and interviewer errors, but difficulties include choosing among the "jungle" of available computer programs (Saris, 1991; Saris & Gallhofer, 2007).[1]

You can read descriptions of the launch information and planned mission highlights at *http://www.nasa.gov/mission_pages/shuttle/shuttlemissions/archives/sts-51L.html*.

Strengths of Telephone Interviews. Phone interviews are less expensive and less time-consuming than personal interviews. A number of phone calls can be conducted during the time it takes to drive to one respondent's location.

The "shocking news" interviews included 10 questions fielded to 538 people conducted over 7 days, a relatively quick pace compared to in-person interviewing. But sometimes phone interviews can be completed even more quickly. A phone survey of 312 respondents for a study titled "How Fast Does News Travel?" about the 1972 shooting of Governor Wallace of Alabama was completed in just over 5 hours on the same day of the shooting. However, the interviews consisted of only three questions. Also, at the time of the shooting the research agency was briefing 12 telephone interviewers for another project, and six interviewers immediately were made available to interview people about the shooting (Schwartz, 1973–74).

In telephone interviewing, several interviewers can work in a central location, where a supervisor can be consulted if necessary and can monitor the interviewing process. Supervision is one critical component of ensuring high quality of data collected by telephone interview (Lavrakas, 1993). And unlike personal interviews, telephone calls don't require the interviewer to travel into unsafe environments. Suppose you wish to interview residents of a high-risk neighborhood who are working with school officials to ensure the safety of their children. Telephone interviews would produce less risk of harm to the interviewer than visiting the residents in their homes. It's difficult for an interviewer to appear relaxed during an interview if personal safety seems threatened. See Miller and Salkind (2002, pp. 314–315) for a telephone survey checklist to help in preparing for a telephone interview.

Limitations and Considerations of Telephone Interviews. If you or someone you know has held a "telemarketing" job selling items over the phone, some of the limitations of telephone surveys probably are obvious. First, many persons dislike unsolicited calls, particularly during meal times. Or they might be in the midst of other activities, and find it difficult or unpleasant to be distracted by a phone interview. Also, some people are reluctant to reveal any information over the telephone to a stranger.

Second, it is difficult to ask complicated questions or explore complex topics by phone. For example, how long can *you* keep 10 response categories in mind, particularly if someone reads them to you? Nor can the telephone interviewer monitor body language or observe clues about the respondent's social setting. And visual aids can't be used in phone surveys.

Third, declining response rates to telephone surveys are said to be due in part to the increasing number of surveys, including Internet e-mail surveys. A voice recording or "electronically contrived" voice might replace a real person, with the respondent asked to punch keys on a phone or other mobile device (Dillman et al., 2009), either of which might make some respondents uncomfortable.

Fourth, phone interviews are a new experience for many people, and most likely need encouragement and support to "get through" an interview (Miller & Salkind, 2002, p. 313). And bogus "surveys" used to disguise sales pitches add to the difficulties of conducting telephone surveys. Respondent comments such as, "Can I call you back later?" and "What are you trying to sell?" indicate *respondent hesitancy*. The first few seconds are crucial for determining whether a successful phone interview will occur.

Another important potential limitation of phone surveys is coverage error. **Coverage error** results from (a) excluding some members of a population from the list used to select the sample, and (b) failing to identify people who are listed more than once. One example of coverage error is using a telephone book to draw a sample of all persons in a community. Not all persons are listed in local telephone books, even if they have a "landline" phone; those not listed are excluded from the sample. And cell phones are not listed at all. On the other hand, some households (and businesses) are listed multiple times because they have more than one phone number.

Other than using a random-digit dialing software program such as CATI, what can the telephone interviewer do to minimize these problems? Strategies include: (1) sending an advance letter about the study and upcoming phone call, (2) calling during time periods less likely to disrupt meals and other known routines and (3) emphasizing the sponsorship and importance of the survey, particularly if it is associated with research or education.

Mail Questionnaire

A third type of survey is conducted by mailing questionnaires to respondents and requesting that they return completed questionnaires by mail. A **mail questionnaire** is *self-administered*, that is, there is no monitoring by any member of the research team. The following excerpt illustrates the use of mail questionnaires to assess behaviors on a highly sensitive topic.

Excerpt: *Identifying Condom Users Likely to Experience Condom Failure*

The rapid spread of the human immunodeficiency virus (HIV) and other sexually transmissible diseases (STDs) during the last decade has led to increased research on the male condom....Anecdotal evidence suggests that a relatively small proportion of condom users are responsible for a disproportionate number of breaks....Because so little is known about the characteristics of such individuals, we cannot predict accurate condom breakage rates for a given user. If simple methods of identifying condom breakers existed, service providers could maximize the impact of their educational interventions by targeting the cohort of users who experience the majority of breaks....

Three hundred couples were recruited for the study from professional organizations and institutions in the Research Triangle Park area of North Carolina....The study protocol required participants and their partners to be in a monogamous heterosexual relationship, at least 18 years old, protected against pregnancy, not practicing behaviors that would put them at risk of STDs (including HIV), and free from known sensitivities to latex....

The 20 study condoms—one from each lot—...were mailed to participating couples along with the study questionnaire, a one-page form on which respondents answered a series of questions on slippage and breakage for each condom and filled in an identifying code from the condom packaging....When the investigators received the completed questionnaires, they paid the participating couples for each condom used....

This analysis is based on 177 couples....The median age of the participants was about 30, and the median education was approximately 15 years....Most of the couples (84%) were either married or living together....

Couples with no condom experience in the year before the study and couples who had experienced condom breakage during that period had relatively high rates of condom failure [13.9% and 13.1%, respectively]...[but] couples who had used condoms in the year before the study without experiencing condom breakage had a failure rate of 5.6%....Couples who were not living together had significantly higher failure rates than their cohabiting counterparts. If the male partner had a high school education or less, the couples experienced significantly higher failure rates than if he had more education. (Steiner et al., 1993, pp. 220–223)

Strengths of Mail Surveys. Mail surveys provide a close approximation to the ideal of complete *confidentiality* for the respondent—completed questionnaires might contain identification such as a name or a code, but the interviewer doesn't reveal any answers to anyone outside the research project. Because of no face-to-face interactions, mail surveys can encourage respondents to share information of a personal or sensitive nature. It's also much cheaper and faster to work with a large sample and cover a large geographic area with a mail questionnaire than with personal interviews, but not so much so when compared with telephone interviews.

Limitations and Considerations of Mail Surveys. What do you think is the greatest problem with mail questionnaires? If you said, "Not answering it," you're right! A major problem usually accompanying mail questionnaires is a low **response rate**—the extent to which surveys are completed and returned. The questionnaire goes directly into the "round file"—the wastebasket.

However, much is known about how to achieve a high percentage of returned questionnaires, as noted in the final section of this chapter titled "Follow Up, Follow Up, Follow Up!" And mail surveys today can achieve a higher response rate than most phone surveys (Dillman et al., 2009, p. 10), due to the increasing problems of telephone interviewing, discussed above.

But low response rates can offset one of the chief advantages of mail surveys—the advantage of *not* revealing sensitive facts in a face-to-face interview. Still, some people with embarrassing or socially unacceptable answers to sensitive questions are less likely to return the survey. A person involved in illegal drug use, for example, may be much less likely to return a questionnaire than are others. Of course, locating and personally interviewing this same person also may be difficult or impossible.

Internet Surveys

E-mail and Web surveys have been used extensively in market research and customer service surveys during the last two decades or so, and also in some areas of academic and government research (Nesbary, 2000). An example of customer service electronic surveys is summarized in NASA's *Functional Leadership Plan, Office of Procurement*, excerpted below.

Excerpt: *Electronic Surveys at NASA*

The Office of Procurement conducts electronic surveys of procurement customers on an ad hoc basis. In the past, we have surveyed Center procurement offices' technical customers to assess how well those offices are satisfying their customers' procurement requirements. We also surveyed NASA contractors to get their feedback on NASA's procurement processes. Two other surveys were used to measure how well the Office of Procurement is meeting its customers' needs. One was sent to Center procurement personnel and the other to customers at Headquarters and senior Center management. Survey results are used to assess the Office of Procurement's performance and to identify opportunities for improvement. (2005 p. 2)

Recently, Internet surveys, also called *Web surveys* or www surveys, have become a much-enhanced version of the e-mail survey, with options such as video and audio, graphics, color and animation (Nathan, 2008, pp. 356–357). Also, responses can be recorded and tallied electronically.

Many informal "surveys" on various topics currently appear on the Internet, in which one or a few questions are posed, and respondents are volunteers. For example, NPR (National Public Radio) asked an intriguing question at its website about the possibility of finding life on other planets (see Table 2). Because the data were from volunteers, the poll wasn't scientific and therefore not generalizable to the general public or to all Internet users.

TABLE 2. Example of an Informal Internet Survey

Will life from another planet be discovered during your lifetime?

The responses were:

Yes	52%	3,187 votes
No	48%	2,933 votes
Total:		6,120 votes

Source: http://www.npr.org/blogs/thetwo-way/2010/12/01/ 131730552/-trillions-of-earths-could-be-orbiting-300-sextillion-stars

Respondents who complete a Web survey use a Web browser such as Internet Explorer or Mozilla Firefox. Figure 1 was constructed as a small Web form. With a Web form, none of the questionnaire text can be altered, and text boxes can be provided for answers to open-ended questions, as in Figure 1 for the "Other" color. Various other devices such as drop-down menus also are available using a Web browser.

Strengths and Limitations of Internet Surveys. Until recently, there was a lot of enthusiasm for the potential of Internet surveys in social science, particularly surveys completed using a Web browser (Dillman et al., 2009). In addition to the graphics and video, audio and similar advantages, reasons for the enthusiasm include the anticipated cost savings from not having interviewers, printing and postage charges, long-distance calls and data entry personnel, as well as shorter time from survey design to results (Dillman et al., 2009; see also Nathan, 2008).

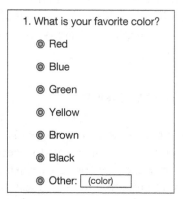

FIGURE 1   Example of a Simple Radio Box for a Web Questionnaire.

Yet interest in the Internet as a mode of survey data collection recently has cooled somewhat, other than for specific populations with high levels of Internet access and computer skills (e.g., members of professional organizations, college students and faculty). Reasons include lack of standards for e-mail addresses, population segments still without computer skills or Internet access and no list of Internet users from which to draw samples (Dillman et al, 2009). Also "cyber crimes" such as computer viruses and identity theft, along with unsolicited and unwanted e-mails (and unfamiliar Web links from unrecognized sources), have led to "increasingly widespread distrust of Internet communications" (p. 9).

Similar to how e-mail, text messaging ("texting") and instant messaging are changing the nature of communication, Internet surveys, despite their potential problems, are making phone and mail surveys more difficult. Internet surveys also are quickly moving toward replacing face-to-face interviewing (Nathan, 2008, p. 356).

As mentioned in the opening section of this chapter, another change in survey research is taking place. Because of the increasing difficulties of administering single-mode surveys (i.e., only phone or personal interviews), technology is being used to transform questionnaires from one survey type to another. For example, one part of a sample might be sent a mail questionnaire, while others are sent an e-mailed or Web version, and perhaps a third group will be contacted using CATI (computer-phone) technology. This *multimode survey* approach is described as "respondent driven"—doing a valid survey while giving respondents a choice (Dillman et al., 2009, p. 11). But there is a downside—persons preparing Internet surveys not only must have survey research experience but also highly advanced technical knowledge "far beyond that required for the design of conventional survey instruments" (Nathan, 2008, p. 357). Of course, the researchers can hire technical experts to construct the forms. Numerous commercial firms specialize or have units that specialize in Web-survey development (e.g., Qualtrics).

The limitations of Internet surveys—particularly the coverage and "distrust" problems—remain serious barriers. Internet access is growing rapidly, however, so we might expect coverage to improve with time, along with better ways to overcome the distrust issue. Regardless of survey type, the basic principles of survey research presented in this chapter still apply, particularly the need for reliable, valid and useful data from samples.

PREPARING THE SURVEY INSTRUMENT

Writing (or even selecting) questions for a survey is not nearly as easy as it might seem! How *does* one decide which questions to select (or write)? The answer: (a) Decide what variables are important for your project, and (b) decide what indicators (questions) you need to measure the variables.

Survey questions are divided into two parts: (1) stem, and (2) response options. The **stem** asks the question, and the **response options** contain the answer choices presented to respondents.

Use Questions from Available Sources

A good rule for preparing survey questions is to *avoid "reinventing the wheel"—don't repeat errors others have already identified about your topic.* Read several recent social science journal articles about your topic; particularly helpful might be articles that used surveys as a method of data collection. Check to see what questions these authors used that might be useful for your survey; questionnaire items seldom are copyrighted. For standard items, like demographics (e.g., race and age of respondent), see how major surveys ask these questions and check the Census wording.

As you read published studies, look for three important components: (1) *theory* (how researchers identify the relationship among their selected variables, including the control variables), (2) *operationalization* (how they turned abstract concepts into variables) and (3) *research findings* (the results of the studies). Often theory is about general topics that also might include your specific interest. Suppose you're interested in alcohol abuse among preteens. Look for theory about substance abuse more generally, or, more generally still, about deviant behavior of any type, or still more generally, about norms, roles and sanctions.

Questionnaires or the full text of question wording is available online for many major surveys. The URLs for three locations are given:

Inter-University Consortium for Political and Social Research (ICPSR): *http://www.icpsr.umich.edu/icpsrweb/ICPSR/index.jsp*

General Social Survey (GSS): *http://www.norc.org/GSS+Website/*

National Crime Victimization Survey (NCVS): *http://bjs.ojp.usdoj.gov/index.cfm?ty=dcdetail&iid=245*

ICPSR is the most general site. It is a distribution center for thousands of data collections.[2] Both the GSS and NCVS sites are linked from ICPSR.

Whether you need to modify some questions or response categories from major surveys or write your own questions, keep the following principles in mind.

Open-ended versus Closed-ended Questions. Questions may be open-ended or closed-ended. In the case of **open-ended questions**, respondents write in an answer, generally in a blank space in the response section of the question.

A familiar type of open-ended question is the essay question on a test. Essay questions require space for more extensive answers than a word or phrase. In survey research, open-ended questions are practical only on a self-administered questionnaire or a Web survey, unless responses are tape-recorded. On an Internet Web form, text boxes can be made to automatically expand to accommodate long responses.

Although it is tempting to ask respondents to "add your comments and suggestions," interpreting answers to open-ended questions is time-consuming. Consider how much time it likely takes your professors to read 50 or more half-page answers to one essay (open-ended) question. Also, answers to open-ended questions might be unrelated to the question asked, and handwritten answers can be difficult to read.

In **closed-ended questions**, respondents are asked to check one (or more) response(s) in a list. The list of responses is called the response options (e.g., female/male, yes/no, strongly agree...strongly disagree and so forth). Figure 2 shows two examples of the same question, one with an open-ended response and one with closed-ended responses. Which example do you think is preferable in most studies?

What is your sex (**female or male**)?	_____	Open-Ended
	Female [ ]	
What is your sex (**check one**)?		Closed-Ended
	Male [ ]	

FIGURE 2   Open-Ended and Closed-Ended Options for the Same Question.

Closed-ended questions are preferable for recording gender and other well-known response options, such as race/ethnicity and age. In general, choose closed-ended questions when possible. They require less respondent effort and ensure uniformity of responses. Uniformity also reduces errors (e.g., those associated with open-ended questions) and speeds working with the completed surveys.

Regardless of type of questions and responses, be consistent in your directions to respondents for answering survey questions. Some of the examples in this chapter show checkboxes for responses, and some use a "circle one" instruction. Either method works, but usually it is better not to mix them in one survey. If you've taken an exam in which a couple of true/false questions are followed by a couple of multiple-choice questions, followed by an essay question, followed by a couple of true/false questions, you'll likely appreciate the importance of consistency!

Composing Your Own Questions (or Modifying Others)

Preexisting questions might not closely fit the purpose of your survey or the people you want to survey. For example, a question for adults might not be understood by preteens (or vice versa). And responses on an interview guide might require modification for use on a self-administered questionnaire (e.g., deleting a "not applicable" response option).

Many principles apply to writing good survey questions. These include (but are not limited to) principles in the following summary. Many of the principles discussed in this section are adapted from Dillman (2000; 2009).

Simplify Words and Phrases. Keep the length of questions (and their response options) as short as possible and still communicate your intent. For example, compare the pairs of synonyms in Table 3 below (Dillman, 2000, p. 52).

TABLE 3. Comparison of Simpler and More Complex Synonyms

Simpler	More Complex
Tired	Exhausted
Honest	Candid
Most important	Top priority
Free time	Leisure
Work	Employment

Also, spend time on sentence structure until the sentences are simple and accurate. For example, simplify

We are interested in finding out how satisfied you are with your cable TV company. There's been a lot of controversy about cable prices lately, and so this question is very important to us. [Response categories would follow.]

to

How satisfied or dissatisfied are you with your cable TV company? [Response categories would follow.]

Write Complete Sentences. For example, avoid "questions" like

Highest degree?
    [ ] Less than high school
    [ ] High school degree
    [ ] Associates degree (2-year college)
        [Other response categories would follow.]

Instead, use a complete sentence with clear instructions to the respondents:

What is the highest educational degree you have completed? (Check one.)
    [ ] Less than high school
    [ ] High school degree
    [ ] Associate degree (2-year college)
        [Other response categories would follow.]

State Both Positive and Negative Sides in the Question Stem. Particularly for rating scales, avoid questions like "How much do you agree with...." Instead ask, "How much do you agree or disagree with...." Otherwise, you probably are leading respondents to agree more than to disagree.

Use Caution with Questions on Sensitive Topics. Sensitive topics include child abuse, drug use, sexual behavior and criminal behavior. *Ask about these topics only if they are important to your study, and you have approval from your institutional review board or IRB.*

If you do ask about a sensitive topic, phrase your questions carefully—avoid emotionally charged words. Table 4 shows two examples (Dillman, 2000, p. 75). Which question is likely to produce less emotional response, particularly if the respondent *has* shoplifted something? The second question obviously is preferred, as it avoids the word "shoplifting."

TABLE 4.   Two Examples of a Question about a Sensitive Topic

Have you ever shoplifted anything from a store?
    [ ]   Yes
    [ ]   No
Have you ever taken anything from a store without paying for it?
    [ ]   Yes
    [ ]   No

Except in rare circumstances, avoid open-ended questions with sensitive topics, including questions about income and wealth. In a personal interview, a card can be handed to respondents showing a complete listing formatted like the partial list in Table 1, above. Respondents are asked to report only a code associated with the dollar range containing their income. Moreover, there is no need to deal with illegible responses such as "30,00" (is the respondent reporting $30 per hour or $3,000 per month, or $30,000 per year?) or illegible numbers handwritten by respondents.

Avoid Double-Barreled Questions. Who should provide sex education? Look at the question in Panel 1 of Table 5. What is the correct answer if the respondent thinks parents should provide sex education, but schools and churches should not? Technically, the correct answer is "No." But many respondents likely will not recognize this, and the researcher probably wants to know the answer for each of the groups. This is an example of a **double-barreled question**. The question should be split into three distinct questions—one asking about parents, one about schools and a third about churches, as shown in Panel 2 of Table 5.

TABLE 5.   Two Examples: One Double-Barreled Question and One Not Double-Barreled

Panel 1: Double-Barreled Question

Do you think parents, schools, and churches should provide sex education for youth ages 13–19? (Circle one.)

Yes

No

Panel 2: Improved Version of Double-Barreled Question, Separated into Three Questions

Do you think the following groups should provide sex education to youth ages 13 to 19? (Circle yes or no for each group.)

Parents	Yes	No
Schools	Yes	No
Churches	Yes	No

Use Specific Quantities in Response Categories, Tailored to Respondents. How much is "a lot" or "some"? In short, avoid using questions with vague quantities in the response options, as shown in Panel 1 of Table 6. The response categories in Panel 1 are virtually useless for estimating time on homework. It's difficult to know what the question measures, but probably it reflects frustration with homework as much as the amount of time spent on it. Instead, ask something like the question shown in Panel 2.

The options in Panel 2 are listed in reverse order according to the time spent on homework. It probably is more natural to show the smallest number of hours first. The reverse order in Panel 2 might tend to inflate the amount of time spent on homework. An experiment could be conducted to find out. Assign at random half of respondents to a form using one order and the other half to use the other order. This is an experiment with random assignment, and, if the sample is a probability sample, it also is random selection—a powerful test.

TABLE 6. Examples Showing Need for Specific Quantities

Panel 1: Question with Unclear Stem and Response Options.

How much time do you spend on homework?

- [ ] A lot   ☐
- [ ] Some   ☐
- [ ] A little   ☐
- [ ] Almost none   ☐

Panel 2: Improved Version of Question from Panel 1.

During a typical week, Sunday through Saturday, how much time do you spend on homework? (Check your best estimate.)

- [ ] 12 hr or more
- [ ] At least 8 hr but less than 12
- [ ] At least 4 hr but less than 8
- [ ] Some time, but less than 4 hr
- [ ] None at all

With time-span questions, the general principle is, Use the same length of time interval for all respondents and have it cover a comparable time span. For example, "the past four days" span a weekend for some respondents but only weekdays for others, depending on which day of the week they completed the survey (*reliability issue*). Although estimating for a "typical week" might be difficult for respondents, it's probably best not to mention "last week." Time spent on homework might vary from week to week.

Use Nonreactive Response Options. An ad reads, "Seventy-five percent of visitors to the World Auto Show rated the NEW 'Extreme Machine' as either 'thrilling' or 'bold'! Perhaps—but did the rating depend on the response options? **Reactive response options** can lead the respondent to an incorrect response (*measurement error*) and should be eliminated.

For example, avoid response options like those shown in Table 7. The question in Table 7 violates several important principles that we've described in this chapter: (1) The response options aren't mutually exclusive. The machine might be thrilling, bold, *and* the respondent likes it a lot, all at the same time. (2) The first two response options are adjectives seemingly designed to "lead" or influence the respondent. And, they aren't ordered or even comparable. Which is ranked higher—"thrilling" or "bold"? (3) The options are not balanced. Three out of five are positive, one is neutral, and only one is mildly negative.

TABLE 7. Example of Reactive Response Options

What is your reaction to the new 2005 Extreme Machine?

    [ ] Thrilling

    [ ] Bold

    [ ] Like it a lot

    [ ] Neutral

    [ ] Don't care for it

Proofread! Spelling errors, typos and omissions slip past even the best survey researchers. Sometimes this can look embarrassingly unprofessional. Sometimes it can be much worse, leading to potentially serious response errors. For example, suppose you present a list of medical conditions to respondents, asking them to indicate which conditions they have. If diabetes (or any other condition, especially one associated with other health problems) is omitted from the list, the quality of the results—reliability, validity and ultimately usefulness—is seriously degraded.

Finally, the need for validity and reliability of responses must be balanced against the difficulty of getting people to participate. To help address both concerns, pretest all questions and the complete survey form before the main survey is conducted, as discussed later in this chapter. Table 8 presents a summary of each principle for constructing survey questions.

TABLE 8. Summary of Principles for Constructing Survey Questions

Question Stem	Response Options
Look for questions from major existing surveys, tailored to respondent and/or survey type	Consider response options from major existing surveys, tailored to respondent and/or survey type.
Simplicity	Simplicity
Use complete sentences, with clear instructions to respondent.	
	Use specific response-option quantities tailored to respondents.
	Use balanced-response options.
	Use nonreactive response options.
Avoid double-barreled questions.	
Use care with sensitive topics.	
Use both positive and negative sides of opinions.	Include both positive and negative sides.
Proofread!	Proofread!

LAYOUT OF A SURVEY FORM

Probably you are now thinking that writing good questions is not as easy as it seems! Assembling them into a survey form that will convince respondents to answer honestly all of the questions is just as difficult. Think of yourself as a respondent. What does it take to get *you* to go to the trouble of completing a questionnaire, phone interview or any other type of survey?

In preparing the layout of a survey form, consider two types of decisions: (1) In what order should the questions appear? (2) How should the pages and completed document be formatted (e.g., layout of questions and pages, where to put instructions, what font and font size to use, what colors to choose and whether and how to use graphics). Such decisions apply mostly to self-administered questionnaires (paper and electronic), but a well-laid-out interview guide simplifies the interviewer's task.

Question Sequencing

A "must" for getting survey respondents to share their information is *trust*. Generally, to encourage participation and valid responses, put easy-to-answer questions, nonthreatening questions and interesting items at the beginning of a survey. General warm-up questions might help build rapport with the interviewer (Weisberg, Krosnick, & Bowen, 1996) or create a positive attitude toward a questionnaire.

The First Question. Dillman (2000, p. 92) argues that the *first question* is the most important question on the survey because it often determines whether the survey will be completed. He gives three criteria for selecting it. The first question should (1) be easy to answer, (2) apply to everyone and (3) be interesting. He mentions age as an example that meets only two of the three criteria—which two? Although Dillman's argument is directed toward self-administered surveys, the point also is applicable to interviews. Even on an exam, the first question you read might encourage (or discourage) you about how well you will do, and might even determine whether you complete the exam.

Figure 3 shows an example of a short, self-administered questionnaire about an environmental topic. Question 1 applies to everyone, and it might be at least mildly interesting, but is it easy? Also, is it possible for more than one option to fit some respondents? If so, the response options are not mutually exclusive. Also, it's not clear what option 3 means. Does "interest/professional affiliation" refer to one reason or two?

Order of Other Questions. After the first question(s), in general, question sequencing follows the below pattern:

simpler → more complex, more sensitive, etc. → simpler

Wind Energy Questionnaire
Survey Research Laboratory
University of Illinois

The Survey Research Center of the University of Illinois is studying public attitudes toward sources of energy, particularly energy machines. As part of this study, would you please fill out this short questionnaire pertaining to wind energy?

(Please circle one code number for each question unless otherwise specified.)

1. Why did you come to see this wind machine? (Circle one.)

   Was in the area and heard about it   1
   Saw it from the road, was curious   2
   Made a special trip to see it because of interest/
       professional affiliation with the subject area . . .   3
   Had other business at this base   4
   Other (specify) _____

                      _____

2. If this wind machine were NOT here, would this area be

   More pleasing   1
   No different   2
   Less pleasing   3

   •

   • (questions omitted here)

   •

11. Are you presently

   Employed   1
   Retired/disabled   2
   Homemaker   3
   Student   4
   Temporarily unemployed   5

THANK YOU FOR YOUR COOPERATION.

FIGURE 3   Example of a Short, Self-Administered Questionnaire (First and Last Sections).
Source: Sudman, Seymour and Norman M. Bradburn. (1982). *Asking questions.* San Francisco: Jossey-Bass. Copyright ©1982. Reprinted by permission of John Wiley & Sons, Inc.

If sensitive questions are needed, put them toward the end of the instrument, for two reasons. (1) Respondents should be interested in the questionnaire by the time they get to them, if you did your job well. (2) By the end of the questionnaire, respondents have invested sufficient time in it that they are inclined to finish it (Dillman, 2000). Of course, some respondents might quit before they finish, thereby omitting possibly the most important questions. Questions providing demographic data, such as employment status, age, or level of education, frequently are placed near the end of the survey or sometimes last, as is the case in Figure 3.

Group Similar Questions, but Cautiously. Regardless of the specific order of questions, it usually is important to group questions of a similar topic, perhaps with an introductory sentence such as: "Next are some questions about...."

Be careful here, however. Asking several questions in a row *with the same response options formatted into a "matrix"* can lead respondents to take the "route of least resistance." Examples are checking all "No" boxes on a health questionnaire in a doctor's office even if one has had the condition or checking "disagree strongly" to each question about sex education as illustrated in Figure 4.

1. Please indicate how strongly you agree or disagree that each of the following groups should provide sex education to junior-high school students? (Check one for each group.)

	Strongly agree	Agree	Neither agree nor disagree	Disagree	Strongly disagree
Community sports program	[ ]	[ ]	[ ]	[ ]	[✔]
Youth clubs	[ ]	[ ]	[ ]	[ ]	[✔]
Schools	[ ]	[ ]	[ ]	[ ]	[✔]
Churchs	[ ]	[ ]	[ ]	[ ]	[✔]
Parents	[ ]	[ ]	[ ]	[ ]	[✔]

FIGURE 4 Example of Possible Response Set Answers from a Matrix Format.

Although it's possible the respondent in Figure 4 "disagrees strongly" with every question, it's also possible the answers primarily are due to what is called **response-set error**—the tendency to select the same answer to many questions when asked in a row, regardless of the question content or accuracy (validity) of the answers.

One approach to avoiding response-set error (*measurement error*) is to vary the content of the questions, so that "agree–disagree" has different meanings for some questions than for others. For example, "strongly agree" to "I love baseball" means just the opposite of "strongly agree" to "I hate baseball." But be cautious here also—respondents can react to something positive (or negative), regardless of the question itself.

Survey Appearance and Other Layout Details. An interviewer can be trained to negotiate through difficult sections of an interview guide, but the respondent trying to complete a self-administered questionnaire does not have this training. Still, mistakes are less likely if the interview guide is laid out in an easy-to-follow format.

Figure 5 illustrates some recommendations for formatting a self-administered questionnaire (Dillman, 2000). The figure shows two of the six questions about liberal–conservative leanings asked on a recent National Election Survey (NES). NES data are collected by interview; the guide in Figure 5 is a sample questionnaire page adapted from the NES. (The introduction to the six questions is verbatim form the NES questionnaire.)

In the next several questions, please rate yourself, political candidates and political parties on the seven-point liberal-conservative scale (selected questions shown below).

1. Where would you place yourself on this scale or haven't you thought much about this?

[ ] Extremely liberal
[ ] Liberal
[ ] Slightly liberal
[ ] Moderate; middle of the road
[ ] Slightly conservative
[ ] Conservative
[ ] Very conservative
[ ] Don't know
[ ] Haven't thought much about it

1. What about George W. Bush? Where would you place him?

[ ] Extremely liberal
[ ] Liberal
[ ] Slightly liberal
[ ] Moderate; middle of the road
[ ] Slightly conservative
[ ] Conservative
[ ] Very conservative
[ ] Don't know

FIGURE 5 Sample Questionnaire Page.

Source: Adapted from National Elections Survey, 2000.

The sample questionnaire page in Figure 5 also illustrates some important principles. (1) Use short lines; (2) put instructions immediately before the question(s) to which they apply or, perhaps better yet, within each question; (3) provide sufficient empty space so the pages don't appear too "busy" and (4) use an easy-to-read font size matching the needs of prospective respondents. The sample in Figure 5 may not illustrate all these points equally well; which aspects do you think might be improved?

Finally, be sure to thank the respondent for participating. The thank-you could appear in large bold font and centered at the end of the survey, if you can do it without adding another page to the instrument—**Thank You!**

PRETESTING THE SURVEY

Be sure to distinguish between the survey pretest terminology used in this chapter and the same terminology used to indicate a measurement taken before an experimental treatment is administered. The term *pretest* in an experiment, or any before-and-after study, refers to measurements of the outcome variable (dependent variable) prior to administering the treatment, quite distinct from a survey pretest which is a try-out of the survey done before the main survey.

Would you buy a car never having driven it (or one like it)? In survey research, a survey **pretest** is "trying out" the survey on some respondents who are similar to those to be included in the main sample.

The survey pretest can help to identify problems with the directions for completing the questionnaire, identify confusing questions and response categories, indicate potential **nonresponse** problems, and determine how long it takes respondents to complete the survey.

Researchers sometimes use pretest "think-alouds" to identify problems with questions. Think-alouds ask respondents to describe what they are thinking about each question and its response options as they answer it (Groves, 1996).

The Pretest Survey Sample

Regardless of survey type, the pretest should duplicate all questions and steps in conducting the main survey as closely as possible. For example, if the survey is a telephone survey, draw a small sample of numbers from your main list of numbers. Then conduct the entire interview for the pretest. If the survey is a mail questionnaire, mail it to a small sample drawn from the main sample and go through the same follow-ups. And if it is a personal interview, interviews should be conducted with a sample pulled from the main sample.

The pretest data should *not* be combined with the main survey data. And respondents selected for the pretest *must be excluded* from the main sample.

If you're contacting respondents more than once, be sure you can match responses from the same respondents collected at different times. If you are using a computer for data analysis, check the procedures for getting the data into the computer and do some preliminary analyses to be sure you haven't left something out or misdefined a variable.

Finally, if you make many changes after a pretest, a second pretest is needed!

CONDUCTING THE SURVEY

A Brief Guide to Interviewing

The following summary of interviewing procedures is adapted from the interviewer's manual of the Survey Research Center, University of Michigan (Frankfort-Nachmias & Nachmias, 1996, p. 240). Most of the points apply to both personal interviewing and telephone interviewing.

The opening moments often decide the success or failure of an interview. During that time, the interviewer must legitimize the study and spark enough interest to persuade the respondent to answer accurately all the questions. Therefore, at the beginning of the interview session: (1) Tell respondents who you are and who you represent; (2) tell respondents what you are doing in a way that will stimulate interest in your survey; (3) tell respondents how they were chosen and (4) adapt your approach to the situation, and try to create a relationship of confidence and trust between each respondent and yourself.

During the interview, keep in mind the following techniques.

- *Follow the interview guide*—but how closely? Recall that unstructured interviewing is informal, semistructured includes probes but permits a fair amount of leeway and structured interviewing does not permit much deviation from the prepared guide. Nonetheless, each respondent should be asked the questions in the same order. Ask every question, and repeat any question that is misunderstood.

- *Display a relaxed manner.* Read each question slowly and crisply so respondents have time to think about the question and formulate an answer. This is especially important in telephone surveys. The respondent can't watch the interviewer pronounce words.

- *End the interview on a positive note such as a simple-to-answer question, and thank the respondent.*

Legitimizing the Survey

Suppose you received a mail survey from the Oval Office of the White House. How about if a survey came from your local Sewer Board? The point is obvious. The sponsor of the survey has a lot to do with how seriously prospective respondents view it. If you're doing a survey for your methods class (or for any other course), you might mention your university or college to prospective respondents. But, first consult your instructor about the need for IRB approval. And you might be able to use university letterhead if you get permission. Most organizations, including colleges and universities, restrict use of their logos and letterheads.

The Cover Letter. As a consideration to your prospective respondents and to improve response rates, a **cover letter** should be sent out, regardless of the mode of administration: telephone, personal interview, mail or Web form. Time it to arrive during *the week prior to* the arrival date of a mail questionnaire or the first interview attempt. It should be brief, no more than a page, and contain the following content.

- *Sponsor of the study.* Include this information in the cover/introduction letter, questionnaire, follow-up reminders and thank-you letters (for both paper and electronic surveys). For interview surveys, mention the sponsor in the introduction.

- *Purpose.* How the survey will contribute to the community, organization/agency and so on? Two to four sentences should suffice.

- *Voluntary nature.* If the survey isn't required by law, it's voluntary and this should be mentioned.

- *Confidential or anonymous.* Nearly all surveys ensure confidentiality (neither respondents' answers nor their identity is revealed outside the research team), and some surveys are anonymous (research team never knows the identity of respondents). Be sure to emphasize whichever applies.

- *Questions.* Provide a phone number or e-mail address where prospective respondents can get more information.
- *Thank you.* Thank prospective respondents in advance.

Follow-up, Follow-up, Follow-up!

A 100 percent response rate is seldom achieved in survey research. More important, it has been found repeatedly that only one attempt to contact prospective respondents leads to unacceptably low response rates, often in the range of 10–20 percent for mail surveys. One review of studies using questionnaires finds response rates from a low of 11 percent to a high of 95 percent (Miller & Salkind, 2002, pp. 298–300).

Low response rates mean fewer cases for data analysis and also suggest the possibility of *nonresponse error*—potential differences between individuals who complete and return the survey and those who don't. We say "possibility of nonresponse error" because there is no information from those who don't complete a survey, so it is impossible to compare answers of nonrespondents to those of respondents. However, miserably low response rates can be improved dramatically by follow-ups.

One interpretation is that a mail survey response rate of 50 percent is adequate and 60 percent is good, depending on the population and topics (Babbie, 1999, p. 240). Typically today, phone interviews require 20–30 follow-ups—a very large increase compared with a few decades ago; recall that the *Challenger* explosion study reviewed earlier included at least seven callbacks. For mail questionnaires, a total of five or six attempted contacts with cover letter probably is sufficient (Dillman, 2000).[3]

Regardless of survey type, effective initial-contact strategies to encourage participation include the following: (a) personalizing the contact (e.g., using respondents' names in the cover/introduction letter); (b) providing a brief prenotice letter/e-mail and a detailed (but not-too-detailed) cover letter and (c) providing a respondent-friendly questionnaire with clear, easy-to-answer questions arranged for easy response (Dillman, 2000, pp. 150–153).

The Question of Incentives. Do inducements such as money, discount coupons, a free item or a copy of the final survey report increase response rates? A token money payment, no more than ten dollars paid in advance, can improve response rates, *but follow-ups work better* (Dillman, 2009). If used, an inducement is announced in the cover/introduction letter.

Surveys and Theory Go Together

Despite limitations of surveys, complex theories have been developed and hypotheses tested using survey data that would be impossible to obtain otherwise. Let's look at an interesting summary from a national study about parental employment and child rearing. It illustrates the close connections between theory and survey research.

Based on previous research, Kohn and his collaborators proposed a theory that the primary reason for class differences in child-rearing values is parental education and what they call "occupational self-direction." According to the theory, working-class jobs tend to be repetitive, with little room for variation. In contrast, middle-class jobs require individual decision making (Kohn, 1977; Kohn & Slomczynski, 1990).

Using personal interviews, Kohn and collaborators conducted a U.S. national survey of 4,105 employed men not in the armed services. Closed-ended questions were developed and refined in subsequent pretests. Particular attention was paid to describing parental occupation and to the measurement of child-rearing values. They achieved a fairly good response rate of just over 73 percent.

The main findings support the theory: Working-class parents emphasize obedience for their children, and middle-class parents emphasize self-direction. Middle-class parents tend to have more education than do working-class parents, and middle-class parents have jobs permitting/requiring more occupational self-direction and decision making than do working-class parents. These differences in education and occupation are reflected in child-rearing values.

Many national surveys, such as the General Social Survey, collect information related to many topics. In contrast, the Kohn National Survey was designed primarily to test a set of theoretical ideas about the relationship between education, work and child-rearing attitudes. And despite the limitations of surveys, it's difficult to imagine conducting a national study to test hypotheses without surveys.

SUMMARY

A survey is a method for collecting information about people by directly asking them questions. The three primary modes of administering a survey are personal interview, telephone interview and mail questionnaire. Newer types of surveys include e-mail, Web or Internet surveys and multimode surveys.

The main strength of personal interviews is their flexibility in probing for details; personal interviews also foster high participation rates. But personal interviews are expensive, time-consuming, and not well suited for asking sensitive questions. Compared with personal interviews, telephone interviews are quick and cheap. But they're easier to decline, don't permit visual cues and aren't well suited for long, complex surveys. Mail questionnaires are well suited for surveys about sensitive topics. Mail questionnaires also are comparatively cheap to administer—there's no labor cost for interviewers. But return rates tend to be low, and the multiple follow-ups needed to achieve an acceptable response rate extend the time it takes to complete a research study using mail questionnaires.

Conducting a survey is relatively easy; however, getting high-quality data from a survey is not easy. The relative advantages of the four modes of survey administration must be evaluated. Questions must be selected with care and composed to ensure accurate and complete responses. The questionnaire, particularly mail questionnaires and Internet forms, must be laid out in an attractive layout. This chapter summarizes several guidelines for writing and formatting a questionnaire. Proofread everything—more than once! Pretesting the survey also is a must. And follow-ups are essential.

Nonresponse error, coverage error and measurement error, dropout in longitudinal surveys and use of nonexperimental data can affect conclusions based on survey data. Nonresponse error comes from differences between individuals who complete and return a questionnaire and those who do not. Coverage error refers to incorrect summaries due to omission of part of the population from the list from which the sample was selected or to inclusion of some people more than once in the sample frame. Measurement error refers to incorrect answers to questions on the survey. Incorrect cause-and-effect conclusions due to use of nonexperimental designs is an ever-present concern with survey data.

The chapter concludes with a review of the Kohn National Survey to illustrate the close relationship between theory, survey data collection and data analysis. The survey was designed specifically to test some very interesting hypotheses about the relationship between parental social status and child-rearing practices and philosophy. Despite their limitations, surveys provide much valuable data and form the basis for critically important social research.

YOUR REVIEW SHEET

1. Thinking about the interviews with adoptive parents, what are some strengths of personal interviews? What are some reasons why personal interviews might not be the best method of data collection? Use the study of adoptive parents as a starting point, but don't confine your answer solely to that setting.

2. State two limitations that an interviewer planning telephone surveys would have to consider. Summarize two strengths in your own words.

3. State two limitations that an interviewer considering Internet surveys would have to consider. Summarize two strengths in your own words.

4. Write a double-barreled question not discussed in the chapter. Rewrite it to avoid the problem.

5. How might a researcher reduce response-set answers when grouping questions on a similar topic?

6. Write another type of question other than those of Questions 4 and 5 that could produce a problem. Rewrite it to avoid the problem.

7. What are Dillman's three criteria for selecting questions to present first on a survey? Write a survey question on the topic of Internet browsing that meets his criteria.

8. What is perhaps the greatest problem with mail questionnaires, and why? How can this problem be minimized or overcome?

9. Why is nonresponse error a problem for survey researchers? What can be done to decrease it?

10. Some researchers prefer to put more complex, sensitive questions at or near the end of the survey form. What is a possible problem with this approach? What are Dillman's arguments in favor of it?

11. What can a survey pretest tell the researcher?

12. Write a balanced assessment of the strengths and weakness of surveys.

END NOTES

1. In addition to CATI, there are other kinds of computer-assisted data collection mentioned by Saris (1991): Two are CAPI (computer-assisted personal interviews) and CSAQ (computerized self-administered questionnaires). Saris and Gallhofer (2007) include CASI (computer-assisted self-interviewing) and Web surveys.

2. ICPSR currently holds more than a half-million data files, and the collection is growing rapidly (*http://www.icpsr.umich.edu/icpsrweb/ICPSR/org/index.jsp*, accessed March 6, 2011).

3. The validity of causal research is not as threatened by nonresponse and coverage errors as are descriptive studies. If a cause-and-effect relationship based on theory is properly specified, it operates in all subpopulations.

STUDY TERMS

anonymity Completed surveys that do not contain any information that identifies respondents, either directly or indirectly (respondents are anonymous). Compare to confidentiality.

closed-ended question Questions with a list of predefined answers, usually called response options (e.g.,...$10,000–$12,499, $12,500–$15,000...for income). A familiar example is a multiple-choice question on an exam. The list of options with most closed-ended questions is short, but this is not always true. State of residence normally contains at least 51 response options (50 states and DC) and sometimes includes U.S. territories. And date of birth on a drop-down menu in a Web survey contains thousands of options, divided into 12 months, up to 31 days and dozens of years.

computer-assisted telephone interviewing (CATI) Phone interview process using random-digit dialing and automated recording of responses; speeds data collection and virtually eliminates transcription errors.

confidentiality Completed surveys contain information identifying the respondents, but the researcher does not reveal any answers of individual respondents (keeps their information in confidence). Compare to anonymity.

coverage error Error due to omitting some part of the population from the sample list and/or including some people more than once.

cover letter Letter that accompanies or precedes a survey. It introduces and describes the purpose of the study and its social contribution, mentions the sponsor, tells why the respondent was selected, lists a contact person (for questions and mailback), contains a statement about anonymity or confidentiality, and says "thank you."

double-barreled-question Question that is really more than one question. For example: Do you like mom *and* apple pie? The correct answer is yes only if you like them *both*.

focus group A semistructured interview that includes several people.

generalization To extend what has been observed to situations or persons not observed

interviewer effect Bias resulting when a respondent chooses incorrect answers because an interviewer is present, for example, to impress or irritate the interviewer.

mail questionnaire Type of survey that collects information by mailing a questionnaire to respondents, who return the completed questionnaire by mail.

mail survey A survey that collects information by mailing a questionnaire to respondents.

nonresponse (*nonresponse error*) Failure of selected sample members to complete all or part of a survey or interview. Nonresponse error is the differences of averages, variation, and so on between individuals who complete and return a questionnaire and those who don't.

open-ended questions Questions requesting respondents to write in a response. A familiar example is an essay question on an exam.

personal interview Survey in which data are obtained from respondents while face to face with the interviewer.

pretest Small preliminary survey to check for problems with questions, response options and procedures such as length of time needed to complete a survey. The pretest sample should be similar to the target population for the main survey. *Note:* the term *pretest* used to describe experiments does not mean the same thing as pretest of a survey. A pretest in an experiment is a measurement of the outcome variable before the treatment is administered. In contrast, a *survey pretest* is a preliminary check for problems and procedures.

probe Follow-up question used in a semistructured interview to clarify responses that are incomplete or to elicit a response when one was not offered.

reactive response options Response categories of a question that lead the respondent to an incorrect response.

response options List of responses to a closed-ended question, e.g., single, married, divorced.

response rate The extent to which surveys are completed and returned, usually given as a percentage of all potential respondents initially contacted. One interpretation is that a mail survey response rate of 50 percent is adequate and 60 percent is good, depending on the population and topics.

response set (response error) Tendency of respondents to select the same answer to many/all questions in a matrix (arrangement of similar questions), no matter what the respondent's opinion is, for example, always answering "strongly agree" (or "strongly disagree," or "neutral").

self-administered questionnaire Survey completed by the respondent, usually obtained by mail, in the absence of the researcher, or administered in a group setting such as a classroom.

semistructured interview Face-to-face survey with a set of questions that can be expanded by using probes.

stem (of a question) The part of a survey item that asks the question. It should be a complete sentence.

structured interview Survey that is administered by an interviewer. Questions are read verbatim to the respondent and answers usually are recorded by the interviewer into one of a set of closed-ended options (although open-ended response categories also can be used).

survey Tool for gathering data which poses questions to a sample of individuals. Four types are mail questionnaire, personal interview, telephone interview and Internet questionnaire.

telephone interview A survey administered by telephone.

unstructured interview A loosely organized survey somewhat similar to a "conversation," but only the respondent provides the content (information). The interviewer usually has one broad question/topic with follow-up questions but doesn't necessarily repeat the follow-ups word-for-word. Nor does an unstructured interview use a question–answer format typical of a structured interview.

EXERCISES

Exercise 1. Evaluation of Research: Personal Interview

Directions: Refer to the excerpt on "open adoption" in the first section of this chapter to answer the following questions. *Note:* The article combines elements of an evaluation report and basic research, but is discussed here as an evaluation report.

Factual Questions

1. How did the researchers select the respondents to be interviewed?

2. How important was open adoption to the 21 respondents in the study? Why?

Questions for Discussion

1. Why might parents refuse to be interviewed for the study? How could nonresponse of parents affect the findings about attitudes toward open adoption?

2. The full article reported that the interviewer read the questions while the respondent followed along on an interview form. In what ways might this strategy assist the interviewer? How might potential problems arise?

3. What types of information might an interviewer be able to observe about adoptive parents during a personal interview that direct questions might not reveal?

4. Suppose an interviewer wearing torn jeans and an old sweatshirt approaches well-dressed parents. What effects is this likely to have on the interviewing process?

Exercise 2. Evaluation of Research: Telephone Interview

Directions: Refer to the excerpt on "shocking news" in this chapter to answer the following questions.

Factual Questions

1. What led Mayer and colleagues to select telephone interviewing?

2. How did questions asked of respondents allow Mayer and colleagues to answer their research questions?

Questions for Discussion

1. Is a telephone survey advantageous in this study? Briefly explain, taking into account the perspectives of both interviewers and respondents.

2. Evaluate Mayer and colleagues' choice of random-digit dialing to collect the data for their study.

3. If the phone interviews were obtained between 5:00 P.M. and 10:00 P.M., what are the advantages of interviewing during this time? What are the limitations?

4. The interviews were completed by alternating male and female heads of household. Why did they alternate female and male heads? Were heads of household appropriate persons to interview? Briefly explain.

5. Review at least one other potential limitation of this study not mentioned in the previous questions.

6. Briefly describe another nationally significant event that could be examined using a similar approach. If you were to conduct the research, how would you use Mayer and others' study to develop your survey?

Exercise 3. Evaluation of Research: Mail Questionnaire

Directions: Refer to the excerpt on "at-risk coital partners" in this chapter to answer the following questions.

Factual Questions

1. State the research question in your own words.

2. What group(s) of respondents was/were selected for the study?

3. How many returned the questionnaires? What is the response rate? Is this a high, medium or low rate of response for mail questionnaires? Explain briefly.

4. Suggest at least two strategies to increase the response rate for this study.

Questions for Discussion

1. Offer one possible reason why the rate of questionnaire return was not higher than it was.

2. Explain to a person not familiar with survey research methods at least two advantages and two limitations of mail questionnaires.

3. Write a short dialogue for a semistructured interview that would be appropriate for use with respondents who had completed the condom study. Use the Lady Gaga concert dialogue as a model. (Review semistructured interviewing in the text.)

Exercise 4. Skills Building: Writing Questions

Directions: Find two phone or personal interview questions on an existing major survey about a topic that interests you. These could be found at Internet sites like the GSS (*http://www.norc.org/GSS+Website*) or NCVS (*http://bjs.ojp.usdoj.gov/index.cfm?ty= dcdetail&iid=245*).

Questions

1. Write the original questions. Be sure to include the website source (URL) for each question.

2. Revise these questions for use in a *self-administered questionnaire*.

3. Explain how you followed good formatting principles for a self-administered survey.

4. What construct are you trying to measure with these questions? How well do you think your questions reflect this construct (face validity)? Why?

5. Compared with the interview mode of data collection, do you think you need more or fewer questions about the same construct to achieve acceptable reliability and high validity with your self-administered questionnaire? Why?

Exercise 5. Skills Building: Unstructured Interviewing

Directions: Decision Resources, Inc., has hired you to conduct four unstructured interviews as a pilot project for a larger study. The goal of the pilot project is to develop initial insights about how TV viewing habits differ between young people and middle-aged people.

Surveys

Conduct four unstructured interviews, two with persons who are at least 19 years old but no older than 25, and another two with persons who are approximately 40–60 years old. Careful note taking is important; your notes should be readable. Be prepared to hand in completed interview guides for the four interviews. Don't rewrite these unless your instructor requests.

Before beginning this exercise, review carefully the Code of Ethics forms in Appendix A. If you do not understand any of the ethical expectations, check with your instructor before proceeding with this exercise.

1. Write a brief interview guide with open-ended questions—one main question and four or five one-sentence follow-up questions—appropriate for an unstructured interview about TV viewing preferences. The follow-up questions are used if the respondent doesn't mention this information spontaneously. Write open-ended questions about preferred time slots or favorite shows, preferred content (comedy, mystery, sports), preferences for cable or a satellite dish and something about commercials. *Be sure to use open-ended questions that require more than yes/no or one-word responses.* (Look back at the Lady Gaga example.)

2. Remember: Unstructured interviews are "conversations" with a main question and follow-up questions. You only provide "direction," and the respondent provides "content." For example, don't suggest answers or respond to comments (e.g., *don't* say, "I like that, too," or "that's good").

3. Prepare a short introduction about the project. Read aloud or paraphrase this introduction at the beginning of each interview. Mention sponsor, purpose of the study, voluntary nature and confidentiality. And thank the respondent. Remember to use "everyday" language and avoid jargon. It is a good idea to have a classmate or your instructor review your introduction before beginning the interviews.

4. For each interview, record identification information. *Be very careful to keep this information confidential.* No one but you should ever be able to connect a respondent's identity with what the person said during your interviews. Nor should anyone but you know whom you interviewed.

5. Using the following outline, write your interview form; make enough copies for each interview—

Interview number: _____ (Write this number at the top of each page of notes for each interview, and number each page after the first.)
Respondent: (first name or pseudonym, age, other relevant information)

Location:

Date:

Introduction:

Interview: (use "I" for Interviewer and "R" for Respondent). Insofar as possible, keep a word-for-word record of respondents' answers and comments, especially their key points (you can use common abbreviations/symbols such as: &, @, tv, ads, am/pm, texting shorthand...).

Write a short statement summarizing your findings for Decision Resources, Inc. Include (a) a summary of respondents' TV viewing preferences, (b) an evaluation of whether there are noticeable differences in TV preferences by age and, if so, (c) a few sentences describing the main differences between young and middle-age respondents.

Note: One strategy for analyzing your notes is to photocopy them and cut the *copies* into parts, one for each comment made by a respondent. First, write the age group on your summary of each comment made by each respondent, so that you can identify the age group of each comment after cutting them apart. Or, you can enter your notes into a word-processing program or spreadsheet. *Again, be very careful not to associate any respondent's true identity with the notes you enter.* Then, for each idea, sort the notes into two stacks, one for young respondents and one for older respondents. This permits you to make comparisons between age groups. You might sort the notes more than once, depending on the idea you are analyzing.

6. Summarize what you learned from the pilot study that could be implemented in a larger study using unstructured interviews.

Exercise 6. Skills Building: Semistructured Interviewing

Directions: Decision Resources, Inc., has offered you a small contract to work on a larger study (see Exercise 5). If you are a new hire, welcome! In either case, your task is to prepare and conduct *semistructured interviews.*

Before beginning this exercise, review carefully the Code of Ethics forms in Appendix A. If you do not understand any of the ethical expectations, check with your instructor before proceeding with the exercise.

Be prepared to hand in your original completed interview guides for the four interviews. Don't rewrite these unless your instructor requests you to.

1. Write a sequence of six to eight questions with probes for a semistructured interview If you completed Exercise 5, base these questions on responses you got during those interviews. Otherwise review the directions to Exercise 5.

2. Next, select four persons, two aged 19 to 25 and two aged 40 to 60 (but not the respondents of Exercise 5). Interview these four people using your semistructured interview guide. Write the *exact words* of the respondent next to your list of questions and probes.

   Respondent: (first name, age, other relevant information)

   Location:

   Date:

   Interview: (use "I" for Interviewer, "R" for Respondent, and "P" for probe). Insofar as possible, keep a word-for-word record of respondents' answers and comments, especially their key points (can use common abbreviations/symbols such as: &, @, tv, ads, am/pm ....).

   Introduction: (revise your Introduction from Exercise 5, if needed)

3. Briefly summarize your findings.

4. If you completed both types of interviews, compare the strengths and limitations of unstructured and semistructured interviewing. If not, describe the strengths and limitations of the semistructured format.

Questions

1. Which survey type is used to collect PSID data? Briefly mention two or three details about ISR's data collection facility that the video shows.

2. Why are potential PSID interviewers brought to "a central location," the ISR?

3. How does field researcher Lorraine Kelley say she is able to keep her respondents in the PSID over time, given that, as she admits, "people (respondents) get tired" of doing the survey?

4. "Panel study" research follows the same individuals over time, surveying them at least twice. Why does the video say panel data are so important in understanding key social issues such as whether or not people's earnings consistently increase over time? Be sure to mention the importance of collecting intergenerational data.

5. What do PSID data reveal as a highly important predictor of one's future economic status? Is this finding consistent with, or in opposition to, common beliefs of Americans? Briefly discuss why only the PSID data have been able to provide this information.

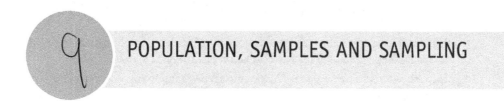

POPULATION, SAMPLES AND SAMPLING

INTRODUCTION: LOOKING AT HOW THE SOCIAL WORLD WORKS

Suppose you read the following headline in your local newspaper: "Research finds the U.S. public increasingly approves of the changing role of women from home-maker to labor market participant." Would you want to know more about the details of the research, such as who provided the views that represent the "U.S. public"?

A Sampling Riddle

As you read the excerpt, jot down in your own words what you think is the authors' main point and their justification of it.

Excerpt: *Attitudes toward Women in Paid Employment*

> A fundamental and profound shift in public expectations of women's roles at work and at home has been well documented....
>
> Despite minor misgivings..., Americans seem generally sanguine [optimistic] about the broadening of women's roles from the home to the workplace and beyond. (Huddy, Neely, & Lafay, 2000, p. 309)

How is this finding justified or documented? It wasn't a question asked on the U.S. Census, which attempts to query every U.S. citizen. So if no one has obtained information from *all* citizens about attitudes toward women's roles, can changes in attitudes be "well documented"? The information was obtained from a sample, and sample sizes seldom exceed 2000—to describe some 215 million adults. How can the results from so few generalize to so many? This is the main sampling riddle for the remainder of the chapter.

Goals of This Chapter

The primary goal of this chapter is to answer the "sampling riddle." The answer is closely related to several additional "little mysteries":

  ■ Why not just study everyone (take a census) to correctly describe a population?

- How is it possible to say anything about how much a sample differs from its corresponding population using information just from the sample?

- How big a sample size is needed? Does the needed sample size depend on the size of its population?

- What is the difference between a "probability sample" like the one used in the above study by Huddy and his coauthors and a "haphazard sample"?

- Why is a probability sample preferred? When can a haphazard sample be justified?

After reading this chapter carefully, you should know the answers to these questions. This chapter begins with the first little mystery—why not just study everyone?

WHY NOT STUDY EVERYONE?

In many instances, testing destroys the tested items, for example, testing light bulbs to find out their expected lifetime. Frito-Lay, the snack-food people who bring us "Wavy Lay's" potato chips and other goodies, can't check every single potato that growers might wish to sell to them. There are too many potatoes to test, and it would be prohibitively expensive. They need to take samples of the potatoes.

A *census* is a complete count of a population. Because the Constitution mandates a census of the U.S. population every 10 years, the federal government tries to count every citizen. On April 17, 2013, the website of the Census Bureau estimated the U.S. population to be 315,692,101 persons (*http://www.census.gov*). The 2010 U.S. Census cost the government $14 billion (Groves, 2010). If we had to pay this much for a survey, the decennial census might be the only survey ever done!

The U.S. Census is a major operation. Every household in the country must be listed. Every institution that houses people must be identified such as prisons, nursing homes, children's homes and mental hospitals. Then there are homeless people who do not live in any dwelling but by law must be counted. Next, the data must be collected, then computer processed and then distributed to the many individuals, agencies and businesses that make use of census data. When there are over 315 million entries, every seemingly minor operation truly is a massive undertaking.

The question, "Why take a sample instead of a complete count?" answers itself, for people, potatoes and many other items (although the reasons differ). In the case of survey research, usually the choice is between selecting a sample and doing no study, because money and time costs nearly always rule out a complete count. Of course, not all populations are as large as the entire U.S. population. Even for your hometown, surveying all persons generally exceeds a reasonable budget. Consequently, nearly all surveys are based on samples rather than on a census.

The next sections of the chapter review basic concepts about drawing correct conclusions from sample data (inference). *Statistical inference* means to estimate population numbers using numbers calculated from a sample. For example, we might sample U.S. residents to estimate the percentage of the U.S. population who stream video of TV shows and movies from the Internet, who get an annual checkup from a health care provider, or who are looking for a new job.

The final sections of the chapter summarize different types of sampling methods and draw important distinction between a probability sample and a nonprobability sample.

BASIC CONCEPTS

In sampling language, **element** refers to the objects to be described, such as people, families, cities, magazine ads and so forth. And in qualitative research, elements might be social interactions.

A **population** is a collection of elements. And a **sample** consists of some, but not all, of the elements in a population. The population for a study is defined according to the goals of the study and often is restricted by practical limitations. Many survey populations are limited to "all U.S. civilian adults, 18 years old and older, living in the continental U.S. and not living in an institution."

There are two major types of samples: a *probability sample* and a *nonprobability sample*. For a **probability sample**, each element in its population has a known, non-zero probability (chance) of selection into the sample. For example, suppose there are 30 students in your class. Your instructor writes each student's name on a separate piece of paper, places the paper slips in a hat, thoroughly mixes the slips and pulls one out. That person gets to answer the next question posed by the instructor. What's the chance your name is drawn?

Of course, your chance is 1 in 30—a known probability of being selected that is greater than zero, and it is known for every student. This type of probability sample is called a **simple random sample (SRS)**. With an SRS, each element has the *same known chance of selection and so does each possible combination of elements*. For example, if the teacher draws two names from the hat, every *pair* of students has the same chance of selection. There are several other types of probability samples described later in the chapter.

Probability samples are drawn to calculate a **sample statistic** to estimate the corresponding *population* number, called a **population parameter**. Figure 1 provides examples of population parameters and sample statistics.

Sampling error is the difference between a statistic calculated from a sample and its equivalent population parameter. An example is the difference between an average fish weight for a sample (the sample statistic) from an aquarium, and the average weight of all fish in the aquarium (the population parameter). **Sampling variability** is the variation among samples from the same population. Of course, in practice, only one sample is taken. You have to imagine what *would* happen if many samples were drawn in order to understand the idea of sampling variability.

Population: collection of all elements

Population parameter: Examples include:
- the mean of a population (e.g., average fish weight for all fish in a population, such as in an aquarium)
- average family size, (e.g. for the U.S. adult population)
- the population percentage (or proportion), such as the percentage (or proportion) with a college degree
- the difference between group averages in a population (e.g. mean hourly wage of people with an without a college degree).

Sample: some (but not all) of the elements in a population

Sample statistic: Examples include:
- the sample mean (e.g. average fish weight of a sample)
- the sample percentage (or proportion) who are female/male
- the difference between two groups (e.g. sample hourly wage of adults with college/no college degree).

FIGURE 1   Population and Sample: Definitions and Examples.

A probability sample requires **a sampling frame**—a list of each element in the population. A sample is drawn from this list. *Every element in a given population must be listed, and listed only once.* For example, a roster of your methods class should list only once each student enrolled in the course, and not omit any enrolled student.

Creating an accurate sample frame usually is difficult. Often some elements are missing—homeless persons in a city, for example. Also, people move, people get married and divorced, some go to college and come home for the summer, and lists aren't necessarily updated.

In short, if one wishes to generalize information from a sample to its population, generally a probability sample is needed. But as we'll see in this chapter, sometimes a probability sample simply isn't possible, such as for homeless people, people in "secret" relationships and others such as illegal drug users.

SIX BEAUTIFUL FISH AND THE SAMPLING DISTRIBUTION

First, consider drawing samples of fish from a small fish bowl containing just six fish. In this instance, the population is very small, so it would be easy to just include them all. But we want to illustrate the way sampling works, and that is much easier with a small population (Figure 2).

Table 1 shows a list of the six fish by name, weight of each fish, average weight and the standard deviation of the weights of all six fish.

Imagine that each student in the class goes fishing and catches two fish, producing a sample with $n = 2$. For this experiment, the second fish in each sample must be drawn *before* replacing the first fish. Next each student weighs the two fish and quickly puts them back in the bowl (this is a catch-and-release fishing trip). The next step is to calculate and record the average weight for the two fish.

FIGURE 2 Population of Six Beautiful Fish.

Finally, combine all two-fish average weights and calculate an average of those means—that is, add up all sample average weights and divide by the number of samples.

Likely some of the samples are duplicates of each other, that is, contain the same two fish. If the class is larger than 15 students, duplicate samples are guaranteed; there are just 15 different possible samples with this small population.[1] However, if we had obtained all possible unique two-fish samples (no duplicates), we could calculate the correct *mean of the sample means*. What number would that calculation produce? It would be 3.5 oz.—which is the population mean.

TABLE 1. Population List of the Six Beautiful Fish and Their Weights

Name	Weight (oz)
Goldie	5
OrangeMan	3
Blackie	2
YellowOne	4
BigOne	6
LittleBrother	1
Population Mean (average weight—known only if *all* fish are weighed)	3.5
Population Variance	2.917
Population Standard deviation	1.708

The distinction between the population mean and the mean of all possible sample means is critical. The fact that their numerical values are the same is due to the simple random sampling procedure. Not all sampling methods guarantee this equivalence. When the average of a sample statistic over all samples equals its corresponding population parameter, the statistic is **unbiased**. Let this distinction sink in a moment before reading on. It's fundamental to much of what follows.

Now look at Table 2, which shows all possible (unique) two-fish samples. Since the first fish was not put back before selecting the second fish, no sample contains the same fish twice. This procedure is called **sampling without replacement**.

TABLE 2. List of All Possible Fish Samples of Size $n = 2$

	Fish in Sample				
Sample	Fish 1	Wt.	Fish 2	Wt.	Average Weight for the Sample (oz)
1	Goldie	5	OrangeMan	3	$(5 + 3)/2 = 4.0$
2	Goldie	5	Blackie	2	$(5 + 2)/2 = 3.5$
3	Goldie	5	YellowOne	4	$(5 + 4)/2 = 4.5*$
4	Goldie	5	BigOne	6	$(5 + 6)/2 = 5.5*$
5	Goldie	5	LittleBrother	1	$(5 + 1)/2 = 3.0$
6	OrangeMan	3	Blackie	2	$(3 + 2)/2 = 2.5^†$
7	OrangeMan	3	YellowOne	4	$(3 + 4)/2 = 3.5$
8	OrangeMan	3	BigOne	6	$(3 + 6)/2 = 4.5*$
9	OrangeMan	3	LittleBrother	1	$(3 + 1)/2 = 2.0^†$
10	Blackie	2	YellowOne	4	$(2 + 4)/2 = 3.0$
11	Blackie	2	BigOne	6	$(2 + 6)/2 = 4.0$
12	Blackie	2	LittleBrother	1	$(2 + 1)/2 = 1.5^†$
13	YellowOne	4	BigOne	6	$(4 + 6)/2 = 5.0*$
14	YellowOne	4	LittleBrother	1	$(4 + 1)/2 = 2.5^†$
15	BigOne	6	LittleBrother	1	$(6 + 1)/2 = 3.5$
	Mean of the means (average of 15 sample means)				3.5
	Variance				1.167
	Standard deviation (standard error of the mean)				1.080

*Deviates from the population mean by more than 1/2 oz—positive difference.

†Deviates from the population mean by more than 1/2 oz—negative difference.

Count the number of mean fish weights less than 3 oz. *and* the number more than 4 oz. (±½ oz. from the population mean of 3.5 oz.). Altogether there are eight. Therefore, 8 of the 15 sample means have more than a half ounce *of sampling error*.

Why report every possible two-fish sample, as in Table 2? It is a step toward understanding the ideas of statistical tests for using sample information such as average fish weight to estimate the average weight of all six fish. In practice, only one sample is drawn. So use the two-fish samples in Table 2 to imagine what would happen if there were repeated samples in real research.

Statisticians are very clever. If they know the probability of selecting each population element from a population, they can figure out the distribution of a statistic. The list of each possible value of a sample statistic and its associated probability is called a **sampling distribution**. Table 3 shows the sampling distribution for all possible two-fish samples. Usually the sample size is designated by the lower-case letter *n*; so in this case ($n = 2$). Because of SRS (simple random sampling), each of these two-fish samples has the *same* chance of being selected.

TABLE 3. Sampling Distribution of Fish Mean Weights for Size $n = 2$

Mean wt (oz)	1.5	2.0	2.5	3.0	3.5	4.0	4.5	5.0	5.5
Probability of Mean									
Fraction	1/15	1/15	2/15	2/15	3/15	2/15	2/15	1/15	1/15
Decimal	0.067	0.067	0.133	0.133	0.200	0.133	0.133	0.067	0.067

In Table 3 the top row lists each of the nine possible average weights for two-fish samples from our six-fish population. For example, one sample average is 1.5 oz (Blackie and LittleBrother; see Table 2), another sample average is 2.0 oz (OrangeMan and LittleBrother) and so forth. The second and third rows give the probability, in fractions (which is exact), and in decimal form (which is rounded). Table 3 shows an example of *sampling variability*—variation among random sample means from the population mean.

So what have we learned about sampling from studying this contrived example? The example reveals several important principles about an SRS.

1. *As the distance increases (in either direction) between any sample mean and its population mean* (here, 3.5 oz.), *the number of samples with that specific sample mean declines.*

In Table 3, compare the number of samples with sample means at each end (or "tail") of the sampling distribution to the number of sample means at the *center* of the distribution. In Figure 3, Panel B shows a bar chart of this tendency to cluster in the middle for $n = 2$.

2. *An SRS provides unbiased statistics.* When the mean of all sample means equals the population mean, the sample mean is an **unbiased statistic**. That is, there is no tendency for samples to overestimate or underestimate the mean of that population. For our six fish, the mean of all sample means and the population mean are exactly the same—3.5 oz.

3. *When all possible samples are equally probable, as with an SRS, each element has an equal probability of being selected into a sample and so does each combination of elements.*

In Table 3, each individual fish appears five times in the list of 15 pairs. So, the probability of being selected for each fish is 5/15 = 1/3, or approximately 0.33. And each pair of fish also appears just once.

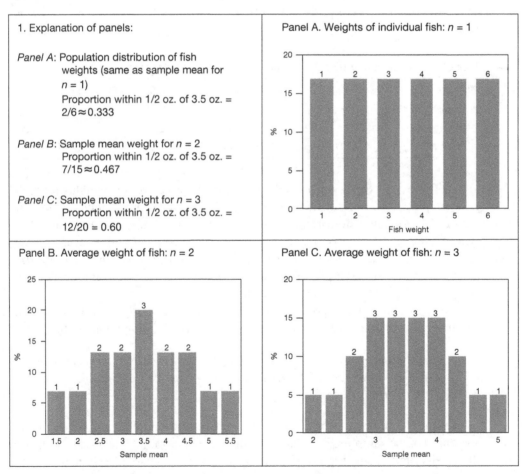

FIGURE 3   Bar Charts Showing Distributions of Fish Weights.

Sample Size Affects the Sampling Distribution

Figure 3 shows three bar charts. Panel A shows the distribution of fish weights for the population; there's just one fish at each weight. This distribution is flat—the probability for selecting each fish is the same for each fish as for each other fish. In contrast, the distribution of the means of the two-fish ($n = 2$) samples shown in panel B isn't flat; the sample means begin to cluster around the center of the distribution. This clustering is more pronounced for samples consisting of three fish ($n = 3$), shown in panel C. The upper-left panel of the table describes the other three panels. It also reports the proportion of sample means within ½ oz. of the true population mean, 3.5.

The general principle illustrated in Figure 3 is:

As the sample size increases, the mean sample fish weights cluster closer and closer around the population mean.

Variance and Standard Deviation

The variance and a closely related measure, the standard deviation, play a central role in how the sampling distribution is used to generalize the results from a sample statistic (e.g., sample average 2-fish weights) to its population parameter (in the fish example, the average fish weight is 3.5 ozs.).

Variance measures dispersion or "spread" of a set of numbers—how much the numbers differ from each other. Variance is defined as the average squared distance from the mean of a set of numbers. For example, imagine each fish weighs the same as the population mean of 3.5 oz. Therefore, each difference between the population mean and the weight of any one fish is zero. Thus, the variance also is zero.

But suppose the differences among the fish weights increase, so that Goldie's weight is 6 oz., rather than 5 oz., Blackie's weight is 1, instead of 2, and LittleBrother's weight is 0.25 oz, rather than 1 oz. The variance of this set of numbers now increases, because the variance is a number that summarizes these differences.

The **standard deviation** is just the square root of the variance. The square root brings the scale back toward the original scale. There are many possible measures of dispersion, but the standard deviation is by far the most important because of its use in generalizing from samples to populations.

The standard deviation can be calculated for any list of numbers. When the list is from a sample, the result is called a **sample standard deviation**. It summarizes differences among the numbers in a *single sample*. When the list is for an entire population, the result is called the **population standard deviation**, and it summarizes differences among the numbers in the entire *population*.

The standard deviation calculated for all possible sample means such as in Table 2, the result is called the **standard error** of the mean. It summarizes how much *sample means are scattered around the population mean*. An often-missed point about the standard error of the mean is that since the difference between each individual sample mean and its population mean is *one* instance of sampling error, the standard deviation calculated for *all sample means* summarizes sampling error. That's why it is called the standard error of the mean.

For the six fish, the population standard deviation is 1.708, and the variance is 2.917. Look back at Table 2 which lists the standard deviation and variance for samples with $n = 2$. They are standard error = 1.080 and variance = 1.167. For the samples with $n = 3$, the standard error and variance are 0.764 and 0.583. The following tabulation summarizes these results. Also, we can see that variation around the population mean declines as the sample size increases.

	Standard deviation (Standard Error)	Variance
Population	1.708	2.917
Sample, $n = 2$	1.080	1.167
Sample, $n = 3$	0.764	0.583

The Central Limit Theorem

As Table 2 illustrates, with just six fish in the population, it's fairly easy to list all 15 possible unique samples containing two fish and to calculate the probability of each one.

But think of an aquarium containing 100,000 fish. Suppose the new goal is to draw just *one sample of 100 fish* to estimate an average fish weight for all 100,000 fish. Say they are all the same species, so we are not "mixing apples and oranges." What is the sampling distribution for all possible sample means with $n = 100$?

Clearly, listing all possible 100-fish samples (or all their possible sample means) like we did for the six fish isn't feasible. Indeed, the number of possible $n=100$ samples is, for practical purposes, infinite. *Replacement* means returning each selected element to the population before drawing another sample. By using mathematical logic, statisticians have found an especially remarkable rule: the **central limit theorem**:

For an SRS (with replacement), as the sample size increases, the distribution of the sample means bunches in the middle to form a normal sampling distribution, regardless of the shape of the population distribution.

In addition, the mean of this sampling distribution is the same as the mean of the population, and the standard error equals the standard deviation of the population, divided by the square root of the sample size. These two relationships do not depend on the central limit theorem, however. But they do depend on simple random sampling.

In Figure 3, we see "bunching" in the middle of the sampling distribution beginning to happen with the fish example, starting with $n = 2$ and a little more bunching with $n = 3$. And the calculations of the mean and standard errors turn out exactly right. That is, the mean of the sample means equals the population mean, and the standard errors decline with increasing sample size like they are supposed to do.[2]

This happened using a population with a perfectly flat distribution—quite different than a normal distribution. Even with a flat distribution, if $n = 30$ fish in a sample, the distribution of the mean would look very much like a normal distribution.

Of course, with a population size of just 6, it is impossible to draw a sample of $n = 30$ unless the sampling is done with replacement—each fish is put back into the fish bowl before the next one is caught. An equivalent way to think about this is to toss a fair die 30 times and calculate the average of the numbers from the 30 tosses.

Let's look briefly at sampling distributions. The **normal distribution** is symmetric around its highest point, which also is its mean. The vertical axis is proportional to the probability (chance) of obtaining a given value listed on the horizontal axis—but *which* normal sampling distribution? There are an infinite number of normal distributions, one for each possible pair of mean and standard deviation.

One particular normal distribution is used extensively—the **standard normal distribution**. It is defined as a distribution with mean = 0.0 and standard deviation (and variance) = 1.0. Figure 4 below shows two plots of the standard normal distribution.

To convert any variable to standardized form (so its mean is 0 and standard deviation is 1), *subtract the sample mean score from each individual value (e.g., subtract 3.5 ozs. from the weight of each individual fish) and divide the result by the standard deviation* (e.g., of fish weights). The result is called a **standard score** (or *z*-score because it often is denoted by the letter *z*). Why should variables be standardized? Comparisons can be made with variables measured on different scales, such as age (measured in years) and income (measured in dollars).

Many variables in everyday life, such as heights and weights of people, conform approximately to the normal distribution. Also, tests such as SAT scores or attitude scores based on the sum or mean of many indicator questions tend to be distributed according to the normal curve. Since tests and attitude scores are constructed as sums or means, their normal distribution is almost built in to their definition. The central limit theorem strongly indicates they are normally distributed.

Not all statistics generate a normal sampling distribution. However, the sample mean is one that does so. There are many other distributions to handle a variety of statistics. The *t*-distribution is used when the sample standard deviation is substituted for the population standard deviation.

Table 4 summarizes the sampling distribution terms we've discussed.

TABLE 4.   Summary of Sampling Distribution Terms

Sampling Distribution	List of each possible value of a sample statistic from a population and its associated probability (keeping sample size constant)
Central limit Theorem	For an SRS with replacement, as the sample size increases, the sampling distribution of the sample mean bunches in the middle to form a normal distribution, *no matter* the shape of the population distribution
Normal Sampling Distribution	A specific sampling distribution that is symmetric around the mean of the distribution, sometimes informally called the "bell-shaped curve," but there are many distributions that *look* bell-shaped
Standard Normal Distribution	One specific normal distribution with a mean = 0 and a standard deviation (and variance) = 1.0
Standard Error	Standard deviation of a sample statistics such as the sample mean over repeated samples
Sampling Variance	Square of the standard error
Sampling Variability or Variation	An informal term referring to differences among values of a sample statistic such as the mean in repeated samples. The standard error and sampling variance are specific measures of sampling variability.

Applying the Sampling Distribution to Hypothesis Tests

How can we know how much a sample differs from its population using information from only the sample?

The short answer is this: *With a probability sample, the sample mean and standard deviation can be used as "stand-ins" for the (unknown) population mean and standard deviation.* Thus, an estimate of the entire sampling distribution—each possible value of a sample statistic of a population and its probability—can be calculated, *if* we wanted to. In practice, however, the calculations are used as the basis of hypothesis tests and confidence intervals. It's not necessary to estimate the entire sampling distribution.

Suppose you don't know whether men or women have more favorable attitudes toward the goal of economic, social and political equality for women and men (women's movement), but you don't think they are the same. So you hypothesize as follows:

The percentage of women who report favorable attitudes toward the women's movement is not the same as the percentage of men who report favorable attitudes.

This hypothesis is an example of a **research hypothesis.** Since the research hypothesis doesn't say whether men or women have a more favorable attitude toward the women's movement, it is *nondirectional*. It is just the opposite of the **null hypothesis,** which is stated as "no difference."

No difference by gender in attitudes toward the women's movement.

TABLE 5.   Percentage "Very Favorable" or "Mostly Favorable" to the Women's Movement, by Gender and Year

Year	Women	Men	Total
1991	77.5	73.9	75.7
(*n*)	(936)	(932)	(1868)
1995	81.6	74.5	79.4
(*n*)	(831)	(368)	(1199)
1998	72.8	73.9	73.4
(*n*)	(556)	(541)	(1097)

Source: Data from Huddy, Neely and Lafay 2000, p. 221, with "don't know" responses omitted. The rows designated *n* give the sample sizes

In this example, the sample statistic to test the null hypothesis is the percentage *difference* between women and men who support the women's movement.

Table 5 shows data for three years. It contains the information needed to calculate percentage differences between the genders for each year. Each difference is an estimate obtained from its sample of the gender difference in the U.S. population for that year.

None of these sample differences is exactly zero—but this does not necessarily mean none of the population differences is zero. A statistical test helps decide whether the difference between women and men in the sample is *large enough that it unlikely is due to sampling error*. A calculated probability called a *p*-value estimates the chance of finding a difference in a sample at least as large as the observed sample difference, *if* the population difference were zero.

However, the *p*-value never is exactly zero. Therefore, it is necessary to specify a threshold—how small must the *p*-value be to reject the null hypothesis and thereby support the research hypothesis that women and men do, in fact, differ. Rejecting the null hypothesis supports the research hypothesis, but does not "prove" it. When the null hypothesis is rejected, we say the difference is **statistically significant.**

Statistically significant is *not* the same as real-life importance. A very small sample difference may be statistically significant if calculated from a very large sample but be entirely meaningless otherwise. For example, with a sample size of 20,000, a $0.04 per hour difference between two groups probably is statistically significant, but it is so small we don't care.

The threshold for rejecting the null hypothesis is called the **level of significance.** The most commonly used level of significance in social research is 0.05 (5 in 100). The calculated *p*-values for Table 5 are as follows:

1991: difference = 77.5–73.9 = 3.6; $p = 0.075$

1995: difference = 81.6–74.5 = 7.1; $p = 0.007$

1998: difference = 72.8–73.9 = −1.1; $p = 0.682$

Only one of these *p*-values is below the level of significance, 0.05. Therefore, the null hypothesis of "no difference between genders" is rejected for 1995, but not for 1991 or 1998. In general, this type of procedure is called a **statistical test, or, sometimes, a test of statistical significance.**

The test for a nondirectional research hypothesis is called a **two-tailed test.** Recall from earlier discussion that the left and right ends of a sampling distribution are called "tails." With a two-tailed test, the probability for the level of significance is split between the left and right tails, as illustrated in the left-hand panel of Figure 4. That is, a large difference in *either direction* leads to rejecting the null hypothesis. One-half of the level of significance, $p < 0.05$, is allocated to negative differences (left tail) and the other half to positive differences (right tail). So the area under the curve in each tail for this case is $0.05/2 = 0.025$.

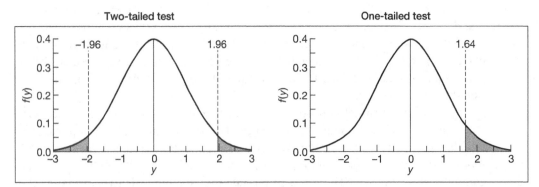

FIGURE 4   Standard Normal Distributions with Shaded Areas Corresponding to Probability of 0.05, Two-Tailed and One-Tailed Tests.

A directional hypothesis seems natural for gender differences in attitudes toward the women's movement:

Women are more likely than men to report favorable attitudes toward the women's movement.

The null hypothesis now is directional:

Women are no more likely than men to approve the women's movement.

But now the null hypothesis will be rejected only if the sample percentage of women with favorable attitudes exceeds the sample percentage of men by a large enough difference that it is unlikely due to sampling error. Now the entire level of significance is allocated to the *right tail* of the sampling distribution, as shown in the right-hand panel of Figure 4, and the statistical test is called a **one-tailed test.**

Reallocation of the level of significance to one tail of the sampling distribution changes the probability calculations. The revised calculations for Table 5 are given here:

1991: difference = 77.5–73.9 = 3.6; $p = 0.038$

1995: difference = 81.6–74.5 = 7.1; $p = 0.003$

1998: difference = 72.8–73.9 = –1.1;

The numbers above the dotted lines in Figure 4 are the z-scores corresponding to the level of significance. For example, the –1.96 above the left tail in the left panel is the value of the standard normal distribution below which 2½ percent of the distribution lies.

With a one-tailed test and level of significance of $p < 0.05$, the null hypothesis is rejected for 1991 and 1995, but still not for 1998. Why not? The direction of difference is wrong for 1998—the percentage of women favoring the women's movement is slightly less than the percentage of men favoring the movement. Therefore, we do not need to calculate a p-value.

That the null hypothesis is not rejected for 1991 using a two-tailed test—but is rejected using a one-tailed test—illustrates the additional statistical power of a one-tailed test.

Applying the Sampling Distribution to Confidence Intervals

How *can* we know how much a sample statistic differs from its population parameter using information from just the sample? With a probability sample, the sample mean and standard deviation can be used as "stand-ins" for the (unknown) population mean and standard deviation. The calculations are used as the basis of hypothesis tests and confidence intervals.

Probably the most natural way to summarize the size of sampling error is to report a pair of numbers. The numbers are a *lower boundary* and *upper boundary*, along with a probability that the unknown population value lies between the two boundaries. The pair of numbers is a **confidence interval.** The greater the difference between the pair of numbers, the less precise the sample estimate of the population value. Larger samples shrink the confidence interval and thus improve the precision of the sample estimate.

The confidence interval includes an associated p-value (probability) that the population parameter is between the two numbers. The **p-value** is called the **level of confidence** and is selected in advance of the study. Often the level of confidence is expressed as a percentage, such as a 95 or 99 percent level of confidence.

Note that the 95 percent level of confidence corresponds to the 0.05 level of significance for a two-tailed test. The 95 percent confidence intervals for the percentage of males in the population calculated from the data in Table 5 are given here:

		95% Confidence Intervals	
Year	Percentage Male (Sample Data)	Lower Interval Boundary (%)	Upper Interval Boundary (%)
1991	49.89	47.62	52.16
1995	30.69	28.08	33.31
1998	49.32	46.35	52.28

For 1991, the probability is 0.95 that the correct percentage of males in the population is between 47.62 percent and 52.16 percent. For 1995, the probability is 0.95 that the correct percentage of males is between 28.08 percent and 33.31 percent. In 1998, the boundaries are 46.35 percent and 52.28 percent.[3]

The confidence intervals for 1991 and 1998 do contain the known correct percentage of the population that is male (about 49.1%). But the interval for 1995 is way off the mark, suggesting some abnormality in sampling methods for that year.

The lower and upper limits of a confidence interval convey a sense of the *precision* of the sample statistic in estimating the population percentage in a way not indicated by a statistical test. It contains more information than a statistical test does. Nonetheless, most ongoing research relies primarily on statistical tests but also usually reports standard errors which are a pretty close substitute for confidence intervals and don't take up so much space in a table.

Notice that there is a wider confidence interval for 1995 ($33.31 - 28.08 = 5.23\%$) than for 1991 ($52.16 - 47.62 = 4.54\%$). Why do the intervals differ between the two years? Look at sample sizes in Table 5. The size of the 1991 sample is $n = 1,868$, but only $n = 1,199$ in 1995, illustrating the point that *the larger the sample size, the narrower the confidence interval.*

In summary, with a probability sample, the sample mean and standard deviation can be used as "stand-ins" for the (unknown) population mean and standard deviation.

Now we need to know *how big a sample is needed?*

How Big a Sample Is Needed?

If a small sampling error is required, a large sample is needed. But before a sample size can be found, one must decide the size of the sampling error acceptable for the statistical tests and/or confidence intervals of a project. Table 6 shows the sample size needed when the population percentage for a variable is 50 percent (e.g., 50% of all people in a population have ever tried fishing). It displays confidence intervals for sample sizes between ($n = 100$) and ($n = 2,000$).

TABLE 6. Ninety-five percent Confidence Intervals for Sample Sizes When the Population Percent = 50 percent

Sample Size (*n*)	Lower Bound (%)	Upper Bound (%)	Sampling Error (%)
100	40.20	59.80	9.80
200	43.07	56.93	6.93
1,000	46.90	53.10	3.10
1,500	47.47	52.53	2.53
2,000	47.81	52.19	2.19

The first row in Table 6 shows the 95 percent confidence interval for $n = 100$, meaning that the chance is 95 in 100 that the true percentage is somewhere between 40.20 and 59.80—probably not precise enough for most work. If $n = 2,000$, the 95 percent confidence interval narrows to 47.81 at the lower bound and 52.19 at the upper bound, noticeably better. The last column of Table 6, titled "Sampling Error" is just half the difference between the upper and lower boundaries.

You may be surprised that multiplying the sample size by 20 (100×20) does not reduce the width of the confidence interval more than indicated in Table 6. These numbers illustrate why sample sizes seldom exceed 1,000 or 2,000. The size of the sampling error does not go down as quickly as the sample size increases. For example, doubling the sample size from 100 to 200 does not halve the error: $6.93/9.8 = 0.7071$ (which is the square root of ½). And the ratio of the width of the confidence interval with $n = 100$ to the width for $n = 2000$ is $9.80/2.19 = 4.47 = \sqrt{20}$

Does Size of the Population Matter? Surprisingly, population size matters only if the sample size is a large proportion of the population and sampling is done without replacement, which is the case with the six-fish example (see endnote 2). For example, a probability sample of 1,000 adults gives essentially as good an estimate for the entire U.S. adult population (about 210 million) as it does for a small state like Delaware, with an adult population of about 600,000.

There is an important assumption, however: Variation from variables in a study (e.g., fish weights, people's attitudes, etc.) is roughly the same across relevant groups in the population. Take the case of approval ratings of a newly elected president. Variation in approval ratings is higher across the United States as a whole than in any single state because of well-known regional variations in political attitudes.

Table 7 summarizes some terms associated with generalizing the results from a sample to a population.

TABLE 7. Summary of Some Terms in Statistical Inference (Generalizing Information from a Sample to Its Population)

Hypothesis Test	Formal approach for using sample data to decide whether a specific hypothesis about a population number is correct.
	In social research, hypothesis tests usually are used to decide whether a relationship in a sample is large enough that it is a fair bet the variables are related in the population.
Null Hypothesis	Testable statement that a population parameter equals a specific value or lies in a specified range, for example, a difference is greater than zero. Often the null hypothesis states that the difference between two percentages or means is zero or no greater than zero, sometimes informally called the "no-difference" hypothesis.
Research Hypothesis	Usually opposite to the null hypothesis, generally the research hypothesis claims a relationship is not zero. In most cases it specifies the direction of the relationship.
Level of Significance	Prespecified probability associated with a statistical test. If the calculated probability is no larger than the level of significance, the null hypothesis is rejected. Usually this means the research hypothesis is supported.
Confidence Interval	Lower and upper boundary and an associated probability that a population parameter, such as a population mean or percentage, lies between the two boundaries. This probability is called the level of confidence.
Level of Confidence	Prespecified probability associated with a confidence interval. The most common level of confidence in social science is 0.95 (95%).

TYPES OF PROBABILITY AND NONPROBABILITY SAMPLES

Types of Probability Samples

Simple Random Sample (SRS). The simplest probability sample is the one we have considered up to now: a simple random sample (SRS). Recall from earlier discussion in this chapter that a simple random sample is a sample for which every possible sample of a given size has the *same chance, greater than zero, of being selected*. This implies that the chance of selecting every element is a constant. The example of a slip of paper for each of 30 students drawn from the professor's hat produces a simple random sample. Each student has the same 1/30 chance of selection. If two students are selected, every pair has the same chance of being selected. If three students are selected, every triplet has the same chance of selection.

Systematic Sample. Think of a listing of 100 students, alphabetized by their student ID number. To get a sample of 10 from the list, choose a random start 1 through 10 and take every 10th student thereafter. In general, select every kth person from the list, where k is the ratio of the population size (N) to the sample size (n): $k = N/n$, rounded down to a whole number.[4]

As with an SRS, every *element* of the population has the same chance of selection with systematic sampling. But, in contrast to an SRS, every sample of size *n* does not have the same chance of selection. Consider: If every 5th person is selected, person 1 will never appear in the same sample with person 2, for instance.

A systematic sampling scheme can work well for small samples. *But people must be listed in random order, meaning that you have to be careful how the list is arranged.* Suppose you are taking every 10th person, and the list is composed of couples, with the female always listed first, for example, take every 10th person who enters the building at the junior-senior prom. If the random start is with an odd number, all selections are female; if the start is an even number, all selections are male.

Stratified Sampling. Often, an SRS isn't possible. Consider a study of the relationship between cancer and church attendance. The research hypothesis is this: People currently fighting cancer attend church more frequently than people not fighting cancer.

Based on information from the National Cancer Institute (Weir, et al., 2002), an SRS of *n* = 500 from the adult U.S. population would contain two to three persons who currently have cancer, and they are likely to be 55 years old or older. Clearly, two persons with cancer aren't enough for any useful comparisons. Moreover, older people are more likely than younger people to have cancer *and* are more likely to attend religious services even if they don't have cancer. So the effects of age and religion are likely to be confounded.

This situation calls for a stratified sample. A **stratified sample** is one for which the population is divided into two or more groups, called strata (singular form is stratum), in a way that guarantees each element of the population fits into exactly one stratum.

For the church attendance/cancer study, two stratification variables are needed: age and cancer. These two variables are needed because both church attendance and cancer risk increase with age. We need to compare church attendance for those with cancer to those without cancer *within* each age group, thereby keeping age approximately constant. A stratified sample using this scheme and with *n* = 500 gives enough cases in each age category to permit the needed comparisons. Not all stratified samples require two stratification variables. Decisions about stratification are specific to each survey. Table 8 shows a schematic of this sampling scheme. There are 12 cells in the table, and 12 cannot divide into 500 an even number of times. The 42 cases per cell produce a sample size of 12 × 42 = 504. (42 cases per cell may not be sufficient for some comparisons, but it's a lot more than 2.)

TABLE 8.   Tabulation Showing Sample Sizes for Age and Cancer

Cancer	Age Group					
	20–29	30–39	40–49	50–59	60–69	≥70
No	42	42	42	42	42	42
Yes	42	42	42	42	42	42

Stratified sampling schemes are used routinely in complex surveys for two reasons: (1) to improve the accuracy of comparisons among strata compared to an SRS, as in the cancer and church attendance study, or (2) to improve the accuracy of sample estimates for the combined strata (two or more categories or strata). If the number of people sampled for each stratum is proportionate to the population size of each stratum, the stratified sample is at least as accurate as an SRS for estimating statistics for the entire population (not comparisons between strata), and usually is more accurate.

Cluster Sampling and Multistage Sampling. Imagine assembling a complete list of every person in New York City, or the state of California, or the entire United States. The task is impossibly costly and difficult. By the time such a list is complete—if it could be compiled at all—it's almost sure to be obsolete. The U.S. Census Bureau is required to compile such a list every 10 years. But it has resources far beyond what any other agency or institution ever has available. And still every census is fraught with controversy about undercounting.

For these reasons, nearly all surveys of large populations do not use individual persons as the **primary sampling unit (PSU)**. Examples of PSUs include households, city blocks, schools and school districts.

The idea of a **cluster sample** is to sample clusters rather than individuals. For example, the National Education Longitudinal Study (NELS) is a survey of students who were in the eighth grade in 1988 and followed every 2 years through 1994. The fourth follow up took place in 2000. NELS used schools as the primary sampling unit National Center for Education Statistics (NCES, 2013). If NELS had surveyed *every student in the selected schools*, the sample would be called a cluster sample, where a cluster consists of all students in each selected school.

Instead, NELS sampled just 24 students (plus an oversample of two or three Asian and Hispanic students within each selected school). Selection of a sample of schools was the first stage, and selection of a sample of students in each selected school was the second stage. Since a *sample of students in each school* was taken, rather than all students in each school, the NELS sample is a **multistage sample** specifically a two-stage sample.

What's the difference between a cluster sample and a stratified sample? A stratified sample is one that samples elements from *every* stratum; the strata are not sampled. A cluster sample is one that *samples clusters*, rather than taking all of them. This distinction may seem inconsequential, but it isn't. Stratified samples usually are more accurate than an SRS for a given sample size. But cluster and multistage samples usually are less accurate than an SRS.[5]

Types of Nonprobability Samples

Using samples to draw conclusions about populations relies on having a probability sample. In the real world of social research, real probability samples are rare. At best, samples are approximations to probability sample, strictly defined.

Nonetheless, the *principles* of probability sampling are important benchmarks for evaluating "real-world" samples.

In disaster research or for a study of homeless populations, for example, a probability sample is not feasible. There is no sampling frame (list of everybody in the population). But often nonprobability samples provide quite useful information, but they must be interpreted cautiously, as the following examples reveal. So if a probability sample is preferred, then when can a nonprobability sample be justified?

Quota Sample. Suppose your methods instructor assigns a project that requires groups in the class to collect data from undergraduates on the campus. This is the research hypothesis:

Married students are less likely than single students to engage in binge drinking.

Your group decides to interview 100 students. Because most students are not married, the decision is to interview 50 married and 50 single students, to ensure including enough married respondents. So far, this procedure sounds like a stratified sample, stratified by marital status. What's the difference?

With a **quota sample**, individuals within the "strata" *aren't sampled at random*. All that's required is to get a predetermined number of interviews from each of the strata. But without some caution, this procedure can lead to poor results.

Suppose, for example, your group decides to go to the local pub to do the interviews. You interview all 50 of your quota of single students and only two married students, because there were only two married students in the pub, both males. So the next night your group fans out and knocks on doors in the married student housing units. This strategy doesn't violate any rule of quota sampling. All that's required is 50 single and 50 married students. The result is overwhelming support for the hypothesis. But, wait—the difference between married and single students in this sample is seriously biased, favoring support of the hypothesis! Why?

Hopefully in practice, few quota samples are this extreme. But they do tend to underrepresent "reluctant" respondents. For example, in a telephone survey designed to learn about time spent on homework, just keep calling until you complete your 10 interviews with high school students. The potential for biased estimate of time spent on homework with this strategy is obvious. But it's a lot cheaper than repeated attempts to contact 10 specific respondents selected at random from a sampling frame.

Purposive Sample. Suppose you need information about drug use and AIDS risk. Could you identify a population of all drug users? A **purposive sample** often is selected to meet specific criteria. A purposive sample is justified for studies in which it is impossible to list all elements of the population or for very small samples, where random sampling error is likely to be unacceptably large, negating the benefit of a random selection process.

A study of an urban soup kitchen population describes risky behaviors and attitudes. The research team chose a kitchen that serves meals to food stamp recipients in the Manhattan section of New York City.

According to soup kitchen staff, about 60 percent of the clients are drug users or alcoholics. Majority of them are not in treatment and spend their days on the street. At night they live in shelters, sleep in subways and doorways, or stay with friends (Schilling, El-Bassel, & Gilbert, 1992, p. 353).

A primary task of the counselors working at the soup kitchen is referring clients with alcohol or drug problems to treatment and community services. The researchers relied on the counselors to refer clients to their study who had a history of drug use. Although the researchers used counselors as knowledgeable "experts" for identifying members of the sample, the study cannot be generalized in any precise way beyond the particular soup kitchen in the study. Whether the results generalize to other soup kitchens depends on informal judgment of those who read the study. Undoubtedly something valuable is learned by this type of work, but it is does not provide a solid basis, for example, to estimate the percentage of people who frequent soup kitchens who are drug addicts.

Theoretical Sample. In theoretical sampling, field researchers record observations about an event, look for patterns or regularities in the observations and often propose generalizations of the patterns observed in specific settings. The generalizations are used to develop theory.

Sometimes theoretical sampling is called "grounded theory," because the theory is derived from (grounded in) the observed behaviors of social life.

Snowball Sample. Another type of nonprobability sample is a **snowball sample.** The name loosely describes the strategy used to recruit participants. A few participants are used to locate others, who in turn provide additional leads, until the target sample size is reached.

The snowball procedure is particularly useful when the population cannot be defined in advance, but a few initial contacts can be located who fit the study criteria and who are willing to provide additional leads. The next excerpt is an interesting example of snowball sampling designed to study secret relationships.

Excerpt: *Secrecy and Status in Forbidden Sexual Relationships*

A feature of cross-sex secret, forbidden sexual relationships is that they are typically constructed between *status unequals*...(unequal by) age, class, or marital status....

The data come from intensive interviews with 65 single women who had or were having long-term (over a year) intimate relationships with married men....The frequently reinstituted "snowball" sampling procedure generated an extensive list of potential interviewees from a wide variety of social networks. After 48 interviews with a diverse set of women over a period of five years, saturation was experienced....

[T]wo stages of intimacy emerge: (1) exchanging secrets about the self or "Becoming Confidantes" and (2) creating mutual secrets or "Becoming a We." The man's marital status, reinforced by his gender and socioeconomic status, has major effects concerning time constraints, expectations of temporariness, and privacy. These lead to intense feelings, idealization, and trust, which enhance the woman's commitment to perpetuating the relationship. The relationship is perpetuated through the construction of mutual secrets (rituals and property), which are imbued with intense symbolic significance. The strategies used to conceal the relationship increase the woman's dependence on it and reduce her power within it. Secrecy protects the interests of the powerful. (Richardson, 1988, pp. 209–211)

When does snowball sampling end? It ends usually when all leads have been exhausted, a predetermined number of participants has been obtained, the pattern of findings suggests "saturation" (replication of information from respondents) or some combination of these situations.

As with all nonprobability samples, the findings properly apply only to the sample studied and not to a larger population, because there is no way to know the probability of selecting every eligible person. Also, observations in a snowball sample are dependent on each other; each interviewed person suggests whom to include next. Variation in these samples therefore likely is smaller than variation in the larger society.

Haphazard Sample. A **haphazard sample** (or **convenience sample**) is any sample that isn't a probability sample—the probability of selection of each element is not known. When little or no information is available on a topic, a nonprobability sample often provides invaluable information. The choice frequently is between a nonprobability sample and no sample.

Disaster research usually relies on nonprobability samples. It's impossible to construct a reliable sampling frame, list of all population elements, for studying people who just survived a disaster like a hurricane or flood, or the destruction of the World Trade Center in New York City. But avoiding research because a probability sample is impossible would result in many valuable insights lost. The alternative might be complete ignorance or reliance on rumors and speculation.

As nonprobability excerpts reveal, it is a rare sample that is of interest for its own sake. We nearly always intend some sort of generalization beyond a particular sample. But, a nonprobability sample is nearly certain to generate larger sampling error than a probability sample. Most of them probably also contain substantial bias. Kalton (1983) gives a succinct summary of the disadvantages of nonprobability sampling. He is particularly hard on quota samples.

On the other hand, as shown in this chapter, nonprobability samples often provide useful information that would not be available to purists who insist on a probability sample or nothing. So be skeptical of findings from nonprobability samples, but don't necessarily dismiss them.

SUMMARY

This chapter begins with a sampling riddle: *How can the results from one sample provide precise information about the larger population from which it was drawn, such as 100,000 fish in an aquarium, or to a large population like all U.S. residents, some 311 million people?*

Using statistical procedures to estimate "how close" the sample information is to the corresponding population information is called statistical inference. The idea of a sampling distribution is the foundation of statistical inference. To understand the concept of sampling distribution, you must imagine many repeated samples from a population. Of course, real-world studies almost never take more than one sample, *but understanding sampling distributions depends on imagining what would happen if repeated samples were taken.* That is the point of the example taking samples of two fish from the population of six fish. We studied what happens to the sample estimate of the average fish weight when repeated small samples of fish were drawn.

Sampling distributions describe how specific sample statistics, such as the sample mean (e.g., of the weights of two-fish), vary over repeated samples. One of the amazing results of sampling theory is that the entire sampling distribution of a sample mean, and many other statistics, can be estimated *using only one sample.*

The **normal sampling distribution** depends on just two numbers, the population mean and population standard deviation. Moreover, the *sample* mean and standard deviation can be used as "stand-ins" for an unknown population mean and standard deviation. Then, an estimate of the sampling distribution could be calculated. But, practical interest doesn't focus on the entire sampling distribution. Rather, the calculations are used as the basis of the two main types of statistical inference: hypothesis tests and confidence intervals.

A statistical test is used to see whether a sample difference is big enough so we are willing to bet it didn't arise by chance in the peculiar sample we have in hand. A statistical test starts with a null hypothesis that usually states there is no relationship between two or more variables in the population. The research hypothesis states there is a relationship. A probability called the p-value is calculated from sample data and compared to the level of significance, typically 0.05 or below. The p-value estimates the chance of finding a sample relationship equal to or greater than the relationship in the sample, *if* there were no relationship in the population? If the calculated p-value is at or below the level of significance, reject the null hypothesis, thereby (usually) supporting the research hypothesis.

If the sample relationship is statistically significant, then we make an implicit bet that there is a relationship in the population. But it is a bet, not a certainty!

A two-tailed hypothesis test is used when the research hypothesis indicates a relationship that isn't zero, but it doesn't state a direction for that relationship. Therefore, the p-value is split between the left and right tails of the sampling distribution (0.025 or less in each tail for $p \leq 0.05$). When a direction is indicated, the hypothesis test is a one-tailed test, and the p-value is concentrated in one tail of the sampling distribution, in the right tail if the hypothesized difference is positive and the left tail if it is negative.

A second method of statistical inference is called a confidence interval. A confidence interval presents a lower and an upper boundary, and an associated probability. The probability specifies the chance that the population parameter is in the interval between the lower and upper boundaries. The probability that the population parameter is within the specified interval is called the level of confidence.

A probability sample provides a known probability (chance) of selecting each element in the population, and the probability is greater than zero. A simple random sample is the most elementary probability sample. For an SRS, the probability of selection is the same for each element of the population and for each combination of elements, as the six-fish example illustrates.

A stratified sample is one in which the population is divided into two or more strata (groups). Each element in the population of interest fits into exactly one stratum, and elements are selected from *every* stratum. In a cluster sample, the population also is divided into groups, called clusters, so that each element fits into just one cluster. In contrast to a stratified sample, some, *but not all*, of the clusters are included in the sample; all elements in selected clusters are in the sample. In a multistage sample, elements are sampled within the clusters.

The difference between a stratified sample and a cluster sample is subtle. But it is very important. Usually, stratified samples give better sampling accuracy than an SRS of the same size, and an SRS generally produces better sampling accuracy than cluster samples of the same size.

Several types of nonprobability (or haphazard) samples are used in social research: quota, theoretical, snowball and purposive samples. Nonprobability samples are likely to contain bias, and even if they don't, we have no way to know that they don't. Consequently, generalizing from a sample to its population isn't, strictly speaking, justified. However, a probability sample often is nearly impossible to select. So the choice is between no information and some information—perhaps a lot of information from a nonprobability sample. Data from nonprobability samples obviously should be considered with caution, but should seldom be rejected as "worthless."

YOUR REVIEW SHEET

1. Why do we take a sample instead of a complete count? Explain in your own words.

2. Suppose there are 20 students in your research methods class. Your instructor writes each student's name on a separate piece of paper, places the paper slips in a hat, thoroughly mixes the slips and pulls one out. What is the probability (in fraction and decimal form) that your name is drawn? Show your calculations.

3. Define probability sample.

4. Distinguish between the terms *statistic* and *parameter*. Give an example of each.

5. Define sampling distribution. Explain why sampling distributions indicate the chance a sample statistic will be in error by as much or more than any specified amount.

6. What can be done to help ensure an accurate sampling frame? Consider both duplicate elements and omissions.

7. Define simple random sample, systematic sample, stratified sample and cluster sample.

8. Why choose stratified sampling? Mention two main reasons.

9. What is the difference between a "random" (probability) sample and a nonrandom sample?

10. Why is a probability sample preferred over a nonprobability sample? Summarize the shortcomings and strengths of nonprobability samples.

11. Although the soup kitchen study of drug risk provides a clear rationale for the sampling strategy and appropriate use of the counselors as knowledgeable persons, it is difficult to know how well the results generalize to the population. It's even difficult to define what the population is. Why?

12. In the fish example, why aren't there 15 different sample mean weights? There are 15 distinct samples.

13. Suppose the differences among the fish weights increase. What happens to the standard deviation and the variance? Why? What is the relationship between the standard deviation and the variance?

14. How can the central limit theorem help us if we need to know the population standard deviation before using it?

15. Does the needed sample size depend on the size of the population? Briefly explain.

END NOTES

1. If class size is much less than 15, each student should draw a couple of samples.

2. In most real-world situations, the population is so large that there is no practical difference between sampling with and without replacement. The rule given in the text for finding the standard error of the mean (divide the population standard deviation by the square root of the sample size) applies to sampling *with* replacement or to sample sizes that are a very small fraction of the population size. In the fish example, though, sampling was done *without* replacement and the sampling fraction is quite

large, $2/6 = 1/3$ for $n = 2$. The text formula has to be modified to take this into account. Define upper case N to mean the size of the population. Then to find the variance of the mean, multiply the population variance by $(N - n)/(N - 1)$ and divide by $n = 2$ to get the variance of the sample means: $(6 - 2)/(6 - 1) \times 2.917 \div 2 = (4/5) \times 2.917 \div 2 = 1.167$. The standard error of the mean is the square root of the variance: $\sqrt{1.167} = 1.080$. These numbers, calculated from the theoretical formulas, exactly match the numbers calculated from the data in Table 2.

3. More precisely, this means that for a very large number of samples, 95% of the confidence intervals calculated from them contain the true population value.

4. With a fractional k (e.g., $144/10 = 14.4$), one approach is to choose a random start between 1 and 144, increment by 14 and treat the list as circular until 10 units are selected. In this example, if the random start is 1 through 18 and you take every 14th person, you don't need to wrap around to the beginning of the list. For higher starting numbers you do. This is because $144/10 = 14.4$. Each selection falls 0.40 short of dividing the list into equal segments. Multiply this by ten selections $0.40 \times 10 = 4$, and $14 + 4 = 18$.

5. The accuracy of a stratified or cluster sample is measured by comparing the sampling variation for sample statistics like the mean or percentage to sampling variation of the same statistic calculated from an SRS.

Sample designs like stratified samples, cluster samples and multistage samples complicate the statistical analysis. Unbiased estimates of population parameters like the population mean reading score in the NELS, for example, require sampling weights. And correct estimates of p-values require specialized software.

STUDY TERMS

central limit theorem The distribution of the mean (or sum) of independent measurements all of the same distribution goes to the normal distribution as the number of cases increases, irrespective of the distribution of the individual measurements. An important application of the central limit distribution is to sampling. As the sample size increases, the distribution of the sample mean goes to the normal distribution. The mean of the samples over all samples equals the mean of the population, and the standard deviation of the samples over all samples equals the population standard deviation divided by the square root of the sample sizes. These latter two points are true by basic math and do not depend on the central limit theorem. But they are crucial to inference from samples to populations.

cluster sample *Groups* of individual *elements* (clusters) are sampled instead of individual elements. Each individual in selected clusters is included in the sample. Schools might form the clusters for a sample of students, for example.

confidence interval Numbers between a lower and upper boundary and an associated probability that a population parameter (e.g., a mean or percentage) lies between the boundaries. The probability is called the *level of confidence*. The boundaries are estimated from sample data, given a specified level of confidence.

element Objects comprising a *population* that you are describing. Examples of elements include people, families, households, cities, church congregations, cemetery markers, magazine advertisements and fish.

haphazard sample (or *convenience sample*) Any sample that isn't a probability sample. The probability of selection of the elements is unknown.

hypothesis test Procedure using sample data to decide whether a statement about the population is correct. In social research, hypothesis tests usually are used to decide whether a relationship from a sample is large enough that it is a fair bet the variables are related in the population.

level of confidence Prespecified probability associated with a confidence interval. The most common level of confidence is 0.95 (95%).

level of significance Prespecified probability stating the p-value required to reject the null hypothesis. The most commonly used level of significance is 0.05 (5 in 100). If the estimated probability from the data is smaller than the level of significance, reject the null hypothesis. Otherwise, do not reject it. Rejecting the null hypothesis generally supports the research hypothesis.

multistage sampling Sampling clusters and elements within clusters, for example, sample households within city blocks, people within households.

nonprobability sample A sample for which the probability of selection of each element is not known.

normal sampling distribution Sampling distribution that is symmetric around the mean of the distribution. It is defined by a specific mathematical formula. The normal distribution is "bell-shaped," but certainly not all bell-shaped curves fit the definition of a normal distribution.

null hypothesis Testable statement that a statistic for a population from which a sample was drawn equals a specific value. In social research, the null hypothesis (sometimes informally called the "no difference" hypothesis) usually states there is no relationship between the independent and dependent variables.

one-tailed test A hypothesis test of a relationship between variables in which the direction of the relationship is predicted in advance of the test. The entire probability of the level of significance is put in one tail of the sampling distribution rather than being split between the two tails. A one-tailed test gives more statistical power to reject a false null hypothesis.

population Collection of elements to be described—for example, all people comprising a religious group or all fish in a fish bowl—or elements of any other known collectivity.

population parameter (parameter) A number such as a percentage, mean or the difference between percentages describing the entire *population*.

primary sampling unit (PSU) A collection of elements, such as people or fish, to be sampled as a single unit. Examples of PSUs include households, city blocks and schools. In cluster sampling, PSUs are sampled rather than individual elements.

probability sample Sample for which the probability of selection is known and greater than zero for each element in a population.

purposive sample Nonprobability sample selected to meet specific criteria of a study, such as all drug users in a soup kitchen population.

p-value Estimate of the probability of observing a sample statistic with a greater deviation from the null hypothesis than the observed statistic if the null hypothesis were correct.

quota sample Nonprobability sample that takes a prespecified number of elements from each of several subgroups of the population (e.g., 100 male and 100 female, or 50 protestants and 50 Catholics). A quota sample differs from a stratified sample because the elements are selected informally by the researcher within each subgroup, but are selected by probability sampling with stratified sampling.

research hypothesis Usually opposite to the null hypothesis. In most instances, the research hypothesis states that there is a relationship; the null hypothesis states there is no relationship.

sample Some part of a population, generally selected with the idea of calculating a sample statistic to estimate the corresponding population parameter.

sample statistic Number calculated from a *sample*, such as the sample mean (average), sample percentage (or sample proportion), sample standard deviation or the difference between sample means or percentages for two groups.

sampling distribution List of each possible value of a sample statistic from a population and its associated probability, such as average weights from all possible two-fish samples in a population.

sampling error Difference between a sample statistic and population parameter when a sample is used to describe the population, for example, the difference between the average number of children in families in a sample of the U.S. population and the correct, but usually unknown, average in the entire population.

sampling frame Complete list of each element in the population. A sample is drawn from this list. Consequently, getting a probability sample depends on the list being complete, with no duplicate entries.

sampling variability Variation from sample to sample of a sample statistic such as the mean. A second two-fish average weight likely is not the same as the average of the first sample.

simple random sample (SRS) The most elementary probability sample; every possible sample of a given size has the same chance of being selected, implying that every element also has the same probability as every other element.

snowball sample Nonprobability sample obtained by relying on a few participants to identify other participants, who in turn provide additional leads, until the target sample size is reached.

standard deviation Measure of dispersion of a variable—how much the numbers differ from each other. The standard deviation is the square root of the variance. A *sample* standard deviation summarizes variation in a single sample. A *population* standard deviation summarizes variation in the population. The standard deviation of many samples of means is called the standard error of the mean. It measures variation from sample to sample of the sample mean.

standard error A special name given to the standard deviation when the numbers are a sample statistic such as a sample mean or proportion.

standard normal distribution Normal distribution with a mean = 0.0 and a standard deviation (and variance) = 1.0.

standard score (*z*-score) A variable transformed to ensure that it has a mean of zero and a standard deviation of one. Standard scores are obtained by subtracting the mean of the original variable from each value and dividing the result by the standard deviation of the original variable.

statistically significant Term used to describe a sample statistic whose *p*-value is less than or equal to the level of significance. Usually a finding of statistical significance supports the research hypothesis.

statistical test A procedure usually used to decide whether a sample relationship between variables is big enough to justify the conclusion that the relationship exists in the population.

stratified sample Sample taken by selecting elements from *each* of two or more groups called strata (singular form, stratum). The strata are defined so that each element fits into exactly one stratum. So strata define a variable used for a specific purpose of sampling. Compare/contrast to a cluster sample.

theoretical sample Nonprobability sample often used by field researchers who directly observe social events, often used to develop a theory to guide future research. Sometimes called "grounded theory," because the theory is derived from (grounded in) the observed behaviors of social life.

two-tailed test Statistical test for a nondirectional hypothesis. The probability associated with the level of significance is split between the right and left tails of the sampling distribution.

unbiased statistic Unbiased implies no systematic tendency to overestimate or underestimate the population parameter. It is a statistic whose mean over all possible samples equals the corresponding population parameter. For example, the mean of all possible sample means equals the mean of the population, as shown in the fish example.

variance Measure of how much the numbers in a list differ among themselves (dispersion). It is defined as the average squared distance from the mean.

EXERCISES

Exercise 1. Evaluation of Research: Nonprobability Sample

Directions: Refer to the excerpt on "secrecy and status in forbidden relationships" (Richardson study) in this chapter and answer the following questions.

Factual Questions

1. Describe the study participants. Why were these individuals selected?

2. How were initial participants located?

3. What evidence does the author give to suggest that the snowball procedure provided an adequate sample?

4. How does the author characterize the generalizability of the study? To what population (if any) do you think the results generalize? Briefly defend your answer.

Questions for Discussion

1. Briefly describe the sampling strategy in your own words.

2. Evaluate the usefulness of the sampling strategy to address the study topic. Are there other strategies that might be more useful? Why or why not?

3. How did the author decide to end sampling? Briefly discuss pros and cons of this approach.

Exercise 2. Skills Building: Taking an SRS (without Replacement).

Directions: Below is a list of the social science and natural science faculty at the small but prestigious AP University, located in the mythical state of North California.

Suppose you want to know whether social science (SS) or natural science (NS) faculty members are more likely to ask students questions during class lectures. You have resources to observe the classes of only a small number of faculty members, so you must rely on a sample.

(SS) Nadia Adams	(SS) Charles Criscione
(SS) Timothy Ames	(SS) AmyJo Domst
(SS) Nancy Ames	(SS) Joyce East
(NS) Denise Antosh	(NS) Ronald Ensign
(SS) Quinn Ardillo	(NS) Len Fenniello
(NS) Gordon Bak	(NS) Arlene Fintzel
(SS) Walther Barreca	(NS) Grace Germaine
(NS) Heath Battaglia	(NS) Lea Goo
(NS) Julia Belliotti	(NS) David Gora
(NS) Brian Benkelman	(NS) George Griffiths
(SS) Anita Bentham	(NS) James Huyck
(SS) Betty Berry	(NS) Vivian Johnson
(SS) Carol Bleecher	(SS) Robert Joseph
(SS) Fritz Bohlen	(NS) Margaret Krzal
(NS) Carolyn Boorady	(SS) Alexis Lagana
(NS) Nancy Benton	(SS) Gary Lanze
(SS) William Branicky	(NS) Sandy Liedke
(SS) Linda Brescia	(SS)Marcia Mackay
(SS) Glenn Cave	(SS) Anthony Maitland
(NS) Bonny Christner	(NS) Karen Paige

1. Assign a number to each member of the population of faculty. (Assign numbers down the columns.) How many faculty members are in this population?

2. Select a 20 percent SRS (without replacement) from this population. How many faculty members will be in the sample? Show your calculation.

Exercise 3. Skills Building: Stratified Random Sample

Directions: A stratified sample is one for which the population is divided into two or more groups, called strata, in a way that guarantees each person (or other element) fits into exactly one stratum. Part of the sample comes from *each* of the strata. The strata themselves are not sampled. For this exercise, the population is defined as all SS and NS faculty members. Faculty in other disciplines are excluded from this population.

1. Suppose you want to know whether SS or NS faculty members at AP University ask more questions of students during class lectures. You decide to sample an equal number of SS and NS faculty members. What is your stratification variable and what are its strata?

2. Sort the list into two lists, one for NS and one for SS. Number each consecutively starting at 1.

3. Using the random numbers table, take a 20 percent random sample of *each list separately*. You need to select two sets of numbers from the random numbers table. How many faculty members are in each sample? Write the names and numbers of selected faculty members in your stratified sample. This question has been intentionally omitted for this edition.

4. Looking at the faculty list of names, what potential problem might you have in trying to stratify by gender?

5. Suppose the sample size were large enough (and you could resolve the potential problem suggested by Question 4), how could you arrange the faculty list to stratify by science field *and* gender? How would you select the sample?

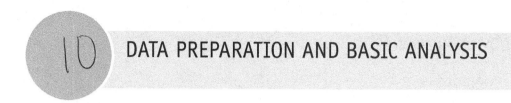

DATA PREPARATION AND BASIC ANALYSIS

INTRODUCTION: LOOKING AT HOW THE SOCIAL WORLD WORKS

What makes some people happier than other people? This chapter explores data analysis using a variable designed to reflect respondents' state of happiness. This chapter begins by examining the relationship between "happiness" and religion."

Then, the chapter reviews some of the basic aspects of data preparation and presentation.

Goals of This Chapter

This chapter discusses the need for *comparison* in research—and in everyday life. The first goal of this chapter is to show how to use tables to display a relationship between two variables.

A second goal of this chapter is to strengthen your skills for *evaluating competing claims* that you encounter daily, such as the belief in wearing a magnet to reduce carpal-tunnel pain. To help avoid jumping to (false) conclusions, a two-variable table is a useful "box" for helping to recognize the nature of claims.

A third goal is to *recognize what data are needed to make a persuasive case.* Unfortunately, most important questions can't be answered definitively with any data that conceivably could be obtained. At decision time, however, we just have to go with the best information we can locate and try not to fall into the "sticky-theory" trap.

A fourth goal of the chapter is to *introduce basic procedures of quantitative (numbers-based) data analysis.* Data analysis, whether qualitative or quantitative, can help in gaining an appreciation of the research process as a whole.

Finally, *understanding the basics of data analysis can help prepare you for graduate education in the social sciences and for employment in many professional jobs.* A growing number of jobs in public service agencies in city, state and federal governments, as well as private business of all types, require numbers-based research skills.

A STUDY OF HAPPINESS

Happiness

Almost by definition, a study of "happiness" has a certain basic interest. The General Social Survey (GSS), a large national survey about the attitudes, beliefs and behaviors of U.S. adults, includes the following question about happiness (Davis et al., 1972–2008):

Taken all together, how would you say things are these days—would you say that you are very happy, pretty happy, or not too happy?

The distribution of answers to this question is:

Very happy	32.9%	3445
Pretty happy	55.6	5828
Not too happy	11.5	1209
Don't know	—	8

NOTE: First column contains percentages; second column contains frequencies (number of cases) (Davis, Smith, 2007, p. 277). The frequencies and percentages are estimated using the GSS dataset sampling weight, *wtssall.* "Don't know" is excluded in subsequent tables. The data are from the five most recent GSS survey years: 2000, 2002, 2004, 2006 and 2008.

A recent article points out that "…numerous studies find religion to be closely related to life satisfaction and happiness" (Lim & Putnam, 2009, p. 914). Table 1 shows the relationship between religion and the GSS measure of happiness using combined data from the five most recent GSS surveys.

Table 1 shows that people who report no religion (column labeled "None") are *less* likely to say they are "Very Happy" than are those who report involvement with a religion. How do we read the table to know this?

TABLE 1. Happiness Percentages by Type of Religion

Happiness	Type of Religion					
	Protestant	**Catholic**	**Jew**	**Other**	**None**	**Total**
Not Too Happy	10.8	11.1	13.7	12.4	13.8	11.5
Happy	53.6	57.1	48.6	55.5	61.0	55.6
Very Happy	35.7	31.8	37.7	32.1	25.2	32.9
Total	100	100	100	100	100	100
(N)	(5,353)	(2,700)	(194)	(640)	(1,560)	(10,447)

Look across the columns within the row labeled "Very Happy." Compare the percentage 25.2 percent in the last column to all the other percentages in that row.

The 25.2 percent of those with no religion who say they are "Very Happy" is noticeably smaller than all the other percentages in the row. And the other percentages in the "Very Happy" row are similar to each other. So the GSS data support the finding about happiness and religion cited and replicated by Lim and Putnam.

The *dependent variable is placed first in the title, followed by the independent variable.* Although not all published tables follow this convention, it simplifies reading the tables and is used in this chapter. Therefore, *read the title of a table first.* If there is a **control variable**, it is stated last in the title.

Table 1a collapses the five religious categories into just two categories: Religion: (1) No, and (2) Yes. Similarly, the three categories of happiness are combined into just two: Very Happy: (1) No, and (2) Yes.

TABLE 1A. Happiness Percentages by Type of Religion (in a "2 x 2" Table)

Very Happy	Religion		
	No	Yes	Total
No	74.8	65.7	67.1
Yes	25.2	34.3	32.9
Total	100%	100%	100%
(**N**)	(1,560)	(8,887)	(10,447)

Table 1a is a "2 × 2 table"—meaning there are only *two rows* and *two columns.* The rows labeled "Total" and "(N)," and the column labeled "Total" are called "marginals" of the table. We will ignore them for now; marginals are discussed later in this chapter.

To read Table 1a, look across the columns and compare 25.2 percent to 34.3 percent. These percentages show that 34.3 percent of those with a religion say they are "Very Happy" compared to just 25.2 percent of those who have no religion, a difference of 9.1 percent.

Of course, we cannot tell whether people become happy because they are religious or happy people become religious because they are happy. This is the chicken-and-egg problem—which is cause and which is effect? Also we must still consider confounding variables—possible alternative explanations to happiness other than religion.

THE DATA MATRIX: TABLE FOR UNPROCESSED DATA

Data analysis starts with the **raw (unprocessed) data**, which is a listing of the value of every variable for every case. The data are represented in a two-dimensional table or matrix called the **data matrix**. The data matrix nearly always is stored electronically; it contains too much detail to be very informative by itself. However, it's important to understand its organization so you can effectively summarize it.

Data matrices come in an ever-increasing variety of formats. These include an Excel file, a comma- or tab-separated text file, a text file with no separators and proprietary formats used by statistical software (e.g., SAS, SPSS or Stata). Figure 1 shows an image of a small subsample of the GSS data stored in Excel. The names of the variables are listed in the first row, and there are 30 cases; therefore, the spreadsheet contains 31 rows. The variable names are those listed in the GSS documentation. Most statistical software can read an Excel file formatted in this way. The software automatically assigns the variable names appearing in the top row.

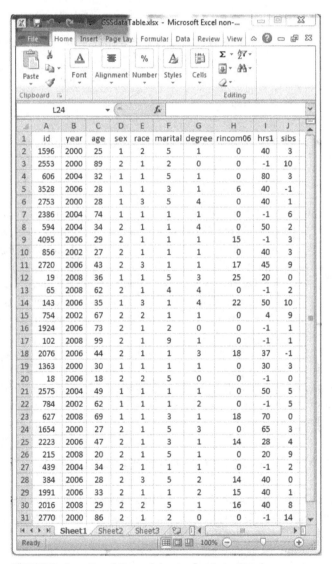

FIGURE 1 Excel Spreadsheet of a Data Matrix.

The Excel version of the data is comparatively easy to read and understand. One row per observation follows the header row containing the variable names, and one Excel column contains each variable. This is the standard format, but there are others. For example, data sometimes include multiple observations per person, one corresponding to each occasion when people were surveyed.

The most basic format of a data table is a text file with no separators, as shown in Table 2. The format is an efficient way to store data because it does not waste space. Large data collections such as the GSS still often are distributed in this format and other formats as well. Computer code can be written to read the data. The line/ruler at the top is not part of the data matrix. It is there to help you identify locations of the numbers.

TABLE 2.   ASCII Text Data Matrix

```
----+----1----+----2----+-
15962000251251 040 3
25532000892120 0-110
 6062004321151 080 3
35282006281131 640-1
27532000281354 040 1
23862004741111 0-1 6
 5942004342114 050 2
4095200629211115-1 3
 8562002272111 040 3
272020064323111745 9
  1920083611532520 0
  652008622144 0-1 2
 1432006351314225010
 7542002672211 0 4 9
19242006732120 0-1 1
 1022008992191 0-1 1
20762006442113183 7-1
13632000301111 030 3
  182006182250 0-1 0
25752004491111 050 5
 7842002621112 0-1 5
 62720086911311870 0
16542000272153 065 3
22232006472131142 8 4
 2152008202151 020 9
 4392004342111 0-1 2
 38420062823521440 0
19912006332112154 0 1
201620082922511640 8
27702000862120 0-114
```

In a data matrix stored as an ASCII text file with no separators, the term *column* has a special meaning. Unlike most other contexts, such as the Excel version of the data and printed tables, *a column in this style of a data matrix is just one character (number or letter) wide*. Any one-digit number takes just one column, any two-digit number requires two columns, and so on. A variable like gender represented by one-digit codes (e.g., 1 if the person is male and 2 if female) requires just one column. But a variable like age spans two or possibly even three columns in a text-file data matrix with no separators.

A *field* is a sequence of adjacent columns used to represent a single variable; a field is like a column in a spreadsheet or a printed table. A field may contain either numeric data, like age, weight, number of siblings, or "character data," such as a name, or comments from open-ended survey questions.

The data in Table 2 contain the same information, minus the variable names, as the Excel version shown in Figure 1. They both contain a subsample of the GSS data with 30 observations and 10 variables.

As in the Excel version of the data, the layout of the data matrix generally follows the format of Table 2. Each row of the matrix contains information for a different case, and each field (not column) represents a different variable. In the GSS dataset, each case is a person; therefore, each row of the data matrix contains a profile for one person. Cases also can consist of units like classrooms, schools, school districts, households and geographical units like states, cities or countries. For example, in a text file with no separators containing census data for U.S. cities, each row represents one city, and the field for population size spans eight columns.

The numbers in Table 2 and Figure 1 require a **codebook** to provide a key that defines the meaning of the numbers and codes, and their location (columns spanned) in the ASCII text version of the data with no separators. Figure 2 shows an abbreviated codebook for the GSS sample in Table 2. For each variable, the codebook gives a short variable name (*Variable*), identifies the field/columns spanned (*Columns*), includes a short description (*Label*) and defines the meaning of each value (*Values*). The values indicate meanings of valid responses and codes indicating a missing response. In this example, the id and year variables have no missing values, and, for example, 98 and 99 indicate missing data for age. Short variable names, like `age`, `sex`, `marital`...are used in statistical software to identify the values of the variable for all observations.

The variable names are those used in the GSS documentation. If you use variable names that do not match those in the original documentation, keep a log that includes the original variable names in case you need to check the information about a variable. If you do the work with statistical software, we strongly recommend using the variable names in the documentation. Create new variables with names that suit you. This makes your work self-documenting and makes it unnecessary to keep a log of variable names.

Variable	Columns	Label	Values
Id	1–4	Respondent ID number	ID number
Year	5–8	Year of the survey	4-digit year
Age	9–10	Respondent age	Age in years 98 = DK 99 = No answer
Sex	11	Respondent gender	1 = Male 2 = Female
Race	12	Respondent race	1 = White 2 = Black 3 = Other
Marital	13	Marital status	1 = Married 2 = Widowed 3 = Divorced 4 = Separated 5 = Never married 9 = No answer
Degree	14	Highest educational degree	1 = Less than HS 2 = HS grad 3 = Associat/Jr college 4 = BA 5 = Graduate degree 8 = DK 9 = No answer
Rincom06	15–16	Respondent annual income in 2006 dollars	1: < $1000 2: 1000–2999 3: 3000–3999 4: 4000–4999 5: 5000–5999 6: 6000–6999 7: 7000–7999 8: 8000–9999 9: 10000–12499 10: 12500–14999 11: 15000–17499 12: 17500–19999 13: 20000–22499 14: 22500–24999 15: 25000–29999 16: 30000–34999 17: 35000–39999 18: 40000–49999 19: 50000–59999 20: 60000–74999 21: 75000–89999 22: 90000–109999 23: 110000–129999 24: 130000–149999 25: 150000 or more 26: Refused 98: DK 0: N/A*
Hrs1	17–18	Hours worked last week, all jobs	Hours worked 98 = DK 99 = No answer
Sibs	19–20	Number of siblings	Number of siblings 98–DK 99 = No answer 0: N/A*

*rincom06 was included only for survey years 2006 and 2008

FIGURE 2   Codebook for Subsample of the GSS Data.

Coding the Data

Data coding refers to converting responses into codes (numeric or otherwise). For surveys with short questionnaires, closed-ended questions and a small sample of respondents, it's possible to print the codes directly on the questionnaires. Figure 3 shows an example of "edge coding." The researcher can look at the questionnaire to either prepare a data sheet or enter the data directly into a computer file such as an Excel spreadsheet.

```
┌─────────────────────────────────────────────┐
│  A. What is your gender (check one):         │
│         [  ] Female                    (1)   │
│         [  ] Male                      (2)   │
│  B. Do you consider yourself (check one):    │
│         [  ] Strong Republican         (1)   │
│         [  ] Weak Republican           (2)   │
│         [  ] Independent               (3)   │
│         [  ] Weak Democrat             (4)   │
│         [  ] Strong Democrat           (5)   │
│         [  ] No party identification   (9)   │
└─────────────────────────────────────────────┘
```

FIGURE 3   Portion of a Sample Questionnaire, with Edge Coding.

Cleaning the Data

Raw data sometimes are described as "clean" or "dirty." "Dirty" data contain errors such as incorrect reading of responses on a questionnaire, incorrect transcription of a personal interview comment, assigning a wrong code to a response category and other human errors. Suppose a completed questionnaire contains the following questions and responses:

Question 1: Do you ever drink alcoholic beverages?

[✓] No, never (total abstainer)

[ ] Yes

Question 2: Do you ever drink alcoholic beverages more than you think you should?

[ ] No

[✓] Yes (at least sometimes)

Clearly, the respondent provided inaccurate information for one of the two questions—but which is the correct answer? In the absence of other information, usually both answers would be considered incorrect.[1]

After coding the raw data, the data always contain coding errors. Therefore, whatever the method used to collect the data—audiotapes from personal interviews, mail surveys, personal interviews, coding sheets in content analysis—the coded data must be checked carefully for errors before proceeding to the next step. For example, if you have assigned a score of 1 for female and 2 for male and find a case with a score of 3 for gender, it's an obvious error.

If entering data using a computer program, the data should be entered twice, and the two files should be compared by a computer; although this double-entry step often is not followed in practice, it is essential and should not be skipped.[2] Summarize all data-cleaning procedures in the research report.

UNIVARIATE ANALYSIS

Suppose your supervisor asked you to summarize the findings of her survey that contains 50 questions and 200 respondents. How many numbers would you have to examine? The answer is, $200 \times 50 = 10,000$ different numbers. However, 200 respondents and 50 variables are much smaller than most survey datasets such as the GSS.

Consider this: The "happiness" study used GSS data containing 14,927 observations and 5,364 variables—80,068,428 numbers in total! Chances are high that you never would make much sense of it without simplification.

A few well-chosen statistics provide summaries of data that would be impossible to garner by looking at the raw data. Examination of one variable at a time is called **univariate analysis**. Examples of univariate statistics include percentages and frequencies, which can be calculated for any type of variable (nominal, ordinal, interval and ratio). Univariate summaries such as measures of the "center" of a distribution (e.g., mean, median and mode) and measures of dispersion (spread or scatter) around the center of a distribution (such as the standard deviation) apply to interval or ratio variables. The mode is suitable for any variable.

Univariate Frequencies and Percentages

For nominal and many ordinal variables, a **univariate frequency distribution** or **frequencies** is the most-often reported one-variable summary. Frequencies usually include the count (raw number) and percentage for each variable category, and often the cumulative frequencies and percentages. Sometimes, categories for numeric variables such as respondents' age are collapsed into fewer categories (e.g., age intervals 18–24, 25–39...) and summarized by counts and **percentage**.

Percentages are obtained by counting the number of cases in each category of a variable, dividing by the total number of cases, and multiplying by 100. The result is frequency "per 100" (or *relative frequency*).

Why use percentages? *Percentages are essential when comparisons are needed among groups with unequal counts of respondents.* The subsample of the GSS in Table 4a contains 11 men and 19 women. Seven men and 13 women reported they did not continue their education after high-school graduation, suggesting that women are much more likely to stop their education with a high school diploma than are men. Converting to percentages, however, suggests a small difference—percentage for men: $100 \times 7/11 = 63.6\%$, percentage for women: $100 \times 13/19 = 68.4\%$.

Table 3 shows two sets of frequencies and percentages from the data matrix of 30 cases in Figure 2, one set for the variable named `marital` and one for `degree`.

TABLE 3. Frequencies and Percentages from the GSS Dataset, Subsample of 30 Cases

Value	Marital	
	Frequency	Percentage
(1) Married	13	43.3
(2) Widowed	3	10.0
(3) Divorced	3	10.0
(4) Separated	1	3.3
(5) Never Married	9	30.0
(9) No Answer	1	3.3
	30	100

Value	Degree	
	Frequency	Percentage
(0) Less Than HS	4	13.3
(1) HS Grad	16	53.3
(2) Associate/ Jr. College	3	10.0
(3) BA	3	10.0
(4) Grad Degree	4	13.3
	30	100.0

Univariate frequencies are very useful, and they should be the first level of data analysis. For example, they can detect data errors, such as a code of "3" for gender, mentioned earlier. Therefore, before doing any other data analysis, check frequencies for each variable. For continuous variables such as age (with many unique values), check statistics such as the mean, median, mode and minimum and maximum values.

For every variable, check the minimum and maximum for values outside the valid range of the variable. In the GSS sample, for instance, if the maximum value of age is 99, it means you have not defined 99 to be missing. It should be defined as missing because 99 is the missing-data code.

Univariate Summaries for Numeric Data

For interval or ratio variables, univariate summaries include (1) **measures of central tendency** such as the mean, median and mode; and (2) **measures of dispersion** (or scatter), such as the standard deviation.

The most-often used measure of "center" of a distribution of values of a variable is the *mean*. It's the arithmetic average: Add up the values of one variable for all cases (e.g., all persons) and divide by the total number of cases.

Another measure of "center" is the *median*, the number that divides in half the distribution of values of a variable when the values are arranged in order, low to high. The median is particularly useful when a distribution is *skewed*—a distribution that has more cases at one end than at the other.

The distributions of income and wealth are examples of skewed distributions—there are many more poor people than rich people. The mean U.S. household income in 2011 was $69,677, and the median was $50,054 (U.S. Census Bureau, 2012). In general, the median is lower than the mean when data are skewed to the right like income, and this difference for the United States is a measure of that skew.

The *mode* is defined as the most frequent value. A distribution can have more than one mode—bimodal, trimodal, and so on.

The *standard deviation* is the most-often used measure of *dispersion* or "spread"—how much the values of a variable differ from the mean and, therefore, from each other. The *variance* is the average of the squared differences between the mean and each value; the standard deviation is just the square root of the variance.

BIVARIATE TABLE

A **bivariate table** shows the relationship between two variables, such as the relationship between happiness and religion in this chapter. In a bivariate table, nearly always one of the variables is considered to be the independent variable and the other the dependent variable. While the independent variable is the variable that we think is the cause, the dependent variable is the variable thought of as the effect—caused by the independent variable. For example, level of education affects income; here level of education is the independent variable and income is the dependent variable. Income depends on education, though not completely.

A bivariate table *displays univariate percentages for the dependent variable side by side, one for each category of the independent variable.* Look at Table 1 again. The first column shows the percentages of the three happiness categories for Protestants, the second column shows the percentages of the happiness categories for Catholics and so on. Each column shows the univariate percentage for one religion or no religion.

Now, look for the two univariate frequencies for all religions combined. They are displayed on the "margins" of the table, one at the right edge or margin, and one at the bottom margin of the table. They are called **marginals** (short for marginal frequencies or percentages). In Table 1, the last two rows, labeled "Total" and "(*N*)," show 100 percent and the number of observations in each religious group, and the last column, labeled "Total," displays the percentage in each happiness category for all religions combined.

Tally Sheet

To construct a bivariate table from raw data without using a computer, first do a count or tally of responses for each case; then convert the tally marks to frequencies and calculate percentages. Table 4 shows a completed **tally sheet** for gender and degree using the data matrix in Figure 1.

TABLE 4.   Tally Sheet Using Data from Figure 2

Degree	1 Male		2 Female	
(0) Less than HS	(1,1)		(1,2)	||||
(1) HS Grad	(2,1)	⊮ ||	(2,2)	⊮ ||||
(2) Associate/ Jr. College	(3,1)	|	(3,2)	||
(3) BA	(4,1)	|	(4,2)	||
(4) Grad degree	(5,1)	||	(5,2)	||

The small pair of numbers in parentheses (e.g., (1,2) in Table 4) are *cell labels.* The first number designates the *row number.* The second number designates the *column number.* They are used to identify the cells later.

After the tally is completed for all cases, count the marks in each cell and enter the total in the cell. However, the subsample is small—10 cells in the table and only 30 observations—so collapse degree into two categories: (1) high school or less, and (2) junior college degree or higher. This reduces the table to a 2 × 2 table.

TABLE 4A. Tally Sheet Using Data from Table 2

Degree	Male	Female	Total
High School or Less	7	13	20
Jr. College or Higher Degree	4	6	10
Total	11	19	30

NOTE: Tally marks have been converted to numbers.

To produce the **row marginals**, add the entries in each row; for the **column marginals**, add the entries in each column. Table 4a shows the completed tally, with degree collapsed into the two categories, tally marks converted to numbers and marginal frequencies included.

Check all calculations! The sum of the row *marginals must* equal the sum of the column marginals. In Table 4a, the row marginals are 20 and 10, and the column marginals are 11 and 19. *Each adds to* 30, the total number of cases.

Calculating Percentages for Tables: Two Rules

In a two-variable table, there are three possible percentage bases (denominators)—

- *row totals* (20 and 10 in Table 4a)
- *column totals* (11 and 19 in Table 4a)
- *grand total* (30 in Table 4a)

Each base tells something about the data, but in nearly all cases, *only one* indicates directly what we really want to know: *How the dependent variable differs among categories of the independent variable.* In order to choose the correct percentage base, it is useful to look at two rules for how to calculate and interpret bivariate percentages.

Rule 1: Calculate percentages within categories of the independent variable.
Rule 1 requires looking at the table, deciding which variable is the independent variable and observing whether it is the column or the row variable. Rule 1 eliminates row totals and the grand total.[3]

Why? In this example, we wish to compare the percentage of males who continue their education beyond high school to the percentage of females who do so. Using the row totals as the percentage base does not tell us what we want to know. For example, $7/20 \times 100$ tells us the percentage of people who did not continue schooling beyond high school who are males, *not* the percentage of males who did not continue schooling beyond high school.

So in Table 4a, the base (or denominator) we need is the *column total*, because gender is the independent variable and it's the column variable—the value of gender changes across the columns. Gender is the independent variable because we know that gender might affect the highest degree earned, but degree has no influence on whether one is female or male!

For the *cell percentages*, divide each cell frequency by the base for that cell, in this case, the column total, and multiply by 100. The calculations (rounded to one decimal place) for Table 4a are

Cell (1,1): percentage $= (7/11) \times 100 = 0.636 \times 100 = 63.6\%$

Cell (1,2): percentage $= (13/19) \times 100 = 0.684 \times 100 = 68.4\%$

Cell (2,1): percentage $= (4/11) \times 100 = 0.364 \times 100 = 36.4\%$

Cell (2,2): percentage $= (6/19) \times 100 = 0.316 \times 100 = 31.6\%$

For *row marginals*, the calculations are

Row margin 1: percentage $= (20/30) \times 100 = 0.667 \times 100 = 66.7\%$

Row margin 2: percentage $= (10/30) \times 100 = 0.333 \times 100 = 33.3\%$

Next, assemble the results into a presentation quality table, like Table 5

NOTE: To save space and reduce clutter in the table, Table 5 doesn't display cell frequencies; *however, the percentage bases should always be reported.* In principle, multiplying each percentage by its percentage base and moving the decimal back two places to the left reproduces the cell frequency. Although, in practice, this calculation often is subject to substantial rounding error.

More important, the size of the base (denominator) used to calculate each percentage gives a quick indication of how stable the sample estimate of the population percentage is. Larger bases provide greater sample stability.[4]

Rule 2: Compare percentages across categories of the percentage base.

If Rule 1 is followed, this rule translates into *compare percentages across categories of the independent variable.* Failure to follow Rule 2 leads to entirely bogus interpretation of a table!

So how do we read Table 5? Rule 2 says, compare percentages across categories of the independent variable, which in this table are in the *columns*. For higher degree (Jr. college or higher), 36.4 percent of males had a higher degree and 31.6 percent of females had a higher degree, a 4.8 percent difference between the genders.[5]

TABLE 5. Percentages for Educational Degree by Gender

Degree	Male	Female	Total
No Higher Degree	63.6%	68.4%	66.7%
Jr. College or Higher Degree	36.4%	31.6%	33.3%
Total	100%	100%	100%
(*N*)	(11)	(19)	(30)

When there are only two categories of the dependent variable, usually you only need to discuss percentages in one category. For example, you don't need to discuss gender differences for both rows in Table 5—if 36.4 percent of males do have a higher degree, then you know that 63.6 percent *do not* have a higher degree (100–36.4% = 63.6%). And the percentage difference in the top row is just the negative of the percentage difference in the bottom row—top row: 63.6–68.4 = −4.8; bottom row: 36.4–31.6 = 4.8.

Table 6 shows what the computer software program SAS® (*www.sas.com*) does with the table for degree and sex using the full GSS dataset sample for survey years 2000 through 2008 (using the SAS default settings and unweighted data).

To understand Table 6, note that the labels under degree" are defined as:

"Frequency": The top entry in each cell is the cell frequency, or the number of cases in the cell; for example, the cell [1,1] frequency is 4314.

"Percent": The second number in each cell is a percentage using the total number in the table ($n = 14899$) as the percentage base. As we've just seen, this seldom is a good choice. You might as well look at the cell frequencies.

"Row Pct": The third number in each cell is the row percentage. This means the row marginals are used as the percentage base.

"Col Pct": The last number in each cell is the column percentage. The column marginals are used as the percentage base. These percentages are the ones we have been considering thus far.

TABLE 6. SAS Output for Educational Degree by Gender (Sex)

Table of Degree by sex

Degree	sex		
Frequency Percent Row Pct Col Pct	Male	Female	Total
No higher degree	4314	5574	9888
	28.95	37.41	66.37
	43.63	56.37	
	64.78	67.65	
Jr college or higher	2345	2666	5011
	15.74	17.89	33.63
	46.80	53.20	
	35.22	32.35	
Total	6659	8240	14899
	44.69	55.31	100.00

Frequency Missing = 28

To read Table 6, *follow Rule 1:* Compare the percentage of males to the percentage of females who earned a higher degree. Therefore, compare the "Col Pct" percentages between male and female. Comparing the "Col Pct" within each column provides no comparisons between men and women.

The Bivariate Percentage Table (Transposed)

Some published tables are arranged with the independent variable as the row variable, and this appears to be the standard in some academic disciplines. In this case, how would you calculate the appropriate percentages? Rule 1 to the rescue!

Rule 1 says, "calculate percentage within categories of the independent variable." So, use the *row* totals as the percentage base. Table 7 shows what Table 5 looks like *transposed*, with gender as the row variable and degree as the column variable. ("Transpose" means to interchange the rows and columns.) So now, the percentages add to 100 percent in each *row* instead of each column.

TABLE 7. Educational-Degree Percentages by Gender, Transposed

Gender	No Higher Degree (%)	Jr. College or Higher Degree (%)	Total (%)	(N)
Male	63.6	36.4	100	(11)
Female	68.4	31.6	100	(19)
Total	66.7	33.3	100	30

To read Table 7, remember Rule 2: *Compare percentages across categories of the percentage base,* which in this table are the rows: 36.4–31.6% = 4.8%, exactly the same difference we found in Table 5.

Comparing Tables 5 and 7 illustrates another important point:

Find the percentage base before reading the rest of the table.

Creating New Variables

Combining variable categories and creating composite variables are two ways to create new variables.

1. *Combine (collapse) variable categories.* Researchers often combine categories of a variable. Table 5, for example, shows a version of the GSS variable named degree collapsed into two categories: (1) no degree beyond high school, and (2) junior-college degree or higher. Collapsing categories in this case was necessary to create a usable table, because the sample size (30) is small.

More generally, why combine variable categories? Some surveys allow six or eight response options for a question about race and 20 or 30 for ethnicity, and the U.S. census uses many more. Consider trying to evaluate a table containing 30 rows and 30 columns, for example!

But note that combining categories hides details, such as how many respondents report a particular religion. Refer to Tables 1 and 1a. Table 1a only tells the percentages who report and don't report a religious preference, but nothing about types of religion, as in Table 1. Part of the "art" of doing research is condensing excessive detail without losing essential information. In this example, little information was lost by collapsing religion into two categories, because the percentage differences in "Very Happy" are small among the religious categories other than "None."

In addition, note that you can combine categories, but it's impossible to "un-combine" them, unless the original dataset retains all the original detail. When collapsing categories of a variable, create a new variable for the collapsed version and keep the original uncollapsed variable. For example, keep the variable `degree` and create another variable named `degree2` to contain the dichotomous version.

2. *Create composite variables, such as an index.* Another frequently used transformation is combining more than one variable. One type of *composite variable* is called an **index**. Which variables might one combine? Items are chosen for their *face validity*—that is, they appear to measure components of the same concept.

Suppose there are six questions asking whether respondents own various electronic devices like a laptop computer, a cell phone, an iPad, ..., each scored (1 = yes) or (0 = no). Create an index defined by the number of electronic items owned. A person who answers "yes" to all six gets a score on the composite measure of six; a person who checked five gets a score of five and so on. The new variable is then included in the analysis. Do you think there is an association between owner's age and the number of electronic items owned?[6]

Now for the fun part—data analysis!

SUMMARY

This chapter opens with a couple of examples of bivariate tables. The data for these examples come from recent survey years of a major national survey, the General Social Survey.

The second section describes the organization of the data matrix. Regardless of whether one uses computers or hand calculations, the data matrix is the starting point for data preparation and for the analyses. The data matrix is a rectangular array, usually one case is listed on each row and one variable listed in each column, or sequence of adjacent columns called a "field." The codebook is the key for deciphering the data matrix. It gives the names and descriptions of every variable, the meaning of each value of the variable (e.g., 1 = strongly disagree...5 = strongly agree) and specifies the field where it appears in the data matrix, first column and ending column, or first column and field width, when the data are stored in ASCII text format without field separators.

Data often are stored in formats where a column is defined as the contents of one variable, no matter how many numbers or characters its values contain. For example, age and wage each would take one column in an Excel spreadsheet.

The chapter also describes how and why data are coded and cleaned. All data contain errors when first assembled. Use univariate statistics and sometimes bivariate tables to help spot errors. Univariate statistics reporting the minimum and maximum value of each variable also help to spot out-of-range values.

The third section of the chapter discusses how to use the data matrix and its codebook to construct a univariate percentage distribution and calculate univariate statistics like the mean and standard deviation. Converting frequencies to percentages "standardizes" them to indicate how many per 100 (relative frequency).

The fourth section describes how to construct and read a two-variable percentage table. The main purpose of a bivariate table is to check for a relationship between two variables. It usually is laid out to compare percentage distributions of the dependent variable between categories of the independent variable.

The final section of the chapter briefly explains how to create new variables from raw data in preparation for data analysis.

YOUR REVIEW SHEET

1. Propose at least one social science explanation for the relationship between gender and education that is not discussed in the chapter. Summarize procedures for testing your hypotheses.

2. What is the first step in data preparation? Provide specific examples.

3. How should one handle inconsistent answers, like this example?

   Question 1: Do you ever drink alcoholic beverages?

   > [✓] No, never (total abstainer)

   > [   ] Yes

   Question 2: Do you ever drink alcoholic beverages more than you think you should?

   > [   ] No

   > [✓] Yes (at least sometimes)

   Explain, in your own words.

4. What is the purpose of a tally sheet? How should it be set up?

5. Summarize two types of data transformations reviewed in this chapter and describe the purpose of each.

6. Why combine categories of a variable? Describe an example from Table 8 (in the "Exercises" section).

7. No matter how variables are collapsed for analysis, the master dataset always should retain all details. Why is this important? Describe an example of the major difficulty that might ensue if you do not.

8. Even knowing what each number stands for, a data matrix is not very informative by itself, particularly when there are many cases and many variables. Why not?

9. If column totals are the percentage base, the percentages should be compared across *columns*, but not across *rows*. Why? State the two rules for reading a bivariate percentage table. What is the rationale for each rule? Repeat your explanation for a transposed table—percentages add to 100 in each row.

10. In Table 1 the percentage base is the column total. Why not use the row total? Summarize the argument for using column totals (happiness) in Table 1a as the percentage base.

END NOTES

1. A quick way to check for inconsistencies like this is to examine a cross-tabulation between variables that are related by definition, like the two in this example. Look for nonzero entries in the inconsistent cells like the cell showing responses for the "no" category of question 1 and the "yes" category of question 2.

2. The SAS statistical package includes a procedure designed for comparing every value in two files. Data entered into a spreadsheet are easy to read into a SAS dataset. Other statistical packages, such as SPSS, can easily be programmed to compare files (use update).

3. The percentages based on the grand total are barely, if at all, more informative than the frequencies. It's difficult to learn anything about a relationship by comparing either frequencies or percentages based on the grand total.

4. The data in Table 4 are a small subsample of the 14,927 cases in the GSS sample for years 2000, 2002, 2004, 2006, and 2008. Therefore, there is likely to be fairly large sampling error in the table. But, in this instance, the percentages in the subsample match the percentages in the full sample quite closely. The maximum difference between the percentages in Table 4 (subsample) and those in the corresponding table calculated from the full sample is 1.9.

5. There is one exception to rule 1: Use categories of the independent variable as the percentage base. The exception arises when the sample is stratified on the dependent variable. Medical studies sometimes use a sample split half-and-half between people who have a rare risk factor or disease such as lung cancer and people who do not ("case-control study"). The researchers want to study potential effects of smoking on the risk of developing lung cancer, but simple random sample of any reasonable size would not include enough people with lung cancer to permit the analysis. In this situation, calculating (unweighted) percentages with the independent variable, smoker, as the percentage base would lead to highly misleading comparisons.

6. Items used to define an index sometimes are weighted unequally, and the weighted scores are added together. Differential weighting of items comprising an index sometimes is done to reflect the importance of the items in measuring the construct. Suppose you decide to create an index of "violence victimization" based on reports of incidents like "ever hit," being "severely beaten," or being "attacked with a weapon." You judge these incidents to be of unequal severity. You could assign a score of 4 to being "attacked with a weapon," 3 to being "severely beaten," 1 to "ever hit," and 0 to none of these. Then, add the weighted scores for each individual to form an index of "violence victimization"—a new variable. Skipping one number (2) in a sequence is unusual. Here it represents a judgment that being attacked with a weapon and being severely beaten both are substantially more serious than being "ever hit," and are closer to each other in severity than they are to being ever hit.

STUDY TERM

bivariate table Table comprised of two variables. Cell frequencies indicate the number of cases which match the column and row label of the cell (e.g., the number of cases which are both Protestant and "Very Happy" in Table 1).

codebook A listing of all variables in a data collection with each variable accompanied by (1) a short "variable name," (2) a brief description, (3) the location (field or columns spanned) and (4) the meaning of each value. Codebooks for survey data also often contain the exact wording of the survey question, the univariate frequency distribution of each variable, a description of the sampling plan and execution and other useful comments.

column marginals Totals for each column, shown in the last row of a bivariate table.

data coding Converting information, usually from words or answers on a questionnaire, from its original collected form into labels for variable categories. For example, for computer analysis you might assign a code of 1 to people who are married, 2 to people who are widowed, and so on.

data matrix Two-dimensional table used to organize and retrieve raw data. Rows represent cases; fields (composed of one or more adjacent one-character columns) represent variables. This is the most used layout of a data matrix, but other organization sometimes is used. For example, when a survey includes data from the same respondent at two or more times, each row of the data matrix might contain a profile for one respondent at one time point.

frequency distribution (univariate frequency distribution) A univariate summary including the count and percentage for each category of *one* nominal, ordinal, or collapsed interval variable.

index Composite measure often created by averaging or summing two or more variables for each case.

marginals (or marginal frequency distributions) Univariate frequency distributions for variables in a bivariate table that are displayed at the edges, or margins, of the table.

measure of central tendency A statistic (or parameter) that summarizes where numbers in a distribution tend to concentrate. Examples include the mean, median and mode.

measure of dispersion A statistic (or parameter) that summarizes how much numbers in a distribution are spread out. Examples include the standard deviation and variance.

percentage Frequency per 100, obtained by counting the number of cases in one category of a variable, dividing by the total number of cases for all categories, and multiplying the quotient by 100.

raw (unprocessed) data A listing of the value of every variable for every case (data that are just in from the field).

row marginals Row totals shown in the last column of a bivariate table.

tally sheet Blank table with labels for the variable categories, used to prepare tables manually.

univariate analysis Examination of statistics such as the mean, standard deviation and frequency distribution, which describe one variable at a time.

univariate frequency distribution List of the number and percentage in each category of one variable, as in Table 3.

EXERCISES

Exercise 1. Skills Building: Univariate Analysis 1

Directions: Use the information in Table 8 to produce the univariate distributions for sex and degree. Split "degree" into two categories, high school or less (0, 1) and junior college or more (2, 3, 4) Be sure to review the rules for calculating percentages. Show your calculations.

Note: Be sure to omit any missing values for age (98 and 99) and degree (9).

TABLE 8.   Data Matrix of 50 Cases from the GSS Dataset

id	year	age	sex	race	marital	degree	wrkstat	rincom06	happy
1502	2006	34	2	1	3	3	6	11	2
3290	2006	25	1	1	1	1	1	17	2
982	2008	39	1	1	3	1	1	26	1
471	2006	38	1	1	3	2	1	22	2
1109	2006	45	2	1	1	4	3	19	1
1279	2006	40	1	1	1	3	1	23	1
3846	2006	43	2	1	1	3	1	22	0
3295	2006	81	1	1	2	0	5	0	2
1094	2008	70	2	1	1	4	5	0	1
743	2008	49	2	2	3	1	5	0	2
1869	2006	69	2	1	1	1	5	0	2
448	2006	57	1	1	3	1	1	20	0
3110	2006	31	1	1	1	1	1	15	2
3113	2006	38	2	1	1	3	7	0	2
719	2008	41	1	1	5	1	1	0	2
755	2008	36	1	1	5	3	1	14	3
139	2006	51	1	1	1	3	1	23	2
765	2006	23	2	3	5	1	1	11	0
1555	2006	99	1	1	9	1	1	99	1
256	2006	65	2	3	1	1	5	0	0
115	2008	56	1	1	1	1	1	21	2
3837	2006	38	2	1	1	2	1	17	0
241	2008	66	1	1	1	3	5	0	2
223	2006	33	1	3	1	1	1	11	2
2645	2006	30	1	1	5	4	1	17	1
1933	2008	21	1	1	5	1	6	0	1
1343	2008	49	1	1	3	1	1	99	2
203	2006	58	1	1	5	3	5	0	3
1572	2008	60	2	1	1	1	7	0	2
210	2006	51	1	2	1	1	3	20	2
621	2008	48	2	1	1	3	1	20	1
1211	2008	43	1	2	1	0	1	15	2
1240	2006	47	1	1	3	1	1	20	2
1153	2008	34	2	1	1	3	7	0	2
3417	2006	77	2	1	5	4	5	99	2
2579	2006	21	2	1	5	1	2	10	1
3497	2006	26	1	1	5	0	1	19	2
368	2006	22	1	3	5	1	1	14	0

id	year	age	sex	race	marital	degree	wrkstat	rincom06	happy
693	2008	43	1	3	1	4	1	25	2
1343	2006	51	2	1	3	3	1	18	2
2973	2006	33	2	3	1	1	7	98	1
343	2008	40	2	2	1	1	2	2	1
824	2008	25	2	2	5	1	7	12	2
650	2006	51	2	2	4	1	1	9	3
4290	2006	29	2	3	1	3	7	0	0
2400	2006	54	2	1	1	2	1	19	0
3873	2006	62	1	2	1	0	8	0	2
1122	2008	36	2	2	5	1	6	12	3
1883	2008	41	1	1	3	1	1	14	2
1442	2008	31	1	3	5	0	1	20	2

The values of all variables except wrkstat and happy are defined in Figure 3. The values for these two variables are as follows:

> happy 0 = NA
>
>> 1 = Very happy
>>
>> 2 = Pretty happy
>>
>> 3 = Happy
>>
>> 8 = Don't know
>>
>> 9 = No answer
>
> wrkstat 1 = Working full time
>
>> 2 = Working part time
>>
>> 3 = With a job, but not at work because of temporary illness, vacation, strike
>>
>> 4 = Unemployed, laid off, looking for work
>>
>> 5 = Retired
>>
>> 6 = In school
>>
>> 7 = Keeping house
>>
>> 8 = Other
>>
>> 9 = No answer

Exercise 2. Skills Building: Univariate Analysis 2

Directions: Use the information in Table 8 to produce the following univariate statistics. Be sure to review the rules for calculating percentages. Show your calculations.

> Mean age
>
> Median age
>
> Frequency and percentage distribution for sex
>
> Frequency and percentage distribution for marital
>
> Frequency and percentage distribution for wrkstat

Mean, variance and standard deviation of `female`. Create a "dummy" variable by assigning a 1 to females and 0 to males. Call this variable `female` (categories are female = 1, and male = 0).

$$\text{Variance: } s^2 = \frac{\sum_i^n (x_i - \bar{x})^2}{n}$$

In this formula, the variable x is the value of female (0 or 1) for each case; $\bar{x}$ is the mean of female, n is the number of cases ($n = 50$ in Table 8), and Σ stands for "add up," starting with the first observation and ending with the last one (i goes from 1 to n). (The standard deviation is just the square root of the variance.)

Note: Most statistical texts use $n - 1$ instead of n in the denominator of the formula for the variance. Also, nearly all software uses $n - 1$ by default. Using $n - 1$ produces an unbiased estimate of the population variance. It's not the sample variance, although it often is defined loosely as such. The instructions use n here for a definite reason.

Questions

1. Compare the mean of the variable called female to the percentage distribution for sex. What correspondence do you see?

2. Compare the variance of female to the product of its mean $\times$ (1-mean). They should be equal to each other. If not, check for calculating errors. (This comparison is the reason for using n instead of $n - 1$ to calculate the variance.)

3. Suppose you had constructed a variable called male instead of female, and assigned a 1 to males and 0 to females. What do you predict about the mean and variance for male?

Exercise 3. Skills Building: Univariate Analysis 3—Calculating Percentages

Directions: Read the following paragraph and then answer the questions that follow.

Suppose you have data for a sample of 25 men and 50 women. You find that 5 men and 10 women approve of buying a new SUV. When you look only at the raw numbers, you might misinterpret the results and say: *Women are more likely than men to approve of buying an SUV.* After all, 10 women are more than 5 men. But, the percentages are the same: 20 percent of women and 20 percent of men approve:

Men: $5/25 = 1/5 \Rightarrow 20\%$
Women: $10/50 = 1/5 \Rightarrow 20\%$

1. In your own words, explain to your 12-year-old cousin why he or she should compare percentages, not raw numbers.

2. Add an example of your own (exclude gender and all other variables in Table 8). Use an example with unequal frequencies, such as for gender in the above paragraphs. Use hypothetical (but sensible) numbers. Show your calculations for percentages.

3. Summarize your information in a table like Table 1 or Table 1a. Include a title for your table.

Exercise 4. Skills Building: Preparing a Bivariate Table

Directions: Use the data in Table 8 to prepare the bivariate tables below (Tables 9 and 10). Use the GSS dataset variable `marital` to define married; check the codebook, Figure 2. Your tally table should show your tally marks, cell frequencies and row and column totals (column totals go inside the parentheses). Table 10 requires calculating percentages. Show all calculations. Then, answer the questions below.

Note: Be sure to omit any missing values for age (98 and 99) and `marital` (9).

TABLE 9. Tally for Married by Age Over 41[*]

Married	Age < 41	Age > 41	Total
1 (Yes)	(1,1)	(1,2)	
2 (No)	(2,1)	(2,2)	
Total	100% (*n*)	100% (*n*)	100% (*n*)

[*] Median age = 41

TABLE 10. Percentage Married by Age over 41

Married	Age < 41	Age > 41	Total
1 (Yes)	%	%	%
2 (No)	%	%	%
Total	100% (*n*)	100% (*n*)	100% (*n*)

Questions

1. Write a concise summary of the relationship (if any) you observe in Table 10.

2. Why should Table 10 display column percentages instead of row percentages or percentages based on the total number of cases in the table?

3. Explain how you calculated the percentages in Table 10

DATA ANALYSIS 2: DESCRIBING, EXPLAINING AND EVALUATING

INTRODUCTION: LOOKING AT HOW THE SOCIAL WORLD WORKS

Data suggest that people who report affiliation with a religion are happier than people who say they have no religion. What other variables might affect happiness?

Goals of This Chapter

The main emphasis of this chapter is on the three-variable table, also called a **trivariate table**. The trivariate table is set up so that *a bivariate relationship can be examined within each category of a third variable*—the **control variable**.

The three-variable table is the simplest form of *statistical control* of possible confounding variables. A researcher is able to assign people either to the treatment(s) or to the control category (e.g., placebo group). If random assignment is used, *physical control* is a powerful substitute for controlling all possible confounding variables. However, when data are from natural settings, the researcher does not have physical control over the independent variable. People cannot be assigned at random to variables like age, gender, ethnicity, income, residence, and so on. Therefore, *statistical control* must serve as a substitute for physical control.

This chapter introduces the use of statistical controls in three-variable percentage tables. This type of statistical control provides a foundation for understanding more advanced methods, such as comparisons among means and basic multivariate regression analysis.

The chapter also introduces statistical tests for (1) checking a relationship in a table, (2) simultaneously comparing several means and (3) performing basic regression analysis.

Happiness and Marriage

Many studies suggest that married people are happier than people who are not married. The diagram summarizes this relationship. The arrow indicates a proposed effect of marriage on happiness.

married → happiness

From Chapter 11 of *Research Methods and Society, Foundations of Social Inquiry,* Second Edition. Linda Eberst Dorsten, Lawrence Hotchkiss. Copyright © 2014 by Pearson Education, Inc. All rights reserved.

TABLE 1. Percentages for Happiness by Marital Status

	Married		
Very Happy	No	Yes	Total
No	78.5%	57.9%	67.1%
Yes	21.5	42.1	32.9
Total	100	100	100
(*n*)	(4,680)	(5,804)	(10,484)

Table 1 uses the GSS data to examine this relationship. The dependent variable is the two-category variable defined by "Very Happy," Yes or No.

The table shows that, similar to published research reports, married people (42.1%) are more likely to report they are happy than are those not married (21.5%). But there might be alternative explanations—confounding variables—that need to be controlled before deciding that marital status does, in fact, affect happiness. Before reading further, list at least two possible confounding variables—that is, variables that might affect both marriage *and* happiness thereby generating a correlation between them that is *not* due to the effect of marriage on happiness.

TESTING BIVARIATE RELATIONSHIPS: ELABORATION ANALYSIS

Past research shows that household income is positively related to being married and also to happiness. So it is possible that the positive relationship between being married and being very happy is due to the fact they *both* are affected by level of household income. The schematic looks like this:

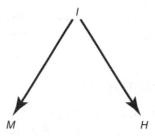

If the diagram correctly describes the real world, we need to control for household income while studying the relationship between marital status and happiness.

There are many income categories in the GSS dataset. To simplify, income categories are collapsed at the median. Therefore, Table 2 is a "2 × 2 × 2 table" that presents the trivariate relationship.[1]

TABLE 2. Percentages for Happiness by Marital Status, Controlling for Household Income

Very Happy	Income below the Median Married			Income at or above Median Married		
	No	**Yes**	**Total**	**No**	**Yes**	**Total**
No	81.3%	63.1%	73.9%	72.5%	55.3%	60.0%
Yes	18.7	36.9	26.1	27.5	44.7	40.0
Total	100.0	100.0	100.0	100.0	100.0	100.0
(*n*)	(2,897)	(1,980)	(4,877)	(1,167)	(3,118)	(4,285)

First, notice that Table 2 contains *two bivariate tables, side-by-side*. Each of these tables is called a *partial table*; it is only a part of the complete trivariate table. Until you are familiar with reading trivariate tables, *it is a good idea to cover all but one partial table with your hand or a piece of paper.* Read the visible partial table; then cover the other partial table(s) and read the one that is now uncovered.

So now, cover the right-side partial table. The partial table on the left shows that *for people with below-median income*, those who are married are more likely to report being very happy than those not married: 36.9 percent versus 18.7 percent.

Now cover the left-side partial table and uncover the right-side partial table. The partial table on the right side shows the relationship between marital status and happiness for those with household income at or above the median. *For people with income at or above the median*, those who are married also are happier than those not married: 44.7 percent versus 27.5 percent.

Table 2 shows that the relationship between married and being very happy is *not* due to the effect of household income. Why not? The percentage differences are fairly large: 18.2 percent (36.9 – 18.7%) and 17.2 percent (44.7 – 27.5%). Also the differences are in the same direction in both partial tables—married respondents were more likely to report they were "Very Happy" than were respondents who were not married, for both income groups.

The next step is to compare the relationships in these two partial tables to the *original bivariate relationship* in Table 1. The three percentage differences are as follows: 20.6 percent (in the original bivariate table) and 18.2 percent and 17.2 percent in the two partial tables—differences that are similar to each other. *The married–happy relationship is only slightly reduced when income is controlled.*

So what do we conclude? The partial relationships between marital status and happiness *cannot be due to income, because income is controlled (held constant) by the two income categories defining the partial tables.* And the relationship between marital status and happiness also remains nearly as high as in the bivariate table. Of course, income is not completely constant here, because income varies a lot within the two categories: above and below the median household income.

But the table illustrates the main idea of controlling for a possible confounding variable. More advanced methods do not require collapsing the income variable.

Before sharing this information with your best friend or spouse, however, consider two other points.

1. The direction of the effect between marriage and happiness is unclear—which is the cause and which is the effect? Does marriage affect happiness, or are happy people more likely to get married, or some of both?

2. Also, in analyses not presented here, the relationship between happiness and marriage is almost entirely due to the fact that happily married people are very likely to report being "Very Happy" generally. Married respondents who did not think their marriage was happy were quite unlikely to report being "Very Happy" in general. Also, most married people reported they were very happily married. That's why the married people in these tables show up as being noticeably more likely to say they are very happy in general than are unmarried people.

TYPES OF BIVARIATE RELATIONSHIPS

When a control variable is added to a bivariate relationship, as in the above section, we call the process **elaboration**—we are elaborating ("expanding upon") the original bivariate relationship. There are four types of possible elaboration outcomes: (1) replication, (2) explanation, (3) interpretation and (4) specification, also called statistical interaction.

Replication

Each **partial relationship** matches the original bivariate relationship—*the control variable does not change the original relationship.* The bivariate relationship remains after adding the control variable. Real-world data seldom match this pattern exactly, but the previous example showing the married-by-happy relationship controlling household income is a close approximation of **replication**.

Explanation

Explanation loosely means that a bivariate relationship is "explained away" when a control variable is added. Explanation is the name of the result when a spurious relationship is present—one in which *two variables are related only because they both depend on another variable,* which affects both of them. The bivariate relationship is *explained* by the dependence of both variables on a causally prior variable. An example of spurious relationship can be seen in a dress-beard-sex example. Sex affects whether or not one wears a dress *and* whether or not one wears a beard.

Important point: The single most important reason for using control variables is to check for a spurious relationship. In Figure 1, the variable Z affects *both* X and Y, but X has no effect on Y, and Y has no effect on X. The common dependence of *X* and *Y* on *Z* generates a non-zero bivariate correlation between *X* and *Y*, but the partial relationship between *X* and *Y*, controlling for *Z*, *is* zero.

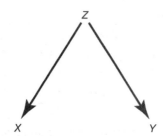

FIGURE 1   Diagram of a Spurious Relationship.

As an example of explanation, suppose that the dependent variable *Y* is "NFL football fan" (yes or no), *X* is a two-category variable for height of each survey respondent (short = less than 5´9,˝ and tall = 5´9˝ or taller), and the control variable *Z* is sex (male or female).

Table 3 displays the bivariate relationship between the two variables labeled height and NLF fan. The data in Table 3 are hypothetical, designed to illustrate a spurious relationship and generated by computer.

TABLE 3.   Percentages of NFL Football Fans by Height

NFL Fan	Height		Total
	Short	**Tall**	
No	74.2%	26.7%	50.3%
Yes	25.8	73.3	49.7
Total	100	100	100
(*n*)	(7,423)	(7,504)	(14,927)

The relationship in this table is fairly strong. Over 74 percent of "tall" people are NFL fans compared to just 26.7 percent of "short" people; the percentage difference is 47.5 percent (74.2 − 26.7). An association this strong is unusual in real data. This one is exaggerated to emphasize the point.

But controlling for gender as shown in Table 4, the relationship between NFL fan and height nearly vanishes. Again, cover one partial table at a time to read the trivariate table.

Clearly, the partial tables show that the relationship between NLF fan and height is nearly zero (17.1 − 15.0 = 2.1, and 84.1 − 85.1 = −1). That is, tall people are more likely to be NLF fans *only because men are taller on average than women,* and *men are more likely to be NFL fans than are women.* Moreover, the directions of effect in this scenario are unambiguous. Sex is not caused by height, and height is not caused by whether or not one is an NFL fan.

TABLE 4.   Percentages of NFL Fans by Height, Controlling for Gender

NFL fan	Women			Men		
	Short	Tall	Total	Short	Tall	Total
No	85.0%	82.9%	84.6%	14.9%	15.9%	15.7%
Yes	15.0	17.1	15.4	85.1	84.1	84.3
Total	100.0	100.0	100.0	100.0	100.0	100.0
(N)	(6,284)	(1,216)	(7,500)	(1,139)	(6,288)	(7,427)

The patterns to look for with explanation elaborations are (1) a strong bivariate relationship, and (2) no relationship in the partial tables (percentages *differences* are zero or close to zero).

A fairly strong bivariate relationship combined with near zero partial relationships requires that the control variable is related to *both* the dependent and the independent variable, and these two relationships must be stronger than the relationship in the bivariate table showing the relationship between the dependent and independent variables.

These requirements imply that sex could not account for the relationship between marriage and happiness. Since each marriage includes one woman and one man (usually), marriage cannot be related to sex.

Interpretation

Interpretation refers to an **intervening-variable model**—a cause-and-effect chain—with the control variable Z in the middle. Figure 2 displays a diagram of the intervening-variable model.

$$X \longrightarrow Z \longrightarrow Y$$

FIGURE 2   Diagram of an Intervening-Variable Model.

Here is an example of interpretation elaboration (the intervening-variable model): We know from everyday-life observations that *women in the United States are more likely to wear "long" hair than are men.* This is a bivariate relationship between one's gender and wearing long hair. We are pretty sure that the female XX chromosome does not carry a gene for choosing to let one's hair grow long. So it is likely that a possible intervening variable accounts for this relationship: gender differences in socialization about which gender should wear long hair.

To examine this bivariate relationship, suppose you could devise a study about socialization experiences promoting long hair and repeatedly check a sample of girls and boys while they were growing up. You likely would find that the relationship between gender and wearing long hair is zero (or near zero) within categories of "socialization experiences" (the control variable) favoring/not favoring wearing long hair. If it is, then the data support an intervening-variable model: Gender affects socialization which then affects the decision to wear long hair. We have *interpreted* the relationship between sex and wearing long hair.

Both explanation and interpretation make the same prediction: a nonzero bivariate relationship and zero partial relationships. So what's the difference? It is in the logic of cause-and-effect: Gender does affect wearing long hair, but only indirectly through socialization. But height does not affect whether one is an NFL fan—the bivariate relationship is spurious, due to the common dependence of both height and NFL fan on gender.

Specification

Specification, also called **statistical interaction**, means that a relationship between two variables differs *within categories of a third variable*—the relationship is *specified* to hold only in some contexts, or to be different in different contexts. Think, for example, about the relationship between baldness and gender: There is a near-zero association at young ages, but the association steadily increases as people age. Here is another example of statistical interaction: Employment affects whether one returns to a life of crime for men 26 years old and older but not for younger men (Uggen, 2000).

ADDITIONAL ANALYSIS METHODS

Imagine a bivariate table for two ratio variables, such as age by years of schooling. To include categories for all ages and all years of education, a bivariate table likely would contain more than 1,000 cells. For example, 18 years of schooling $\times$ 72 possible ages (between 18 years and 90 years) = 1,296 unique categories and, thus, cells in that percentage table!

We could collapse the categories (values) for both age and schooling down to manageable size. Age could be split at the median, and schooling could be split at 12 years to produce a 2×2 table. But a lot of potentially important detail is covered up, particularly when categories are collapsed to this extreme degree. For example, two continuous variables with correlation 0.75 are correlated about 0.54 if each is dichotomized at their mean.[2]

Another problem with using many control variables is that it is time-consuming to read many tables—one trivariate table for *each* control variable. More importantly, such results do not produce adequate evaluation of two-variable tables. The idea of control demands *simultaneous controls*. What's needed is one table showing the joint relationship of the dependent variable, independent variable, and *all control variables simultaneously*.

Imagine what the table might look like with only a few control variables—just five two-category variables produce a table with 32 cells. Each additional two-category variable doubles the number of cells. So, six two-category variables require 64 cells, seven require 128 cells and so on. Clearly, some simplifications are essential. The remainder if this section briefly reviews other methods for summarizing relationships.

TABLE 5. Mean Annual Earnings ($1,000s) by Gender

	Gender		
	Female	**Male**	**Total**
Earnings	33.8	58.1	46.9
(*n*)	(1,565)	(1,722)	(3,287)

Bivariate Table of Means

If the dependent variable is *numeric* like earnings or wage, and the independent variable is *categorical*, like gender or race, a useful device is to calculate the dependent-variable mean score for each category of the independent variable. A simple diagram of a hypothesis with a numeric and a categorical variable is:

gender → earnings

Table 5 shows an example using mean (average) annual earnings in $1,000s as the dependent variable and gender as the independent variable. The earnings data come from the GSS data for survey years 2006 and 2008 combined.[3]

Table 5 reveals a substantial difference between the average annual earnings of men and women. For women, average annual earnings were about $33,800, compared to $58,100 for men—a difference of $24,300 per year. The "*n*" is the number of cases for each gender and the total cases with both genders combined. It is important to report the sample size for each statistic to provide the reader an indication of the stability of the statistic.

Table 5 reports sample means, showing a bivariate association between gender and annual earnings. Here, annual earnings is a ratio variable. Table 1 also shows a bivariate association, between married and happiness. The dependent variable happiness is an ordinal variable, collapsed from three levels into two categories. Both tables show a bivariate relationship.

More about Statistical Control

Gender is not the only variable that affects earnings. What is one other variable that might account for the difference in earnings shown in Table 5?

One possible variable is work status, which can be defined as a nominal variable with two categories: "work full time" and "work part time."

Men earn more than women because they are more likely to work full-time than are women.

The initial hypothesis was "Men earn more than women." The revised hypothesis implies that the gender difference in earnings disappears after controlling for work status. This hypothesis is expressed as an intervening-variable model:

$$gender \rightarrow wrkstat \rightarrow earnings$$

The diagram illustrates an *intervening-variable model*: Gender affects wrkstat, which, in turn, affects earnings. That is, women are more likely to work part time than are men, and that reduces their annual earnings compared to men. The intervening-variable model suggests that controlling work status will produce an *interpretation elaboration.*

Table 6 shows the relationship between gender and earnings separately for full-time and part-time workers.

TABLE 6. Mean Annual Earnings ($1,000s) by Gender, Controlling for Work Status

	Work Full Time Gender			Work Part Time Gender		
	Female	**Male**	**Total**	**Female**	**Male**	**Total**
Earnings	38.2	61.0	51.2	17.3	31.6	22.3
(n)	(1,246)	(1,554)	(2,800)	(319)	(168)	(487)

Table 6 reveals a surprise—the data do not support the intervening-variable model. The original bivariate relationship between gender and earnings remains whether or not one works full time. But the relationship is much stronger for full-time workers. Rather than an intervening-variable model, the data support *specification elaboration*—specifying *how* the strength of the relationship depends on work status. The specifications shown in Table 6 are as follows:

- For full-time workers, the bivariate relationship is nearly unchanged: Men earn an average of $61,000 and women earn an average $38,200, which is a difference of $22,800 more per year for men, close to the difference in the bivariate table, Table 5, which is $24,300.

- For part-time workers, the partial relationship is much smaller than in the bivariate relationship: $31,600 for men and $17,300 for women, a difference of just $14,300 per year (compared to the bivariate, $24,300). But the earnings difference between the genders remains.[4] No simple diagram represents this situation.

There's a "built-in" relationship between earnings and whether one works full time or part time, because earnings is defined by wage × hours. So suppose we study hourly wage instead of annual earnings—are there still gender differences in wage? The GSS data permit only a *very* rough estimate of hours worked in a given year; consequently, the analyses with wage as reported next should be viewed as an illustration.[5]

Table 7 reports hourly wage by gender, controlling for work status. It shows that for those who work full time, men earn about $4.75 more per hour than women; the gender difference is $2.40 more for those who work part time. (The wage difference for men is close to the wage difference by gender of $4.32 when employment status is *not* controlled—$23.13 – 18.81 = $4.32). But the wage difference for women is less, 22.54 – 20.14 = 2.40.

TABLE 7. Average Hourly Wage by Gender, Controlling for Work Status

	Work Full Time Gender			Work Part Time Gender		
	Female	Male	Total	Female	Male	Total
Hourly Wage	18.43	23.18	21.12	20.14	22.54	20.89
(*N*)	(933)	(1,128)	(2,061)	(249)	(111)	(360)

The findings in these two analyses make an important point: *Findings can depend on the way a variable is defined.* It is analogous to different crime rates reported from surveys of crime victimization and from police records. Neither result is wrong, but the reader needs to be aware that each paints a different picture. In studies of pay equity, we prefer the analysis using hourly wage.

Regression Analysis

The 2006 earnings variable in the GSS dataset contains 25 income ranges. A percentage table with the 25 income categories, two categories for gender, and two categories for work status has 100 cells ($25 \times 2 \times 2$)! Clearly, such a table is too big to evaluate easily.

Using mean earnings reduces the table to four cells and two comparisons, one for full-time and one for part-time workers (Table 7). This is a useful simplification. But almost any dependent variable you can think of probably is influenced by many variables. Therefore, useful data analysis must include many control variables—and remember, they must be included as *simultaneous controls*. Ten or even 20 variables are a modest number when considering the complexity of the social world.

Some further simplifying techniques are essential. Recall that the business of science promotes *parsimony* or simplification—extract the essential patterns out of what otherwise looks like chaos.

The most basic and most often used simplification with several control variables is a statistical method called *linear regression analysis*, usually shortened to just "regression analysis" or "regression." Don't confuse regression analysis with the threat to internal validity called "regression to the mean." Regression to the mean refers to cases at either extreme of a distribution drifting back toward the arithmetic mean with repeated overtime measurements (e.g., remedial reading test scores or poor/excellent sports performance).

Regression analysis is a method of predicting the value of a dependent variable using at least one "predictor variable." Predictor variable is another name for independent variable. In regression, the term *control variable* appears infrequently; predictors in a regression include all variables that are part of the regression analysis except the dependent variable. When one predictor variable is the focus of attention, it is the independent variable, and all other predictor variables are control variables. Technically, however, in regression analysis there's no difference between an independent variable and a control variable. The only difference is the researcher's focus.[6]

Regression analysis combines the values of all the independent variables into a single prediction of the value of the dependent variable, for each observation. The effect of each predictor derives from its importance in generating the prediction. It's easy to see how this works from an example.

Suppose we wish to estimate the effects on hourly wage from the predictors *age*, education (`educ`) and gender, choosing the category `female` for the nominal variable and assigning it arbitrary values: 1 = female, 0 = male. Estimated hourly wage is calculated by a linear equation:

$$predicted\ wage = a + b_{age}\ age + b_{educ}\ educ + b_{fem}\ female$$

The symbols a, b_{age}, b_{educ}, b_{fem} stand for constant numbers. The constant number represented by the letter a is called the *intercept*. It does not measure the effect of any variable but is essential to produce accurate predictions.

The letters b with a subscript are called *regression coefficients*. Each coefficient gives an estimate of the effect of the predictor variable on the dependent variable, *simultaneously controlling* for all other predictor variables in the regression model. For instance, with education and gender constant, b_{age} indicates the predicted increase in wage for each year one gets older.

The equation is called "linear" because plotting the predicted dependent variable by any one of the predictors with the remaining predictors constant produces a straight line. For example, plotting predicted wage by age for women with 16 years of schooling produces the sloping straight line on the plot, Figure 3.

The linear equation in this example says, Multiply the value of each predictor variable (age in years, years of schooling and female [1 = female, 0 = male]) by its corresponding regression coefficient and add their products to the intercept to get the predicted hourly wage.

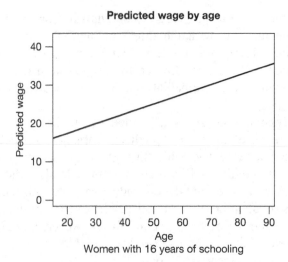

FIGURE 3 Plot of Predicted Wage by Age for Women with 16 Years of Education.

The regression coefficient for age is 0.25. For constant education and gender, the equation predicts that each year one gets older, wage increases by 25 cents. That's the slope of the line in Figure 3. This implies that wage increases by $6.25 from age 25 to age 50, for example, for constant education and gender (and zero inflation).

The regression coefficient for education (years of schooling) is 1.90. This means, controlling for both age and gender, the predicted wage increases by $1.90 an hour for each year of additional schooling (2,006 dollars)—$7.60 more for a college graduate compared to a high school graduate. For the standard number of hours worked per year (2,080 hours), the difference is $15,808 more for a college graduate per year.

The intercept and regression coefficients are estimated from the data by picking the values that give the most accurate predictions for the entire sample. "Most accurate" is defined by minimizing the sum of the squared prediction errors. Details of their calculations are beyond the scope of this chapter; however, the constants are easy to obtain using statistical software.

Regression analysis is a flexible tool. It can be adapted to many nonlinear patterns in data and easily accommodates categorical variables. Linear regression works when the categorical variables are the predictors. For categorical dependent variables, a type of regression called logistic regression is the most-often-used alternative.

"Dummy" Variables in Regression Analysis. Regression uses mathematical procedures that require ratio or interval-level variables. Therefore, nominal variables such as gender and work status need to be converted. A **"dummy" variable** is a nominal variable with only two categories for which the two codes are the numbers 0 and 1. To do this analysis, define two dummy variables:

Female   = 1 if the respondent is female, 0 if the respondent is male

Part time = 1 if respondent is working part time, 0 if working full time
         [Others (e.g., retired) are omitted from this analysis.]

These are the two predictor variables in the equation estimating the effects of gender and work status on wage:

$$predicted\ wage = a + b_{fem}\ female + b_{pt}\ parttime$$

In regression analysis, include a dummy variable for female or male, but not both. Including both is redundant; if you know a respondent is female, you know she is not male. For the same reason, include a dummy variable for part-time *work or* full-time work, but not both.[7]

Table 8 displays the estimated effects on wage from this regression using the GSS data. The regression equation appears at the top of the table in three formats. The last one shows the numerical estimates of the intercept and the slope regression coefficients for the two predictors. The column labels display both the value of the dummy variable, female, and the categories, male (0) and female (1). The same double-labeling appears in the row labels for work status. The cells of the table show the predicted wage for each combination of female and part time.

TABLE 8.   Regression Coefficients for Hourly Wage by Gender and Work Status

Predicted wage = intercept + slope$_1$ × female + slope$_2$ × parttime
= a + b$_{fem}$ female + b$_{pt}$ parttime
= 23.05 − 4.43 female + 0.89 parttime

	Gender	
Work Status	**Female (female = 1)**	**Male (female = 0)**
Full Time (*part time* = 0)	18.61	23.05
(*n*)	(933)	(1,128)
Part Time (*part time* = 1)	19.51	23.94
(*n*)	(249)	(111)

The value of the regression coefficient for *female* is −4.43. This means, controlling for full-time or part-time work, the regression analysis estimates women earn $4.43 less per hour than men earn. And the regression coefficient for part time is 0.89, implying that part-time workers get a slightly higher wage, by 89 cents, than full-time workers, controlling for gender. The estimated effect of part-time work, however, is small and could easily be due to sampling error if the effect were zero in the population.[8]

MORE ABOUT STATISTICAL TESTS

All data in this chapter come from the five most recent GSS sample survey years, except wage and earnings data, which are limited to the 2006 and 2008 GSS surveys. You can be quite sure none of these *sample statistics* (such as percentage, mean, difference between means, or regression coefficient) exactly equals the corresponding *parameter* in the entire U.S. population. Some questions about **statistical inference** are given here:

1. In a bivariate or trivariate table, how can one decide whether the *sample* relationship is large enough to be confident it is not due to sampling error?
2. For *differences among several sample means*, how can one decide whether differences are large enough to be confident they are not due to sampling error?
3. With sample estimates of *regression coefficients*, how can one decide whether the magnitude of the coefficient is large enough to be confident that it is not really zero, and its nonzero value in the sample is just due to sampling error?

An auxiliary question arises for each of these questions: *How confident do we want to be?* It is not possible ever to be certain; science does not use the word "prove" because it suggests being able to project current research findings into the future, which is unknown. The solution to these questions lies in the use of statistical tests.

The next subsection briefly reviews three types of tests:

1. chi-square test for a two-variable table
2. *t*-test and *F*-test to compare means
3. *t*-test and *F*-test for the results from regression analysis.

These descriptions are intended only to introduce you to the basic concepts in statistical inference for tables, means and regression, and give you some exposure to the terminology. Except for chi-square, details about how to calculate statistical tests are beyond the scope of this chapter.

Chi-Square Test for Tables

There are three ways the term *chi-square* is used:

■ *chi-square statistic*—a statistic calculated from a sample table (and often from other types of sample data)

■ *chi-square distribution*—a probability distribution analogous to the normal distribution but with a different shape

■ *chi-square test*—a statistical test based on using the chi-square statistic with the chi-square probability distribution

The chi-square test is used with cross-tabulations. The term *chi-square* (pronounced **kī square**) comes from the Greek letter *chi* and from a sum of squared numbers. It is denoted by χ^2 in statistics.

The chi-square test is carried out by calculating the chi-square statistic from cell frequencies of a crosstab using data from a sample. The calculated chi-square statistic is used with the chi-square distribution to find the *p*-value (probability value). (Most statistics textbooks include an appendix of probabilities for the chi-square distribution; nearly all statistical software (SPSS, Stata, SAS, etc.) prints *p*-values for chi-square. If the *p*-value is below a threshold called the *level of significance* (most often 0.05), reject the null hypothesis of no relationship in the table.

Rejecting the null hypothesis with the level of significance of 0.05 means that the chance of getting a sample value of the chi-square statistic as big as the one observed is 0.05 or less if the variables in the table were, in fact, not related in the population. Not related means all the percentage differences are exactly zero.

Nearly always, rejecting the null hypothesis supports the research hypothesis. For example, the null hypothesis for Table 1 states that there is no relationship between being married and reporting that you are "Very Happy." Rejecting it supports the research hypothesis that marriage tends to improve one's sense of well-being.

The level of significance is an arbitrary threshold set by the investigator. It is the answer to the question *How confident do you want to be?* In theory, one can set the level of significance to any probability number, from just above 0 to just under 1. But in practice there are fairly rigid conventions. Usually the level of significance is set to 0.05 in theoretical research. This means that if you reject the null hypothesis, you have a 5 percent chance of being wrong. Other often-used values of level of significance are 0.02, 0.01, 0.001 and, occasionally with small samples, 0.10.

If something of critical importance is riding on the conclusion, then the level of significance might be set much lower than 0.05—for example, a DNA match to determine whether a defendant will be sentenced to death.

Table 9 shows the calculations of the chi-square statistic for the married $\times$ happy table, Table 1.[9] Column 3 contains the "Expected Cell Frequency." These entries are the frequencies that would occur if all the percentage differences in the table were exactly zero, that is, if there were no relationship between the two variables in the table.

The formula for expected frequency is:

Expected frequency = row total $\times$ column total/total sample n.

If any expected frequency is less than 5, the chi-square statistic does not follow the chi-square distribution very closely, and the chi-square test is not accurate. In practice this means that it often doesn't work for small samples and/or large tables. Other methods do exist for doing the test (e.g., Fisher's Exact Test).

TABLE 9.   Chi-Square Calculations for Table 1

Cell	Observed Cell Frequency	Expected Cell Frequency	Squared Difference $(O-E)^2$	Squared Difference/ Expected Freq.
(1,1)	3,675	3,141.72	284,387.56	90.52
(2,1)	1,005	1,538.28	284,387.56	184.87
(1,2)	3,363	3,896.28	284,387.56	72.99
(2,2)	2,441	1,907.72	284,387.56	149.07
Sum	10,482	10,482		$\chi^2 = 497.45$
				$p < 0.0001$ (with 1 degree of freedom)

NOTE: All calculations rounded to two digits.

The chi-square statistic measures the difference between observed and expected frequencies. The magnitude of the chi-square statistic increases with the degree of relationship in the table. However, chi-square also depends on the sample size and the number of cells in the table, so it is not a good measure of the strength of a relationship. Several measures of the strength of a relationship in a bivariate table are available.[10]

For the data in Table 9 the chi-square statistic is $\chi^2 = 497.45$ with an associated *p*-value very close to zero (much less than 0.0001). This means the probability is nearly zero of obtaining a χ^2 as large as 497.45 for a 2×2 table if there were no relationship between happy and married in the population. Therefore, declare the relationship in Table 2 to be **statistically significant**—a good bet there is relationship between happy and married in the population, a very good bet in this instance.

T-Test and *F*-Test for Comparing Means

Recall that Table 5 shows the difference in average annual earnings between women and men to be $24,300 per year. Is the difference big enough to be due to a relationship in the population and not sampling error? Many people would say, yes. But people have a definite tendency to interpret *sample* relationships as if the same relationship existed in the *population*.

The *t-statistic* can be used to test the null hypothesis that the difference between two means is zero. For the difference between annual earnings of women and men, the *t*-statistic is $t = 13.09$, $p < 0.0001$ (calculation omitted). Therefore, the chance of finding a difference of $24,300 between men and women is less than 1 in 10,000 (much, much less in this instance) if the two genders had equal annual earnings in the U.S. population. This difference is statistically significant, meaning unlikely due to sampling error. If you guessed that the difference is significant, in this example you were right!

What should be done when there are more than two means to be compared simultaneously? Stated another way, the question is, Do a set of means differ from each other? The F-statistic is designed for this type of test. The analysis of variance (ANOVA) is a statistical method that, in part, organizes groups of F-statistics and associated calculations involving comparisons of several means.

Table 10 reports an example containing five means, one for each of five categories of educational degree. The question is, Do these five means differ enough to attribute the differences among them to something besides sampling error? An **F-test** and its associated p-value, reported at the bottom of the table, indicate that these differences are very unlikely to be due to sampling error. Again, the p-value is very, very close to zero.

TABLE 10. Average Annual Earnings ($1,000s) by Highest Educational Degree Completed

Average Annual Earnings	Highest Educational Degree				
	Less than High School	High School Diploma	Associate Degree (Two Year College)	BA Degree	Graduate Degree
$1,000s	23.534	35.693	39.937	62.120	86.761
(n)	(319)	(1,632)	(309)	(654)	(373)

$F = 110.20$, degrees of freedom $= 4, 3,282$, $p < 0.0001$

Not surprisingly, we conclude that annual earnings *are* related to the highest educational degree one has completed—rejecting the null hypothesis of no differences supports the research hypothesis that education makes a difference in earnings.

T-Test and *F*-Test for Regression

The same ideas for statistical tests among means apply to regression analysis. There is an F-test indicating whether *any* of the regression coefficients is significant and a t-test associated with *each* regression coefficient. The t-test associated with each coefficient indicates whether the associated effect is statistically significant. The regression F-test follows the same logic as the F-test applied to means.

For the regression using three variables to predict wage (age, number of years of schooling and gender), and the second regression using two variables (gender and work status), the F-test shows that both are highly statistically significant—that is, their p-values are much below 0.05. The t-tests associated with the regression coefficients for age, schooling and gender also are significant in the first of these two regressions. However, in the regression using just gender and part-time work to predict wage, only the regression coefficient for gender is statistically significant.

Summary

This chapter opens with examples of bivariate and trivariate tables. The first example presents a bivariate table between happiness and marital status, both two-category variables. The table shows a fairly strong relationship.

Next, the relationship between marriage and happiness is tested by controlling for family income, split at the median. The original relationship in the bivariate table holds up with little change for both low- and high-income couples.

There are four main outcomes in a three-variable table:

1. *Replication*: The original bivariate relationship is replicated in each of the categories of the control variable.

2. *Explanation*: The control variable is causally prior to both the independent and dependent variables in the bivariate table, and the partial relationship between the presumed independent variable and dependent variable is zero within categories of the control variable.

3. *Interpretation*: The independent variable in the bivariate table directly affects the control variable, and the control variable directly affects the dependent variable. Therefore, the independent variable does affect the dependent variable, but indirectly. The predictions for the partial relationships of this model are the same as for explanation. The original bivariate relationship is nonzero, but it is zero within levels of the control variable.

4. *Specification* (or *statistical interaction*): The relationship between the independent variable and the dependent variable is different in different levels of the control variable. The bivariate association between the independent variable and the dependent variable could be negative, zero, or positive when the three-variable table contains interaction.

Perfect examples of these ideal types are difficult to find in real data. The marriage–happiness relationship under control for income is a close approximation to replication. The computer-generated tables with NFL fan as the dependent variable, height (short, tall) as the independent variable, and gender as the control variable illustrate the idea of explanation. The relationship between height and NFL fan disappears for each gender.

An example of an **intervening variable** uses the dependent variable wear "long" hair, the independent variable gender and control variable socialization. Gender affects socialization for wearing long hair, which, in turn, affects whether one does or does not wear long hair.

Interpretation also is called the intervening variable model, and socialization is the intervening variable in this example. If the intervening variable model is correct in this example (and we had a good measure of socialization), the relationship between gender and hair length would disappear after controlling for socialization.

An example of specification, also called statistical interaction, is the relationship between gender, bald head and age. The difference between men and women at young ages is negligible. It increases with age.

Following the examples of three-variable tables, the next section of the chapter introduces two more advanced methods of data analysis: (1) comparisons among means, and (2) regression analysis. The research question is, Do males have higher earnings or higher hourly wages than females? Regression analysis and its extensions are designed for research involving simultaneous analysis of many variables. Multiple regression combines at least one and usually several variables to predict the dependent variable. Constants in the regression equation indicate the effect of each predictor (independent variable) on the dependent variable.

The final section of the chapter presents a brief introduction to using statistical tests with tables, comparisons among means and regression. Statistical tests provide a method for making inferences from a sample to its population based on probability calculations. The chapter briefly introduces three types of statistical tests: The chi-square test for a bivariate table, the F-test and t-test applied to analyses of means and the F-test and associated t-test applied to regression.

This chapter illustrates the central role data analysis plays in understanding our social world! The exercises that follow allow you to gain additional practice in data analysis: calculating and reading percentage tables and evaluating a data table.

YOUR REVIEW SHEET

1. Why should percentages within categories of the independent variable (i.e., *within* the percentage base) not be compared? Explain.

2. How are univariate distributions used in social science research?

3. Why are cell frequencies seldom included in a bivariate or trivariate table?

4. Can Table 1 be transposed without losing any information, so that the "General Happiness Measure" is the column variable and "Marital Status" is the row variable? If you did transpose the table, what rule would you use for computing percentages and interpreting the percentages?

5. How can the title of a table provide clues about which are the independent, dependent and the control variables?

6. Suppose you have 10 control variables. What is the main problem with constructing 10 three-variable tables instead of one table including all 10 control variables simultaneously?

7. What is the key to understanding Table 2 and trivariate tables in general?

8. Can variables with more than two categories be included in a table? Briefly explain.

9. What is a good strategy for studying a relationship when the dependent variable is numeric and the independent variable is categorical?

10. Suppose you want to examine simultaneously the effects of age, gender and work status on wage. What analysis method is appropriate? Briefly discuss.

11. Explain what it means to declare the relationship in Table 1 "statistically significant."

12. What feature of Table 6 indicates there is statistical interaction present? Summarize the interaction in Table 6. Answer these same two questions for Table 7.

13. Explain in your own words the purpose of statistical tests.

END NOTES

1. The total sample sizes in these tables do not all match. This is because of missing observations. Each observation that is missing on any variable included in a table is omitted from the table. Therefore, the number of observations in a table is less than or equal to the minimum of nonmissing observations for each variable included in the table.

2. Assuming both are normally distributed.

3. Annual earnings is an estimate of the total earnings ($\times$ \$1,000) from one's principal occupation during the year prior to the survey. Respondents were presented a list of income ranges and asked to check the range that contained their income. Dollar estimates for tables in this chapter were calculated by taking the midpoint of each interval. The top interval is \$150,000 or more. Due to the high skew in income, the estimate for the top boundary was set to 500 (\$500,000), implying a midpoint of $(150 + 500)/2 = 325$. (For your instructor: Separate log-likelihood fits by gender to the log-normal distribution implied that an even higher upper boundary might be justified.)

To keep up with inflation, the GSS periodically updates the income categories. The most recent update refers to 2006 dollars. It is difficult to compare earnings estimates between years with differing sets of income categories. Earnings and income data for survey years 2006 and 2008 used the same 2006 income categories. The analyses reported here use only 2006 and 2008 data.

To avoid unnecessary complication later, the sample used to construct Table 10 includes only people who were working full-time or working part-time.

4. It's interesting, however, that the ratio of men's to women's annual earnings is higher for those working part time than for people working full time ($61/38.2 \approx 1.60$, $31.6/17.3 \approx 1.83$).

5. Wage was estimated by the product of weeks worked with either: (1) hours worked "last week" or (2) usual hours worked if the respondent was not working the week prior to the survey due to vacation, illness, or other temporary situation other than layoff. Several estimates were extremely high (maximum $3333.33). Most of these outliers were associated with very few hours worked in the year. Wage was capped at $125/hr. for the analyses reported here. Also, note that the GSS question refers specifically to earnings from the respondent's main occupation.

6. This is true of multiway tables as well, but it's not apparent from the way they are laid out in this chapter. If you compare column one to column two in Table 2, for instance, you see the relationship between the GSS happiness variable and marital status for income below the median. Although it is not as convenient, you also can see the relationship between income and happiness controlling for marital status by comparing across the two halves of the table. For instance 18.7 percent of *unmarried* people with income below the median report being "Very Happy" compared to 27.5 percent of unmarried people with income above the median who report being "Very Happy," a difference of $27.5 - 18.7 = 8.8$. Similarly, for *married* people, the difference between those above and below the median income is $44.7 - 36.9 = 7.8$. In these comparisons, being married has a stronger relationship to happiness than does income.

7. It's just as acceptable to define a dummy variable male: $1 = $ male, $0 = $ female. Using male instead of female reverses the sign of the regression coefficient. Using female indicates how much less females earn than males, controlling for part time. Using male, instead, indicates how much more males earn per hour than females. Similarly, a dummy variable can be constructed indicating full-time work instead of part-time work. Again, the only difference is a sign reversal on the regression coefficient. The intercept also changes but generally is not relevant to the research hypotheses.

Generally, a nominal variable with any number of categories can be used as an independent variable in regression by including a dummy variable for each category except one. Because of the rule that the categories of a variable must be mutually exclusive and exhaustive, at most, one of these dummy variables can be 1; the rest must be 0. If they all are 0, then the respondent must be classified into the category without a dummy variable in the regression. Either way, the computer knows which category fits the observation.

8. Note how close the predicted hourly wage in Table 8 is to the average hourly wage in the corresponding cells in Table 7. The differences arise because the regression is defined so that the statistical interaction is exactly zero. Since there is very little interaction in Table 7, it matches the predicted values from the regression quite

closely. This is one of the main ways regression analysis simplifies a display of means for every combination of categories of many predictor variables, by assuming statistical interactions to be zero. Regression can, however, accommodate interactions. It is quite flexible in this regard, permitting one to include some of the possible interactions and omit others—when more than two predictors are included, there is more than one interaction to consider.

9. The "observed" frequencies are weighted frequencies, weighted by the GSS weight variable `wtssall`, rounded to whole numbers. But, for pedagogical purposes, the calculations are standard textbook calculations that do not account for the cluster and stratification in the GSS samples.

10. One often-used measure is called Cramer's V. It is calculated by dividing chi-square by $n \times (k-1)$ and taking the square root of the result—where n is the sample size and k is the lesser of the number of rows or number of columns. Cramer's V ranges from 0, no relationship, to 1, perfect agreement between row and column variables. For the example in Table 9, Cramer's V is 0.218, which shows that a very big sample can produce a very small p-value even when the magnitude of the relationship is modest.

STUDY TERMS

chi-square distribution A theoretical probability distribution used in many applications for statistical inference, probably most often in testing for a relationship in a bivariate table.

chi-square test (bivariate table) Statistical test done by calculating the chi-square statistic for a sample cross-tabulation and comparing it to the probability from the chi-square distribution.

chi-square statistic (for a bivariate table) Number calculated from the sample cell frequencies for a cross-tabulation (and many situations other than cross-tabulations not reviewed in the chapter).

control variable (in table elaboration) Variable that contains a bivariate table within each of its categories.

dummy variable Two-category variable that takes a value of 0 or 1, often used as an independent variable in regression analysis.

elaboration Process of studying the relationship between two variables by observing their relationship within each category of one (or more) control variable(s).

explanation The bivariate relationship between two variables is due to their common dependence on a third variable. The bivariate relationship is called spurious—not due to an effect of the independent variable on the dependent variable. The relationship between the dependent variable and independent variable is zero within categories of the variable that affects both of them, the control variable.

F-test Statistical test to assess whether sample differences among two or more means are likely due to sampling error, or whether all predictors in a regression analysis combine to produce a significant relationship between the dependent variable and the combination of all the predictors together.

Data Analysis 2: Describing, Explaining and Evaluating

interpretation/intervening-variable model The independent variable does affect the dependent variable, but only indirectly acting through the control variable. A bivariate relationship exists, but it is zero within categories of the control variable. Compare/contrast to explanation.

intervening variable A variable that is affected by the independent variable and affects the dependent variable. In the pure intervening variable case, the bivariate relationship between the independent variable and the dependent variable vanishes (is zero) when the intervening variable is controlled statistically, as in a three-variable table. See **interpretation**.

regression analysis (linear regression analysis, regression) Method of predicting the value of the dependent variable using a linear formula and one or more independent variables, such as

$$predicted\ wage = a + b_{fem}\ female + b_{pt}\ parttime$$
$$predicted\ wage = a + b_{age}\ age + b_{educ}\ educ + b_{fem}\ female.$$

Usually, regression analysis is done with statistical software program, such as SPSS or SAS.

partial relationship Association between the independent and dependent variables within one category of a control variable (or one cell in the crosstab of two or more control variables); in tabular analysis, a partial table and in regression, a partial slope coefficient.

replication Possible outcome of elaboration. Each partial relationship matches the original bivariate relationship. The control variable has no effect on the bivariate association. For example, happiness by married controlling for gender.

sampling error The difference between a sample statistic and the corresponding population parameter—for instance, the difference between the percentage female in the GSS sample and the percentage female in the adult U.S. population.

specification/statistical interaction Possible outcome of elaboration. The relationship between the independent and dependent variable is different in different categories of one or more control variables. For example, the relationship between gender and bald head increases with age.

statistical inference Process of drawing conclusions about a population using data from a sample of that population.

statistically significant Sample statistic deviates from the null hypothesis by a large enough amount to trigger rejection of the null hypothesis. The size of the difference required to reject the null hypothesis is determined by a probability called a p-value. If the calculated p-value is no larger than the level of significance, reject the null hypothesis. In social research, the most-used level of significance is 0.05. Usually, but not always, rejecting the null hypothesis supports the research hypothesis.

statistical test A procedure for making a decision as to whether a population value of a statistic is some stated value, called the null hypothesis. Usually the null hypothesis states no relationship between two variables. Statistical tests are the primary technical method of statistical inference in use in most research.

t-**test** A statistical test used for many statistics, for example, to compare two sample means or test a regression coefficient against a null hypothesis that it is zero (no partial relationship).

trivariate table A table that includes three variables: independent, dependent and control.

EXERCISES

Exercise 1. Skills Building: Bivariate Table

Data Matrix of 50 Cases from the GSS Dataset

id	year	age	sex	race	marital	degree	wrkstat	rincom06	happy
1502	2006	34	2	1	3	3	6	11	2
3290	2006	25	1	1	1	1	1	17	2
982	2008	39	1	1	3	1	1	26	1
471	2006	38	1	1	3	2	1	22	2
1109	2006	45	2	1	1	4	3	19	1
1279	2006	40	1	1	1	3	1	23	1
3846	2006	43	2	1	1	3	1	22	0
3295	2006	81	1	1	2	0	5	0	2
1094	2008	70	2	1	1	4	5	0	1
743	2008	49	2	2	3	1	5	0	2
1869	2006	69	2	1	1	1	5	0	2
448	2006	57	1	1	3	1	1	20	0
3110	2006	31	1	1	1	1	1	15	2
3113	2006	38	2	1	1	3	7	0	2
719	2008	41	1	1	5	1	1	0	2
755	2008	36	1	1	5	3	1	14	3
139	2006	51	1	1	1	3	1	23	2
765	2006	23	2	3	5	1	1	11	0
1555	2006	99	1	1	9	1	1	99	1
256	2006	65	2	3	1	1	5	0	0
115	2008	56	1	1	1	1	1	21	2
3837	2006	38	2	1	1	2	1	17	0
241	2008	66	1	1	1	3	5	0	2
223	2006	33	1	3	1	1	1	11	2
2645	2006	30	1	1	5	4	1	17	1
1933	2008	21	1	1	5	1	6	0	1
1343	2008	49	1	1	3	1	1	99	2
203	2006	58	1	1	5	3	5	0	3
1572	2008	60	2	1	1	1	7	0	2
210	2006	51	1	2	1	1	3	20	2
621	2008	48	2	1	1	3	1	20	1

id	year	age	sex	race	marital	degree	wrkstat	rincom06	happy
1211	2008	43	1	2	1	0	1	15	2
1240	2006	47	1	1	3	1	1	20	2
1153	2008	34	2	1	1	3	7	0	2
3417	2006	77	2	1	5	4	5	99	2
2579	2006	21	2	1	5	1	2	10	1
3497	2006	26	1	1	5	0	1	19	2
368	2006	22	1	3	5	1	1	14	0
693	2008	43	1	3	1	4	1	25	2
1343	2006	51	2	1	3	3	1	18	2
2973	2006	33	2	3	1	1	7	98	1
343	2008	40	2	2	1	1	2	2	1
824	2008	25	2	2	5	1	7	12	2
650	2006	51	2	2	4	1	1	9	3
4290	2006	29	2	3	1	3	7	0	0
2400	2006	54	2	1	1	2	1	19	0
3873	2006	62	1	2	1	0	8	0	2
1122	2008	36	2	2	5	1	6	12	3
1883	2008	41	1	1	3	1	1	14	2
1442	2008	31	1	3	5	0	1	20	2

The values of all variables except wrkstat and happy are defined in Figure 3. The values for these two variables are as follows:

`happy` 0 = NA

1 = Very happy

2 = Pretty happy

3 = Happy

8 = Don't know

9 = No answer

`wrkstat` 1 = Working full time

2 = Working part time

3 = With a job, but not at work because of temporary illness, vacation, strike

4 = Unemployed, laid off, looking for work

5 = Retired

6 = In school

7 = Keeping house

8 = Other

9 = No answer

Directions: Table 11 below shows the bivariate crosstab between higher degree (at least a junior-college degree) and married. Replicate this table using the sample in the Data Matrix of 50 Cases from the GSS Dataset observations in table above. Prepare two tables: (1) One showing tally marks and frequencies in the same cells, and (2) a complete bivariate table matching the format in Table 11.

TABLE 11. Percentage Who Earned a Junior-College Degree or Higher by Marital Status

	Married		
Higher Degree	**No**	**Yes**	**Total**
No	73.0%	61.8%	66.7%
Yes	27.0	38.2	33.3
(*n*)	100.0	100.0	100.0
Total	(6,501)	(8,387)	(14,888)

The GSS variable `degree` must be collapsed into a dichotomy, and the GSS variable `marital` also must be collapsed into a dichotomy.

Be sure to omit missing values, if any.

1. Summarize the relationships in your table of 50 cases (or less if any missing observations).

2. Calculate expected frequencies for your table. Use the frequency counts, not the percentages. Are any of these frequencies less than 5? What implication does your answer have for a chi-square test applied to your table?

3. Compare/contrast your table based on the subsample to Table 11. Chi-square for your table is 2.64, $p = 0.1040$. Is the relationship in your table statistically significant? Why or why not?

4. What implications do you see for the sample size needed to detect the relationship in Table 11.

Exercise 2. Skills Building: Trivariate Table

Directions: Table 12 shows the trivariate crosstab between higher degree (at least a junior-college degree) by married, controlling for gender. Replicate this table using the subsample of 50 GSS observations in the unnumbered table in Exercise 1.

1. Summarize the relationships in the two partial tables.

2. Compare and contrast the percentages in your table to those in Table 12.

3. Calculate expected cell frequencies in each of your two partial tables. Are any of them less than 5? If so what implication does that have for a chi-square test applied to each partial table?

4. What difficulty with multivariate tables emphasized in the chapter does your trivariate table illustrate?

TABLE 12. Percentage Who Earned a Junior-College Degree or Higher by Marital Status, Controlling for Gender

	Women			Men		
	Married			Married		
Higher Degree	No	Yes	Total	No	Yes	Total
No	73.2%	63.3%	67.7%	72.8%	60.3%	65.6%
Yes	26.8	36.7	32.3	27.2	39.7	34.4
(*n*)	100.0	100.0	100.0	100.0	100.0	100.0
Total	(3,602)	(4,456)	(8,058)	(2,899)	(3,932)	(6,831)

Exercise 3. Skills Building: Reading a Percentage Table

Directions: Refer to Table 1 when answering the following questions. Review the rules for calculating and reading percentages.

Factual Questions

1. What is the independent variable in Table 1? What is the dependent variable?
2. What is the percentage base (row totals, column totals, total *n*)?
3. Are the percentages in Table 1 calculated correctly? Explain, using Rule 1 for calculating percentages. Mention any ambiguities you see about deciding which variable is the independent variable.
4. Summarize the findings shown in Table 1.

Questions for Discussion

1. Provide a brief social science explanation for the findings.

Exercise 4. Skills Building: Table of Means

Directions: Use the data in the unnumbered table given in Exercise 1. Split the variable named `marital` into three categories (1) never married, (2) married, (3) married before, but not now. Calculate the mean age for each of these three marital status categories. Omit missing values, if any. Show your calculations. Construct a bivariate table similar to Table 10 to show your results.

1. Suppose you were asked to make a judgment as to whether these means differ enough to be statistically significant. What is your judgment?
2. Do you think that the mean for single (never married) persons is significantly different from the means for those who were married, or divorced, separated or widowed?
3. What is the dependent variable in this table, and what is the independent variable?
4. Propose a generalization to apply to a table of means of the rule for a bivariate percentage table: Use categories of the independent variable as the percentage base. Does your table follow this rule?

Exercise 5. Evaluation of Research Article: Data Tables

Note: Some students can benefit from reading a complete journal research article. Although crosstab analysis now is used infrequently in published scholarly articles, one article using trivariate tabular analysis is Fiorentine and Cole (1992).

Directions to students: Read the article referenced above and answer the questions below. Your instructor will tell you how to obtain the article.

Factual Questions

1. What is the dependent variable in Table II in the article? What is the independent variable? What is the control variable? Explain the reason for your answers.

2. How many males perceive their chances of medical school admission as excellent if they had a high GPA? How many females? Show your calculations. (*Hint:* Convert percentages into frequencies.)

3. How many partial tables are shown? Briefly describe each, using the control variable category name for each.

Questions for Discussion

1. Look at the percentages in the "competitive GPA" category for males and females and the frequencies obtained for Question 2 for each gender. Briefly explain the advantage of calculating percentages for cross-classifying tables versus looking at the frequencies.

2. Assume that a percentage difference of 10 percent or greater indicates a "substantively important" relationship between the two variables. Is there a *substantively* significant relationship between gender and estimates of admission?

3. Based on your answer to the previous question, do you agree or disagree with the authors that "there was no gender difference in estimating the chances of admission to medical school"? Explain your answer.

PREPARING THE REPORT

INTRODUCTION: LOOKING AT HOW THE SOCIAL WORLD WORKS

"She looked at the lips that seemed to suggest...."

Unlike romance novels, detective stories and many forms of popular writing, which are produced for the pleasure of individuals, writing about research results is undertaken to contribute to general human knowledge and welfare. For example, disaster research has found that procedures followed "on the ground" often don't conform to plans for managing disasters (Quarantelli, 1997). Victims are likely to be transported by private vehicles to the most familiar hospital, regardless of disaster plans, resulting in an uneven distribution of patients among hospitals. At the hospitals, the less seriously injured usually arrive first and therefore tend to be treated first. Also, new groups providing emergency medical services often emerge during disasters, and established institutions such as hospitals often are underutilized.

Findings about services during disaster times are potentially very useful for community leaders and the general public. The heightened concern about public security after September 11, 2001, reinforces the need for successful management of disasters, whether human or natural in origin. But without appropriate research and dissemination of the findings, knowledge about disasters would be known only to the disaster victims, a few of their family and friends and local relief workers.

If the research findings don't support a well-formulated hypothesis or theory should they be reported? Yes—they *should* be. Negative findings tell researchers where *not* to look and inform policymakers what *doesn't* work (Harrison & McNeece, 2001). But this important point generally is overlooked in the popular press, and often by journal editors and reviewers. It is much easier to publish a paper based on "positive findings" than one in which the theory is not supported by the data.

Goals of This Chapter

When you set out to complete a term paper, what questions come to your mind? Probably these two questions: "What should I write about?" and "How should I organize it?"

This chapter summarizes the final step in the research process: **dissemination** of scientific research results. It illustrates an important contrast between the way commonsense information spreads among individuals and the public nature of science. The chapter also describes key issues encountered by authors of scientific reports, and gives instruction about how to write a scientific report for this course and other courses—or for publication.

Most people find it difficult to write—*do you*? Where does one learn how to write a scientific-style report? Start by reading what others have written, such as the excerpts from journal articles and monographs. Often finding a topic and getting organized are the most difficult parts. This chapter offers advice on both counts.

RESEARCH REPORTS: FOUR EXAMPLES

This section summarizes and describes the organization of (1) a research-based journal article, (2) an evaluation report, (3) a monograph and (4) a government document. The summaries are intended to convey three key aspects of report writing:

1. the *importance and variety* of formal research reports
2. the *organization* of the reports
3. the *content* of the reports

Of course, there are many types of scientific reports other than the four mentioned here, far too many to summarize them all; these four provide an overview.

Also, you will learn about a more visual type of research dissemination than papers or presentations—the poster display—that is increasingly important in class activities and at professional conferences.

Journal Articles and Similar Papers

Perhaps the most prestigious and important way to disseminate research results in most social science disciplines is publication in a scholarly refereed journal (Thyer, 2001, p. 504). "**Refereed journal**" refers to a periodical that publishes only papers that have passed an intensive review process called "**peer review**." Peer review means each submission to the journal is evaluated by a panel of experts for importance and accuracy. Reviewers include faculty and other scholars closely associated with the academic discipline of the journal. For example, a sociologist might review articles in *Marriage and the Family*, *Criminology* or *Social Problems*.

A few examples of refereed journals and their social science discipline are given here:

- *American Sociological Review, Social Forces* (sociology)
- *Social Work* (social work)
- *Criminology, Journal of Research on Crime and Delinquency* (criminology/justice)
- *Marriage and the Family, Journal of Social Issues* (family and human relations)
- *Addiction, Social Problems* (human services)
- *American Economic Review, Journal of Human Resources* (economics)
- *American Political Science Review, Journal of Politics* (political science)

In contrast, articles published in popular-press magazines, such as *Newsweek, Sports Illustrated, Ebony* and *Marie Claire*, typically are not subject to the formal peer review used by scientific journals. Popular-press magazines (1) contain articles about current issues for the general public, (2) seldom are based on original scholarly research and (3) typically have no list of sources used by the author to write the article. Most articles in the popular press do undergo informal review by an editor and possibly one or two others, but they are not subject to the lengthy formal review process required for publication in a refereed journal. And publication deadlines in popular-press magazines would not permit formal reviews that can require months to complete.

Who chooses the experts to review articles submitted to refereed journals? The journal editor does, based on specializations needed to evaluate each specific article. For example, a qualitative research article on "social-class inequality in education" submitted for publication to the journal *Social Forces* calls for reviewers with expertise about class inequality, education and the relationships between education and class inequality. Also, reviewers may be selected, in part, for their expertise in specialized research methods used in the article, whether qualitative or quantitative.

The chief job of peer reviewers is to evaluate the article. They identify strengths and weaknesses, suggest revisions and recommend to the journal editor whether to publish the paper. Often papers are revised multiple times before publication, and many are not published. It can take up to a year or longer to obtain a publication decision from a journal. The goal of the peer-review process is twofold: (1) select only the best submissions for publication, and (2) improve the quality of selected papers.

Example of a Journal Article: *Inbreeding and Infant Mortality among the Amish, Revisited.* This study investigates effects of inbreeding on infant mortality among the Amish residing in Lancaster County, Pennsylvania (Dorsten, Hotchkiss, & King, 1999). It relies on unusual data—information for up to 12 generations of Amish families.

The research paper appeared in the scholarly journal *Demography*, published by the Population Association of America (PAA). According to the PAA website,

> *Demography* is the official journal of the Population Association of America. It is an interdisciplinary peer-reviewed periodical that publishes articles of general interest to population scientists. Fields represented in its contents include geography, history, biology, statistics, business, epidemiology, and public health, in addition to social scientific disciplines such as sociology, economics, psychology, and political science. Published quarterly, it includes theoretical and methodological articles, commentaries, and specialized research papers covering both developed and developing nations. (*http://www.jstor.org/pss/2648113*)

The findings of the inbreeding paper are interesting: The higher the level of inbreeding, the less likely a newborn is to survive the first year of life. But more important to social scientists, sociodemographic variables such as parents' church, district of residence and year of child's birth also influence the risk of infant death, even with statistical control for inbreeding. Although the findings properly apply to the Amish community, the research likely was published in the journal *Demography* because it extends accumulating knowledge about the effect of sociodemographic variables on infant mortality.

What are the components of a scholarly article like the inbreeding study? As with nearly all scholarly papers, the inbreeding article contains an abstract. The **abstract** is a summary of the research report. The rest of the paper follows a fairly standard format. The major sections are shown as run-in headings in the next paragraphs.

Introduction. The introductory section doesn't display a heading. It begins by identifying a gap in current knowledge and states how the paper contributes to filling the gap.

> An unresolved issue in research on child survival is the extent to which familial mortality risk in infancy is due to biological influences net of sociodemographic and economic factors, such as household economic status, household health-related knowledge and attitudes, parental competence in child rearing and genetic viability....
>
> We extend prior research on familial mortality risk in the first year of life by using the inbreeding coefficient to predict perinatal, neonatal, and postneonatal mortality. (Dorsten, et al., 1999, p. 263)

Usually the introduction is brief. Even though the typical introduction is short, it must focus precisely on a known issue or present a concise explanation for *why* readers should be interested in a new issue.

"Unobserved Measures and Recent Familial Mortality Research." This is the "literature review," even though it's not called that. The paper summarizes earlier papers investigating possible bias in estimating the effects of socioeconomic variables on infant mortality due to omission of an explicit measure of inbreeding.

In short, the literature review focuses narrowly on the main "reason for being" of the paper. The research question for the paper is: *Has past research overestimated effects of variables like education and earnings on infant mortality, due to lack of control for genetic influences like inbreeding?* To find out, the partial solution is to include an explicit measure of inbreeding in the analysis.

"Data and Methods." This section describes the sample—how the sample was collected, how many cases it contains, and how many potential cases were eliminated and why. The sample was taken from church records of the Old Order Amish. All cases of infant death were included, plus a sample of survivors. This section also describes each variable, so that readers know exactly how it's defined.

The description must do more than just list the names of variables; for example, it is not sufficient to list gender as a variable without describing how it is defined for the study. Readers must know what code is assigned to male and female in order to interpret the results.

"Findings." The summary of findings is organized around a sequence of tables fairly typical in journal articles.

- *Table 1.* The first table presents univariate statistics for each variable in the study: mean, standard deviation, and minimum and maximum values.

- *Table 2.* The second table shows bivariate relationships between the inbreeding coefficient and the three time periods of infant mortality: Perinatal mortality, neonatal mortality, and postneonatal mortality.[1]

- *Table 3 through Table 5b.* The remaining tables display the main findings, which are estimates of the effects of inbreeding and the other independent variables on three outcomes: perinatal, neonatal and postneonatal deaths.

"Discussion." The final section of the paper summarizes the findings. The data indicate that inbreeding affects neonatal and postneonatal mortality but not perinatal mortality. The discussion section emphasizes the main point and offers possible reasons for the exception for perinatal mortality. The final conclusion of the study is:

> In summary, we find that inbreeding increases the risk of neonatal and postneonatal mortality. Yet, the findings of the present study also reaffirm the relevance of incorporating social, demographic, and cultural measures in studies of child survival. We find clear evidence of the impact of these measures, even in a population [with a high level of intermarriage] in which biological influences are expected. (p. 270)

Evaluation Reports

Applied or *evaluation research* assesses the effectiveness of social programs. Unlike basic research, evaluation research focuses on whether intended outcomes of policy and practice were achieved in a specific setting.

The evaluation report provides results primarily for practitioners and policy-makers. However, individuals involved with a social intervention ("stakeholders") don't necessarily agree on an outcome, its definition and measurement or even the length of time required to achieve it. Thus, an evaluator must consider viewpoints of those involved, such as appropriate outcomes and how to measure them, how to implement the intervention and variables other than the intervention needed for the analysis.

Example of an Evaluation Report: *Evaluation of a School-Based Pregnancy-Prevention Program.* Let's look at a social intervention program designed to make pregnancy-prevention information and contraceptive technology available to inner-city adolescents (Zabin et al., 1986). The evaluation was designed to assess the school-based intervention by comparing changes in knowledge, attitudes, behaviors and pregnancy rates between students who were offered pregnancy-prevention services and students who were not offered these services.

Students in the schools with the pregnancy-prevention program were in the "experimental group." The rest were in the "control group." Data were collected from students through self-administered questionnaires. The article suggests that the two school-based clinics did influence student behaviors and attitudes, as anticipated. The primary goal of the evaluation was to assess the contributions from the specific program included in the evaluation, but the researchers conclude other schools might benefit from similar programs.

The article by Zabin and coauthors appeared in the professional journal *Family Planning Perspectives* (now *Perspectives on Sexual and Reproductive Health*), published by the Alan Guttmacher Institute:

> *Perspectives on Sexual and Reproductive Health* (formerly *Family Planning Perspectives*) provides the latest peer-reviewed, policy-relevant research and analysis on sexual and reproductive health and rights in the United States and other industrialized countries. For more than three decades, *Perspectives* has offered unique insights into how reproductive health issues relate to one another; how they are affected by policies and programs; and their implications for individuals and societies. (*http://www.guttmacher.org/journals/aboutper.html*)

The evaluation article doesn't contain an abstract; the sections of the paper are summarized below.

Introduction. As with the *Demography* paper, the introduction is not preceded by a heading, but it's much longer than the introduction to a typical journal article. It describes in detail the participating schools, the characteristics of the sample of students, the survey instrument, sample attrition (dropout) and the components of the pregnancy-prevention program.

Remember, evaluations assess specific programs in specific settings. Therefore, a detailed description of the setting is needed.

"Some Methodological Problems." This section describes methodological problems of the study and notes that these problems are typical in school evaluations. As you might expect, one of the problems was student absence from school on the days the surveys were administered. Another problem was students in the study moving in and out of the school attendance areas. The survey was administered four times, about a year apart, to the same students.

"Changes in Knowledge and Attitudes." The paper contains no section titled "Findings." The findings are split into three sections. "Changes in Knowledge..." is the first one. It reports differences between experimental and control schools in changes of attitude and knowledge over the 4 years of the study. The findings are mixed, but appear to show small positive effects of the program on knowledge about contraception and reproductive health, and little or no effects on attitudes.

"Changes in Behavior." Changes in sexual behavior are reported in this section. Effects on age at first sexual intercourse were small, but effects on attending the clinic and use of contraceptives were substantial. Junior-high boys in the experimental school made as frequent use of the clinic as did girls.

"Pregnancy Rates." The final section summarizing the findings focuses on the likelihood of becoming pregnant. The data indicate a strong impact of the program on the risk of pregnancy among sexually active females—the program reduced pregnancy risk.

"Conclusions." The authors conclude the program was effective. Appropriate for an evaluation, they mention the specific location and time of the evaluation:

> The brief, though intensive, pregnancy prevention program introduced in two Baltimore schools has demonstrated significant changes in several areas of adolescent knowledge and behavior—changes that have major implications for the formulation of public policy and for program design. (p. 124)

They generalize the findings beyond the Baltimore schools in the study and recommend:

> In conclusion, these findings suggest the efficacy of a program with pregnancy prevention as an explicit objective. Such a model requires a program and a staff capable of addressing a wide range of reproductive health issues. (p. 125)

Monographs and Books

Translated literally, a monograph means "one writing." For social science research, this definition translates into the following statement: A book-length publication that focuses on a narrow research issue, often based on a large research project.

How does a monograph differ from a book? A monograph usually is shorter in length. Monographs and books are prepared by some researchers so that they have a complete collection of their work in one place, rather than as several articles in different journals, although some also publish individual articles from a study (Thyer, 2001, p. 506).

Example of a Monograph: *Sidewalk.* Duneier's (1999) study titled *Sidewalk* was published as a monograph. Recall that Duneier shows how street vendors and panhandlers in Greenwich Village, New York, solve many problems of daily life, including lack of access to public restrooms.

The general progression of the chapters is from descriptions of specific subgroups of people to their daily life on the city streets. This monograph is divided into three sections, which the author calls "parts."

Part 1: The Informal Life of the Sidewalk: Three chapters: "Book Vendors," "Magazine Vendors" and "The Men without Accounts."

Part 2: New Uses for Sidewalks: One chapter: "How Sixth Avenue Became a Sustaining Habitat."

Part 3: The Limits of Informal Social Control: Four chapters: "Sidewalk Sleeping," "When You Gotta Go," "Talking to Women" and "Accusations: Caveat Vendor?"

Duneier shares two concerns with his readers: Should he use pseudonyms (aliases) to protect the privacy of the people he wrote about? And how could he assure each person the right to an "informed decision" about whether to be in the book?

Duneier didn't conduct covert (nonparticipant) observation, but his method of getting "informed consent" nevertheless is quite interesting:

> I brought the completed manuscript to a hotel room and tried to read it to every person whose life was mentioned.... [However, m]ost people were much more interested in how they looked in the photographs than in how they sounded or were depicted. (Duneier, 1999, pp. 347–348)

Government Reports

The last example of a research report is particularly noteworthy. It illustrates how research sometimes offers cause-and-effect conclusions about critically important topics that can't be examined using random assignment experiments, due to ethical and practical constraints.

Example of a Government Report: ***The U.S. Surgeon General's Report on Smoking and Health.*** The massive report of the Surgeon General's Advisory Committee on Smoking and Health, published in 1964, is a landmark government publication. It relied on data from many sources, including questionnaires and interviews; retrospective data from the subjects' histories and studies that followed subjects contacted before the onset of disease and followed until their death or the study ended. The Committee also consulted autopsy studies revealing damage to internal organs of people and controlled experiments with animals. In addition, it relied on members' expertise related to medicine, biology, chemistry, psychology and statistics.

The Surgeon General's report resembles a monograph in many respects: It is a monograph in length and focuses on a narrow range of research questions. It consists of two parts, 15 chapters and 387 pages.

But there are important contrasts between a government report and a monograph. First, it's rare for more than three or four authors to collaborate on a monograph. The Surgeon General's report lists 10 members of the Surgeon General's Advisory Committee on Smoking and Health plus the then-surgeon general, and the then-assistant surgeon general, vice-chair. Second, government reports often do not contain original research. The Surgeon General's report is based on research existing *prior to* the time of its publication. This is a distinctive difference between a government report and a monograph.

The committee consisted of highly capable experts in a mix of fields such as internal medicine, mathematical statistics, clinical pathology, genetics, cancer, biology and cardiopulmonary disease. The report is too lengthy to summarize in detail. But you can get a sense of its breadth and depth by looking at the main part of its table of contents:

Part I. Introduction, Summaries and Conclusions

Chapter 1	Introduction
Chapter 2	Conduct of the Study
Chapter 3	Criteria for Judgment
Chapter 4	Summaries and Conclusions

Part II. Evidence of the Relationship of Smoking to Health

Chapter 5	Consumption of Tobacco Products in the United States
Chapter 6	Chemical and Physical Characteristics of Tobacco and Tobacco Smoke
Chapter 7	Pharmacology and Toxicology of Nicotine
Chapter 8	Mortality
Chapter 9	Cancer
Chapter 10	Non-Neoplastic Respiratory Diseases, Particularly Chronic Bronchitis and Pulmonary Emphysema
Chapter 11	Cardiovascular Diseases
Chapter 12	Other Conditions
Chapter 13	Characterization of the Tobacco Habit and Beneficial Effects of Tobacco
Chapter 14	Psycho-Social Aspects of Smoking
Chapter 15	Morphological Constitution of Smokers

Chapters 3 and 4 of the report are of particular interest. They contain a lengthy review of the struggle with the issue of identifying cause-and-effect results between smoking and health without controlled experiments. The arguments concerning the causal effects of smoking tobacco convey a sense of the serious work that can go into a government document. The argument starts by noting an association between tobacco smoke and the likelihood of an early death.

> The array of information from the prospective and retrospective studies of smokers and nonsmokers clearly establishes an association between cigarette smoking and substantially higher death rates. (U.S. Public Health Service, 1964, p. 30)

But, the survey data consulted by the Committee exhibited several problems. For example, the average nonresponse rate was 32 percent for the seven prospective studies. The Committee estimated that nonresponse may have led to overestimation of a relationship between smoking and health problems.

The Committee, nonetheless, concluded in specific instances that a causal connection does exist between smoking and disease. For example:

> Cigarette smoking is causally related to lung cancer in men; the magnitude of the effect of cigarette smoking far outweighs all other factors. The data for women, though less extensive, point in the same direction. (U.S. Public Health Service, 1964, 31)

In the absence of experiments with humans, how was the committee able to draw these types of conclusions? Certainly, the variety of evidence was an important factor. In addition—research must *control (as far as possible) variables that might cause people both to smoke and to contract diseases associated with tobacco smoke.*

Therefore, the Committee reviewed studies with controls for a number of possible confounding variables, including age, occupation, urban–rural residence, exercise, drinking habits and religion. And it's pretty clear that lung cancer doesn't cause people to smoke. The balance of evidence fairly strongly indicates a causal connection between smoking tobacco and various ailments.

The Poster Display

Have you ever looked at posters in school projects, on display in public places like supermarkets or even in class presentations? What do you recall about their appearance?

A common tendency with posters is *clutter!* Posters should be as sparse as possible, yet convey all the information that is necessary to understand the project.

As Stoss (2010) emphasizes, "The poster presentation is NOT the pasting of a scholarly article on poster board or foam-core and standing by to defend the results reproduced in miniature on the 'poster' "...Rather, it should be a "...well-designed, eye-catching, and engaging...display of research or scientific information" (p. 1, "Poster Presentations"). Stoss offers visual examples of a "good" and a "bad" poster at *http://library.buffalo.edu/asl/guides/bio/posters.html*, as well as websites to locate poster design tips, sample poster sessions, graphics and poster software, books and journal articles and even tips on managing poster presentation "disasters."

Typically, posters include the following:

- Title of the project (in larger letters) and name and affiliation of the researcher(s)
- Objectives of the research
- Theory and hypothesis (if relevant to the project)
- Background information (e.g., sample/population and field site, if applicable)
- Data, method of data collection and method of analysis (keep these brief)
- Findings (generally limit to easy-to-read graphs or a few simple tables)
- The most important conclusions from the study, highlighted.

Each of these topics can be separate sections of the poster put on letter-sized paper. Each section should have a heading, such as "Findings." Use easy-to-read print. Some presenters use colored construction paper to matte each poster section; others use colored paper or color printers to print the individual posters. See the sample illustration in Figure 1.

What about technical project details, such as mathematical equations or special computer software? Consider your audience. Also, each academic discipline has its own set of standards that you should follow. Contact your faculty mentor to ensure that you are following the correct format.

In general, neatly display each individual poster section with a logical progression of ideas. Place your title in a "banner" format near the top. If using individual sections, hang them near eye level, particularly those most important to explain the research.

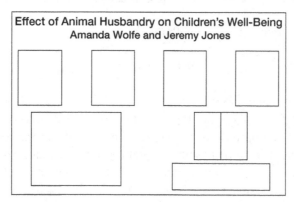

FIGURE 1   Example of a Poster Layout.

If you have access to a poster printer and Microsoft PowerPoint, you can develop a professional-style poster. (e.g., see information about technical requirements, design, layout, etc., at *http://sph.washington.edu/practicum/ppposter_3c.asp*, University of Washington School of Public Health, 2010). Other websites offer links to media software such as *Photoshop* and *InDesign* and even to websites that will print and ship your poster to you (e.g., *http://www.hsl.unc.edu/services/mdstudio/howdoi.cfm*) (Health Sciences Library, UNC-Chapel Hill, 2010).

At a **poster presentation**, the researcher usually is present to answer questions during at least part of the viewing time. Find out in advance whether you need to bring a large piece of posterboard to display your individual poster sections and whether to bring pushpins, tape, and so on. Additional details about poster presentations are included in a later section of this chapter.

A BRIEF GUIDE TO REPORT WRITING

Getting Started—and Following Through

Here are some suggestions about writing reports about qualitative research, derived from Wolcott's (2001) book titled, *Writing Up Qualitative Research*. The suggestions generally apply to most scholarly writing.

1. *You are "telling a story," and your own writing style can be used.* If you don't have a writing style (or don't know whether you have one), a good approach is to think about what *you* would need to know in order to understand your own project if someone else were describing it to you. How can you make your topic interesting to your readers? Try stating your research problem in the form of an interesting question, for example:

> *"Are children who assume responsibility for care of pets more likely than other children to develop an interest in community volunteering?"*

Or, you might get started with this:

> *"The purpose of this study is. . . . "*

As Wolcott points out, if you are stuck here, then perhaps the problem is "focus," meaning your topic likely is too broad. If you said something grandiose like "The purpose of this study is to solve the crime problem," you definitely lack focus. The "broad-topic" problem is common among many writers. Take time at the beginning to narrow your topic; it will save much frustration! Remember, knowledge advances in "baby steps." Look at published research articles as models. You don't want to "re-invent the wheel."

2. *Begin writing early, even before beginning data collection.* You always can change words, sentences, paragraphs and sections of a paper. Use short sentences and paragraphs. Perhaps start by describing existing research you read and details of how you plan to obtain your data. Wolcott suggests writing an early draft, even before beginning the research—you don't have to show it to anyone. Just getting some ideas on paper (or into the computer) helps to clarify your thinking and getting past the "blank canvas" problem that some painters face—the worry that the first brush stroke is so important it must be "perfect." Having something on paper, even if most of it is changed, will encourage you to work on it.

You also might talk with another student or a professor about your research. Explain your goals and how you plan to collect data. Or, try writing to yourself in order to help pin down your thoughts. For example, if your goal is to describe adoptive parents' perceptions of the infant adoption process, how will you locate adoptive parents, how will you obtain data from them and what do you think you might find?

Be sure to: (1) use headings and subheadings to organize ideas, (2) check all references for accuracy and (3) identify the citation style needed. Check with your instructor about the use and preferred style of headings. Rules for citation and the format of references vary by discipline (and professional journal).

Here's an often-forgotten step—keep an accurate record of what you read *and* the full **citation** and reference information for each source. And, check references and citations for accuracy. You will not want to scramble for this information when you are finishing your paper!

Citations are references within the body of a paper to a source of an idea, fact or quotation. *The Sociology Student Writer's Manual* (Johnson et al., 2002) also contains a chapter on citations based primarily on the ASA *Style Guide*. **References** appear at the end of a document as a list of sources cited in the paper. You might create a computer file with this information, including direct and indirect quotes. Or you can use individual note cards.

Cite *all* sources of ideas, quotes and information not widely known—everything other than your own thoughts and information that is "common knowledge" (e.g., television watching is common in many households) and basic knowledge presented in many sources (e.g., personal computers vary in cost).

Like all writers, you need to read and revise your written drafts several times. Also, use "spell-check" in your word-processing program—but don't use it blindly.

Components of a Qualitative Report

The organization of qualitative (meaning-based) reports varies considerably by topic and theoretical preferences of the author. And, there is considerably more variety in writing qualitative reports than quantitative ones. Consequently, the content of sections about methods and analysis of qualitative reports generally are comparatively long narrative accounts.

Lofland and Lofland (1995) present an outline that resembles the major topic headings of most qualitative scientific reports. The sections presented by Lofland and Lofland are given below:

- *Abstract.* The abstract contains a succinct, paragraph-length summary of the paper.

- *Introductory paragraphs.* The introductory section of the report states the main theory or thesis. Lofland and Lofland advocate stating it in the form of a proposition or relationship, using nontechnical terminology. In addition, the early paragraphs often state the relationship of the topic to social problems.

- *Early overview.* Following the statement of the thesis, inform the reader about the organization and content of the rest of the report.

- *Literature review.* Include a review of studies similar to yours, and tell how they relate to the research you are reporting.

- *Data sources.* This section is important. Fieldwork is highly varied. Inform readers how you identified your sample or social setting, how you gained access, whether you informed participants you were doing research about them, about social conflicts between you and your subjects, about your emotional reactions and feelings of stress, about emotional entanglements between you and your subjects and how you recorded your observations. This section may require several pages or, in a monograph, may take an entire chapter.

- *Main body.* This section presents a summary of observations and some type of analysis. Clearly describe how the data and your analysis of it relate to the main thesis/theory stated in the introductory section. Make the connection explicit for the reader. Subdivide this section for ease of reading and reorganize the subheadings until you "get them right."

- *Summary and conclusions.* Include a titled section that summarizes the study, states your conclusions, discusses implications for theory and proposes additional research to complement what you've done. Mention both the strengths and weaknesses of your research.

- *References.* List a complete reference for each citation in the text. Verify that each reference is complete and accurate, and follows the prescribed format.

Components of a Quantitative Report

If you've collected quantitative (numerical) data, follow the outline for journal articles shown in the subsection in this chapter titled "Journal Articles and Similar Papers." You don't need to follow the headings exactly. Your report must include all the components, however.

An abstract is optional—ask your instructor. Do include the following topics using specific headings that fit your paper.

- *Introduction.* This section should give a to-the-point overview of the purpose of the study.

- *Focused literature review and theory.* Cite only studies directly relevant to your paper. Perhaps a good general motto here, particularly as you finalize your paper, is, *When in doubt, leave it out.*

  You might split this discussion into two or three sections, each with its own heading, depending on the nature of the study. For example, if there is controversy in the literature about some aspect of your study, you may need to devote a short section to describing the controversy and how you resolved it. Finally, state your hypotheses.

- *Data.* Describe your data. If you developed a questionnaire or completed interviews, describe the questions for your key variables and explain how they reliably measure what you intend them to measure (validity). Describe the sample. How did you (or others) select it, and how were the data collected—by mailed questionnaire, by telephone interview, by in-person interview or by observation? If you are doing secondary analysis using data from a large dataset like the General Social Survey, some of these details can be omitted. Instead, cite the documents related to the data (e.g., the codebook).

  Precisely define each variable so the reader knows exactly what the numerical values mean. For example, "marital status" (1 = married, 2 = divorced, 3 = widowed ...) and "age" measured in years. If you collapse age into a few categories, explain how you combined categories and explain how you determined the age intervals (e.g., split age at its median).

- *Method.* Describe the method(s) of analysis you used. This description should be brief, but provide enough information to show that you know what you're doing.

- *Findings.* Put your numerical results in tables. Just as in a journal article, "Table 1" should display univariate statistics like means, standard deviations and frequencies for each variable in the study. For nominal scale variables with many categories (e.g., 10 ethnic groups), include a frequency distribution, but display it compactly.

  For a student paper, the remainder of the tables likely consist of bivariate and trivariate tables. Include chi-square tests of significance for each table. You could also try some more advanced statistics, with guidance from your instructor.

  Write some discussion to summarize the results in your tables. Highlight the major results; do they support your hypotheses? What are the major exceptions, if any? Summarize the results in a table so readers can see at a glance what you've found. But *don't* repeat every number in every table—would *you* like to read such detail? Consider using Excel to create your tables and paste or link them into Word, if you have access to these programs.

- *Discussion and conclusions.* Are your main hypotheses supported? If they are, discuss what the results imply. If they aren't, speculate about possible reasons (but don't be too sure about the reasons). Remember: One study never "proves" anything. Discuss reasonable "next projects," for example, to test your speculations about why your hypothesis was not supported.

◼ *References.* Find out from your instructor the required format for a quantitative report.

THE CLASS OR CONFERENCE PRESENTATION

Experienced presenters know that all materials for a presentation should be completed at least one week prior to the presentation date. You'll have time to attend to any last-minute details and can arrive at the session confident you are ready!

Papers presented at professional conferences generally are written in a format appropriate for a journal article. Sometimes these are read, but it's usually better to give an oral presentation that isn't read word for word. If you have the software and time to prepare it, an electronic slide show outline provides a good set of notes for you and the audience. A one-page outline is shown in Figure 2.

> **Effect of Inbreeding on Early Childhood Mortality: Twelve Generations of an Amish Settlement**
>
> Introduction
>   Overview of Lancaster Amish Settlement
> Recent Familial Mortality Research
> Data and Method of Analysis
> Findings
> Conclusions and Implications
>   Next Steps

FIGURE 2   *One-Page Outline of a Paper for Presentation.*

Prepare in advance to answer questions. Think what you might ask if *you* were in the audience, and consider answers that would satisfy you. Also, ask your instructor, classmates or another person to serve as a practice audience. Practice will help you become comfortable discussing the details of the project. Your practice audience might ask some tough questions about your research; that's part of its function. Make notes of topics you are unsure how to answer, and do a little prep work on these topics before the presentation. Students who have presented papers and posters say that prior practice does help on the day of the presentation.

Find out the time allotted to your presentation and practice staying within that time limit. You want to keep your audience wishing to know more. For poster presentations with individual sections, lay out the sections approximately the way they will appear for the presentation. Check with your instructor or the organizer of the poster session about the space you will be allotted and other details, such as whether you need push pins, tape and so on. Get to the site early and, if possible, look over the room assigned for your presentation or poster displays. "Expect surprises" is a good motto.

You might ask your instructor whether to make some copies of your study's abstract to hand out. If needed, include the title of your presentation, your name, institution and e-mail address.

Maybe you will become famous!

SUMMARY

This chapter summarizes the final step in the research process: the report of findings. It illustrates an important contrast in the way individuals learn compared with the way scientific knowledge accumulates. As we have emphasized repeatedly, a critical feature of science is that the findings are public and subject to formal peer review.

This aspect of scientific research certainly does not guarantee accurate results, but it does comprise a built-in corrective mechanism.

The primary focus in this chapter is on the written report. The written report is the most important mode of dissemination; other forms of reports typically begin with a written draft. The chapter begins with four examples of the major types of written reports: (1) journal article, (2) evaluation report, (3) monograph and (4) government report. It also describes the poster display, a visual presentation increasingly seen at professional and student research conferences.

The next section of the chapter discusses insights and general guidelines for getting started and following through with the writing process. Then the chapter reviews components of reports for qualitative research and reports for quantitative research. The chapter ends with some considerations for oral presentations in class and at professional conferences.

YOUR REVIEW SHEET

1. What are the main forms of written documents of social science research described in the chapter? Briefly describe each.
2. Where could one look to learn how to write a scientific research report?
3. Why are scholarly journals probably the most important and prestigious sources for publishing research results?
4. What are the components of an empirical journal article using quantitative data? Summarize briefly the contents of each component.
5. Evaluation reports do not follow the same format as empirical journal articles like the *Demography* paper. Summarize the main ways they differ.
6. What is a monograph? How does a monograph differ from a book and from a book-length government report?
7. Describe some strategies for developing your own writing style.
8. Where can one look to find out what already is known on a topic? Be specific.
9. Why do you think writers use headings (and subheadings) in a paper?
10. What is a very common "error" in summarizing data tables?
11. What information should be included on a poster for a professional poster session?
12. In getting ready for a class or conference presentation (including poster displays), how can one prepare for questions that others might ask?
13. What is plagiarism? What steps should you take to avoid plagiarism?

END NOTES

1. Perinatal death refers to death in the first week for infants born alive. Neonatal death refers to death of infants who survived the first week but died within a month of birth. Postneonatal death refers to death of infants who survived the first month but died within the first year after birth.

STUDY TERMS

abstract Summary of the research; if used, it is presented at the beginning of a research report and seldom exceeds a paragraph or two in length.

citation Reference in the text of a paper to a source of an idea, fact, or quotation—any material or idea that isn't "common knowledge" or the writer's own thinking. Sources include journal articles, evaluations, monographs, government documents and so forth. Compare with references.

dissemination Spread or diffusion. In science, dissemination refers primarily to informing the scientific community and practitioners about research findings.

evaluation report Written document summarizing findings of an evaluation. The primary audience usually consist of professionals with an interest in the social intervention.

government report Written document produced or sponsored by a government agency. Often it does not contain original research. Rather, it reviews research existing prior to the time of its publication. This is a distinctive difference between a government report and a monograph.

monograph Literally translated, "one writing." More precisely, a monograph is a book-length document written on one scientific topic. In social research, a monograph presents a detailed report of an extensive research program of study.

peer review The process through which each submission to a journal is evaluated by a panel of experts for importance and accuracy.

plagiarism Quoting or summarizing in writing someone else's ideas without crediting the source.

poster presentation Dissemination method using posters to summarize research findings, usually at a professional conference; to answer questions, the researcher usually is present at least part of the time period the poster is available for viewing.

refereed journal Scholarly periodical that publishes only peer-reviewed papers. Issues are published several times a year, usually monthly, bimonthly or quarterly.

references Alphabetized list of sources cited, including Internet resources and personal communications, appearing at the end of a document; compare with **citation.**

EXERCISES

Exercise 1. Skills Building: Writing a Research Report Using Quantitative Data

Directions: Use an exercise that your instructor assigns. If you have not collected data for an exercise in this course, you may use data you collected for another course; check with your instructor. Otherwise, use the data in Table 1.

Table 1 contains frequencies for three variables: gunchild, gunadult and gender.

The order of the list of variables identifies their type: (1) dependent variable, (2) independent variable, (3) control variable. The variables gunchild and gunadult are derived from the GSS questions:

Have you ever been threatened with a gun, or shot at? (1 = yes, 2 = no) IF YES: Did this happen to you as a child or as an adult? (1 = child, 2 = adult, 3 = both)

TABLE 1. Frequencies for Gunadult, Gunchild and Gender

	Gunchild = yes Gender = male	Gunchild = yes Gender = female	Gunchild = no Gender = male	Gunchild = no Gender = female
Gunadult = yes	152	20	2148	925
Gunadult = no	358	145	5685	9868

Source: General Social Survey, cumulative data file 1972–2000 cumulative file (Davis, Smith, & Marsden, 2003). This table is for survey years: 1973, 1975, 1976, 1978, 1980, 1983, 1984, 1986, 1991, 1993 and 1994. Table entries are frequencies.

If you use the data in Table 1, report the following tabulations in your paper:

1. Univariate frequencies:

   `gender`

   `gunchild`

   `gunadult`

2. Bivariate tables:

   `gunchild` ✕ `gender`

   `gunadult` ✕ `gender`

   `gunchild` ✕ `gunadult`

3. Trivariate table:

   `gunadult` ✕ `gender` ✕ `gunchild`.

Prepare a short report of your research in the format of a journal article. The paper should include (1) an introduction, (2) a statement of the research question and thesis (or hypothesis), (3) description of the method of data collection, (4) how you analyzed the data, (5) your findings, (6) what you conclude about your research and (7) limitations of your study. If your instructor requests, add a title page, references and brief literature review.

Exercise 2. Skills Building Web Project: Locating Online Journals

Directions: Perform the following searches and obtain the requested information. Write a paragraph describing what you have learned about locating online journals. Print your search results and be ready to hand it in with this exercise.

1. Search 1. Connect to the Internet and go to the Google search engine (*http://www. google.com*). Conduct a search for "social sciences index/abstracts with full text: journal list." How many full-text journals are listed at this site? Write the names of three full-text journals that are professionally reviewed.

2. Search 2. Type in the following URL: *http://www.loc.gov/*. Which organization sponsors this website? Click on "Readings Rooms" under "Visit the Library." Next, click on "Newspaper & Current Periodical." Or, go directly to *http://www.loc.gov/rr/news/*. Find and list two magazine and newspaper sources with full text available online.

3. Search 3. Return to *www.google.com*. Conduct a search to find out the sociology and psychology journals the University of California Press publishes Which are e-journals? Which e-journal was online first, and what was the date?

13 APPLYING PRINCIPLES OF SOCIAL SCIENCE METHODS TO EVERYDAY LEARNING

INTRODUCTION: LOOKING AT HOW THE SOCIAL WORLD WORKS

Picture a "skull-and-crossbones-type" picture on the cover of a popular magazine—although perhaps eye-catching—would you expect a sober, balanced assessment of an important social issue in the lead article?

The cover of an issue of *Sports Illustrated* (*SI*) shows a baseball crossed with two hypodermic needles, suggesting that steroid use in professional baseball is widespread—and that it's a big problem. It seems to imply a *big, bold* exclamation point!

But what is the evidence for these implications? What does such a cover picture have to do with the use of steroids? And how much credibility are you willing to put in the "confessions of an MVP (most valuable player)"?

This *is* only the cover, however. Maybe the story presents enough supporting evidence to justify the hype. The story was published in 2002. Since that time much additional evidence has surfaced. Part of this chapter reviews the content of the story and other evidence, with the intent of evaluating how well the combined evidence backs up the implications of the cover.

Goals of This Chapter

Every day each of us is bombarded with numerous claims and counterclaims about many issues—steroids in baseball, global warming, the impact of violent TV video games on real violence, immigrants and immigration and a bewildering assortment of consumer choices. Whether commercial advertising for prescription drugs or political arguments about "welfare," these claims share important features:

- Generally it is impossible to find definitive evidence in support of one view over competing views, and
- Many sources of information generally have a monetary interest in getting your attention and persuading you about something.

From Chapter 13 of *Research Methods and Society, Foundations of Social Inquiry,* Second Edition. Linda Eberst Dorsten, Lawrence Hotchkiss. Copyright © 2014 by Pearson Education, Inc. All rights reserved.

The study of methods in the social sciences teaches how to conduct and evaluate believable research results. But do social science standards of evidence apply *only* to research?

Whether zero percent—or any percent—of professional baseball players take steroids has to do with sampling accuracy and accuracy in measuring key variables. And, supposing many players do take steroids and/or other performance-enhancing drugs, how much of a problem is that? The answer to these questions depends on scientific information about the safety of the drugs, their effectiveness in improving performance and ethical principles. It is important to separate questions of fact from those of ethics and to avoid "sticky-theory" opinion.

Specifically, *how can standards in social research be applied to everyday decision making and learning?*

This chapter isn't a definitive guide to everyday issues, obviously. Rather, it attempts to achieve two objectives: (1) reinforce your skills about how to look for important criteria in decision making, and (2) illustrate how to apply basic principles of social research methods. The principles in social science research provide standards for assessing the many claims we hear each day. Unfortunately, on the one hand the evidence indicates we should withhold judgment—probably much more often than most of us do. On the other hand, we often cannot wait for convincing evidence before something must be decided.

The chapter summarizes five everyday situations and illustrates how to apply your methods skills-set to better understand these situations. For additional skills building, exercises at the end of the chapter ask you to break down each situation into the social research components in this chapter. *We strongly suggest you* (a) *read the exercises first, and then* (b) *read (and re-read) the chapter, making notes while you read about how to answer the exercises. Or you might answer the exercises while you re-read.* Following these suggestions will clarify how the five situations and related exercises use social science standards, which will help you evaluate other claims in your everyday life.

STEROIDS IN BASEBALL

What are steroids, and why might they be a problem? A steroid is a complex chemical substance consisting primarily of hormones. Anabolic steroids are the class of steroids taken by athletes to improve their performance.

Side-effects of steroids can be serious. *WebMD*, an Internet website providing health information, summarizes potential side-effects for one particular form of anabolic steroid—androstenedione, popularly known as "andro," infamous because of its use by the great home-run hitter, Mark McGwire.

Q: Since AN [androstenedione] is widely available and the FDA hasn't stopped stores from selling it, why is there so much concern about it, as reflected in the media?

A: Because AN is classified as a dietary supplement, it is not regulated by the FDA the way prescription drugs are (*WebMD*, 2002).

This same *WebMD* Web page catalogs the many serious risks associated with AN:

- The quantity of AN in dietary supplements varies, ranging from none to excessive dosage. Product labels do not indicate the quantity of AN.

- In high dosages typically used by athletes, AN may lead to numerous threats to the user's health, including problems with the liver, behavioral problems, sexual dysfunction, infertility, increased risk of heart disease, reduced supply of HDL (the "good" cholesterol) and muscle disorders.

- AN is likely to combine with other drugs users may be taking to produce still more medical complications.

Steroids in fairly high doses have been used to treat medical conditions and in scientific trials designed to assess their effects on performance and health (Yesalis, 2000, pp. 6–7). The risks cited by *WebMD* arise because steroids often are not taken with care, and users often lack accurate knowledge about correct dosage and the safe versions of steroids (there are dozens of variants of steroids).

There are at least two issues implied by the *Sports Illustrated* lead story: How widespread (prevalent) is the use of steroids in professional baseball? And how dangerous is their use to the health and welfare of the player?

Prevalence of Steroid Use

The *Sports Illustrated* article makes strong claims. It says use of steroids and other performance enhancers are "rampant" in professional baseball. And steroid use in professional baseball has "grown to alarming proportions." Sources for these claims include a baseball MVP and "other sources" (Verducci, 2002, p. 34).

Are these claims thorough and balanced, as science advocates? Neither the wording nor the content of the opening statement gives us much confidence that they are.

The evidence consists solely of a sequence of testimonials and lengthy quotes from ballplayers, both major and minor league. Ken Caminite, the MVP referred to in the excerpt, is quoted estimating that 50 percent of players do it, but he later retracted that estimate (*New York Times*, 2002). Jose Canseco is quoted as estimating that 85 percent use some kind of enhancer.

In short, the article doesn't contain an accurate estimate of the prevalence of steroid use in baseball.

What does an accurate estimate of steroid use require? A *survey* of all professional baseball players or a *probability sample* combined with repeated medical tests for many drugs is needed. Since the tests aren't always correct, they should be supplemented by *anonymous* self-reports from players. Careful development of a questionnaire or interview schedule combined with extraordinary efforts to gain the confidence of the players in the study also are required. Obviously, a popular magazine like *Sports Illustrated* isn't going to conduct such a study—though it might have commissioned one from a reputable research institution.

How damaging to the main theme of the story is the absence of a good numerical estimate of the prevalence of steroid use? Knowledge about sampling and qualitative methods suggests that much useful information isn't readily quantifiable and doesn't necessarily derive from a scientific survey. However, an editorial in *The New York Times* judged the *Sports Illustrated* (*SI*) story to be credible, and calls for action based on it. The editorial says that ubiquitous use of steroids by baseball players is documented in "compelling detail" by the *SI* article (*New York Times*, 2002, p. A14).

Why was *The New York Times* editorial staff convinced? Of course, we don't know, but we can assume that it's because of extensive quotes from ballplayers and others in the sport. Some of the descriptions of how to obtain steroids and other drugs, based on *interviews* with players, contain so much detail that it's not likely that they were concocted on the spot for the reporter. It appears that "something is going on out there," even if we aren't able to quantify it exactly.

Still, *Sports Illustrated* doesn't describe its methods. How did it *select* the sample of players it interviewed? How many players refused to be interviewed? Were questions *leading the respondent* to an answer, producing biased information? Is the sample of interviewed players large enough to give an accurate estimate of the prevalence of steroid use in baseball?

We don't know the answers to these questions. But we do know that *Sports Illustrated* and the journalist have their own interests for reporting spectacular findings. Maybe reporters selected players they already knew informally were steroid users. Given the high-pressure environment of the media, this is a plausible scenario—but, again, we don't know.

Nonetheless at the time the article was published, the public seemed convinced that there was some problem with steroid use in baseball, but it was unclear how serious it was. Since that time, substantial additional evidence has surfaced supporting the original opinion. But there also may be reason to be skeptical of all the hype associated with the issue. The question is: Is strict prohibition of performance-enhancing drugs, along with severe punishment for their use, the best policy?

Dangers of Steroid Use

The *SI* article mentions two types of health risks associated with steroid use: (1) injury and, (2) impaired body functions. The evidence of these risks comes primarily from (a) anecdotal (personal story) cases of specific players, (b) interviews with doctors who specialize in sports medicine, (c) informal references to research findings and (d) league statistics showing an increase in time and money spent on disability.

Caminiti, for example, won the MVP award in 1996, the year he started taking steroids. In the years after 1996, he was injured a high percentage of the time and never approached the MVP level of performance again. A lengthy, graphic quote from Caminiti recounts the problems he encountered because his body virtually shut down production of natural testosterone.

More generally, *SI* cites medical research that indicates steroid consumption damages the heart and liver, leads to hormone imbalance, is associated with strokes and aggressive behavior, increases cholesterol levels and diminishes sexual function (Verducci, 2002, p. 36).

But most of the article is devoted to the informal information and doesn't convey a good indication of how widespread these problems likely will be, given the usual dosages taken by ballplayers.

The article also attributes increased player injuries and days on the disabled list to steroid use. It cites four types of evidence: (1) opinions of a couple of sports managers and an orthopedic physician, (2) an increase in the number of players on the disabled list, (3) a 20 percent increase in the average number of days on the disabled list comparing the 2001–2002 season to 1997 and (4) a 130 percent increase over 4 years in the cost to owners for pay to players who were unable to play due to injuries (Verducci, 2002, p. 44).

How *useful* is this evidence of health risks? Each piece of evidence, taken separately, is not very convincing. The medical evidence cited in the article is weak and does not match what is known in the scientific and medical literature, which is not nearly as extensive as you might expect. Research published in academic sources before the *SI* article (2002) and later do not lend strong support to the claim that steroid use has major impact on any of these aspects of health (Friedl, 2000; Hoffman & Ratamess, 2006; Yesalis, 2000).

It also is important to recognize that the findings depend on the type of steroid and how it is measured (*operational definition*). Generally, the type of steroid taken orally (17-alkylated) does increase the risk of liver cancer. There is little debate about this effect. But no serious short-term health effects of injected steroids are documented. The scientific literature as of 2000 had not conducted research into long-term effects (Friedl, 2000).

The evidence in the *SI* article about sports injuries is especially inconsistent, and could be due to many variables not under **physical control** or **statistical control**. Only one comparison year is used in each mention of a percentage increase, generating some suspicion that the *comparison* year might have been picked deliberately to emphasize the main point (**selection bias**). In particular, it would be useful to know the natural variation in these rates from year to year and to see trend lines over several years. Is the trend markedly up, despite yearly fluctuations? We also need to scrutinize carefully other events that might account for sharp changes in the trend line (*history*).

Even with a marked increasing time-trend line, attributing it to steroid use would be difficult. Many *variables* might affect such a trend, and it would be difficult to identify and measure them. This is the problem of a *history effect* (as an *intervening variable*).

Convincing evidence requires *comparisons* of the injury rate of individual players who do and do not take steroids. Except in *randomized experimental designs*, variables such as age, position, playing time, number of at bats, injury rate prior to starting to take steroids and race/ethnicity must be *controlled*.

In an extensive review of the scientific and medical literature, Friedl (2000) concluded that effects of steroid use on tendon ruptures was not established. In a similar review, Hoffman and Ratamess (2006) report the same conclusion. However, animal studies do suggest that very high doses may deteriorate ligament tissues. We conclude, however, that the *SI* evidence about injuries is not very convincing.

Sizing It All Up

So what are we to make of the question of steroids in baseball and, more generally, in any competitive sport? Should they be banned, allowed but regulated or allowed without regulations?

There are two aspects to these questions: facts and ethics. Questions of scientific fact include the effects of steroids on the health and injuries of users, and knowing how much steroid use contributes to improving athletic performance. Questions of ethics (and opinion) have a different vantage point: Do you believe threats to athletes' health and well-being are acceptable or unacceptable, *and* do you believe any performance advantages steroid users might gain is fair or unfair competition?

It is not easy to determine the facts about effects of steroid use. There are many varieties of steroids and they do not all have the same effects. There are many potential effects. Effects are not the same for men as for women; nor are they same for adults as for teens and preteens. Good scientific study of steroid effects in humans is difficult to carry out. The following list attempts to summarize current findings:

- It is fairly well established that steroid use by men increases secondary male features such as baldness, hair growth except on the scalp, and deep voice.
- It is well established that steroid use increases upper body strength, particularly when combined with weight lifting. Effects on other muscle groups are not documented and appear to be small, or none.

- The competitive advantage of steroid use to weight lifters and body builders is well established. But it is not clear that much advantage is gained in other sports, including baseball. Apparently, the main muscles controlling hitting power and pitch speed are in the legs. The arms and torso serve primarily as connectors. For example, the extensive Web page about steroids in baseball authored by Eric Walker contains data that show each of the eras of increased hitting power in baseball is preceded by an event such as increased liveliness of the ball. The scientific literature does not find any advantage of steroid use in endurance sports such as distance running (Walker, 2011, *http://steroids-and-baseball.com/*).

- Steroid use may lead to acne in both sexes, but this effect is reversible after steroid use ends.

- In men, steroid use may cause female-appearing breasts to develop. This happens in a minority of men but is not reversible except by delicate surgery.

- Steroid use by men reduces sperm count and shrinks the testicles. Steroids have been experimented with as a male contraceptive, with mixed success. This effect is reversible with cessation of steroid use.

- It is often claimed that heart and cardiovascular disease is a consequence of steroid use, but the evidence for this claim is very weak.

- Several documented effects occur in women: Emergence of secondary male sex characteristics including deepening voice, muscle growth, hair growth, shrinking breasts and enlargement of the clitoris. These effects are not reversible.

- An increased risk of liver cancer is associated with oral ingestion of steroids but not with injected steroids. The reason is that the types of steroids taken orally are modified to prevent the liver from removing them before they enter the blood stream. The modification is the causative agent.

- Very little is known about the long-term effects of steroid use on humans. Several studies with animals report very harmful effects of high doses, including shortened lives.

- Teenage steroid users, particularly boys, are at risk of stunting their growth. The steroids cause an increase of testosterone in the body. When a threshold is reached, it triggers the bone growth plates to close prematurely.

Ethical concerns also are complex. The arguments in favor of banning steroids are that we should protect the health and well-being of members of society, including athletes, users gain an unfair advantage in competitions, use by some athletes prompts other athletes to become users and use by athletes encourages youth also to become users. And, steroid effects on youth are more serious than effects on adults (see above).

Those opposed to banning steroids pose several arguments.

- Steroids, when used sensibly, pose less threat to individual health and well-being than other substances that are not banned, particularly tobacco and alcohol.

- Adults must be given the right to decide for themselves whether the risks are worth the benefits, just as they are in many other risky activities, such as tobacco use, alcohol use, parachute jumping, mountain climbing and so on.

- Many circumstances give some athletes an "unfair" advantage over others. Access to the best coaches, best equipment, best training methods all give those with access an advantage over those without access. What is the difference between these inequalities and those resulting from steroid use by some, but not all, athletes?

- Steroid use may be "unnatural" but so is most of athletics. The rules of all competitions were manufactured by people and are not natural. Fiberglass poles for pole vaulting, high-tech materials such as body suits worn by swimmers and high-tech tennis rackets are all unnatural.

- It is impossible to exercise effective control over steroid use. The attempt to do so has prompted athletes to try all manner of unregulated substances, often in very high doses. It has stimulated an ever-growing list of new substances designed to avoid tests. A resulting black market is flourishing. Also, athletes use a number of tricks to avoid detection.

The arguments against rules and legislation to make steroids a "controlled substance" (make non-prescription steroid use illegal) tend to be drowned out by media (e.g., the *SI* article) and politics. For example, the Mitchell Report (2007) was commissioned by the Commissioner of Baseball to assess the use of steroids in major league baseball. By this time, steroid use in baseball had become something of a scandal. But the report does not contain a balanced assessment of the problem. Much of the report simply presumes steroid use must be prevented and offers many recommendations about how to do it. The NPR (National Public Radio) report on baseball titled "The Tenth Inning" contains some coverage of steroid use. It simply assumes that the scandal surrounding steroid use is based on strong science and makes no mention that there *is* an opposing viewpoint.

Also, there is a long history of mistrust of mainstream medicine by athletes. This mistrust apparently is due in part to early claims by prominent medical people that steroids do not help build strength—a claim that many athletes knew very well from experience is not true. Few, if any, argue that steroids should be entirely unregulated. But to do effective regulation, steroid use would have to be supervised by physicians or other trained medical personnel, and for this to work, athletes would have to be persuaded to trust medical people.

The issues related to steroid use in baseball and other sports are complex, and it is not clear just what the best policy is. The purpose of this section you've just read is to demonstrate the interplay between science and ethics, show the importance of separating the two domains and illustrate how hype and conventional "wisdom" can obscure important facts and ethical considerations.

GBL (GAMMA-BUTYROLACTONE)

A search of *WebMD* turned up another interesting issue: presence of gamma-butyrolactone (GBL) in dietary supplements. GBL is a strong chemical used in household and industrial solvents. It is also found in dietary supplements where it is claimed to produce many "miracles"—relieve insomnia, produce growth hormones, reduce stress and improve sexual potency. The article makes some serious claims about the dangers of GBL:

Q: What does GBL do to the body?

A: So far, one person who consumed a product containing GBL has died, and 55 others have experienced side effects ranging from vomiting, aggression, and tremors to slowed heartbeat, impaired judgment (causing at least one traffic accident), seizures, breathing difficulties, and coma. (*WebMD*, 2002)

There are two reasons for interest in the GBL article. First, it illustrates the potential importance of *reliable* information. In particular, know that most health supplements are not regulated; many are advertised in a manner implying that they produce "miracles," and many are quite dangerous. The article mentions several product names and listings of chemical ingredients, but it does not give a certain identification scheme, just a list of products and a list of possible chemical ingredients. This is important. New products containing GBL could appear at any time, and old products could reappear under a new name.

Second, the *WebMD* article itself is deficient. It states: "…one person who consumed a product containing GBL has died, and 55 others have experienced side effects?" What is the relevance of these figures? Probably one person who *did not* consume GBL also died and 55 others probably experienced the "side effects" during the same time interval referred to in the quote from *WebMD*. To make an informed judgment, we need to *compare* the numbers of deaths and the 55 other ailments among GBL consumers to the numbers among non–GBL consumers, preferably *controlling* for other risk factors such as age, general health and gender. This is a critical point. The numbers reported in the *WebMD* posting really are meaningless without proper comparisons.

What is called for fits into a *bivariate table*. Think of a table with GBL use as the *independent variable*. The *dependent variable* is died (yes, no) within a specified period of time. The percentages can be compared between users and nonusers across the columns.

The article doesn't even tell us what the *base number* (denominator) is for the 1 death and 55 other ailments. Did 1 person die and 55 get sick out of 56, 100, 1,000, 2,000…who took GBL? The answer makes a big difference in our assessment of the risk; in fact, it's impossible to assess the risk at all without the base number. As the article stands, we are left to assume that probably the numbers would not have been provided if the experts didn't have sufficient information for concern—a very weak presumption.

Omission of the *base of comparison* is a frequent shortcoming in information to the general public. For example, an architect specializing in building skyscrapers was interviewed soon after the World Trade Center was destroyed by terrorists. He was asked to assess the argument that few new skyscrapers should be built because they are vulnerable to air crashes. In response, he argued that high-rise building should not be restricted because most airplanes that crash into buildings do not hit skyscrapers. There are a lot more short buildings than skyscrapers to hit, but there probably also is more air traffic around tall buildings. However, this argument is missing a fundamental ingredient: a *comparison*. We need to know whether the risk of being hit by an airplane is related to the height of a building. It seems like a plausible hypothesis, but the interviewer didn't even notice the lack of a *comparison*.

PONCE DE LÉON AND THE "FOUNTAIN OF YOUTH": HORMONE THERAPY AND WOMEN'S HEALTH

Ponce de Léon was a Spanish explorer who sailed the Caribbean seas searching for the mythical "fountain of youth." He didn't find the fountain of youth, but he did discover Florida. However, Ponce de Léon's exploits illustrate an important aspect of **sticky theory**. People believe what they want to believe and act on those beliefs—disregarding other evidence.

Medicine is an arena particularly likely to generate inflated hopes and beliefs, probably because stricken people so fervently desire to be cured. A best-selling book titled *Feminine Forever* (Wilson, 1966) seems to be a major source of the idea that women can achieve everlasting youth and beauty by taking estrogen (a hormone) supplements at the onset of menopause. Wilson claimed a great medical discovery: Menopause is a curable disease—just take estrogen! He traveled extensively promoting this idea and published his findings in reputable medical journals such as *JAMA* (*Journal of the American Medical Association*). The dust jacket of his book proclaims thus:

> A fully-documented discussion of one of medicine's most revolutionary breakthroughs—the discovery that *menopause is a hormone deficiency disease, curable and totally preventable*, and that every woman, no matter what her age, can safely live a fully-sexed life for her *entire* life. (Wilson, 1966, emphasis in the original)

A number of *observational studies* appeared to support this viewpoint. But it soon was found that estrogen supplements were associated with increased risk of uterine cancer. And later, Wilson's son reported that *Feminine Forever* and Wilson's research were financed by the Wyeth pharmaceutical firm—manufacturer of one estrogen supplement called Prempro, a prescription drug (Kolata, 2002). However, evidence suggested that reducing the dosage of estrogen and combining it with progesterone (another hormone) reduces the risk of uterine cancer to near normal level. Therefore, estrogen alone was recommended for women who had had hysterectomies (removal of the uterus), and estrogen plus progesterone (usually a synthetic called progestin) for women with a uterus.

What was the basis for recommending hormone supplements? Numerous *observational studies* suggested a variety of benefits to combined estrogen and progestin supplements in postmenopausal women, including improved cardio-vascular health and increased bone density. But none of these early studies were based on careful controls using **random assignment** to *treatment* and *control groups*. Instead, each woman (and her doctor) decided whether she should take the supplements. Women who *self-selected* themselves to take the supplements were, on average, of higher income, healthier, less prone to overweight and less likely to smoke (Kolata, 2002). This *self-selection* of healthy women into the group who took hormone supplements created a *positive relationship* between hormone supplements and various health benefits. Self-selection created a **spurious association** *or* relationship, as illustrated in Figure 1.

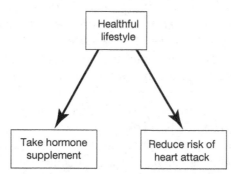

FIGURE 1   Spurious Relationship from Observational Studies of Potential Medical Benefits of Hormone Therapy in Postmenopausal Women.

The Women's Health Initiative Study

In the late 1990s (1997–1998), the Women's Health Initiative (WHI) began two clinical trials to assess the potential benefits to postmenopausal women of hormone supplements (Rossouw et al., 2002). The *treatment* (independent variable) in one of the studies combines estrogen and progestin, and the *treatment* in the other is estrogen alone, limited to subjects without a uterus.

However, on May 31, 2002, the WHI suddenly halted the estrogen–progestin study, some 3 years before its scheduled completion. The research team judged that the risks of the supplements outweighed the benefits. They found slight, but *statistically significant,* elevations in the risk of breast cancer, heart attack, stroke and blood clots in the lungs and legs of those taking the supplements instead of the placebo (WHI, 2002). The differences between the risks of supplements versus the placebo were very small, however. The biggest difference was 18 in 10,000 (0.18%) higher risk for blood clots from taking the supplements. This small effect showed up as statistically significant because of the large sample size.

But the study didn't evaluate the short-term benefits of estrogen–progestin supplements in reducing the often-severe symptoms of menopause—hot flashes, vaginal drying and thinning and urinary-tract infections and incontinence (lost ability to control bladder). Since the increased risks associated with estrogen–progestin supplements are very slight, the benefits still may exceed the risks.

Halting the estrogen–progestin study was a shock to much of the medical community. Previously, the standard had been to recommend hormone supplements for postmenopausal women. These recommendations were based on the extensive *observational studies* noted earlier (Kolata, 2002). Why did the WHI study more than offset earlier evidence of benefits of hormone supplements?

Subjects in a clinical trial are assigned at random to the *experimental* (treatment) and *control groups*. In the WHI study, over 16,600 women were assigned at random to take either (1) a combination of estrogen and progestin supplements or (2) a placebo. Neither the subjects nor the research team knew who was taking the supplements and who was taking a *placebo* (Rossouw, 2002).

With *random assignment*, *all* factors that influence outcomes like heart attack or bone density are, on average, the same at the beginning of the study for both those who took the supplements and those who took the placebo. With over 8,000 women in each group, average differences in all variables affecting the outcomes between the experimental and control groups due to random variation are highly likely to be quite small. (We "expect" them to be zero.) Given appropriate **statistical tests**, differences in health outcomes between those who took supplements and those who took a placebo can be attributed with high confidence to effects of the supplements. But, remember, high confidence isn't the same thing as certainty. Also, high confidence is not the same thing as a strong effect. In this instance, we have high confidence in quite small effects.

Follow-up studies published since 2002 checked to see whether these effects of the hormone supplements persist after the study was halted and all women quit taking the supplements. The findings of one follow-up study, for the most part, show that the effects diminished to near zero during the 2.4-year-period, July 2002 through March 2005 (Heiss, et al., 2008). The Heiss study included all of the outcomes in the original study. A more recent study focused on the effects of the hormone therapy on cardiovascular disease (Toh, et al., 2010). It found a complex pattern of still very small effects.

Another follow-up study published in the *Journal of the American Medical Association* in the April 6, 2011, issue reports results of continued study of 7,645 women who participated in the original WHI study and who had had hysterectomies. The treatment group of these women, therefore, included estrogen-only hormone therapy. This study found the risks and benefits reported in the earlier findings from the WHI study did not persist, except that women taking the estrogen had a statistically significant reduced risk of breast cancer. These benefits were concentrated in younger women in the study, that is, women who were in their 50s when the study began (LaCroix et al., 2011). An editorial in the same issue of *JAMA* raises several questions about the LaCroix study (Jungheim & Colditz, 2011). The authors cite evidence from other research that indicates increased risk of breast cancer among women on estrogen therapy—just the opposite of the findings reported by LaCroix and colleagues!

Shortly after the LaCroix paper and its accompanying editorial appeared, Gail Collins wrote an op-ed piece in *The New York Times* saying, "We got word this week that estrogen therapy, which was bad, is good again" (Collins, 2011). In her typically flippant, humorous style, she managed to express the frustration that many undoubtedly feel about the complexity and ever-changing landscape of medical information.

What do we conclude? First, recall the claims on the dust jacket of Wilson's book:

> A fully-documented discussion of one of medicine's most revolutionary break-throughs—the discovery that *menopause is a hormone deficiency disease, curable and totally preventable*, and that every woman, no matter what her age, can safely live a fully-sexed life for her *entire* life. (Wilson, 1966, emphasis in the original)

It is clear from the facts to date that (1) menopause is *not* a curable disease, and (2) taking hormone supplements after menopause does not provide a path to paradise. To repeat an old adage: *If it sounds too good to be true, it probably is.*

It is not entirely clear just how serious the effects of the hormone supplements are. Whatever harm the supplements do to a woman's health appear to be quite small. An analysis of the Women's Health Initiative data also revealed the supplements may help to prevent hip fractures, but this effect also is small and appears to die out after women no longer take the supplements. That's what the LaCroix study found. The NIH (National Institutes of Health) does not categorically recommend against hormone supplements, but repeats the strong cautions that accompanied cessation of the study in 2002, and recommends that a woman consult with her physician before using the supplements (NIH News, 2010). The editorial accompanying the LaCroix report echoes essentially these same sentiments (Jungheim & Colditz, 2011, p. 1355).

GAMES OF CHANCE AND "OVERDUE" EVENTS

Our fourth application of science principles to everyday life is about games of chance. Many believe events in games of chance depend on recent outcomes in the game—"I'm overdue" (for good luck) or "I'm on a run" (of good luck).

Recent events in games of chance do affect the next outcome—but only in certain circumstances. For example, if you have drawn 45 cards without *replacement* from a 52-card deck and have yet to draw a queen, your chance of getting a queen on the next draw is much higher than it was on the first draw (4 out of 7 versus 4 out of 52). In contrast, the chance of getting a six on the next toss of a single die is unrelated entirely to what happened on the previous roll or on any previous rolls. Similarly, the chance of getting a head on the next coin toss is exactly the same, no matter the sequence of heads and tails on previous tosses. Those who believe otherwise are prone to lose money in games of chance.

Such beliefs also are likely to overinterpret "slumps" in sports. What's a "slump"? Usually, it's just a random string of poor performances—analogous to a string of several tails in a row in the toss of a coin. It doesn't happen often, but it happens. A baseball player hitting 250, for example, has close to a six (5.6) percent chance of going hitless 10 times in a row if his hitting average is entirely unrelated to his recent history of hits and outs. That's not a slump, and it is likely to happen several times in a long career.

True to *sticky-theory* predictions, even some very intelligent people keep painstakingly precise records of the frequencies of numbers occurring in lottery jackpot drawings. As of this writing (December, 2010), the multistate "Powerball" lottery contains five numbers, each drawn from numbers 1 through 59 and one number called the "Powerball" drawn from the numbers 1 through 39, making six numbers total in each drawing. Wilma Pickwin (not named for "Wilma Carstart") checked 590 drawings to find out what numbers would give her the best chance of becoming a multimillionaire. In the same 590 drawings, she tallied frequencies for each of the first five numbers in the drawings and the Powerball number and found the following values occurred most often for positions 1 through 5 in the drawings: 9, 6, 2, 3, 45 and 31 for the Powerball. It's clear that she should bet on 9 for the first number, 6 for the second, 2 for the third, 3 for the fourth, 45 for the fifth and 31 for the Powerball—*right?*

Oops—wrong! Don't forget there's natural *variation* in random events. If you doubt the "natural variation" argument in lotteries and other games of chance, look at Figure 2. The numbers were generated by a computer random-number generator—*a "pure chance" technique giving each number exactly the same chance of* selection*!*

Ms. Pckwin's six numbers and their frequencies were: (9,22), (6,22), (2,19), (3,17), (45,19), (31,23). Since each of the numbers 1 through 59 has an equal chance of occurring, Wilma Pickwin should expect 10 times for each number of the first five picks, and for the Powerball, $590/39 \approx 15.13$. The maximum *frequencies* observed by Wilma Pickwin are pretty far away from these averages. This might make the results of any tally seem credible to a novice. But, in any tally you get a *sampling distribution* of frequencies, some close to the average frequency, and a few distant from it. This is what Figure 2 illustrates! If you tally enough drawings, the maximum frequency is nearly certain to be distant from the *average*, but most of the time the maximum will correspond to a different number each time you tally the frequencies. If Wilma repeats her tally, she will find a much different set of numbers to bet on. Most likely she will find no repeats!

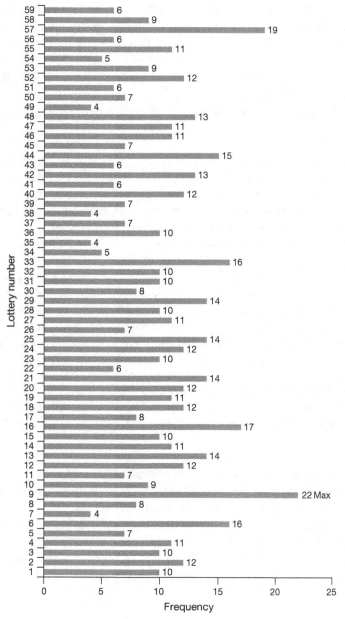

FIGURE 2   Frequency Distribution of Lottery Number Picks: 1, 2, . . . , 59, First Drawing for Wilma Pickwin.

But, it's not impossible to get a repeat, even with equal chance for each number drawn. In this setting, the logic of random events trumps *observation,* because the logic is irrefutable, and we know random fluctuations occur in data.

Statistical tests by Wilma Pickwin for each of the six Powerball numbers support that these numbers were chosen using *random selection* (without *replacement* for each set of 6), with exactly the same chance for each number, from 1 through 59 for the first 5 and 1 through 39 for the Powerball.[1] Another *sample* of 590 numbers will produce similar "evidence" of numbers to bet on, but they will be different than the numbers in Figure 2.

The case of the lottery-number picks illustrates some of the fundamental ideas in the sampling chapter.

- Any one sample contains **sampling error**—probably more error than you expect. In the "population" of lottery numbers, the proportion of each number is exactly 1 in 59 for the first 5 numbers and 1 in 39 for the Powerball. In any sample of 590, then, the "expected" *frequency* is exactly 10 for each of the first five positions and exactly $590/39 \approx 15.13$ for the Powerball. But, there is considerable variation among the frequencies, entirely due to *random variation* in the sample.

- A **statistical test** is a device for making a decision when you can't be sure. In the case of the lottery numbers, the question is: Is the method of drawing winning numbers "fair"? (The operational definition of "fair" is that each number has the same *probability* of *selection* every time.) No matter how many instances of drawings you observe, however, some of the first 5 numbers will be selected more than 10 times in a sample of 590 and some less, as shown quite convincingly in Figure 2. Similarly, some of the Powerball numbers will be selected more than 15 times and some less. A *statistical test* is based on a calculated *probability* that any sample of 590 numbers deviates from being fair so much so that the lottery likely is not fair. According to convention, if the probability is above some prespecified threshold, typically $(p \leq 0.05)$, then make the practical decision to act as if the lottery *is* fair.

None of us make practical decisions by conducting statistical tests of significance. Moreover, there's little you can be certain about in life; yet you have to decide. Good judgment might boil down to an ability to make accurate intuitive *probability* assessments—judgments about the likelihood of what will happen if.…Those with "good judgment" and the ability to avoid *sticky-theory* beliefs might very well stand a better chance of "success" in life! However, even people with good judgment don't always win. That's built into the nature of risk.

CAR RELIABILITY

How easy is it to find good information about the reliability of cars? A major source of car repair data is *Consumer Reports* (*CR*). *CR* publishes data annually from surveys that describe the reliability of most makes and models, including separate reports for different engine and drive-line options (two-wheel drive vs. four). These data are extensive, but how *useful* are they?

Consumers Union (CU) is a nonprofit organization. It accepts no commercial advertising. This is a major advantage over most other sources of information about automobile performance. Nearly all other magazines and websites about automobiles are full of automobile ads.

The CU sample is very large (over 1.3 million vehicles for the 2011 survey), but it's a *nonprobability sample* of subscribers. Moreover, some subscribers didn't return a completed questionnaire, and the *response rate* is not reported. Also, ratings are derived from respondent answers to questions about their vehicles and therefore are subject to "recall error," which translates into **measurement error**. *CR* readers are given no information about how serious measurement error might be.

Data are reported for overall *reliability* and for a list of several categories of problems like "Engine, major"; "Engine, minor"; "Engine, Cooling"; "Fuel system," "Electrical"; "Trans, major"; "Trans, minor" and so on (*Consumer Reports* April, 2011, p. 86f). Each vehicle is rated in each category by a system of small colored circles (or black and gray in the Buying Guide):

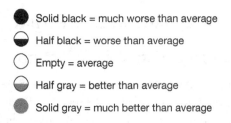

What can be learned from ratings like this? The *sample size* for each make/ model/configuration is much less than the total *sample size*. The sample size for each make/model isn't reported; *CR* doesn't publish the data if the sample size is below some threshold (100). The average sample size appears to be about 400–500. But the number obviously varies substantially among models since some makes and models are much more popular than are others.

At least as important, there's no indication of the costs of the repairs. The difficulty of obtaining good cost data doesn't change the fact that we want to know costs. Also the data contain very limited information about how many miles a vehicle will run before it is entirely worn out. This is an important factor for those who keep a vehicle for most of its useful life. The most recent issue as of this writing of the *Annual Auto Issue,* however, does present a couple of useful charts (*Consumer Reports* Annual Auto Issue, 2013).

Finally, the data don't **control** for probable *selection bias* in the purchase of a vehicle. Why is the Honda Civic, for example, rated more *reliable* than the Chevrolet Corvette? Are Civic drivers more diligent about routine maintenance? Do they drive more conservatively than Corvette owners? If so, we have an example of the *effects of selection* that produce a *spurious relationship* between car model and repair rating—selection because conservative drivers buy Civics instead of Corvettes, and spurious because hard/easy driving affects both the car model and the repair rating.

Granted, *control* for "hard use" would be difficult or impossible to implement. But, again, the difficulty of implementing a procedure is irrelevant to its importance in evaluating the data. On balance, however, it seems likely that *statistical control* for driver "personality" would have a modest impact on the ratings. But, of course, that is our intuitive judgment. You might have a different one.

Do all these criticisms mean the *CR* car reliability data are useless? No! It just means they aren't as *useful* as we wish they are. The fact that *CR* doesn't accept any commercial advertising is an important consideration. No data are perfect, but "not perfect" isn't the same as useless. The standards of evidence in science provide benchmarks to evaluate how skeptical you should be of information you use to make everyday decisions. You always should be skeptical to some degree or another. In short, consult the *CR* data and consult other sources too. Then, as usual, make the best choice you can make in the absence of full information.

WHAT SHOULD SCIENCE'S ROLE BE IN EVERYDAY LIFE?

What is the Appropriate Role for Science in Everyday Life?

We hope you have begun to notice how the same themes about quality of information run through many real-world situations. These critical principles in social science methods apply to nearly every situation—in both scientific research and everyday learning—in which a decision must be made based on information.

SUMMARY

Several important principles of social science methods are illustrated in this chapter. Probably the most important single idea is that everyone faces "mega" information overload and must therefore depend on others for information. Judgments about the quality of that information are crucial. Three important criteria are illustrated:

- Evaluate the expertise/credentials of your sources.
- Pay close attention to possible vested interests—product sponsors, **sticky theory** devotees, someone with an "ax to grind" and so forth—that might affect what is claimed.
- Consider how fully and carefully the methods of data collection and analysis are documented.

The point about credentials and vested interests go hand in hand. Several examples in this chapter emphasize these two considerations. The *Sports Illustrated* story about steroids in baseball obviously was motivated by an interest in selling advertising and copies of the magazine. The book by Wilson claiming everlasting life and love for women who take hormone supplements was, in fact, written by someone with credentials, namely, Robert A Wilson. But he had a definite conflict of interest, since he was on the payroll of the pharmaceutical company that manufactured one brand of the supplements.

Also, in the case of hormone replacements, cause-and-effect claims must be subject to independent review by people with enough expertise to evaluate the claims *and* without vested interest in the outcome. Given the substantial monetary incentives for persuading people they need to purchase something, it's not surprising that often it isn't easy to spot "tainted" information. In contrast, *Consumer Reports* auto repair data aren't motivated by any direct commercial interest in selling one make of automobile instead of another, but it must sell subscriptions to continue its operation.

When in doubt, remember these important principles.

1. Look for a spurious relationship and understand the power of random assignment to avoid misinterpreting every association as if it were a **cause-and-effect** relationship. Think of the hormone supplement case as one example (Figure 1).

2. Insist on a base of comparison—raw numbers seldom are useful reported in isolation. Percentages, for example, tell "how many per 100" died who took GBL. And this should be compared to how many per 100 who died but did not take GBL.

3. Be aware of sampling variability—how results can vary from sample to sample without being due to any systematic process such as bias in a lottery. Figure 2 gives you an example frequency distribution for random draws of numbers with equal probabilities for each number 1 through 59.

4. Pay close attention to potential sources of survey error, such as **nonresponse** error and respondent misreport (measurement error).

5. Consider the advantages and limitations of **qualitative** and **quantitative data**. Many aspects of human affairs are nearly impossible to quantify where qualitative observation may provide a lot of insight. But qualitative data are difficult to replicate. The *SI* story about steroids in baseball is an example of qualitative data that may be useful but also has a number of shortcomings, not all due to the fact it is qualitative data.

6. Watch out for "sticky-theory" choices. One of the most common tactics in commercial advertising and political comments is to systematically pick examples that appear to support one's viewpoint while ignoring contrary evidence. Another name for this operation is cherry-picking.

7. Be aware of the regression to the mean phenomenon. For example, don't be too quick to attribute improvement in your headache to whatever pill you took for it. Likely your headache eventually would have cured itself even if you had taken no pills. Regression to the mean happens to things that wax and wane over time, for example, sports performance (e.g., free throw percentage, batting average, pass completion percentage).

YOUR REVIEW SHEET

1. Summarize how formal social science standards and procedures apply to everyday learning.

2. Summarize the evidence presented by *SI* that steroid use is widespread in major league baseball. What procedures are needed to produce accurate estimates of the percentage of players who use steroids? Does *SI* meet these standards? If not, could one devise a study that would? Explain briefly.

3. How difficult would it be to carry out the study you devised in response to question 2?

4. Summarize and evaluate the evidence relating to sports injuries presented by *SI*.

5. Why was the evidence weak indicating that women should take hormone supplements after menopause? Why is the evidence from the Women's Health Initiative study using random assignment strong enough to offset prior evidence indicating benefits of the hormone supplements?

6. What basic principle of science is violated by the connection between the author of *Feminine Forever* and the pharmaceutical industry, and, more generally, by sources of information about medicinal drugs?

7. How is a "run" of good luck in cards similar to a hitting "streak" in baseball? How is this point illustrated in Figure 2?

8. What sampling principles are illustrated by the simulated lottery numbers in Figure 2?

9. What are the main strong points of the *CR* data on car reliability? What are the weaknesses? What important general principle does the text claim is illustrated by the strengths and weaknesses of the *CR* data?

10. In your own words, what are the seven principles of a scientific approach with which to judge the quality of information encountered in everyday life?

END NOTES

1. One of the tests was significant. This is not unusual when multiple tests are done. It does illustrate that a decision based on a statistical tests is a bet, with good odds. But sometimes you lose the bet.

STUDY TERMS

cause-and-effect relationship Change of the cause is followed by a change in the effect, "everything else being equal," as illustrated by *if...then* statements.

control To "hold constant" one or more variables that might be related to both the presumed cause and the presumed effect.

measurement error Difference between an observed value and the "true" value of a variable.

nonresponse Failure of selected sample members to complete all or part of a survey. *Nonresponse error* comes from differences between individuals who complete and return a questionnaire and those who do not.

physical control Control in which the researcher determines the values of all causes thought to affect the outcome. Social researchers have limited ability to use physical controls and must rely on statistical control. Random assignment often is thought of as a control. But it does not set the value of any variable except the treatment variable. It does create an expectation of zero difference between the treatment and control groups of the *average* of all variables other than the treatment variable that might affect the outcome.

qualitative data Information collected from unstructured observation intended to represent meanings, symbols, descriptions, concepts and characteristics of people.

quantitative data Research observations that are converted into numbers.

random assignment A "pure chance" procedure used to determine which subjects are in the treatment group(s) and which subjects are in the control group. The purpose is to improve *internal validity*. (Did the treatment have the effect attributed to it?)

sampling error Difference between a sample statistic and population parameter.

selection bias People decide for themselves whether to engage in an activity such as taking estrogen. The basis of their decision, such as healthy lifestyle, also affects an outcome such as a heart attack. The result is a spuriously low incidence of heart attack among women who took estrogen.

spurious association Non-cause-and-effect relationship between two variables, generated by their common dependence on at least one other variable. (See Figure 1.)

statistical control An approximation of physical control in which a relationship between two variables is observed within constant levels of control variable(s).

statistical test A procedure for making a decision as to whether a population value of a statistic is some stated value, called the "null hypothesis." Usually the null hypothesis states no relationship between two variables. If the null hypothesis is rejected, it implies support for the research hypothesis (in most cases). Statistical tests are the primary technical method of *statistical inference* (process of drawing conclusions about a population using data from a sample).

sticky theory A phrase we invented to capture the widespread observation that people sometimes hold ideas so strongly that they refuse to acknowledge evidence that contradicts their ideas.

EXERCISES

Exercise 1. The Critical Consumer—Issue 1

Directions: Answer each of the questions by referring to the *SI* story about "steroid use in professional baseball."

1. In a brief sentence, define the population for the steroid story.
2. The primary variable in the steroids story is consumption of anabolic steroids. Write two operational definitions of this variable: (a) as a numeric variable, and (b) as a categorical variable with two categories (dichotomous).

3. Write a brief discussion of the difficulties you might encounter getting accurate measures of steroid use in a survey, and with medical tests.

4. The steroid story is primarily a descriptive study, the goal being to describe the extent of use/abuse of steroids in professional baseball. But it also discusses the relationship between steroid use and various health problems. One outcome of steroid use mentioned in the story is reduced production of testosterone. Assume you collapse testosterone production into a dichotomy: (a) normal or above, and (b) below normal. Use the dichotomous version of your steroid-use variable (Question 2) to produce a hypothetical 2×2 table showing percentages supporting the hypothesis that steroid use reduces testosterone production to below-normal levels. (Assume a sample of males.) Describe the relationship in one or two sentences.

5. Suppose the relationship you produced in your answer to Question 4 is observed in real data. Identify and discuss variables that might generate this relationship even if steroid use didn't affect testosterone production. Or argue that it's difficult to explain away this relationship as spurious even if it's not observed in a randomized experiment.

Exercise 2. The Critical Consumer—Issue 2

Directions: Answer each question referring to the story about "hormone therapy and women's health."

1. Identify the dependent variable(s) and primary independent variable in the hormone supplements example. Identify at least one potential control variable.

2. In your own words, describe why early research showing health benefits of estrogen or estrogen–progestin supplements probably mistook a spurious relationship to be a cause-and-effect relationship. In your answer, first define a spurious relationship and draw a path (arrow) diagram illustrating this idea. Then, fill in the path diagram with the names of the variables in the hormone supplement debate.

3. Explain why a randomized clinical trial isn't subject to the same criticism about spuriousness that applies to observational studies.

4. The WHI halted its very large clinical trial ($n > 16,000$) early because of small elevations in health risks for women assigned to take the hormones instead of the placebo. The biggest elevation of risk was for the risk of blood clots: 34 of 10,000 for women taking the supplement versus 16 of 10,000 for women taking the placebo. Why is such a small difference still statistically significant? (*Hint:* If there had been only 1,000 women in the study, do you think this difference (34 vs. 16 in 10,000) would be statistically significant?)

5. Discuss the practical (logistics and funding) and ethical issues you think might arise if a large clinical trial (which uses random assignment) were undertaken to test the following hypothesis:

   a. There's an interaction between hormone supplements and a healthful lifestyle (consisting of a "preferred" diet and regular vigorous exercise). The interaction is because hormone supplements are beneficial for those with the "healthful lifestyle" but detrimental for those who don't follow the healthful lifestyle.

6. Based on your current limited information, do you think the hypothesis in Question 5 is worth the expense? If so, why? Do you think a study to test this hypothesis would pass the IRB (human subjects review board)? Why or why not?

Exercise 3. The Critical Consumer—Issue 3

Directions: Answer the following questions referring to the discussion about "*CR* auto reliability data."

1. Consider the auto reliability data as a relationship between two variables: (a) make of automobile, and (b) frequency of repairs. Which of these two variables is the independent variable? The dependent variable?

2. Which type of variable is make of automobile: nominal, ordinal, interval, ratio? Explain why.

3. Construct a hypothetical two-variable table for make of automobile and cost of repairs, with make of automobile as the column variable. Show a strong relationship in the table. Use just two makes of automobile, and choose one make that has a large, powerful engine and one that has a small engine and gets high fuel economy. What essential feature of a variable is missing from your automobile-make variable?

4. Explain how the difference in repair costs between the two makes in your example might be due to something other than the quality of the make of automobile—that is, to the driving "personality" of the car owners. Construct a three-variable table illustrating your argument.

5. Suppose you were to do a randomized field trial to study the reliability built into five makes/models of automobile. First, discuss how you would operationalize the concept "overall reliability." Then explain how random assignment of the make/model of automobile to subjects in your experiment avoids the spuriousness described in Question 4. Don't forget to describe your procedures for this study, including the records you require participants to keep.

Exercise 4. The Critical Consumer—Issue 4: Independent Peer Review in Everyday Learning

Directions: Write a brief essay about the role of independent peer review in science and how it might apply to practical decisions. Address the following issues:

1. Why is it so difficult to identify a cause-and-effect relationship?

2. Draw on examples in this chapter to illustrate some of the subtle and not-so-subtle ways vested interests may influence conclusions about causation.

3. Contrast the norm of independent review with the influence of vested interests.

Exercise 5. Skills Building: Batting Slumps and Hot Streaks

Directions: Consider Steve Steroidal Massif, a rookie major league baseball player with a 0.300 lifetime batting average (he has, in the past, hit safely 3 times for every 10 times at bat). Steve has a stellar minor league record and has just been "brought up" to his major league parent club to help revive it from its current standing in the cellar of its division. Table 1 shows Steve's first 102 at bats. (This is a little less than 1/5 of a season for a starter.)

TABLE 1. Hitting Streaks—Rookie Big-League Player (0.300 Batting Average)

Total at Bats	Length of Streak	Streak									
10	10	Out	Out	Out	Out	Out	Out	Out	Out	Out	Out
11	1	Hit									
13	2	Out	Out								
17	4	Hit	Hit	Hit	Hit						
18	1	Out									
19	1	Hit									
21	2	Out	Out								
22	1	Hit									
23	1	Out									
24	1	Hit									
26	2	Out	Out								
27	1	Hit									
30	3	Out	Out	Out							
33	3	Hit	Hit	Hit							
34	1	Out									
35	1	Hit									
37	2	Out	Out								
38	1	Hit									
46	8	Out	Out	Out	Out	Out	Out	Out	Out		
47	1	Hit									
48	1	Out									
50	2	Hit	Hit								
54	4	Out	Out	Out	Out						
55	1	Hit									
61	6	Out	Out	Out	Out	Out	Out				
63	2	Hit	Hit								
66	3	Out	Out	Out							
67	1	Hit									
68	1	Out									
70	2	Hit	Hit								
71	1	Out									
73	2	Hit	Hit								
81	8	Out	Out	Out	Out	Out	Out	Out	Out		
82	1	Hit									
86	4	Out	Out	Out	Out						
87	1	Hit									
88	1	Out									
90	2	Hit	Hit								
91	1	Out									
93	2	Hit	Hit								
98	5	Out	Out	Out	Out	Out					
99	1	Hit									
102	3	Out	Out	Out							

1. Suppose you are the manager of this ball club. After Steve's first 10 at bats, would you (a) bench him, (b) send him back to the minor leagues, (c) stick with him at least for the rest of the season? Explain why. Keep in mind that you have seen just the first 10 at bats when you make this decision.
2. Identify the streaks that you consider to be "slumps" in Steve's first 102 at bats.
3. Identify the streaks which you think are "hot streaks" in Steve's first 102 at bats.
4. Explain why the "slumps" are longer than the "hot streaks."
5. Suppose the hitting records in Table 1 were generated at random—as they were, in fact. What implications does this fact have for your answers to Questions 2 and 3? Offer a definition of a streak. (*Hint:* Base your definition on the idea that the chance of getting a hit depends partly on how well the hitter has done in recent at bats.)

Exercise 6. Skills Building: Batter Up!

Directions. Table 2 shows a selection of "streaks" for a veteran player, Grant Greybeard. Grant has a lifetime big-league batting average of 0.300 (same as rookie Steve). Answer the questions below referring to Table 2. Remember, the numbers in Table 2 were made up to look like batting averages using a random number generator.

1. Explain why Grant has more long streaks and slumps than Steve. (*Hint:* Consider number of career at bats in your answer.) Does your answer contain a definite guarantee that Grant will have longer streaks than Steve? Why?
2. Note that out of at least 2,905 career at bats for Grant, only eight are displayed in Table 2. How many more hitting "slumps" as long as 25 do you think might have occurred in Grant's career? Answer in qualitative terms (none, one or two, a few, several, etc.). Explain why.
3. How often do you think people mistake an unusual sequence of events, like a hitting slump or streak, for some mysterious, or not so mysterious, unseen "force" (causal mechanism)? Describe an example you have seen that might illustrate this point, or make up a realistic example if you can't think of one you have seen.

TABLE 2.   Hitting Streaks—Veteran Big-League Player (0.300 Lifetime Batting Average)

Career at Bats	Length of Streak	Streak									
398	18	Out	Out	Out	Out	Out	Out	Out	Out	Out	Out
		Out	Out	Out	Out	Out	Out	Out	Out		
537	6	Hit	Hit	Hit	Hit	Hit	Hit				
565	15	Out	Out	Out	Out	Out	Out	Out	Out	Out	Out
		Out	Out	Out	Out	Out					
997	15	Out	Out	Out	Out	Out	Out	Out	Out	Out	Out
		Out	Out	Out	Out	Out					
1,320	25	Out	Out	Out	Out	Out	Out	Out	Out	Out	Out
		Out	Out	Out	Out	Out	Out	Out	Out	Out	Out
		Out	Out	Out	Out	Out					
1,583	5	Hit	Hit	Hit	Hit	Hit					
2,559	22	Out	Out	Out	Out	Out	Out	Out	Out	Out	Out
		Out	Out	Out	Out	Out	Out	Out	Out	Out	Out
		Out	Out								
2,905	18	Out	Out	Out	Out	Out	Out	Out	Out	Out	Out
		Out	Out	Out	Out	Out	Out	Out	Out		

CODE OF ETHICS

This appendix contains selected excerpts from the Code of Ethics of the American Sociological Association, the Code of Ethics of the American Anthropological Association and the Code of Ethics of the Academy of Criminal Justice Sciences. Website linkages include Council on Social Work Education, the National Organization for Human Services and the National Council on Family Relations.

AMERICAN SOCIOLOGICAL ASSOCIATION CODE OF ETHICS

The American Sociological Association Code of Ethics consists of four major parts:

Introduction
Preamble
General Principles
Ethical Standards

The excerpts in this appendix include the first paragraph of the Introduction and the entire section on General Principles.

The Code of Ethics of the American Anthropological Association contains eight sections:

    I. Preamble
   II. Introduction
  III. Research
  IV. Teaching
   V. Application
  VI. Epilogue
 VII. Acknowledgments
VIII. Other Relevant Codes of Ethics

From Appendix of *Research Methods and Society, Foundations of Social Inquiry,* Second Edition. Linda Eberst Dorsten, Lawrence Hotchkiss. Copyright © 2014 by Pearson Education, Inc. All rights reserved.

This appendix contains Section III, Research.

The Code of Ethics of the Academy of Criminal Justice Sciences (ACJS) and its procedures were developed using the American Sociological Association's Code of Ethics. The ACJS code includes four sections:

    I. Preamble

    II. General Principles

    III. Ethical Standards

    IV. Policies and Procedures

This appendix contains III B, Ethical Standards.

The National Statement on Research Integrity in Social Work from the Council on Social Work Education contains an introduction titled, "Responsible Conduct of Research," along with eight components:

1. Human Subjects and Communities

2. Mentor/Trainee Responsibility

3. Conflicts of Interest and Commitment

4. Collaborative Science

5. Data Acquisition, Management, Sharing and Ownership

6. Publication Practices and Responsible Authorship

7. Peer Review

8. Research Misconduct

This appendix includes the "Responsible Conduct" statement and component 1. The American Sociological Association's (ASA) Code of Ethics sets forth the principles and ethical standards that underlie sociologists' professional responsibilities and conduct. These principles and standards should be used as guidelines when examining everyday professional activities. They constitute normative statements for sociologists and provide guidance on issues that sociologists may encounter in their professional work.

General Principles

The following General Principles are aspirational and serve as a guide for sociologists in determining ethical courses of action in various contexts. They exemplify the highest ideals of professional conduct.

Principle A: Professional Competence. Sociologists strive to maintain the highest levels of competence in their work; they recognize the limitations of their expertise; and they undertake only those tasks for which they are qualified by education, training, or experience. They recognize the need for ongoing education in order to remain professionally competent; and they utilize the appropriate scientific, professional, technical, and administrative resources needed to ensure competence in their professional activities. They consult with other professionals when necessary for the benefit of their students, research participants, and clients.

Principle B: Integrity. Sociologists are honest, fair, and respectful of others in their professional activities—in research, teaching, practice, and service. Sociologists do not knowingly act in ways that jeopardize either their own or others' professional welfare. Sociologists conduct their affairs in ways that inspire trust and confidence; they do not knowingly make statements that are false, misleading, or deceptive.

Principle C: Professional and Scientific Responsibility. Sociologists adhere to the highest scientific and professional standards and accept responsibility for their work. Sociologists understand that they form a community and show respect for other sociologists even when they disagree on theoretical, methodological, or personal approaches to professional activities. Sociologists value the public trust in sociology and are concerned about their ethical behavior and that of other sociologists that might compromise that trust. While endeavoring always to be collegial, sociologists must never let the desire to be collegial outweigh their shared responsibility for ethical behavior. When appropriate, they consult with colleagues in order to prevent or avoid unethical conduct.

Principle D: Respect for People's Rights, Dignity, and Diversity. Sociologists respect the rights, dignity, and worth of all people. They strive to eliminate bias in their professional activities, and they do not tolerate any forms of discrimination based on age; gender; race; ethnicity; national origin; religion; sexual orientation; disability; health conditions; or marital, domestic, or parental status. They are sensitive to cultural, individual, and role differences in serving, teaching, and studying groups of people with distinctive characteristics. In all of their work-related activities, sociologists acknowledge the rights of others to hold values, attitudes, and opinions that differ from their own.

Principle E: Social Responsibility. Sociologists are aware of their professional and scientific responsibility to the communities and societies in which they live and work. They apply and make public their knowledge in order to contribute to the public good. When undertaking research, they strive to advance the science of sociology and to serve the public good.

Source: American Sociological Association. *Code of Ethics of the American Sociological Association.* Available at http://www.asanet.org/about/ethics.cfm (accessed October 24, 2010).

CODE OF ETHICS OF THE AMERICAN ANTHROPOLOGICAL ASSOCIATION

In both proposing and carrying out research, anthropological researchers must be open about the purpose(s), potential impacts, and source(s) of support for research projects with funders, colleagues, persons studied or providing information, and with relevant parties affected by the research. Researchers must expect to utilize the results of their work in an appropriate fashion and disseminate the results through appropriate and timely activities. Research fulfilling these expectations is ethical, regardless of the source of funding (public or private) or purpose (i.e., "applied," "basic," "pure," or "proprietary").

Anthropological researchers should be alert to the danger of compromising anthropological ethics as a condition to engage in research, yet also be alert to proper demands of good citizenship or host–guest relations. Active contribution and leadership in seeking to shape public or private sector actions and policies may be as ethically justifiable as inaction, detachment, or noncooperation, depending on circumstances. Similar principles hold for anthropological researchers employed or otherwise affiliated with nonanthropological institutions, public institutions, or private enterprises.

Responsibility to People and Animals with Whom Anthropological Researchers Work and Whose Lives and Cultures They Study

1. Anthropological researchers have primary ethical obligations to the people, species, and materials they study and to the people with whom they work. These obligations can supersede the goal of seeking new knowledge, and can lead to decisions not to undertake or to discontinue a research project when the primary obligation conflicts with other responsibilities, such as those owed to sponsors or clients. These ethical obligations include:

- To avoid harm or wrong, understanding that the development of knowledge can lead to change which may be positive or negative for the people or animals worked with or studied
- To respect the well-being of humans and nonhuman primates
- To work for the long-term conservation of the archaeological, fossil, and historical records
- To consult actively with the affected individuals or group(s), with the goal of establishing working relationships that can be beneficial to all parties involved

2. Anthropological researchers must do everything in their power to ensure that their research does not harm the safety, dignity, or privacy of the people with whom they work, conduct research, or perform other professional activities. Anthropological researchers working with animals must do everything in their power to ensure that the research does not harm the safety, psychological well-being or survival of the animals or species with which they work.

3. Anthropological researchers must determine in advance whether their hosts/providers of information wish to remain anonymous or receive recognition, and make every effort to comply with those wishes. Researchers must present to

their research participants the possible impacts of the choices, and make clear that despite their best efforts, anonymity may be compromised or recognition fail to materialize.

4. Anthropological researchers should obtain in advance the informed consent of persons being studied, providing information, owning or controlling access to material being studied, or otherwise identified as having interests which might be impacted by the research. It is understood that the degree and breadth of informed consent required will depend on the nature of the project and may be affected by requirements of other codes, laws, and ethics of the country or community in which the research is pursued. Further, it is understood that the informed consent process is dynamic and continuous; the process should be initiated in the project design and continue through implementation by way of dialogue and negotiation with those studied. Researchers are responsible for identifying and complying with the various informed consent codes, laws and regulations affecting their projects. Informed consent, for the purposes of this code, does not necessarily imply or require a particular written or signed form. It is the quality of the consent, not the format, that is relevant.

5. Anthropological researchers who have developed close and enduring relationships (i.e., covenantal relationships) with either individual persons providing information or with hosts must adhere to the obligations of openness and informed consent, while carefully and respectfully negotiating the limits of the relationship.

6. While anthropologists may gain personally from their work, they must not exploit individuals, groups, animals, or cultural or biological materials. They should recognize their debt to the societies in which they work and their obligation to reciprocate with people studied in appropriate ways.

Source: American Anthropological Association *American Anthropological Association Code of Ethics.* Available at http://www.aaanet.org/committees/ethics/ethicscode.pdf (accessed October 24, 2010).

CODE OF ETHICS OF THE ACADEMY OF CRIMINAL JUSTICE SCIENCES

The Code of Ethics of the Academy of Criminal Justice Sciences (ACJS) sets forth (1) General Principles and (2) Ethical Standards that underlie members of the Academy's professional responsibilities and conduct, along with the (3) Policies and Procedures for enforcing those principles and standards.

Objectivity and Integrity in the Conduct of Criminal Justice Research

1. Members of the Academy should adhere to the highest possible technical standards in their research.

2. Since individual members of the Academy vary in their research modes, skills, and experience, they should acknowledge the limitations that may affect the validity of their findings.

3. In presenting their work, members of the Academy are obliged to fully report their findings. They should not misrepresent the findings of their research or omit significant data. Any and all omitted data should be noted and the reason(s) for exclusion stated clearly as part of the methodology. Details of their theories, methods, and research designs that might bear upon interpretations of research findings should be reported.

4. Members of the Academy should fully report all sources of financial support and other sponsorship of the research.

5. Members of the Academy should not make any commitments to respondents, individuals, groups or organizations unless there is full intention and ability to honor them.

6. Consistent with the spirit of full disclosure of method and analysis, members of the Academy, after they have completed their own analyses, should cooperate in efforts to make raw data and pertinent documentation available to other social scientists, at reasonable costs, except in cases where confidentiality, the client's rights to proprietary information and privacy, or the claims of a field worker to the privacy of personal notes necessarily would be violated. The timeliness of this cooperation is especially critical.

7. Members of the Academy should provide adequate information, documentation, and citations concerning scales and other measures used in their research.

8. Members of the Academy should not accept grants, contracts or research assignments that appear likely to violate the principles enunciated in this Code, and should disassociate themselves from research when they discover a violation and are unable to correct it.

9. When financial support for a project has been accepted, members of the Academy should make every reasonable effort to complete the proposed work on schedule.

10. When a member of the Academy is involved in a project with others, including students, there should be mutually accepted explicit agreements at the outset with respect to division of work, compensation, access to data, rights of authorship, and other rights and responsibilities. These agreements should not be exploitative or arrived at through any form of coercion or intimidation. Such agreements may need to be modified as the project evolves and such modifications should be clearly stated among all participants. Students should normally be the principle author of any work that is derived directly from their thesis or dissertation.

11. Members of the Academy have the right to disseminate research findings, except those likely to cause harm to clients, collaborators and participants, those which violate formal or implied promises of confidentially, or those which are proprietary under a formal or informal agreement.

Disclosure and Respect of the Rights of Research Populations by Members of the Academy

12. Members of the Academy should not misuse their positions as professionals for fraudulent purposes or as a pretext for gathering information for any individual, group, organization or government.

13. Human subjects have the right to full disclosure of the purposes of the research as early as it is appropriate to the research process, and they have the right to an opportunity to have their questions answered about the purpose and usage of the research. Members should inform research participants about aspects of the research that might affect their willingness to participate, such as physical risks, discomfort, and/or unpleasant emotional experiences.

14. Subjects of research are entitled to rights of personal confidentiality unless they are waived.

15. Information about subjects obtained from records that are open to public scrutiny cannot be protected by guarantees of privacy or confidentiality.

16. The process of conducting criminal justice research must not expose respondents to more than minimal risk of personal harm, and members of the Academy should make every effort to ensure the safety and security of respondents and project staff. Informed consent should be obtained when the risks of research are greater than the risks of everyday life.

17. Members of the Academy should take culturally appropriate steps to secure informed consent and to avoid invasions of privacy. In addition, special actions will be necessary where the individuals studied are illiterate, under correctional supervision, minors, have low social status, are under judicial supervision, have diminished capacity, are unfamiliar with social research or otherwise occupy a position of unequal power with the researcher.

18. Members of the Academy should seek to anticipate potential threats to confidentiality. Techniques such as the removal of direct identifiers, the use of randomized responses, and other statistical solutions to problems of privacy should be used where appropriate. Care should be taken to ensure secure storage, maintenance, and/or destruction of sensitive records.

19. Confidential information provided by research participants should be treated as such by members of the Academy, even when this information enjoys no legal protection or privilege and legal force is applied. The obligation to respect confidentiality also applies to members of research organizations (interviewers, coders, clerical staff, etc.) who have access to the information. It is the responsibility of administrators and chief investigators to instruct staff members on this point and to make every effort to insure that access to confidential information is restricted.

20. While generally adhering to the norm of acknowledging the contributions of all collaborators, members of the Academy should be sensitive to harm that may arise from disclosure and respect a collaborator's need for anonymity.

21. All research should meet the human subjects requirements imposed by educational institutions and funding sources. Study design and information gathering techniques should conform to regulations protecting the rights of human subjects, regardless of funding.

22. Members of the Academy should comply with appropriate federal and institutional requirements pertaining to the conduct of their research. These requirements might include, but are not necessarily limited to, obtaining proper review and approval for research that involves human subjects and accommodating recommendations made by responsible committees concerning research subjects, materials, and procedures.

Source: Academy of Criminal Justice Sciences. *American Anthropological Association Code of Ethics.* Available at http://www.acjs.org/pubs/167_671_2922.cfm (accessed October 22, 2010).

OTHER SOURCES: CODE OF ETHICS

Council on Social Work Education. *National Statement on Research Integrity in Social Work.* Available at http://www.cswe.org/cms/17157.aspx (accessed October 22, 2010).

National Council on Family Relations. *NCFR Ethical Guidelines.* Available at http://www.ncfr.org/about/board-directors/governance/ncfr-ethical-guidelines (accessed February 2, 2010).

National Organization for Human Services. *Ethical Standards for Human Service Professionals.* Available at http://www.nationalhumanservices.org/index.php?option=com_content&view=article&id=43 (accessed February 7, 2011).

RANDOM NUMBERS

```
83656   04063   80398   01443   83035   98436   34344   54842   67303   53025   75969
55226   65639   61977   73628   43752   83499   69594   25098   32035   91572   95419
42131   05891   63915   64011   16887   27212   31458   94103   97328   90723   86573
92849   85068   67358   06249   13181   64716   95326   14245   74523   03106   48882
41468   78067   80181   43643   24161   42814   99031   20470   19295   01215   00640
43664   57128   57160   87218   27177   45178   22297   05966   74421   13155   38565
37050   41196   37175   53842   86185   84375   28959   41141   17954   51273   26761
08542   95213   98052   27499   78531   52823   59716   24211   39422   35157   21925
79986   50436   87591   59079   58613   85665   34416   73830   66869   97643   87871
91388   61396   98819   30631   75481   05614   05944   35615   54706   44099   62576
60196   25825   49329   79498   24503   67649   77466   30758   89140   45040   01053
89694   51994   63680   39398   39511   49474   60039   41654   59205   01007   39074
49847   17862   34276   07606   80524   22731   32061   77585   98650   10990   72826
12211   13205   31125   93919   93954   70105   76116   57022   09020   85385   37894
67194   81490   20777   44800   82587   53028   04370   09153   89029   06422   81569
77481   19746   72197   19364   76461   38632   65638   13037   38553   67411   33459
30738   31370   86420   93441   80874   75361   82066   32024   21045   79562   11732
61356   35846   75851   44395   18782   06983   20643   96327   61836   06638   57667
32226   58702   63876   82510   18828   81630   07878   19750   08133   71115   20092
85997   38153   60896   16473   00545   82067   29188   05336   06082   40658   73258
86172   40988   16780   22476   68112   77120   53185   81258   28289   07278   80707
38760   75474   72813   12337   79336   06359   92066   22050   28124   95282   66339
86300   93146   77723   92129   53163   88763   03832   69224   54884   80897   35888
92810   81030   19238   92709   20631   83733   31275   88821   74947   09059   60301
25134   59525   14221   38820   66229   67802   22043   42018   32920   01297   13052
31923   64471   20232   91363   26975   54216   57657   90347   76700   61840   45371
73998   01003   83848   88901   12279   30971   61428   05841   03898   76705   87264
22797   60003   80685   49730   78880   15303   10068   61048   04184   76008   66315
27095   52123   54105   32483   14478   20546   06161   40548   91373   50255   27575
05870   24966   31171   72152   38146   03973   68717   90314   90020   34878   63470
85772   23984   45798   92870   43418   01197   33032   02334   36897   03017   47576
57468   53505   80616   25466   52143   62992   03844   52604   96180   53973   44028
25912   33742   58070   04892   11612   30493   46301   73600   83718   28386   79583
86266   91863   87838   00968   29535   71993   67380   72312   40463   82014   01450
```

50759 38617 15003 11281 93078 70255 63022 05396 19757 78770 97208
56556 18955 09374 49988 56507 60799 16558 08251 56224 49584 77914
11308 27433 63391 20840 63178 92661 02289 75891 70838 26963 76483
84698 67943 45977 50908 69606 47668 63175 02293 00069 44329 36712
93269 41441 55492 05119 25284 70199 23433 65402 88286 91629 32158
38300 21372 32623 47898 52419 37181 26555 70333 14116 68229 60680
24515 54756 98362 42265 38198 32419 24455 24880 06822 24784 05283
27938 31176 29184 15306 59645 77326 11101 24301 06860 21850 32932
22861 51810 28318 00576 17777 67082 77992 90160 70706 51887 50316
22873 11845 30492 72230 91947 62766 97146 00610 59044 18665 93799
85031 20386 92706 97812 93233 24678 49628 95138 06619 51205 53389
18877 51724 67881 26647 54818 09871 96241 93508 02266 54945 23379
84242 01266 39119 32252 68032 69887 65174 03783 33704 79469 70585
52008 93862 13852 11353 85547 87310 45205 51621 78267 55812 22271
52335 21619 71798 32117 74995 37439 87536 58094 96583 67415 45620
27672 67672 23388 13963 03676 67998 12209 04033 60946 06020 87430
50984 41809 86148 16902 96736 96926 11212 51191 15678 29103 08662
75935 60573 41730 75508 78857 97498 83175 79845 23121 41916 95881
11463 98121 73403 36674 02775 39050 86712 78903 79682 88278 12061
55470 38903 46724 45176 41896 58435 94998 32343 77143 87913 46501
54818 89850 11356 75960 86016 67012 56528 97744 68149 41525 06154
22947 72975 25318 36889 40500 67642 71540 75932 06431 77831 28353
19472 60253 32521 03492 10374 39136 57610 54906 67419 47628 15161
09375 85464 97763 12024 06378 33163 81695 22605 72944 33054 72383
64351 51692 55417 83112 43291 58873 54971 78175 69760 24844 25659
86012 31436 64457 57833 17913 41133 36677 07138 88008 76681 37004
67136 66737 27586 23354 40511 60167 54610 35470 70830 68452 11130
93198 47443 57490 63550 16244 37266 39933 90510 33159 48280 14057
83192 25220 68735 84890 62475 25643 70904 07909 02373 20143 43122
60209 96177 03304 58655 91463 96611 20733 34072 89613 35380 26548
78292 05555 41000 46767 34841 49637 38891 26440 89800 93333 22912
90623 38130 40563 72870 25534 43918 10598 29281 54531 70767 91354
02186 94414 03176 67854 91327 86080 15978 47489 09992 37406 70160
45851 74363 86769 25740 93833 46671 28706 37552 05179 82126 04411
38340 23094 13147 11542 56312 94153 21496 10281 95083 29618 38774
92554 89553 54387 23123 96235 08526 08819 47492 66211 28228 72377
85766 01097 94316 72452 15367 97437 85653 81037 02389 20076 30133
53493 53625 88094 25227 14310 07919 15816 02502 60935 53444 29137
20729 35315 47692 24043 61322 96382 44162 84999 07327 08172 82586
30495 73185 28024 19456 74391 17915 94739 05314 78026 55611 54213
34545 32776 23764 21911 22214 86621 36246 69886 59447 81476 51165

Appendix: Random Numbers

```
48329  90532  55006  11389  33224  93069  38591  60241  39351  60274  00440
09609  16677  06661  45271  55229  40143  71488  84110  64074  81282  93358
75020  80688  69775  78974  29483  52531  38891  97763  94977  05944  82625
64241  00799  82964  13556  41920  57180  64680  23690  28759  52966  02575
62512  60531  79249  39844  78328  82393  70080  65116  02998  46490  32874
71207  35612  73578  03856  84240  61360  81122  90416  46498  21472  67460
71011  88758  57134  12782  97281  67789  56168  32972  56013  55899  74163
36587  04301  00827  18455  64154  16031  54198  42835  25135  46020  16776
52241  62351  74455  79660  15637  12116  80711  49911  28590  75668  48135
92751  98442  07378  62561  81515  07961  41702  23660  07736  42180  06836
14131  64595  60894  58415  16142  22686  03777  76508  38113  59565  31096
46634  20668  95994  96853  48547  50347  31363  66661  78075  21044  17209
34507  04689  99342  58794  63437  63575  70052  11092  34101  77141  72008
97047  62239  55672  92134  28363  22139  14551  39945  71165  27182  62056
08612  38039  89499  36910  91563  71629  92481  60865  41014  77725  22325
05111  81223  30423  44380  26413  70460  54040  23893  87353  34823  67800
26429  70510  30644  63617  65114  44224  40467  17400  77761  21079  00806
04134  01625  14167  57884  50521  80232  44834  91500  97575  05010  91866
25850  93019  81699  40666  34986  72749  19770  66215  22071  95907  48487
87424  78057  09449  57893  29563  13209  84388  77136  05884  19555  97247
22850  33768  00213  35717  99451  22628  48328  52493  48613  16895  10847
87415  45002  04832  51710  97858  77890  41531  98816  67556  76388  87115
95203  37304  25719  92538  39407  79840  03510  97829  30223  79839  38954
55434  75759  69478  71930  02216  03242  49654  04497  43811  58853  54457
63770  85786  49985  67761  40330  49436  22367  49215  26545  21269  73576
96181  91795  51747  38507  16023  87954  07943  21394  37350  31058  26418
07413  67484  91349  04936  39665  35733  91402  77447  47070  60177  38936
07516  98996  49704  80237  15042  11993  52067  22246  90011  02323  96113
26757  29919  27393  41462  51662  86744  42488  88682  36113  91733  76867
16049  67804  62447  19557  02252  24484  70203  57980  34740  63674  73054
58733  00686  71812  26418  39271  87015  68670  31465  91673  66411  75206
88610  30490  92380  80769  52195  34583  67998  90580  08097  85649  91251
89607  83858  81391  34486  71418  46265  54354  76172  18263  34922  38857
12778  53332  77611  15042  37107  15700  25839  42318  66821  19507  64952
66762  51692  46652  67199  18367  98308  00472  00258  43139  26061  44149
```

INTRODUCTION TO THE GENERAL SOCIAL SURVEY (GSS)

The General Social Survey (GSS) is a repeating survey of U.S. households designed for use by the entire community of social science scholars and *students*. In this respect it is unusual, if not unique, in the United States (Davis, Smith, & Marsden, 2009). Most surveys cover a restricted scope of topics such as consumer attitudes, aspects of aging, drug abuse and income and wealth. And they are collected primarily for use by the principal investigator or for scholars in a narrow range of academic specialties. So the word "General" in the title carries a definite meaning.

The GSS is conducted by personal interview by the National Opinion Research Center (NORC). NORC is a nonprofit survey research corporation affiliated with the University of Chicago.

The GSS is available for download from its producer at NORC, and students and faculty from member institutions of the Inter-university Consortium for Political and Social Research (ICPSR) can download it from the ICPSR website. But users do need a certain amount of expertise to know how to use it. Simpler methods of analysis can be done online at either website and at the well-known SDA analysis website at the University of California, Berkeley. Both ICPSR and Berkeley support analysis of several major surveys.

The initial GSS survey was done in 1972. The interview schedule was short, consisting of just 20 questions. It was conducted primarily to validate the concept. In 1973, the National Science Foundation began funding an annual survey with a complete battery of questions. Each survey contains hundreds of questions. Annual surveys continued through 1993. Subsequently, the sample size was nearly doubled and the survey was conducted biannually. No surveys were conducted in 1979, 1981 and 1992, however, because of lack of funding. In the years before the biannual survey, sample sizes ranged from 1,372 to 1,860. Thereafter, sample sizes lie in the interval 2,765 to 4,510.

The GSS is funded by continuing grants from the National Science Foundation (NSS) and private foundations. The National Science Foundation is a U.S. government agency. Its mission is to fund fundamental research and education, except in health. NSF funding is prestigious and highly prized in the research community. The National Institutes of Health fund medical-related research.

Until the 2006 survey, the GSS sample contained different respondents in each survey; each respondent was interviewed just once. Consequently, researchers could study aggregate trends but not changes in individual people. However, in 2006 the GSS began a longitudinal component which does include reinterviews with a subsample of the same respondents for two successive surveys. The longitudinal design was fully implemented in the 2010 survey.

The GSS has supplied data for thousands of research papers, including journal articles, master's theses and Ph.D. dissertations. In addition, it frequently supports education in undergraduate and graduate college and university classes and provides information to the news media.

SURVEY CONTENT

A guiding principal of the GSS is replication. A large number of core questions are repeated in each survey, with the same wording. Repeated variables include demographic and stratification variables such as mentioned below:

- Age
- Gender
- Race
- Marital status
- Education
- Occupation (prestige, D.O.T. [a description of type of work])
- Industry
- Income
- Hours worked per week
- Employment status
- Residence (region, size of city/town/rural area)
- Geographic mobility (change of residence)
- Nativity (born in the United States?)
- Household composition
- Status variables like education, occupation and income
- Spouse's status variables like education, occupation and income

The GSS also contains many questions about a variety of social and political topics. Examples include the following:

- Party identification (Democrat, Independent, Republican)
- AIDS
- Alcohol consumption
- Alienation
- Race relations and attitudes
- Arrests

- Military (many questions related to the military)
- Attitudes and habits related to the "fine arts"
- Voluntary associations (many questions)
- Religion
- Civil liberties
- Attitudes toward authority
- Attitudes toward social issues like abortion, pornography, women's rights, minorities, euthanasia
- Consumer behavior (e.g., auto purchase, garage sale, price haggling)
- Family finance
- Sign of the zodiac

The last item is kind of amusing. The GSS is designed and executed with the benefit of continual advice from many highly regarded scientists. So why do the GSS data contain the astrological sign of each respondent? Do the experts advising the GSS staff believe researchers might find scientific support for astrology? In 2003, the GSS website said that the astrological sign is included in the data to allow users to test widely held "superstitions" about effects of astrological sign but that, to date, none had been reported. However, this material does not appear to be accessible any longer (April 2011).

Beginning in 1985, a sequence of topical modules has been included. These modules do not appear on each survey but may be replicated periodically. Examples of topics include the following:

- Political participation
- Religion
- Intergroup relations and conflict (questions about, e.g., protest movements, causes of poverty, group wealth)
- Civic duty
- Work and employment (questions about, e.g., corporations and unions, supervision, job control, pay)
- Culture—fine arts
- Multiculturalism

GSS DATA

The GSS data file contains coded responses to each question asked for every survey year. It is organized in one field for each variable and one row for each respondent. Values for questions not asked in a given year are coded missing for every respondent in the years when the questions were not asked. The 1972–2008 data file contains 53,043 observations and 5,364 variables. The number of observations is the sum of the number of completed surveys for all survey years combined up to and including 2008.

Response rates have been about 76 percent, with the lowest 70 percent in 2000 and the highest 82 percent in 1993. The response rates for the last five surveys, however, are just above 70 percent. These rates are among the best that can be expected with a large national survey. The interview currently runs about 90 minutes. So achieving this high response rate is good evidence of the dedication and talent of the NORC survey team.

STATISTICAL FORMULAS

Calculations for the median, mean, mode and standard deviation are shown for the variable "age" in the sample of 30 cases of Figure 2 in the chapter "Data Preparation and Basic Analysis." In all calculations, exclude missing values—no information for a respondent or case on a variable. (Statistical software will do this automatically, but it has to be told that 99, for example, is a missing value for age.)

1	2	3	4	5	6	7	8	9	10	11	12	13	14		15	16	17	18	19	20	21	22	23	24	25	26	27	28	29
18	20	25	27	27	28	28	28	29	29	30	32	33	34	I	34	35	36	43	44	47	49	62	62	67	69	73	74	86	89

Median

Median = 34 (middle value for age)
(bottom numbers are the ages, case numbers are on top).

NOTE: There are 29 cases here, not 30. One of the ages = 99 which is the missing-value code. All the calculations below for age omit the case with age = 99.

Also, since there is an odd number of cases due to the omission of the observation where age = 99, there is no value that falls exactly in the middle. The cases necessarily are split 15 on one side and 14 on the other.

$$\text{Mean: } \bar{x} = \frac{\sum_i^n x_i}{n} = \frac{1258}{29} \approx 43.38 \text{ (average)}$$

$$\text{Mode} = 28 \text{ (most frequent age)}$$

$$\text{Sample variance: } s^2 = \frac{\sum_i^n (x_i - \bar{x})^2}{n}$$

$$\text{Sample std deviation: } \sqrt{Variance} \approx \sqrt{398.9941} \approx 19.9748$$

$$\text{Pop. estimate variance: } \hat{\sigma}^2 = \frac{\sum_i^n (x_i - \bar{x})^2}{n - 1}$$

$$\text{Pop. estimate std deviation: } \sqrt{Variance} \approx \sqrt{413.2439} \approx 20.3284$$

The $\sqrt{}$ symbol stands for square root (e.g., $\sqrt{4} = 2$).

Notice n is in the denominator for calculation of the sample variance, and $n - 1$ instead of n in the denominator of the calculation for the population estimate of the variance and standard deviation. The sample variance is a biased estimate of the population variance. Using $(n - 1)$ gives an unbiased estimate of the population variance. Introductory statistical texts often loosely define the variance using $(n - 1)$ in the denominator.

The symbol x stands for the variable "age." The smallest value of age is 18. The subscripts on x refer to the respondent or case number (here, $1 - 29$). The symbol Σ means "add up." So case $i = 1$, $x_i = 18$; case $i = 2$, $x_i = 20$, etc. (The subscript on Σ indicates to start with case $i = 1$ and the superscript says to include all n cases, here, 29 cases).

GLOSSARY

abstract Summary of the research; if used, it is presented at the beginning of a research report and seldom exceeds a paragraph or two in length.

access Permission or agreement from subjects and/or agencies to conduct research at an observational or field setting.

announce Divulge to potential subjects that they are part of a research study; opposite of covert (hidden) observation.

anonymity The researcher does not know the identity of respondents, and the researcher therefore cannot link data to specific individuals (compare with confidentiality).

applied (evaluation) research Investigation of a social intervention designed to find out whether it works. Evaluation is a goal or objective, rather than a method of data collection (compare with basic research).

archival data Recorded information, usually historical, that is stored in repositories such as libraries or museums.

basic research Investigation for which the goal is to expand the level of knowledge rather than to change or evaluate a social intervention or social policy. The study of the possible effects of maternal schooling on child health is an example (compare with applied research).

bibliography A list of all sources explicitly cited in a paper—books, monographs, journal articles and government reports, as well as general periodicals and newspapers, encyclopedias and dictionaries, Internet resources and personal communications.

bivariate relationship Association between two variables; for example, a bivariate table displays the relationship between just two variables.

bivariate table Cross-tabulation of two variables. See cross-tabulation.

case One instance of the unit being studied, such as persons, couples, social groups and organizations like schools. In this use of the term, for example, each respondent in a survey is a case, and so is each subject in an experiment.

categorical variable A variable with a finite number of categories. The categories are different, but one category is not greater or less than any other category (e.g., gender contains two categories).

categories (of a variable) Classes of a variable; values of a nominal variable, for example, state of residence, with categories: Alabama, Alaska,...Wisconsin, Wyoming.

causal inference Conclusion that an observed relationship is due to the effect of the independent variable on the dependent variable (see also internal validity).

causal relationship A relationship that occurs where current knowledge of the cause reduces uncertainty about the effect some time in the future.

From Glossary of *Research Methods and Society, Foundations of Social Inquiry,* Second Edition. Linda Eberst Dorsten, Lawrence Hotchkiss. Copyright © 2014 by Pearson Education, Inc. All rights reserved.

cause and effect Change of the cause is followed by a change in the effect, "everything else being equal," as illustrated by *if . . . then* statements.

cause-and-effect relationship Manipulation of the cause is followed by a change in the effect, "everything else being equal," as illustrated by *if . . . then* statements. The study of cause and effect is called explanatory research.

cell frequency Number of occurrences of an event defined by the intersection between a column and a row in a cross-tabulation (e.g., the number of women who ever were hit).

central limit theorem The distribution of the mean (or sum) of independent measurements all of the same distribution goes to the normal distribution as the number of cases increases, irrespective of the distribution of the individual measurements. An important application of the central limit distribution is to sampling. As the sample size increases, the distribution of the sample mean goes to the normal distribution. The mean of the samples over all samples equals the mean of the population, and the standard deviation of the samples over all samples equals the population standard deviation divided by the square root of the sample sizes. These latter two points are true by basic math and do not depend on the central limit theorem. But they are crucial to inference from samples to populations.

chi-square distribution A theoretical probability distribution used in many applications for statistical inference, including testing for a relationship in a bivariate table.

chi-square statistic Number calculated from the sample frequencies for a cross-tabulation. (The chi-square statistic and chi-square test apply to many situations other than cross-tabulations.)

chi-square test Statistical test done by calculating the chi-square statistic for a sample cross-tabulation and comparing it to the probability from the chi-square distribution.

citation Reference in the text of a paper to a source of an idea, fact or quotation—any material or idea that isn't "common knowledge" or the writer's own thinking. Sources include journal articles, evaluations, monographs, government documents and so forth. Compare with references.

classical experimental design (pretest-posttest control group design) Experimental design in which pretest–posttest changes for the experimental group are compared with changes for the control group , and subjects are assigned at random to the treatment or control group.

closed-ended question Questions with a short list of predefined answers, usually called response options (e.g., . . . \$10,000–\$12,499, \$12,500–\$15,000 . . . for income). A familiar example is a multiple-choice question on an exam.

cluster sample Groups of individual elements are sampled instead of individual elements. The groups are called "clusters." Each individual in selected clusters is included in the sample. Schools might form the clusters for a sample of students, for example.

codebook A listing of all variables in a data collection with each variable accompanied by (1) a short "variable name," (2) a brief description, (3) the location (field or columns spanned) and (4) the meaning of each value.

column marginals Totals for each column, shown in the last row of a table containing a cross-tabulation.

complete observer (nonparticipant observer) Field worker whose role as a researcher is not known by the subjects.

composite variable Variable created by adding, averaging or combining in some other way two or more other variables. See index (one type of composite variable).

computer-assisted telephone interviewing (CATI) Phone interview process using random-digit dialing and automated recording of responses; speeds data collection and virtually eliminates transcription errors.

concepts (constructs) Variables that are not directly measurable; examples include prejudice, self-esteem, occupational status and intelligence.

confidence interval Lower and upper boundary and an associated probability that a population parameter, such as a mean or percentage, lies between the boundaries. This probability is called the level of confidence. The boundaries are estimated from sample data, given a specified level of confidence.

confidentiality The researcher knows respondents' identities, but does not reveal information in any way that can be linked to individual respondents (keeps their information confidential) (compare with anonymity).

confounding variable A variable producing a spurious (noncausal) association between two variables. For example, gender probably accounts for a strong negative relationship between height and hair length. Gender is the confounding variable.

constant A measure with only one category; all cases fit into one category (compare with variable).

construct validity Method of evaluating validity by observing whether measurements of constructs exhibit relationships with other variables as predicted by theory.

content analysis Conversion of recorded communication into usable form, usually variables. Recorded communication is found in print materials (e.g., books and magazines) in audio and visual recordings, and in electronic text and images, such as those found at computer websites.

content validity Method of evaluating validity that relies on researchers' judgments about whether procedures reflect the construct they are designed to measure.

continuous variable Variable whose values correspond to numbers that lie at any point along a straight line.

control To "hold constant" one or more influences that might be related to both the presumed cause and the effect. The purpose of using controls is to avoid mistaking an incidental or chance "relationship" for a causal relationship (see physical controls and statistical controls).

control group In an experiment, the group that receives no treatment; it is included simply for comparison.

control variable A variable that is held constant; a constant is a measure with one category, and all cases fit into one category (e.g., female gender).

controlled experiment The experimenter determines what is changed, by how much and what is not changed (kept constant).

correlation (Pearson product-moment correlation) Number ranging from −1 to 1, which measures the degree of linear relationship between two variables. A correlation of 1.0 indicates a perfect positive linear relationship. A correlation of −1 indicates a perfect negative linear relationship; a negative relationship means that values of the variables change in opposite directions (one increases as the other decreases). A correlation of 0.0 indicates no linear relationship.

cover letter Letter that accompanies or precedes a survey. It describes the purpose of the study and its social contribution, gives the sponsoring agency, tells why the respondent was selected, lists a contact person (for questions and mailback), contains a statement about anonymity or confidentiality and says "thank you."

coverage error Error due to omitting some part of the population from the sample list, and/or including some people more than once.

criterion validity Method for assessing validity by testing whether a variable predicts a criterion or standard. For example, does self-reported age predict the age calculated from one's birth certificate?

Cronbach's alpha Most general single measure of reliability based on internal consistency. It is calculated by using all of the two-variable correlations between scale items.

cross-tabulation Table displaying the frequencies and/or percentages for every combination of values of two or more variables.

data coding Conversion of information from the form it was collected into predefined values of variables, usually from words or answers on a questionnaire to numbers in a computer file.

data matrix Two-dimensional table used to organize and retrieve raw data. Rows represent observations; fields (composed of one or more adjacent columns) represent variables.

data reduction Summarizing one or more variables, for example, percentage distribution, mean, standard deviation.

dependent variable "Outcome" variable or effect; it *depends* on the independent variable(s).

descriptive field notes Notes that include conversations, the physical setting and details of activities and events.

descriptive research Research intended to present a profile of subjects' characteristics, one at a time, such as in the campus drug study. This drug study does not present comparisons designed to identify causes of drug use.

direct methods Method of data collection in which data are obtained personally from subjects or respondents. Examples include interviews, questionnaires and observation of behaviors. Compare with indirect methods.

discrete variable Variable with a finite number of categories or whose categories correspond to whole numbers (compare with continuous variable).

dissemination Spread or diffusion. In science, dissemination refers primarily to informing the scientific community and practitioners about research findings.

domain coverage Degree to which a set of variables measures the entire range of content (domain) of a construct. A math test for third-graders should cover all the math operations they have learned, not just addition, for example.

double-barreled question Question that is really more than one question. For example: Do you like mom *and* apple pie? The correct answer is yes only if you like them *both*.

dummy variable Two-category variable that takes a value of 0 or 1, often used as an independent variable in **regression analysis**.

elaboration Process of studying the relationship between two variables by observing their relationship within each category of one (or more) control variables.

element Objects comprising a population. Examples of elements include people, families, households, cities, states, church congregations, cemetery markers, magazine advertisements and fish.

empirical test Testing an idea by observing what happens in the physical world.

ethnographic research Investigation based on a broad perspective that emphasizes looking for the meaning attached to social settings by the participants. Ethnographic research is not confined to any method of data collection. But it typically is based on a small number of cases and depends on intensive open-ended interactions with them. The goal is to reveal the meanings and functions of human actions and interactions.

evaluation report Written document summarizing findings of an evaluation. The primary audience usually consists of professionals with an interest in the social intervention.

exhaustive categories Set of categories that accommodate every person or object; no person or object is left unclassified.

experiment Investigation in which a researcher manipulates or changes at least one variable and observes what happens to at least one other variable. The objects of the manipulation in experimental research with people are called subjects.

experimental group In an experiment, the group that receives some type of "treatment."

explanation (type of elaboration) Bivariate relationship exists only due to a control variable that is "causally prior" to both the independent and dependent variables. In the perfect type, the bivariate relationship between the original independent variable and the dependent variable is zero within categories of the control variable (e.g., the sex–beard–dress relationships). The bivariate relationship is called spurious; that is, it is not due to cause and effect.

explanatory research Research with the goal of identifying cause-and-effect relationships (e.g., residence affects contraceptive use). Compare to descriptive research, which does not attempt to discover cause-and-effect relationships.

external validity Degree to which findings are generalizable beyond the experimental or research setting. Random selection is done to improve external validity.

F-**test** A test to assess whether sample differences among two or more means are likely due to sampling error—also applied in other instances such as **regression analysis**.

face validity Judgment of researchers about whether a specific item measures at least part of the construct it is intended to measure. An addition test for third-graders measures skills in addition but not multiplication.

falsifiable Hypothesis formulated so that observations might show it is wrong.

field Location of an observational or ethnographic study. Also, sequence of adjacent columns in a data matrix containing the values of a single variable.

focus group (or focused interview) A semistructured interview that includes several people.

frequency distribution A univariate summary including the count and percentage for each category of a nominal, ordinal or collapsed interval variable.

generalization To extend what has been observed to situations or persons not observed.

government report Written document produced or sponsored by a government agency. Usually it does not contain original research. Rather, it reviews research existing prior to the time of its publication. This is a distinctive difference between a government report and a monograph.

group-administered questionnaire Self-administered questionnaire completed by several respondents at the same time, for example, in a classroom, usually (but not always) with the researcher present.

grouping effects Increased sampling variability when observations or experiments are done with intact groups such as classrooms or schools, due to dependence among subjects in the same group.

haphazard sample (or convenience sample) Any sample that isn't a probability sample. The probability of selection of the elements is unknown.

historical data Data describing the past. Historical research often is used to examine changes over time, such as in pictures or words.

historical research Study based on data in historical records, typically focusing on changes over lengthy periods of time.

history Events or circumstances occurring between a pretest and posttest other than the treatment that might account for observed changes in the outcome, a threat to internal validity in the absence of a comparison group.

human subjects review board See institutional review board.

hypothesis Speculation about how the world works. In science it's usually a proposed causal relationship that, at least in principle, can be checked by observation.

hypothesis test Formal approach for using sample data to decide whether a statement of fact about the population is correct. In social research, hypothesis tests usually are used to decide whether a relationship observed in a sample is large enough that it is a fair bet the variables are related in the population.

independent variable Variable assumed to generate or "cause" variation in another variable.

index (or scale) Variable defined by combining two or more other variables, usually by adding or averaging the values of the components for each person or observation.

indicators Observable variables such as a survey question that partially measure complex, abstract concepts (constructs) such as "self-esteem" or "parental support."

indirect methods Type of observation that does not involve direct contacts between the researcher and the subjects. Examples include content analysis, historical research and unobtrusive observation. Compare with direct methods.

inference See statistical inference.

informed consent Formal statement obtained from research subjects prior to starting the research. The statement affirms that the subject agrees to participate with full understanding of the risks and benefits of participation.

institutional review board (IRB) A formal committee that examines research proposals for potentially harmful impacts on research participants (social, psychological, emotional, physical). The IRB advises researchers about needed changes before research may begin. On college campuses, this group might be called the human subjects review board (or human subjects committee).

instrumentation Change in the measuring instrument between pretest and posttest that is mistaken for a treatment effect; a threat to internal validity.

interaction The possibility that selection into the treatment and control groups occurs in such a way that subjects in the treatment group react differently to some factor than do those in the control group.

internal consistency Comparing more than one measurement of a construct when all the measurements were taken at the same time.

internal validity Degree to which the treatment did, in fact, have the effect attributed to it in the experimental setting; random assignment is undertaken to protect internal validity.

interpretation (type of elaboration) intervening-variable model A bivariate relationship exists due only to a control variable that intervenes between the independent and dependent variables. In the perfect type, the bivariate relationship between the original independent variable and the dependent variable is zero within categories of the control variable. For example, that women on average wear long hair, and men do not, is due to socialization after birth and not due to an inherent difference between men and women.

interval variable A continuous variable whose values are numbers but which does not include a natural zero, such as the Fahrenheit temperature scale.

intervening variable A variable that is affected by the independent variable and affects the dependent variable. In the pure intervening-variable case, the original relationship between the independent variable and the dependent variable vanishes (is zero) when the intervening variable is controlled statistically, as in a three-variable table. Socialization intervenes between gender and hair length, for example.

interviewer effect Bias resulting when a respondent chooses incorrect answers because an interviewer is present, for example, to impress or irritate the interviewer.

items Term used to refer to the individual components of an index. Often the components are variables, each of which summarizes a single question on a questionnaire.

level of confidence Prespecified probability associated with a confidence interval. The most common level of confidence is 0.95 (95%).

level of significance Prespecified probability giving the p-value required to reject the null hypothesis. The most commonly used level of significance is 0.05 (5 in 100). If the estimated probability from the data is smaller than the level of significance, reject the null hypothesis. Otherwise, do not reject it. Rejecting the null hypothesis generally supports the research hypothesis.

linear regression analysis (regression analysis, regression) Method of predicting the value of the dependent variable using a linear formula and one or more independent variables, such as:

$$predicted\ wage = a + b_{fem}\ female + b_{pt}\ parttime$$
$$predicted\ wage = a + b_{age}\ age + b_{educ}\ educ + b_{fem}\ female$$

Usually, the regression analysis is done with a computer statistical software program, such as SPSS or SAS.

mail questionnaire Type of survey that collects information by mailing a questionnaire to respondents, who return the completed questionnaire by mail.

mail survey A survey that collects information by mailing a questionnaire to respondents.

marginals (or marginal frequency distributions) Univariate frequency distributions for variables in a cross-tabulation that are displayed at the edges, or margins, of the cross-tabulation.

maturation Observed changes in subjects between a pretest and posttest that would have occurred with or without the treatment or any other external event(s); maturation may be mistaken for treatment effects and therefore is a threat to internal validity.

measure (or variable) Operational version of a concept; an indicator (e.g., a survey question) with each response assigned a *unique* category or value.

measure of central tendency A statistic or parameter that summarizes where numbers in a distribution tend to concentrate. Examples include the mean, median and mode.

measure of dispersion A statistic or parameter that summarizes how much numbers in a distribution are spread out. Examples include the standard deviation and variance.

measurement error Difference between an observed value and the "true" value of a variable.

model A simplification of reality designed to promote understanding by summarizing essential elements and reducing complexity.

monograph Literally translated, "one writing." More precisely, a monograph is a book-length document written on one scientific topic. In social research, a monograph presents a detailed report of an extensive research program of study.

multistage sampling Sampling clusters and elements within clusters, for example, households within city blocks.

mutually exclusive categories Set of nonoverlapping categories defined so no person or object fits into more than one category.

negative relationship Relationship in which values of two variables move in opposite directions. As the value of one variable increases, the value of the other variable decreases, and vice versa.

nominal variable (categorical variable) Variable that classifies objects or elements into one and only one class or category; the classes simply are different (e.g., color).

nonparticipant observer (complete observer) A researcher who makes observations, usually in public settings, without the subjects being aware they are being studied.

nonprobability sample A sample in which the probability of selecting each element is *not* known, usually due to lack of a comprehensive list of elements.

nonresponse Failure of selected sample members to complete all or part of a survey or interview. Nonresponse error comes from differences between individuals who complete and return a questionnaire and those who do not.

nonresponse error Errors in sample statistics due to differences between individuals who complete and return a questionnaire and those who do not. Those who fail to return a completed questionnaire (nonrespondents) might be different from respondents in ways that influence the results of the study.

normal sampling distribution Sampling distribution that is symmetric around the mean of the distribution. It is defined by a specific mathematical formula.

null hypothesis Testable statement that the population statistic from which a sample was drawn equals a specific value. In social research, the null hypothesis usually states there are no differences in a dependent variable among levels of an independent variable, sometimes informally called the "no difference" hypothesis. Usually rejecting the null hypothesis supports the research hypothesis

numeric variable Interval and ratio variables (sometimes ordinal variables); the numerical values are given their natural mathematical meaning (compare with categorical variable).

observation The term *observation* is used in three ways: (1) to indicate a process for getting information by looking to see what happens, (2) to indicate a profile summary of variables for one individual or other unit (case) such as a college and (3) to indicate observational analysis, which means, roughly, to go out and talk to people, see what they do, stay for a while and see what develops. This latter sense of observation is associated with ethnographic and other qualitative approaches to research.

observational study Unstructured method of data collection in which the researcher visits a field site for an extended time to obtain information by directly watching human social interactions and behaviors.

observed score Value of a variable obtained through procedures such as personal interview or observed behaviors (compare with true score).

one-group pretest–posttest design Design with no control group or comparison group; the researcher observes change between a measurement taken before an event occurs and a second measurement taken after it.

one-shot case study Most basic design, consisting of one observation after an event has occurred or a treatment administered; usually, informal or implicit comparisons are made between the observations in the study and other information not gathered as part of the formal study.

one-tailed test A hypothesis test of a relationship in which the direction of the relationship is predicted in advance of the test. For example, women express more favorable attitudes toward the women's movement than do men. The entire probability of the level of significance is put in one tail of the sampling distribution rather than being split between the two tails. A one-tailed test gives more statistical power than a two-tailed test to reject a false null hypothesis.

open-ended questions Questions requesting respondents to write in a response. A familiar example is an essay question on an exam. A short open-ended question might ask respondents to write down their age or date of birth.

operational definition Collection of rules for obtaining observations that will become a variable.

operationalization Process of converting abstract concepts (e.g., academic achievement, self-esteem) into measurable variables.

ordinal variable One type of variable defined by a set of categories, each of which is either greater than or less than each of the other categories, but with no indication of the magnitude of the differences among the categories (e.g., agree–disagree questionnaire item).

overgeneralization Concluding that a pattern observed in too small a number of instances is typical of other situations not observed. For example, you observe in 100 lottery drawings that the number 22 turns up more often than any other number and conclude that future drawings are more apt to turn up 22 than any other number.

***p*-value** Estimate of the probability of observing a sample statistic with a greater deviation from the null hypothesis than the observed statistic if the null hypothesis were correct.

panel survey Survey in which the same individuals are surveyed at least twice.

parsimony Simplicity; in science, the simpler theory is preferred when two theories make the same predictions.

partial observer Researcher who is observing and participating as a group member but is known as a researcher.

partial relationship Association between the independent and dependent variables within a category of one or more control variables; in tabular analysis, a partial table, in **regression**, a partial slope coefficient.

participant observer Researcher who is completely immersed in the regular activities of the group under study, and usually is known as a member of the group rather than as a researcher.

peer review The process through which each submission to a journal is evaluated by a panel of experts for importance and accuracy.

percentage Frequency per 100, obtained by counting the number of cases in each category of a variable, dividing by the total number of cases for all categories, and multiplying the quotient by 100.

perfect relationship Relationship for which knowledge of one variable reduces uncertainty about the other variable to zero.

personal interview A method of data collection in which information is obtained from each respondent in a face-to-face meeting with the interviewer.

physical controls The researcher determines what is changed, by how much, and what is not changed (i.e., kept constant). Contrast physical control to "control" by random assignment, for which only the expected differences among means of variables are controlled.

physical trace data Data such as paths worn in the grass and fingerprints indicative of subjects' previous activity. Other examples include checking litter containers for cans and bottles to estimate the extent of illegal use of alcohol in public places, and examining rates of repair of public telephones as a measure of vandalism in a community.

placebo Nonreactive agent, such as the sugar pill given in medical research, to provide a "baseline" comparison group in experiments.

plagiarism Quoting or summarizing in writing someone else's ideas without crediting the source.

population Collection of elements to be described—for example, all people comprising a religious group, all fish in a fish bowl—or elements of any other known collectivity.

population parameter (parameter) A number such as a percentage, mean or the difference between percentages describing the entire population.

positive relationship Relationship in which values of two variables move in the same direction. As the value of one variable increases, the value of the other variable also increases.

poster presentation Dissemination method using posters to summarize research findings, usually at a professional conference; the researcher usually is present during viewing of the poster to answer questions.

posttest Measurement of the outcome in an experiment taken *after* the treatment is administered. The posttest must use the same, or equivalent, data collection procedures as used for the pretest.

posttest-only control-group design Random assignment design comparing differences between the experimental group and the control group after the treatment is administered to the treatment group. Subjects are assigned at random to treatment and control groups.

pretest There are two meanings to the term *pretest:* (1) Small preliminary survey to check for problems with questions, response options and procedures. Pretests also are used to determine the length of time needed to complete a survey. The pretest sample should be similar to the target population for the main survey; (2) A measurement taken in a pretest–posttest design taken before the "treatment" is administered (or an event thought to influence the outcome is observed).

primary data Data collected for a specific study. The researcher defines a research question and collects new data tailored to answer the question. Contrast with secondary data.

primary sampling unit (PSU) A collection of elements, such as people or fish, to be sampled as a single unit. Examples of PSUs include households, city blocks and schools. In cluster sampling, PSUs are sampled rather than individual elements.

probability sample Sample for which the probability of selection is known and greater than zero for each element in a population.

probe Follow-up question in an interview used to clarify responses that are incomplete or elicit a response when one was not offered.

purposive sample Nonprobability sample selected to meet specific criteria of a study, such as all drug users in a soup-kitchen population.

qualitative data Information collected from comparatively structured research in which the observations are converted into numbers or predefined categories.

qualitative methods Research methods that do not rely heavily on mathematical and statistical analysis. Qualitative research is multi-method in focus, involving a naturalistic approach to subject matter. Qualitative researchers study people in their natural setting, attempting to make sense of phenomena in terms of the meanings that people bring to them.

qualitative research ("meaning-based" research) A relatively unstructured approach to social science, involving an interpretive, naturalistic method, attempting to make sense of, or interpret, phenomena in terms of the meanings people bring to them.

quantitative data Information collected from comparatively structured research in which the observations are converted into numbers.

quantitative methods Research methods that rely primarily on mathematical and statistical analysis of numeric (numbers-based) data.

quantitative research ("numbers-based" research) Comparatively structured research that usually emphasizes causal relationships among variables, using data represented by numbers.

quota sample Nonprobability sample that takes a prespecified number of elements from each of several subgroups of the population, for example, 100 male and 100 female, or 33 male and 67 female. The subgroups are comparable to strata. A quota sample differs from a stratified sample because the elements are selected haphazardly within each subgroup with quota sampling, but are selected by probability sample with stratified sampling.

random assignment A "pure chance" procedure used to determine which subjects are in the treatment group and which subjects are in the control group. The purpose is to improve internal validity. (Did the treatment have the effect attributed to it)

random selection A "pure-chance" procedure for including subjects in a study. The purpose is to improve external validity.

ratio variable Variable defined by values that are natural numbers *and* zero indicates the absence of some real-world quantity (e.g., wage).

raw data A listing of the value of every variable for every observation.

reactive arrangements Umbrella term covering a variety of experimental manipulations that may not mirror real-world settings; a threat to external validity.

reactive response options Response categories of a question that lead the respondent to an incorrect response.

recording units In content analysis, the basic items to be classified. There are six commonly used types of recording units for text: word, word sense, sentence, theme, paragraph and whole text.

refereed journal Scholarly periodical that publishes only peer-reviewed papers. Issues are published several times a year, usually monthly, bimonthly or quarterly.

references Alphabetized list of sources cited, appearing at the end of a document; compare with bibliography and citation.

reflective field notes Notes that contain the researcher's thoughts, feelings, ideas, problems and so forth.

regression (to the mean) Average for extreme scores at the pretest (either very high or very low) moves closer to the middle score at the posttest, because of imperfect but positive correlation between pretest and posttest scores. Regression to the mean threatens internal validity when subjects are selected for their extreme score, often for remedial treatment, and subjects are not assigned at random to the treatment.

regression analysis See linear regression analysis.

relationship (or association) A relationship exists between two variables when knowing the value of one variable reduces uncertainty about the value of the other variable. Knowledge of gender, for example, reduces uncertainty about hair length.

reliability Consistency of a measure; does the same result occur on repeated measurement in the absence of real change?

replication (type of elaboration) Each partial relationship matches the original bivariate relationship within categories of the control variable (or variables) (control variable has no effect on the bivariate association).

research hypothesis Usually opposite to the null hypothesis. In most instances, the research hypothesis states that there is a relationship.

respondent An individual who answers the questions on a survey; analogous to case in ethnographic/observational research and subject in experiments.

response options List of responses to a closed-ended question.

response rate The extent to which surveys are completed and returned, usually given as a percentage of all potential respondents initially contacted. One interpretation is that a mail survey response rate of 50 percent is adequate and 60 percent is good, depending on the population and topics.

response set Tendency of respondents to select the same answer to many questions, irrespective of the question content, for example, answering "strongly disagree" to every question no matter what the respondent's opinion is.

row marginals Row totals shown in the last column of a table containing a cross-tabulation.

sample Some part of a population, generally selected with the idea of calculating a sample statistic to estimate the corresponding population parameter.

sample attrition Sample loss that occurs when some of those who participated in the first data collection of a panel survey don't participate in later collections (waves). Some reasons for attrition include change of residence, illness or death of respondent and refusal.

sample statistic Number calculated from a sample, such as the sample mean (average), sample percentage (or sample proportion) or the difference between sample means or percentages for two groups.

sampling distribution List of each possible value of a sample statistic from a population and its associated probability.

sampling error Difference between a sample statistic and population parameter when a sample is used to describe the population.

sampling frame Complete list of each element in the population. A sample is drawn from this list. Consequently, getting a probability sample depends on the list being complete, with no duplicate entries.

sampling variability Variation from sample to sample of a sample statistic such as the mean. A second two-fish average weight likely is not the same as the average of the first sample.

scale Group of response options to a question that are arranged in order of intensity or importance (contrast to index).

secondary data Data collected by someone other than the researcher, often for multiple purposes. Prominent examples of secondary data include surveys such as the *General Social Survey* and the U.S. decennial census.

selection The result when subjects choose their independent variable assignment (treatment group or control group) or are selected by a nonrandom process; the most frequent source of a spurious (false) relationship.

selection bias People decide for themselves whether to engage in an activity such as taking estrogen. The basis of their decision, such as healthy lifestyle, affects an outcome such as a heart attack. The result is a spuriously low incidence of heart attack among women who took estrogen.

selection × treatment interaction The situation in which people who are most (or least) sensitive to the treatment recruit themselves into the pool of potential subjects, a threat to external validity.

self-administered questionnaire Survey completed by the respondent, usually obtained by mail, in the absence of the researcher, or administered in a group setting such as a classroom.

semistructured interview Face-to-face survey with a set of questions that can be expanded by using probes.

sequencing Determining the order of survey questions in an interview or on a questionnaire.

serendipity Finding the unexpected, thought to figure prominently in the history of scientific discovery.

simple random sample (SRS) The most elementary probability sample; every possible sample of a given size has the same chance of being selected.

snowball sample Nonprobability sample obtained by relying on a few participants to identify other participants, who in turn provide additional leads, until the target sample size is reached.

social significance (or substantive significance) Importance of an observation for practical applications or social theory. In a cross-tabulation, one indicator of social significance is the magnitude of the percentage difference. Contrast with statistical significance.

sociogram Sociometric method of displaying patterns of interaction, such as friendship networks, cliques and other social networks. It consists of a diagram with circles or squares representing participants, and arrows or lines connecting interacting participants.

specification (type of elaboration) Finding that the relationship between the independent and dependent variable is different in different categories of one or more control variables. Also called statistical interaction.

spurious association Noncausal relationship between two variables, generated by their common dependence on at least one other variable.

standard deviation Measure of dispersion of a variable—the more the values of the variable differ from each other, the higher the standard deviation. The standard deviation is the square root of the variance. A sample standard deviation summarizes variation in a single sample. A population standard deviation summarizes variation in the population.

standard error A special name given to the standard deviation when the numbers are a sample statistic, like the sample mean.

standard normal distribution Normal distribution with a mean = 0.0 and a standard deviation (and variance) = 1.0.

standard score (*z*-score) A variable transformed to ensure that it has a mean of exactly zero and a standard deviation of exactly one, obtained by subtracting the mean of the original variable from each value and dividing the result by the standard deviation of the original variable.

static group comparison A design with no random assignment; comparison is between naturally occurring groups, such as hourly wage between college graduates and noncollege graduates.

statistic A number such as an average calculated from sample data, usually intended to estimate the corresponding population number, like the population average. Examples of sample statistics include the sample mean (average), sample percentage (proportion) and the difference between sample means or percentages (proportions) for two groups.

statistical control An approximation of physical control in which a relationship between two variables is observed within constant levels of control variable(s).

statistical inference Process of drawing conclusions about a population using data from a sample of that population.

statistical interaction Variation among relationships between two variables within categories of one or more control variables.

statistical test A procedure for making a decision as to whether a population value of a statistic is some stated value, called the null hypothesis. Usually the null hypothesis states no relationship between two variables. Statistical tests are the primary technical method of statistical inference.

statistically significant Sample statistic deviates from the null hypothesis by a large enough amount to trigger rejection of the null hypothesis. The size of the difference required to reject the null hypothesis is determined by a probability (*p*-value). If the calculated *p*-value is no larger than the level of significance, reject the null hypothesis. In social research, the most-used level of significance is 0.05.

stem (of a question) The part of a survey item that asks the question. It should be a complete sentence.

sticky theory A phrase we invented to try to capture the widespread observation that people sometimes hold ideas so strongly that they refuse to acknowledge evidence that contradicts their ideas. In science, no norm is stronger than the norm of skepticism, which should overcome sticky-theory thinking. Still, science is conducted by humans; sticky theory creeps in.

stratified sample Sample taken by selecting elements from each of two or more groups called strata (singular form, stratum). The strata are defined so that each element fits into exactly one stratum. So strata define a variable used for a specific purpose of sampling.

structured interview Questionnaire that is administered by an interviewer. Questions are read verbatim to the respondent and answers usually are recorded by the interviewer into one of a set of closed-ended options (although open-ended response categories also can be used).

subjects Objects of the manipulation in an experiment, usually people in social research; analogous to case in ethnographic/observational research and respondent in surveys.

survey Tool for gathering data in which the researcher asks questions of a sample of individuals. Four types are mail questionnaire, personal interview, telephone interview and Internet questionnaire.

t-**test** A statistical test used for many statistics, for example, to compare two sample means or test a **regression** coefficient against a null hypothesis that it is zero (no partial relationship).

tally sheet Blank table with labels for the variable categories, used to prepare cross-tabulations manually.

target population Collection of all people who are eligible to participate as subjects in a study.

telephone interview A survey administered by telephone.

testing The experience of a pretest might influence results on a posttest. For example, the experience of taking a test usually improves performance on a second test. Effects of testing might be mistaken for effects of a treatment (e.g., tutoring), a threat to internal validity.

testing × treatment interaction Situation in which the pretest sensitizes subjects to the treatment, either increasing or decreasing treatment effects. A threat to external validity.

test–retest reliability Correlation between the same measure observed at two time points, in the absence of change in the true score and the "absence of memory."

theme In content analysis, a recording unit as subject/verb/object, such as "Snow covers the grass."

theoretical sample Nonprobability sampling strategy often used by field researchers who directly observe social events, often used to develop a theory to guide future research. Sometimes called "grounded theory," because the theory is derived from (grounded in) the observed behaviors of social life.

theory In brief, a collection of hypotheses about a coherent topic.

treatment In experiments, one category of the independent or treatment variable.

treatment variable (independent variable) In an experiment, the variable that is manipulated (the "treatment"). Analogous to independent variable in nonexperimental research.

trivariate table A table that includes three variables: independent, dependent and control.

true score Correct value of a variable, for example, age = date of last birthday − date of birth on a birth certificate (compare with observed score).

two-tailed test Statistical test for a nondirectional hypothesis. The probability associated with the level of significance is split between the upper and lower tails of the sampling distribution.

unbiased statistic Statistic whose "expected value" (mean of all sample means) equals the corresponding population parameter. Unbiased implies no systematic tendency to overestimate or underestimate the population parameter.

univariate analysis Examination of statistics such as the mean, standard deviation and frequency distribution, which describe one variable at a time.

univariate frequency distribution List of the number and percentage in each category of one variable.

unobtrusive observation Watching behaviors in a way that is "inconspicuous" to the research subjects.

unstructured interview A loosely structured survey that might be thought of as a "conversation." The interviewer usually has a list of questions but doesn't necessarily repeat them word-for-word to respondents or use a question–answer format.

validity Accuracy with which an observed variable measures the concept or construct it is designed to measure.

validity coefficient Correlation between the observed score and the true score.

value (of a variable) Category or number assigned to one variable and one observation. For example, Sally is 5 feet 8 inches tall.

variable Set of categories or numbers defined so that the categories are mutually exclusive (unique) and exhaustive. Each observation (e.g., person, object) fits into exactly one category, and all needed categories are included. An example is gender (two unique categories); other variables include race, age and self-esteem.

variance Measure of how much the numbers in a list differ among themselves (dispersion). It is defined as the average squared distance from the mean.

weighting (of a variable) In calculating an index, multiplying each component by a different numeric constant before calculating a sum or average. The constants are the weights and are chosen to reflect the importance of each component for defining the index.

word sense In content analysis, the meaning of words or phrases constituting a unit (e.g., New York State). Different specific words and phrases often convey the same or nearly the same meaning, for example, "applauding" and "clapping."

References

Academy of Criminal Justice Sciences. (March 21, 2000). *Code of Ethics of the Academy of Criminal Justice Sciences*. Available at http://www.acjs.org/pubs/167_671_2922.cfm (accessed October 22, 2010).

Adorno, T.W., Else Frenkel-Brunswik, Daniel J. Levinson, and R. Nevitt Sanford with collaboration with Betty Aron, Maria Hertz levinson, & William Morrow. (1950). *The Aurhoritarian Personality*. New York. Harper & Brothers.

Alan Guttmacher website. Available at http://www.guttmacher.org/journals/aboutper.html (accessed October 10, 2010).

Allen, Charlotte. (1997). Spies like us: When sociologists deceive their subjects. *Lingua Franca: The Review of Academic Life 7*(November), 31–39.

American Anthropological Association Code of Ethics. (February 1997). Available at http://www.aaanet.org/committees/ethics/ethicscode.pdf (accessed October 24, 2010.)

American Sociological Association. *Code of Ethics of the American Sociological Association*. Available at http://www.asanet.org/about/ethics.cfm (accessed October 24, 2010).

Association of Internet Researchers. (2012). Available at http://ethics.aoir.org/index.php?title=Main_Page (accessed March 16, 2013).

Atkinson, Paul & Martyn Hammersley. (1994). Ethnography and participant observation. In Norman K. Denzin, & Yvonna S. Lincoln (Eds.), *Handbook of qualitative research* (pp. 248–261). Thousand Oaks, CA: Sage.

Axinn, William G., & Jennifer S. Barber. (2001). Mass education and fertility transition. *American Sociological Review, 66*, 481–505.

Babbie, Earl. (1999). *The basics of social research*. Belmont, CA: Wadsworth.

Baron, Naomi S. (1998). Letters by phone or speech by other means: The linguistics of email. *Language and Communication, 18*, 133–170.

Berg, Bruce L. (2001). *Qualitative research methods for the social sciences* (4th ed.). Needham Heights, MA: Allyn and Bacon.

Berg, Bruce L. (2009). *Qualitative research methods for the social sciences* (7th ed.). Boston, MA: Allyn and Bacon/Pearson.

Berger, Arthur A. (2000). *Media and communication research methods: An introduction to qualitative and quantitative approaches*. Thousand Oaks, CA: Sage.

Bourgois, Philippe. (1995). *In search of respect: Selling crack in El Barrio*. Cambridge: Cambridge University Press.

Campbell, Donald T., & Julian S. Stanley. (1963). *Experimental and quasi-experimental designs for research*. Chicago: Rand McNally and Company.

References

Centers for Disease Control. (2011). *U.S. Public Health Service Syphilis Study at Tuskegee.* Available at http://www.cdc.gov/tuskegee/timeline.htm (accessed April 3, 2011).

Chen, Shing-Ling Sarina, G. Jon Hall, & Mark D. Johns. (2004). Research paparazzi in cyberspace: The voices of the researched. In Mark D. Johns, Shing-Ling Sarina Chen, & G. Jon Hall (Eds.), *Online social research: Methods, issues, & ethics* (pp. 157–175). New York: Peter Lang Publishing.

Christakis, Nicholas A., Norma C. Ware, & Arthur Kleinman. (2001). Illness behavior and the health transition in the developing world. In Duane A. Matcha (Ed.), *Readings in medical sociology* (pp. 143–159). Boston, MA: Allyn and Bacon.

Cohen, Brett, Gordon Waugh, & Karen Place. (1989). At the movies: An unobtrusive study of arousal-attraction. *The Journal of Social Psychology, 129*(5), 691–693. Reprinted with permission of the Helen Dwight Reid Educational Foundation. Published by Heldref Publications, 1319 Eighteenth St., NW, Washington, DC 20036–1802. Copyright 1989.

College Prowler website. Available at http://collegeprowler.com/university-of-virginia/drug-scene/ (accessed October 16, 2010).

Collins, Gail. (2011). Medicine on the move. *New York Times*, April 6. Available at http://www.nytimes.com/2011/04/07/opinion/07collins.html?_r=1&nl=todaysheadlines&emc=tha212 (accessed April 8, 2011).

Conger, Rand D., Frederick O. Lorenz, Glen H. Elder, Jr., Ronald L. Simons, & Xiaojia Ge. (1993). Husband and wife differences in response to undesirable life events. *Journal of Health and Social Behavior, 34*(March), 71–88.

Consumer Reports Annual Auto Issue (April 2011). Yonkers, NY: Consumers Union.

Consumer Reports Buying Guide. (2011). Yonkers, NY: Consumers Union.

Corbin, Juliet & Anselm Strauss. (2008). *Basics of qualitative research* (3rd ed.). Thousand Oaks, CA: Sage.

Creswell, John W. (2009). *Research design: Qualitative, quantitative, and mixed method approaches* (3rd ed.). Thousand Oaks, CA: Sage.

Creswell, John W. (2007). *Qualitative inquiry and research design: Choosing among five approaches* (2nd ed.). Thousand Oaks, CA: Sage.

Council on Social Work Education. (June 2006). *National Statement on Research Integrity in Social Work.* Available at http://www.cswe.org/cms/17157.aspx (accessed October 22, 2010).

Davis, James A., Smith, Tom W., & Marsden, Peter V. (2009). General social surveys, 1972–2008: [Cumulative codebook]. Principal Investigator, James A. Davis; Director and Co-Principal Investigator, Tom W. Smith.—Chicago, IL: National Opinion Research Center, 2009. 2,656 pp., 28cm.—(National Data Program for the Social Sciences Series, no. 18).

Davis, James A., & Smith, Tom W. (2007). General social surveys, 1972–2008: [machine-readable data file]. Principal Investigator, James A. Davis; Director and Co-Principal Investigator, Tom W. Smith; Co-Principal Investigator, Peter V. Marsden; Sponsored by National Science Foundation.—NORC ed.—Chicago: National Opinion Research Center [producer]; Storrs, CT: The Roper Center for Public Opinion Research, University of Connecticut [distributor].

Denzin, Norman K. (2004). Prologue: Online environments and interpretative social research. In Mark D. Johns, Shing-Ling Sarina Chen, & G. Jon Hall (Eds.), *Online social research: Methods, issues, & ethics* (pp. 1–12). New York: Peter Lang Publishing.

References

Denzin, Norman K., & Yvonna S. Lincoln. (1994). Introduction: Entering the field of qualitative research. In Norman K. Denzin & Yvonna S. Lincoln (Eds.), *Handbook of qualitative research*, (pp. 1–17). Thousand Oaks, CA: Sage.

Denzin, Norman K., & Yvonna S. Lincoln. (2005). Introduction: The discipline and practice of qualitative research. In Norman K. Denzin & Yvonna S. Lincoln (Eds.), *The Sage Handbook of qualitative research*, (pp. 1–132). Thousand Oaks, CA: Sage.

Desai, Sonalde & Soumya Alva. (1998). Maternal education and child health: Is there a strong causal relationship? *Demography, 35*(1), 71–81.

Diamond, Timothy. (1986). Social policy and everyday life in nursing homes: A critical ethnography. *Social Science and Medicine, 23*(12), 1287–1295. Reprinted with permission from Elsevier Science.

Diamond, Timothy. (1992). *Making gray gold: Narratives of nursing home care*. Chicago, IL: University of Chicago Press.

Dillman, Don A. (2000). *Mail and Internet surveys: The tailored design method* (2nd ed.). New York: Wiley.

Dillman, Don A., Jolele D. Smyth, & Christian, Leah M. (2009). *Internet, mail and mixed-mode surveys: The tailored design method*. Hoboken, NJ: John Wiley & Sons.

Disaster Research Center home page, University of Delaware. Available at http://www.udel.edu/DRC/aboutus/index.html (accessed October 1, 2010).

Disaster Research Center quick response studies page, University of Delaware. Available at http://www.udel.edu/DRC/Quick_Response_Studies/2001_WTC.html (accessed October 2, 2010).

Dorsten, Linda E., Lawrence Hotchkiss, & Terri M. King. (1999). Effect of inbreeding on early childhood mortality: Twelve generations of an Amish settlement. *Demography, 36*(2), 263–271.

Douthat, Ross. (2010). The partisan mind. *New York Times*, November 28, p. A25. Available at http://www.nytimes.com/2010/11/29/opinion/29douthat.html?_r=1&ref=columnists (accessed November 28, 2010).

Drugs in baseball: Editorial. (2002). *New York Times,* June 1, p. A24, col 1.

Duneier, Mitchell. (1999). *Sidewalk*. New York: Farrar, Straus and Giroux.

Durand, John D. (1960). Mortality estimates from Roman tombstone inscriptions. *American Journal of Sociology, 65*(4), 365–373.

Ellis, Carolyn. (1986). *Fisher folk*. Lexington, KY: University Press of Kentucky.

Ess, Charles. (2004). Epilogue: Are we there yet? Emerging ethical guidelines for online research. In Mark D. Johns, Shing-Ling Sarina C., & G. Jon Hall (Eds.), *Online social research: Methods, issues, & ethics* (pp. 253–263). New York: Peter Lang Publishing.

Ferraro, Kenneth F., & Melissa M. Farmer. (1999). Utility of health data from social surveys: Is there a gold standard for measuring morbidity? *American Sociological Review, 64*(2), 303–315.

Fiorentine, Robert & Stephen Cole. (1992). Why fewer women become physicians: Explaining the premed persistence gap. *Sociological Forum, 7*(3), 469–496.

Fontana, Andrea & James H. Frey. (2000). The interview: From structured questions to negotiated text. In Norman K. Denzin, & Yvonna S. Lincoln (Eds.), *Handbook of Qualitative Research* (pp. 645–672).

References

Foster, Gary S., Richard L. Hummel, & Donald J. Adamchak. (1998). Patterns of conception, natality, and mortality from Midwestern cemeteries: A sociological analysis of historical data. *The Sociological Quarterly, 39*(3), 473–489. Copyright 1998, Midwest Sociological Society.

Frankfort-Nachmias, C., & David Nachmias. (1996). *Research methods in the social sciences* (5th ed.). New York: St. Martin's.

Friedl, Karl E. (2000). Effects of anabolic steroids on physical health. In Charles E. Yesalis (Ed.), *Anabolic Steroids in Sport and Exercise,* (2nd ed., pp. 175–223).

Garwood, Jeanette, Michelle Rogerson, & Ken Pease. (2000). Sneaky measurement of crime and disorder. In Victor Jupp, Pamela Davies, & Peter Francis (Eds.), *Doing criminological research* (pp. 157–167). London: Sage.

General Social Survey (GSS). Available at http://www.norc.org/GSS+Website/ (accessed November 20, 2010).

Groves, Robert M. (1996). How do we know what we think they think is really what they think? In Norbert Schwarz & Seymour Sudman (Eds.), *Answering questions: methodology for determining cognitive and communicative processes in survey research* (pp. 389–402). San Francisco, CA: Jossey-Bass.

Groves, Robert. (2010). US census: Unsustainable? *Significance, 7*(4), 174.

Harrison, Dianne F., & C. Aaron McNeece. (2001). Disseminating research findings. In Bruce A. Thyer (Ed.), *The handbook of social work research methods* (pp. 501–512). Thousand Oaks, CA: Sage.

Harvard-Smithsonian Center for Astrophysics. (1987). Posted by *Annenberg Media*, "A private universe." Available at http://www.learner.org/vod/vod_window.html?pid=9 (accessed January 10, 2011).

Health Sciences Library, UNC-Chapel Hill. (February 12, 2013). *Media design studio: How do I...?* Available at http://guides.lib.unc.edu/content.php?pid=210772&sid=1754233 (accessed November 22, 2010).

Heiss, Gerardo, Robert Wallace, Garnet L. Anderson, Aaron Aragaki, Shirley A. Beresford, Robert Brzyski, Rowan T. Chlebowski, Margery Gass, Andrea LaCroix, JoAnn E. Hanson, Ross L. Prentice, Jacques Rossouw, & Marcia L. Stefanick. (2008). Health risks and benefits 3 years after stopping randomized treatment with estrogen and progestin. *Journal of the American Medical Association, 299*(9), 1036–1045.

Hoffman, Jay R., & Nicholas A. Ratamess. (2006). Medical issues associated with anabolic steroid use: Are they exaggerated? *Journal of Sports Science and Medicine, 5*(2), 182–193.

Homans, George C. (1950). *The Human Group.* New York: Harcourt Brace.

Huddy, Leonie, Francis K. Neely, & Marilyn R. Lafay. (2000). The polls—trends: Support for the women's movement. *Public Opinion Quarterly 64*(3), 309–350. By permission of Oxford University Press.

Hurricane Katrina Field Work. (2005). Disaster Research Center, Quick Response Studies. Available at http://www.udel.edu/DRC/projects/Quick%20Response.html (accessed February 10, 2011).

Humanitarian Response to Haiti Earthquake. Disaster Research Center, Quick Response Studies. Available at http://www.udel.edu/DRC/projects/Quick%20Response.html (accessed February 10, 2011).

References

Janesick, Valerie J. (2000). The choreography of qualitative research design. In Norman K. Denzin, & Yvonna S. Lincoln (Eds.), *Handbook of qualitative research* (2nd ed., pp. 379–399). Thousand Oaks, CA: Sage.

Janesick, Valerie J. (1994). The dance of qualitative research design: Metaphor, methodolatry, and meaning. In Norman K. Denzin, & Yvonna S. Lincoln (Eds.), *Handbook of qualitative research* (pp. 209–219). Thousand Oaks, CA: Sage.

Johnson, William A., Jr, Richard P. Rettig, Gregory M. Scott, & Stephen M. Garrison. (2002). *The sociology student writer's manual* (3rd ed.). Upper Saddle River, NJ: Prentice Hall.

Jungheim, Emily S., & Graham A. Colditz. (April 6, 2011). Short-term use of unopposed estrogen: A balance of inferred risks and benefits. Editorial: *Journal of the American Medical Association, 305*(13), 1354–1355.

LaCroix, Andrea Z., Rowan T. Chlebowski, JoAnn E. Manson, MD, Aaron K. Aragaki, Karen C. Johnson, MD, Lisa Martin, Karen L. Margolis, Marcia L. Stefanick, Robert Brzyski, J. David Curb, & Barbara V. Howard, Cora E. Lewis. (April 6, 2011). Health Outcomes After Stopping Conjugated Equine Estrogens Among Postmenopausal Women With Prior Hysterectomy: A Randomized Controlled Trial. *305*(13), 1305–1314.

Kalton, Graham. (1983). *Introduction to survey sampling.* Beverly Hills, CA: Sage.

Kaplan, Karen. (2010). Mining destruction for data to help others. *Los Angeles Times,* February 1. Available at http://articles.latimes.com/2010/feb/01/science/la-sci-disaster-research1-2010feb01/2 (accessed September 6, 2010).

Kendall, Lori. (2004). Participants and observers in online ethnography: Five stories about identity. In Mark D. Johns, Shing-Ling Sarina Chen, & G. Jon Hall (Eds.), *Online social research: Methods, issues, & ethics* (pp. 125–140). New York: Peter Lang Publishing.

Kirk, Jerome & Marc L. Miller. (1986). *Reliability and validity in qualitative research.* Beverly Hills, CA: Sage.

Kohn, Melvin L. (1977). *Class and conformity: A study in values* (2nd ed.). Chicago, IL: University of Chicago Press.

Kohn, Melvin L., & Kazimierz M. Slomczynski. (1990). *Social structure and self-direction: A comparative analysis of the United States and Poland.* Cambridge, MA: Basil Blackwell.

Kolata, Gina with Melody Petersen. (2002). Hormone replacement study a shock to the medical system. *New York Times*, July 10, p. A1.

Kolata, Gina. (2001). Cancer study finds support groups do not extend life. *The New York Times*, December 13, p. A36.

Krueger, Richard A., & Mary Anne Casey. (2000). *Focus groups: A practical guide for applied research* (3rd ed.). Thousand Oaks, CA: Sage

Lavrakas, Paul J. (1993). *Telephone survey methods: Sampling, selection and supervision* (2nd ed.). Applied Social Research Methods Series (vol. 7). Newbury Park, CA: Sage. Copyright ©1993 by Sage Publications, Inc. Reprinted by permission.

LeBesco, Kathleen. (2004). Managing visibility, intimacy, and focus in online critical ethnography. In Mark D. Johns, Shing-Ling Sarina Chen, & G. Jon Hall (Eds.), *Online social research: Methods, issues, & ethics* (pp. 63–79). New York: Peter Lang Publishing.

References

Lim, Chaeyoon & Robert D. Putman. (2010). Religion, social networks, and life satisfaction. *American Sociological Review, 75*(6), 914–933.

Lofland, John & Lyn H. Lofland. (1995). *Analyzing social settings: A guide to qualitative observation and analysis* (3rd ed.). Belmont, CA: Wadsworth.

Lofland, John, David A. Snow, Leon Anderson, & Lyn H. Lofland. (2006). *Analyzing social settings: A guide to qualitative observation and analysis* (4th ed.). Belmont, CA: Wadsworth

Lofland, Lee. (2007). *Police Procedures and Investigations.* Cincinnati, OH: Writer's Digest Books.

Lord, Fredrick M., & Melvin R. Novick. (1968). *Statistical theories of mental test scores.* Reading, MA: Addison-Wesley.

Manski, Charles F., Gary D. Sandefur, Sara McLanahan, & Daniel Powers. (1992). Alternative estimates of the effects of family structure during adolescence on high school graduation. *Journal of the American Statistical Association, 87*(417), 25–37.

Markham, Annette N. (2005). The methods, politics, and ethics of representation in online ethnography. In Norman K. Denzin & Yvonna S. Lincoln (Eds.), *The sage handbook of qualitative research* (3rd ed., pp. 793–820). Thousand Oaks, CA: Sage.

Mann, Chris & Fiona Stewart. (2000). *Internet communication and qualitative research: A handbook for researching online.* London: Sage.

Maxim, Paul S. (1999). *Quantitative research methods in the social sciences.* New York: Oxford University Press.

Mayer, Michael E., William B. Gudykunst, Norman K. Perrill, & Bruce D. Merrill. (1990). A comparison of competing models of the news diffusion process. *Western Journal of Speech Communication, 54*(1), 113–123.

Meltzoff, Julian. (1998). *Critical Thinking About Research.* Practice article 6 (pp. 207–209). Washington, DC: American Psychological Association.

Merton, Robert K., Marjorie Fiske, & Patricia L. Kendall. (1990). *The focused interview: A manual of problems and procedures* (2nd. ed.). New York: The Free Press.

Mitchell, George J. (2007). *Report to the Commissioner of Baseball of an Independent Investigation into the Illegal Use of Steroids and Other Performance Enhancing Substances by Players in Major League Baseball,* Office of the Commissioner of Baseball.

Milgram, Stanley. (1974). *Obedience to authority: An experimental view.* New York: Harper & Row.

Miller, Delbert C., & Neil J. Salkind. (2002). *Handbook of research design and social measurement* (6th ed.). Thousand Oaks, CA: Sage.

Morrow, Betty H., & Elaine Enarson. (1996). Hurricane Andrew through women's eyes: Issues and recommendations. *International Journal of Mass Emergencies and Disasters, 14*(1), 5–22.

Morse, Janice M. (1994). Designing funded qualitative research. In Norman K. Denzin & Yvonna S. Lincoln (Eds.), *Handbook of qualitative research* (pp. 220–235). Thousand Oaks, CA: Sage.

NASA. (2013a). Available at http://www.nasa.gov/mission_pages/shuttle/shuttlemissions/index.html (accessed January 30, 2011).

NASA. (2013b). *Functional Leadership Plan, Office of Procurement.* Available at http://www.hq.nasa.gov/office/codez/plans/FLPs/H-FLP.pdf (accessed January 30, 2011).

References

Nathan, Gad. (2008). Internet surveys. In Paul J. Lavrakas (Ed.), *Encyclopedia of survey research methods* (pp. 356–359). Thousand Oaks, CA: Sage.

National Election Survey. (2000). Available at http://www.electionstudies.org/ (accessed October 24, 2010).

NCES (National Center for Education Statistics). (2013). Available at http://nces.ed.gov/surveys/ nels88/ (accessed October 24, 2010).

National Institutes of Health. (2010). *NIH News*, February 15. Available at NIH News (accessed November 29, 2010).

NPR (National Public Radio). (2010). "Trillions Of Earths" could be orbiting 300 sextillion stars. Available at http://www.npr.org/blogs/thetwo-way/2010/12/01/131730552/-trillions-of-earths-could-be-orbiting-300-sextillion-stars (accessed February 24, 2011).

Nesbary, Dale K. (2000). *Survey research and the World Wide Web*. Needham Heights, MA: Allyn & Bacon.

Norton-Hawk, Maureen A. (2001). The counterproductivity of incarcerating female street prostitutes. *Deviant Behavior: An Interdisciplinary Journal, 22*, 403–417.

Painter, Gary & David I. Levine. (2000). Family structure and youths' outcomes. *Journal of Human Resources, 35*(3), 524–549. Reprinted by permission of the University of Wisconsin Press.

Parcel, Toby L., & Elizabeth G. Menaghan. (1994). Supplemental child care arrangements: Determinants and consequences. In *Parents' jobs and children's lives* (pp. 179–206). New York: Aldine de Gruyter.

Percentages of Children 0-17 Years Living in Various Family Arrangements, 2009. (2010). America's Children in Brief: Key National Indicators of Well-Being. Available at http://www. childstats.gov/americaschildren/famsoc.asp#figure2 (accessed February 17, 2011).

Popper, Karl R. (1968). *The logic of scientific discovery* (Patrick Camiller, Trans.). London: Hutchinson.

Population Association of America website. (1999). Available at http://www.jstor.org/pss/2648113 (accessed 2013).

Population Reference Bureau. (2010). *2010 World Population Data Sheet*. Available at http://www. prb.org/Publications/Datasheets/2010/2010wpds.aspx (accessed October 24, 2010).

Punch, Maurice. (1986). *The politics and ethics of fieldwork*. Beverly Hills, CA: Sage.

Quarantelli, E.L. (1997). Non-medical difficulties during emergency medical services delivery at the time of disasters. Reprinted from *BC Medical Journal, 39*(11), 593–595.

Ramsland, Katherine. (1998). *Piercing the Darkness: Undercover with Vampires in America Today*. New York: HarperPrism/HarperCollins.

Richardson, Laurel. (1988). Secrecy and status: The social construction of forbidden relationships. *American Sociological Review, 53*(April), 209–219.

Ross, Catherine E., & Beckett A. Broh. (2000). The roles of self-esteem and the sense of personal control in the academic achievement process. *Sociology of Education, 73*(4), 270–284.

Ross, Lee & Craig A. Anderson. (1982). Shortcomings in the attribution process: On the origins and maintenance of erroneous social assessments. In Daniel Kahneman, Paul Slovic, & Amos

References

Tversky (Eds.), *Judgment under uncertainty: Heuristics and biases* (pp. 128–152). Cambridge: Cambridge University Press.

Rossouw, J.E., G.L. Anderson, R.L. Prentice, A.Z. LaCroix, C. Kooperberg, M.L. Stefarick, R.D. Jackson, S.A. Beresford, B.V. Howard, K.C. Johnson, J.M. Kotchen, & J. Ockene. (2002). Risks and benefits of estrogen plus progestin in healthy postmenopausal women: Principal results from the women's health initiative randomized controlled trial. *Journal of the American Medical Association, 288*, 321–333.

Rubin, Donald B. (1974). Estimating causal effects of treatments in randomized and nonrandomized studies. *Journal of Educational Psychology, 66*(5), 688–701.

Saferstein, Richard. (2007). Posted by Daily *motion,* What is "trace evidence" and how is it studied in crime scene investigations? Available at http://www.videojug.com/interview/csi-and-trace-evidence-2 (accessed January 11, 2011).

Saris, W.E. (1991). *Computer assisted interviewing*. Newbury Park, CA: Sage.

Saris, Willem E., & Irmtraud H. Gallhofer. (2007). *Design, evaluation, and analysis of question-naires for survey research*. Hoboken, NJ: John Wiley & Sons, Inc.

Schilling, Robert F., Nabila El-Bassel, & Louisa Gilbert. (1992). Drug use and AIDS risk in a soup kitchen population. *Social Work, 37*(3), 353–358.

Schwartz, David A. (1973–74). How fast does news travel? *Public Opinion Quarterly, 37*(4), 625–627.

Shields, Stephanie A., & Beth A. Koster. (1989). Emotional stereotyping of parents in child rearing manuals, 1915–1980. *Social Psychology Quarterly, 52*(1), 44–55.

Siegel, Deborah H. (1993). Open adoption of infants: Adoptive parents' perceptions of advantages and disadvantages. *Social Work, 38*(1), 15–23.

Steiner, Markus, Carla Piedrahita, Lucinda Glover & Carol Joanis. (1993). Can condom users likely to experience condom failure be identified? *Family Planning Perspectives, 25*(5) 220–6. Reproduced with the permission of The Alan Guttmacher Institute.

Stevens, S.S. (1946). On the theory of scales and measurement. *Science, 103*, 677–80.

Stevens, S.S. (1958). Measurement and man. *Science, 127*, 383–9.

Stoss, Fred. (2010). *Poster presentations: Designing effective posters*. (Arts & Sciences Libraries University at Buffalo). Available at http://library.buffalo.edu/asl/guides/bio/posters.html (Accessed November 28, 2010).

Sudman, Seymour & Norman M. Bradburn. (1982). *Asking questions*. San Francisco: Jossey-Bass. Copyright ©1982. Reprinted by permission of John Wiley & Sons, Inc.

The Belmont Report. Available at http://ohsr.od.nih.gov/guidelines/belmont.html (accessed November 30, 2010).

The Ethnograph, Version 5.0. Salt Lake City, UT: Qualis Research Associates. Distributed by Scolari, Sage Publications Software. V6. Available at http://www.qualisresearch.com/ (accessed October 24, 2010).

The National Commission for the Protection of Human Subjects of Biomedical and Behavioral Research, Department of Health, Education and Welfare. (April 18, 1979). *The Belmont Report: Ethical principles and guidelines for the protection of human subjects of research*. Bethesda,

MD: National Institutes of Health. Available at http://www.hhs.gov/ohrp/humansubjects/guidance/belmont.html. (accessed October 24, 2010).

Thyer, Bruce A. (2001). *The handbook of social work research methods.* Thousand Oaks, CA: Sage.

Tierney, Kathleen J. (1998). *The field turns fifty: Social change and the practice of disaster field work.* Preliminary Paper No. 273. Newark, DE: University of Delaware, Disaster Research Center.

Toh, Sengwee, Sonia Hernández-Diáz, Roger Logan, Jacques E. Rossouw, & Miguel A. Hernán. (2010). Coronary Heart Disease in Postmenopausal Recipients of Estrogen Plus Progestin Therapy: Does the Increased Risk Ever Disappear?: A Randomized Trial. *152*(4), 211–217.

Tuchman, Gaye. (1994). Historical social science: Methodologies, methods, and meanings. In Norman K. Denzin & Yvonna S. Lincoln (Eds.), *Handbook of qualitative research* (pp. 306–323). Thousand Oaks, CA: Sage.

Tversky, Amos & Daniel Kahneman. (1982). Causal schemas in judgments under uncertainty. In Amos Tversky & Daniel Kahneman (Eds.), *Judgment under uncertainty: Heuristics and biases* (pp. 117–128). Cambridge: Cambridge University Press.

Uggen, Christopher. (2000). Work as a turning point in the life course of criminals: A duration model of age, employment, and recidivism. *American Sociological Review, 67*(4), 529–546.

University of Washington School of Public Health. *Design and layout.* Available at http://sph.washington.edu/practicum/forms/PosterDesignGuidelines.pdf (accessed April 18, 2013).

U.S. Public Health Service. (1964). *Smoking and health: Report of the advisory committee to the Surgeon General of the Public Health Service.* Washington, DC: Government Printing Office (Publication number 1103). Available at http://profiles.nlm.nih.gov/NN/B/B/M/Q/_/nnbbmq.pdf (accessed October 24, 2010).

Verducci, Tom, with reporting by Don Yaeger, George Dohrmann, Luis Fernando Llosa, & Lester Munson. (2002). Totally juiced. *Sports Illustrated*, June 3, pp. 34–48.

Vidich, Arthur J., & Stanford M. Lyman. (1994). Qualitative methods: Their history in sociology and anthropology. In Norman K. Denzin & Yvonna S. Lincoln (Eds.), *Handbook of qualitative research* (pp. 23–59). Thousand Oaks, CA: Sage.

Vidich, Arthur J., & Stanford M. Lyman. (2003). Qualitative methods: Their history in sociology and anthropology. In Norman K. Denzin & Yvonna S. Lincoln (Eds.), *The landscape of qualitative research* (2nd ed., pp. 55–129). Thousand Oaks, CA: Sage.

Walker, Eric. (2011). Steroids, other "drugs", and baseball. Available at http://steroids-and-baseball.com/ (accessed April 8, 2011).

Weaver, Jim. (1994). Students say drugs obtainable. *The Review, 120*(51), A-3, A-13.

WebMD website. (2002). Available at http://my.webmd.com/content/article/1671.50535 (accessed May 29, 2004).

Webb, Eugene J., Donald T. Campbell, Richard D. Schwartz, & Lee Sechrest. (2000). *Unobtrusive measures* (rev. ed.). Thousand Oaks, CA: Sage.

Weber, Robert Philip. (1990). *Basic content analysis* (2nd ed.). Newbury Park, CA: Sage.

Weir, Hannah K., Michael J. Thun, Benjamin F. Hankey, Lynn A.G. Ries, Holly L. Howe, Phyllis A. Wingo, Ahmedin Jemal, Elizabeth Ward, Robert N. Anderson, & Brenda K. Edwards. (2002). SPECIAL ARTICLE: Annual Report to the Nation on the status of Cancer, 1975–2000, Featuring the uses of Surveillance Data for Cancer Prevention and Control. *Journal of the National Cancer Institute, 95*(17), 1276–1299.

Weisberg, Herbert F., Jon A. Krosnick, & Bruce D. Bowen. (1996). *An introduction to survey research, polling and data analysis* (3rd ed.). Thousand Oaks, CA: Sage.

Weiss, Robert. S. (1994). *Learning from strangers: The art and method of qualitative interview studies*. New York: The Free Press.

Wilson, Robert A. (1966). *Feminine Forever*. New York: M. Evans.

Winship, Christopher & Robert D. Mare. (1992). Models for sample selection bias. *Annual Review of Sociology, 18*, 327–350.

Wolcott, Harry F. (2001). *Writing up qualitative research* (2nd ed.). Thousand Oaks, CA: Sage.

Wolcott, Harry F. (2009). *Writing up qualitative research* (3rd ed.). Thousand Oaks, CA: Sage.

Women's Health Initiative. (June 2002). *WHI HRT Update*. Women's Health Initiative, The WHI homepage. Available at http://www.nhlbi.nih.gov/whi/ (accessed December 4, 2010).

Yesalis, Charles E. (2000). Introduction. In Charles E. (Ed.), *Anabolic steroids in sport and exercise* (2nd ed., pp. 1–13).

Zabin, Laurie S., Marilyn B. Hirsch, Edward A. Smith, Rosalie Streett, & Janet B. Hardy. (1986). Evaluation of a pregnancy prevention program for urban teenagers. Perspectives *on Sexual and Reproductive Health* (formerly published as *Family Planning Perspectives), 18*(3), 119–126. Reproduced with the permission of The Alan Guttmacher Institute.

Index

Page references followed by "f" indicate illustrated figures or photographs; followed by "t" indicates a table.

A

Abortion, 326
Abuse, 5, 13, 79, 101, 156, 159, 308, 324
Adoption, 146-147, 174-175, 279, 356
Age
  and status, 202
  fieldwork and, 116
Alcohol
  addiction, 5
American Anthropological Association, 313, 315, 317, 320, 349
American Revolution, 125
Art
  categories of, 229
  studying, 109
Associations
  military, 326
  voluntary, 326
Authority, 13, 326, 354

B

Base, 6, 79, 101, 164, 178, 225-228, 231-232, 258, 265, 295-296, 305, 311
Baseball, 165, 287-290, 292-294, 300, 304-309, 351, 354, 357
Basic research, 18-19, 21, 25-26, 75, 174, 271, 331
Behavior
  race and, 156
Beliefs
  religious, 91
Bell-shaped curve, 192
Bourgois, Philippe, 101, 349
Buildings, 24, 133, 296
Bureaucracy, 24

C

Capital, 7-9, 92
Capital punishment, 7-9, 92
CARE, 17-19, 58-60, 62, 64, 103-104, 162, 170, 183, 193, 278, 289, 319, 351, 355
Census, 67, 156, 181-182, 200, 218, 223, 229, 344, 352
Chief, 153, 269, 319
Child abuse, 159
Children
  abuse of, 13
  street, 355
  violence against, 86
Class
  characteristics, 59, 149
Classification, 30, 51-53
Community
  action, 131
Competition
  male, 292
Connecticut, 350
Contract, 178, 276
Cooking, 9
Critique, 15
Culture
  aspects of, 25, 118
  describing, 39

D

Data
  qualitative, 37, 44, 98, 100, 105-106, 109-113, 115-120, 126, 128-130, 137, 140, 146, 213, 269, 279-280, 305, 307, 339, 341-342, 350-351, 353, 358
  quantitative, 37, 44, 98, 105, 112, 115-118, 120-121, 126, 128, 130-131, 137, 140, 146, 213, 269, 279-280, 282, 284-285, 305, 307, 342, 350
Data analysis
  ethnography, 110, 113, 116
Data collection
  field notes, 112, 118, 334
  interviews, 19, 24, 100, 112-113, 137, 144, 146, 148, 150, 155, 172, 176, 334
  participant observation, 100, 106, 116-117, 119
  questionnaire, 63, 144, 146, 148, 155-156, 171, 173, 176, 334, 339-340
Death
  age at, 126
  infants, 17, 131, 284
Death and dying, 141
Death penalty, 7, 143
Deception, 114, 128, 137
Deviant behavior, 145, 156, 355
Diabetes, 162
Difference, 12, 14, 53, 58, 61, 63, 69-71, 74, 76-77, 80-81, 86-87, 89, 93, 112, 134, 149, 182-184, 186, 189-190, 192-195, 197-198, 200-201, 204-206, 208-209, 215, 222-223, 226-228, 232, 243, 245-250, 252, 254-256, 259, 261, 266, 275, 285, 294-295, 298, 306-309, 336-339, 341, 343-345
Divorce, 67-68
DNA
  damage, 132
Drinking, 17, 93, 136, 201, 276

E

Economic resources, 17
Ethnic groups, 281
Ethnicity
  status and, 125
Ethnographers, 102, 106, 118
Ethnography
  of communication, 104, 106
Evidence
  measurement, 9, 48, 51, 59, 132, 305-306, 356
  operationalization, 48
  sampling, 210, 288, 290, 302, 305-307
  theories, 7, 39, 42

F

Falsifiable, 39, 43, 335
Family
  adoption, 147, 356
  independent, 68, 256, 354
Features, 105, 113, 131, 287, 292
Field notes, 99, 109-110, 112, 118, 334, 342
Fieldwork
  data analysis, 116
  ethics, 98, 107, 116, 355
  ethics in, 98, 116
  survey research, 355
Flowers, 30
Fraternities, 4
Frequency distribution, 221, 232-233, 281, 301, 305, 336, 347

G

Games
  of chance, 299-300
Gender
  concepts, 30-32, 34-35, 38, 40, 42-44, 59, 135, 333
  roles, 119
  third, 35, 59, 128, 227, 239, 245
Genealogy, 131

H

Head of household, 42
Historical research, 129, 138, 336
Human immunodeficiency virus (HIV), 152
Hurricane Andrew, 79, 119-120, 354
Hurricane Katrina, 37, 100, 352
Hypertension, 51
Hypotheses, 37, 39-40, 44-46, 65, 92, 144, 169-171, 231, 259, 281, 346
Hypothesis, 37-40, 42-46, 58, 64-65, 92-93, 121, 130, 140, 192-195, 198-199, 201, 204, 208-210, 246-247, 253-255, 261, 267, 277, 282, 286, 296, 307-309, 335-337, 339-340, 343, 345-347

I

Influence, 6, 8, 11, 21, 24, 26-27, 48, 58-59, 70-71, 81, 83, 91, 104, 121, 161, 225, 270, 272, 298, 309, 339, 341, 346
Institutions
  primary, 316
International Classification of Diseases, 51
Interview, 23, 51, 63, 66, 110-111, 115, 132, 143-151, 153, 158-159, 163, 165, 167-168, 170, 173-178, 201, 220, 281, 290, 324, 327, 333, 336, 339-341, 344, 346-347, 351, 354, 356, 358
Interviews, 4, 19, 24, 28, 36, 99-100, 103, 110-113, 115, 137, 143-151, 153, 155, 163, 167, 169-170, 172, 175-178, 201-203, 221, 274, 281, 290-291, 334
Intimacy, 203, 353

L

Labor
  child, 170
Laws
  universal, 34
Leisure, 158
Linguistics
  anthropological, 349
Literature review, 270-271, 280-281, 286
Living together, 152-153

M

Marriage
  age and, 143
  group, 130, 239
Measure
  classification, 53
Menopause, 296, 298-299, 306
Mining, 353
Minorities, 23, 143, 326
Mitigation, 100
Modes, 101, 170, 318
Mortality
  infant mortality, 21, 130, 269-271

N

Negotiation, 317
Nonrandom sample, 206
Nonverbal communication, 121
Norm, 9, 12, 24, 309, 319, 345
Norms
  sanctions, 156

O

Observation, 9, 12-13, 18, 32, 40, 43, 68, 75, 97-124, 127, 132, 134-138, 217, 236, 249, 258-259, 274, 281, 301, 305, 307, 328, 331, 334, 336, 339, 342, 344-345, 347, 349, 354
Observations, 9, 14, 18, 28, 37, 79-80, 84, 86, 89-90, 94-95, 97, 100, 103, 107, 109, 112-115, 117, 119-123, 132, 136, 139, 202-203, 217-218, 221, 224, 244, 258, 264, 280, 307, 327, 334-336, 338-342
Operational definition, 32, 43, 128, 291, 302, 340
Operationalization, 45, 48, 63, 156, 340
Oracles, 94

359